Crime Science Series

Edited by Richard Wortley
UCL

Crime science is a new way of thinking about and responding to the problem of crime in society. The distinctive nature of crime science is captured in the name.

First, crime science is about crime. Instead of the usual focus in criminology on the characteristics of the criminal offender, crime science is concerned with the characteristics of the criminal event. The analysis shifts from the distant causes of criminality – biological makeup, upbringing, social disadvantage and the like – to the near causes of crime. Crime scientists are interested in why, where, when and how particular crimes occur. They examine trends and patterns in crime in order to devise immediate and practical strategies to disrupt these patterns.

Second, crime science is about science. Many traditional responses to crime control are unsystematic, reactive, and populist, too often based on untested assumptions about what works. In contrast crime science advocates an evidence-based, problem-solving approach to crime control. Adopting the scientific method, crime scientists collect data on crime, generate hypotheses about observed crime trends, devise interventions to respond to crime problems, and test the adequacy of those interventions.

Crime science is utilitarian in its orientation and multidisciplinary in its foundations. Crime scientists actively engage with front-line criminal justice practitioners to reduce crime by making it more difficult for individuals to offend, and making it more likely that they will be detected if they do offend. To achieve these objectives, crime science draws on disciplines from both the social and physical sciences, including criminology, sociology, psychology, geography, economics, architecture, industrial design, epidemiology, computer science, mathematics, engineering, and biology.

Realist Evaluation for Crime Science
Essays in Honour of Nick Tilley
Edited by Graham Farrell and Aiden Sidebottom

Rebuilding Crime Prevention Through Environmental Design
Strengthening the Links with Crime Science
Edited by Rachel Armitage and Paul Ekblom

Problem-Oriented Policing
Successful Case Studies
Edited by Michael Scott and Ronald Clarkes

For more information about this series, please visit: https://www.routledge.com/criminology/series/CSCIS

Mike Scott and Ron Clarke have made an important contribution to the literature on problem-oriented policing by bringing together successful case studies and making them available to the field. These case studies are an excellent way to share successful ideas with police officers who are always looking for solutions to the persistent problems they encounter in their work. They also reinforce a thoughtful process for identifying, understanding and responding to problems.

Darrel W. Stephens, *chief of police (Ret.), Charlotte-Mecklenburg (North Carolina), St. Petersburg (Florida) and Newport News (Virginia), and former Executive Director, Police Executive Research Forum and Major Cities Chiefs Association*

This book is an indispensable resource from masters of the field, showing generations of police yet to come how they can do problem-oriented policing with insight, imagination and precision.

Lawrence Sherman, *professor of criminology, University of Cambridge*

Sir Robert Peel fathered the first professional police force in 1829, stressing that "the basic mission for which the police exist is to prevent crime and disorder." This book provides inspirational worked examples of how to do that. Sir Robert would have loved it.

Ken Pease, *professor of policing, University of Derby*

This book will prove invaluable because Ron, Mike and the authors of the case studies have re-visited the initiatives, sometimes decades later. This is the acid test of problem orientation. Some chapters reveal resilient and resounding results, others more ephemeral success. However, the analysis and insights of success or ultimate failure allow the reader to learn and hopefully deliver a policing service focused on prevention and wisdom.

Michael Barton, *chief constable (Ret.), Durham Constabulary and visiting professor, Jill Dando Institute of Crime Science, University College London*

PROBLEM-ORIENTED POLICING

Problem-Oriented Policing: Successful Case Studies is the first systematic and rigorous collection of effective problem-oriented policing projects. It includes more than twenty case studies from among the thousands of projects submitted for the Herman Goldstein Award for Excellence in Problem-Oriented Policing. The volume describes in detail the case studies and explains the wider significance of each for effective, efficient, and equitable policing.

This book explores a wide range of problems that fall under five general categories: gang violence; violence against women; vulnerable people; disorderly places; and theft, robbery, and burglary. The case studies tell stories of how police, in collaboration with others, successfully tackled real-world policing problems fairly and effectively. The authors have also drawn out of the case studies the cross-cutting themes and issues they illustrate. The authors prove that the concept can work, bring to life the context in which police and communities addressed these vexing problems, and, ideally, will inspire future problem-oriented police work that builds on these reported successes.

Written in a clear and direct style, this book will appeal to students and scholars of policing, criminology, and social studies; police practitioners and crime analysts; and all those who are interested in learning more about the reality of police problem-solving.

Michael S. Scott is clinical professor at Arizona State University's School of Criminology & Criminal Justice and director of the Center for Problem-Oriented Policing, which produces and disseminates information about how police can effectively and fairly address specific public-safety problems. He was formerly a clinical professor at the University of Wisconsin Law School; chief of police in Lauderhill, Florida; special assistant to the chief of the St. Louis, Missouri, Metropolitan Police Department; director of administration of the Fort Pierce,

Florida, Police Department; a senior researcher at the Police Executive Research Forum (PERF) in Washington, D.C.; legal assistant to the police commissioner of the New York City Police Department; and a police officer in the Madison, Wisconsin, Police Department. In 1996, he received PERF's Gary P. Hayes Award for innovation and leadership in policing.

Ronald V. Clarke is university professor at the Rutgers School of Criminal Justice and associate director of the Center for Problem-Oriented Policing. Before coming to the United States, he worked for fifteen years in the British government's criminological research department, the Home Office Research and Planning Unit. While there, he led the team that originated situational crime prevention and is now considered to be the leading authority on that approach. In 2015, he was awarded the Stockholm Prize in Criminology. His current research focuses on wildlife crimes.

PROBLEM-ORIENTED POLICING

Successful Case Studies

Edited by Michael S. Scott and Ronald V. Clarke

Routledge
Taylor & Francis Group

LONDON AND NEW YORK

First published 2020
by Routledge
2 Park Square, Milton Park, Abingdon, Oxon OX14 4RN

and by Routledge
52 Vanderbilt Avenue, New York, NY 10017

Routledge is an imprint of the Taylor & Francis Group, an informa business

© 2020 selection and editorial matter, Michael S. Scott and Ronald V. Clarke; individual chapters, the contributors

British Library Cataloguing-in-Publication Data
A catalogue record for this book is available from the British Library

Library of Congress Cataloging-in-Publication Data
Names: Scott, Michael S., editor. | Clarke, R. V. G., editor.
Title: Problem-oriented policing : successful case studies / edited by Michael S. Scott and Ronald V. Clarke.
Description: Abingdon, Oxon ; New York, NY : Routledge, 2020. | Series: Crime science series | Includes bibliographical references and index. |
Identifiers: LCCN 2019056091 | ISBN 9781138313897 (hardback) | ISBN 9780367900533 (paperback) | ISBN 9780429457357 (ebook)
Subjects: LCSH: Problem oriented policing—Case studies. | Crime—Case studies. | Police-community relations—Case studies.
Classification: LCC HV7936.P75 P698 2020 | DDC 363.2/3—dc23
LC record available at https://lccn.loc.gov/2019056091

ISBN: 978-1-138-31389-7 (hbk)
ISBN: 978-0-367-90053-3 (pbk)
ISBN: 978-0-429-45735-7 (ebk)

Typeset in Bembo
by Apex CoVantage, LLC

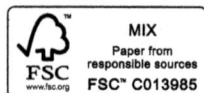

MIX
Paper from
responsible sources
FSC
www.fsc.org   FSC™ C013985

Printed in the United Kingdom
by Henry Ling Limited

Dedicated to Herman Goldstein and to those who have put into practice his vision for better policing.

CONTENTS

FIGURES

TABLES

CONTRIBUTORS

Emmanuel Barthe is an associate professor of criminal justice at the University of Nevada, Reno. His interests include policing, situational crime prevention, and, for the last several years, prescription drug diversion and the effect on other crime problems such as heroin use.

Gisela Bichler, PhD, is a professor of criminal justice at California State University, San Bernardino. Dr. Bichler is an applied researcher, with more than 25 years of experience collaborating with criminal justice agencies, community groups, and city governments to develop solutions to local crime and public-safety issues that invoke stronger place management and situational crime prevention. A major focus of her current research investigates how social networks shape crime opportunities. She explores this topic in considerable detail in a book titled *Understanding Criminal Networks: A Research Guide*, available from the University of California Press. She is founder and director of the Center for Criminal Justice Research—CSUSB.

Kate Bowers is a professor in crime science at the University College London Department of Security and Crime Science. She has worked in the field of crime science for more than 20 years, with research interests focusing on the use of quantitative methods in crime analysis and crime prevention. Her most recent interests are in using big and innovative data approaches in understanding crime problems.

Anthony A. Braga is Distinguished Professor and the director of the School of Criminology and Criminal Justice at Northeastern University. He is a fellow of the American Society of Criminology. Braga is also a past president and fellow of the Academy of Experimental Criminology and the 2014 recipient of its Joan McCord Award. He received his M.P.A. from Harvard University and his Ph.D. in criminal justice from Rutgers University.

Steve Burton worked for 15 years as a senior executive in Transport for London—the local government body responsible for the transport system in Greater London—leading its policing, security, and enforcement function and setting the strategy for policing London's transport system and deploying more than 3,500 officers onto the network. He also has experience supporting and advising on the development of problem solving, performance management, and transport-policing delivery structures in a range of international arenas, including Cape Town, South Africa; Chile; and India.

Sharon Chamard is an associate professor at the University of Alaska–Anchorage Justice Center. She received her Ph.D. in 2003 from the School of Criminal Justice at Rutgers University–Newark. She is interested in conflicts over use of public space and strategies used by local governments to deal with chronically homeless people and chronic public inebriates, the spatial characteristics of homeless encampments, and how social networks among chronically homeless people are related to their willingness to accept services.

Ronald V. Clarke is University Professor at the Rutgers School of Criminal Justice and an associate director of the Center for Problem-Oriented Policing. Before immigrating to the United States, he worked for 15 years in the British government's criminological research department, the Home Office Research and Planning Unit. While there, he led the team that originated situational crime prevention and is now considered to be the leading authority on that approach. In 2015 he was awarded the Stockholm Prize in Criminology. His current research focuses on wildlife crimes.

Gary Cordner, a retired professor and former police officer and police chief, serves as academic director for the police academy/education and training division of the Baltimore Police Department. He received his Ph.D. from Michigan State University, served on the Commission on Accreditation for Law Enforcement Agencies for nine years, and is past editor of *Police Quarterly* and the *American Journal of Police.* He has been affiliated with the Center for Problem-Oriented Policing since its inception and has served as a Goldstein Award judge for more than 20 years.

Deena R. DeVore is a research associate in the tourism safety and crowd science program at the University of Nevada, Las Vegas. Her interests include policing, situational crime prevention, and criminological theory. She studied prescription drug abuse in Nevada under the Harold Rodgers Prescription Drug Monitoring Program grant funded through the U.S. Department of Justice, Bureau of Justice Assistance.

John E. Eck is a professor of criminal justice at the University of Cincinnati. For more than 40 years, he has worked with police to develop better practices. He has studied criminal investigations, problem-oriented policing, and high-crime locations. Eck is co-author (with Ronald V. Clarke) of *Crime Analysis for Problem*

Solvers. In 60 Small Steps. He also assisted the U.S. federal court in the creation of the City of Cincinnati's Collaborative Agreement.

Nkechi Erondu is a research analyst at the Urban Institute's Justice Policy Center in Washington, D.C. She works on projects related to violence prevention, corrections and reentry, and community-driven public-safety strategies, and provides technical assistance to jurisdictions improving justice-system functioning.

Marcus Felson is the originator of the routine activity approach and author of *Crime and Everyday Life*. He has also authored *Crime and Nature* and serves as professor at Texas State University in San Marcos, Texas. He has a B.A. from the University of Chicago and an M.A. and Ph.D. from the University of Michigan and has received the 2014 *Honoris Causa* from the Universidad Miguel Hernandez in Spain. Professor Felson has been given the Ronald Clarke Award by the Environmental Criminology and Crime Analysis group.

Rob T. Guerette is an associate professor at Florida International University. He studies and publishes in the areas of situational crime prevention, problem-oriented policing, transnational crime, and program and policy evaluation.

Kris Henning is a professor of criminology and criminal justice at Portland State University. He earned his Ph.D. in clinical psychology from the University of Vermont, leading to 25 years of teaching and applied research addressing criminal behavior. His work in this area has been supported by local and federal grants, including the National Institute of Justice (Strategic Approaches to Community Safety Initiative) and the Bureau of Justice Assistance (Community-Based Crime Reduction, Smart Policing Initiative, Project Safe Neighborhoods).

Tamara D. Herold (formerly Madensen) is an American crime scientist. She is currently an associate professor of criminal justice and graduate director at the University of Nevada, Las Vegas. She received her Ph.D. with an emphasis in crime prevention from the University of Cincinnati. She uses the crime-science perspective to study the criminological impact of the design and management of places.

David M. Kennedy is a professor of criminal justice at John Jay College of Criminal Justice in New York City. He specializes in practical approaches to public safety.

Stuart Kirby is a professor of policing at the University of Central Lancashire in the United Kingdom. He acts as academic advisor to Her Majesty's Inspectorate of Constabulary and to the National Police Chiefs Council. Prior to becoming an academic he served as a UK police officer, being responsible for the implementation of problem-oriented policing in his force. He has been awarded two Tilley Awards and was a Goldstein Award finalist for his work applying problem-oriented policing.

Johannes Knutsson is professor emeritus at the Norwegian Police University College (Politihøgskolen) and has conducted research for and with the Swedish and Norwegian police since the mid-1970s.

Brandon R. Kooi, Ph.D., is professor of criminal justice at Aurora University in Illinois and past president of the Midwest Criminal Justice Association. He has worked with the Center for Problem-Oriented Policing since 2004 and coordinated the first Illinois state Problem-Oriented Policing conference in 2015.

Joseph B. Kuhns, Ph.D., is a professor of criminal justice and criminology at the University of North Carolina (UNC) at Charlotte. Prior to arriving at UNC-Charlotte in 2003, Dr. Kuhns served as senior policy analyst at the U.S. Department of Justice, Office of Community Oriented Policing Services. Dr. Kuhns has worked on a wide range of research and evaluation projects focused on use of deadly force by and against the police; alcohol, drug, and violent-crime relationships; and the impact of burglary offending and victimization. Dr. Kuhns regularly works with police departments, national associations, and federal agencies to improve policing practices, identify emerging priorities, and enhance officer and community safety.

Nancy G. La Vigne, Ph.D., is the vice president for justice policy at the Urban Institute in Washington, D.C., where she directs the Justice Policy Center. She conducts research on prisoner reentry, criminal justice technologies, crime prevention, policing, criminal justice reform, and the spatial analysis of crime and criminal behavior. Her work appears in both scholarly journals and practitioner publications and has made her a sought-after spokesperson in her areas of expertise.

Gloria Laycock has a BSc and a Ph.D. in psychology from University College London. She is currently a professor of crime science at University College London and was the director of research supporting the What Works Centre for Crime Reduction until 2017. She was awarded an OBE (Order of the British Empire) in the Queen's Birthday Honours 2008 for services to crime policy.

Rick Linden is a professor of sociology and criminology at the University of Manitoba in Canada. He served as chair of the Manitoba Police Commission from 2011 to 2016. He has written more than 60 published papers and reports and is the author or editor of four books, including Canada's best-selling *Criminology* text. His current research interests are in the areas of policing, crime prevention, auto crime, and program evaluation.

Mandy McGregor is a senior operational policy and problem-solving manager at Transport for London (TfL), the local government body responsible for the transport system in Greater London. She is responsible for policy development for transport policing, civilian enforcement, and guiding and supporting problem solving across the TfL/police partnership. She has had a key role in Safer Travel at Night over the last 15 years and in tackling sexual offences on public transport.

Rachel B. Santos, Ph.D., is a professor of criminal justice and co-director of the Center for Police Practice, Policy and Research at Radford University in Virginia. Her interests include conducting practice-based research by implementing and evaluating evidence-based practices as they are incorporated in everyday practice. She seeks to improve crime prevention and proactive crime-reduction efforts by police in areas such as crime analysis, problem solving, accountability, leadership, and organizational change.

Roberto G. Santos, Ph.D., is a tenure-track assistant professor of criminal justice and co-director of the Center for Police Practice, Policy and Research at Radford University in Virginia. He retired from policing as a commander after 22 years of service. He assists local, county, and state police agencies in proactive crime reduction. He conducts evidence- and practice-based research to translate research to police practice, and vice versa, in a variety of areas, including crime reduction, use of force, criminal investigations, organizational change, and leadership.

Karin Schmerler is the program coordinator of the Preventing Repeat Domestic Violence Initiative at the San Diego County District Attorney's Office. Previously, she was senior public safety analyst with the Chula Vista (California) Police Department, where she worked for 17 years on a variety of crime and disorder problems. Schmerler also spent five years as a social science analyst at the U.S. Department of Justice, Office of Community Oriented Policing Services, and seven years as a researcher at the Police Executive Research Forum. She holds a bachelor's degree in public policy studies from Duke University.

Michael S. Scott is a clinical professor at Arizona State University's School of Criminology & Criminal Justice and the director of the Center for Problem-Oriented Policing. Scott was formerly clinical professor at the University of Wisconsin Law School; chief of police in Lauderhill, Florida; special assistant to the police chief in St. Louis, Missouri; director of police administration in Fort Pierce, Florida; senior researcher at the Police Executive Research Forum (PERF) in Washington, D.C.; legal assistant to the police commissioner in New York City; and police officer in Madison, Wisconsin. In 1996, he received PERF's Gary P. Hayes Award for innovation and leadership in policing. Scott holds a J.D. from Harvard Law School and a B.A. from the University of Wisconsin–Madison.

Greg Stewart has worked for the Portland (Oregon) Police Bureau (PPB) since the mid-1990s. His assignments have included patrol, street crimes, investigations, and various support units. He helped create and supervise the PPB's centralized crime analysis unit. He is also an adjunct professor and research analyst for Portland State University's Criminology and Criminal Justice Department.

Nick Tilley is professor in the University College London Department of Security and Crime Science and adjunct professor at the Griffith Criminology Institute in Brisbane, Australia. He has published about 20 books and 200 articles in journals and edited collections, mostly relating to research methodology, policing, and crime reduction. He led pioneering projects implementing problem-oriented policing and partnership in the United Kingdom. The Tilley Award was therefore named after him. He was awarded an OBE (Order of the British Empire) for services to policing and crime reduction in 2005 and elected a Fellow of the Academy of Social Sciences in 2009.

Lisa Tompson is an associate professor at the University College London Department of Security and Crime Science. In recent years, her work has helped to shape the professionalization agenda for the UK police and the infrastructure underpinning this transformation. For five years she worked on the research programme that underpins the UK's What Works Centre for Crime Reduction, for which she and the team won a Chief Constable's commendation in 2015. She has also recently completed a project developing the evidence base to support the introduction of graduate entry into UK Policing.

Stacy Ward has served as the drug abuse prevention coordinator for the Reno (Nevada) Police Department since 2008. Her focus area for the majority of her tenure has been the prevention of prescription drug misuse. In this capacity she has supervised the Reno Police Department's Smart Policing Initiative and the Harold Rogers Prescription Drug Monitoring Program grant project. Stacy formerly served as program analyst for the Nevada Board of Pharmacy's Prescription Monitoring Program, and currently consults as a subject-matter expert for the U.S. Department of Justice, Bureau of Justice Assistance Smart Policing Initiative, wherein she advises other communities that are working on this issue.

Julie Wartell is an independent advisor on public-safety issues relating to crime analysis, problem solving and justice systems. She has performed a wide range of research on and analysis of various crime problems and police-related issues for police departments, prosecutor's offices, and research organizations. She has conducted extensive training and made presentations around the world on topics relating to crime analysis and problem-oriented policing, has edited or authored numerous publications, and currently teaches at the University of California–San Diego. Wartell holds a master's degree from San Diego State University and a Postgraduate Diploma from the University of Cambridge.

Deborah Lamm Weisel served as the research partner for the Chula Vista Domestic Violence project, funded by the Strategic Policing Initiative of the U.S. Department of Justice, Bureau of Justice Assistance. She currently serves in that role for a repeat-domestic-violence initiative at the San Diego County District Attorney's Office. Since 1999, Weisel has been on the faculty of the Administrative

Officer's Management Program at North Carolina State University. She was on the criminal justice faculty at North Carolina Central University until 2019 and a senior researcher at the Police Executive Research Forum in Washington, D.C., for 12 years. Weisel has conducted applied research on a variety of public-safety problems, ranging from gangs and street-level drug dealing to residential burglary and theft from motor vehicles. She holds a doctorate in public policy analysis from the University of Illinois at Chicago.

1

INTRODUCTION

Michael S. Scott and Ronald V. Clarke

Problem-oriented policing is not a new idea; indeed, it has been around for more than forty years with the publication of Herman Goldstein's (1979) classic article outlining the approach. In that article, Goldstein advised police departments to abandon their usual mode of allocating resources for the narrow objectives of patrolling territory, responding quickly to service requests, and detecting criminal activity and instead to focus more directly on addressing the crime and disorder problems that constitute their business. He urged that policing problems were best addressed by coordinating highly specific societal and environmental changes that would, ideally, prevent the problems or, at a minimum, reduce the harm they were causing the public.

Since then, the benefits and practicality of problem-oriented policing have been analyzed in many different publications (see, e.g., Goldstein, 1990; Scott, 2000; Clarke, 2002; Bullock & Tilley, 2003; Bullock, Erol & Tilley, 2006; Braga, 2010; Scott et al., 2017). In this book, we assume that readers are familiar with the concept and we do not explain it further (however, Box 1.1 contains Goldstein's own succinct description as a brief reminder). Instead, we write with the different objective of gathering in one place a collection of successful case studies of problem-oriented policing.

We believe this will be helpful to police, either those who are already engaged in problem-oriented policing but who might learn something from recognized successes or those who are thinking about undertaking it but need proof that it can work. Neither group of officers is likely to have time to search through the hundreds of case studies of problem-oriented policing on the website of the Center for Problem-Oriented Policing (www.popcenter.org), and even if they did, they might not feel confident in judging the success of particular projects. We trust this book will do that work for them.

We also hope the book will be useful to those in the academic world who are teaching or learning about policing. They might know that problem-oriented policing was found to be effective in the systematic review of police research undertaken by the National Research Council (2004) as well as in those undertaken by the Campbell Collaboration (Weisburd et al., 2010) and others (Sherman et al., 1997; Welsh & Farrington, 2002; Telep & Weisburd, 2012). They might also be familiar with the vetting processes of various problem-oriented policing award programs,[1] and they might have heard that Herman Goldstein was awarded the Stockholm Prize in Criminology in 2018 for his work in developing problem-oriented policing. However, we believe this book would also be useful to them as a "go-to" source of detailed accounts of successful case studies that would fill out the dry and abstract conclusions of the systematic reviews mentioned earlier.

In fact, it was Goldstein's Stockholm Prize that was the immediate stimulus for this volume. The award jury asked one of us, Scott, the director of the Center for Problem-Oriented Policing and a onetime undergraduate student of Goldstein, with a subsequent career in policing, to organize a series of panels at the Stockholm Symposium where the prize is awarded. These panels would be intended to convey to those attending the symposium—many of whom are criminologists who would not necessarily be familiar with work on policing—what problem-oriented policing is and how it is put into practice. Scott, in turn, invited the other of us, Clarke, associate director of the Center for Problem-Oriented Policing, to join him in organizing the panels. Clarke is the leading exponent of situational crime prevention, an approach similar to problem-oriented policing but that has its origins in criminology, not in police administration as is the case for problem-oriented policing. In fact, the links between problem-oriented policing and situational crime prevention have grown stronger in recent years, with much intermingling of scholars (Scott & Goldstein, 2012).

We thought the best way for neophytes to learn about problem-oriented policing would be through presentations of a variety of specific projects undertaken by scholars and practitioners, sometimes working together, and this comprised the panels we organized. Subsequently, we invited symposium presenters to write up their presentations as chapters for this volume to share these examples of effective problem-oriented policing with an audience far wider than was able to attend the Stockholm Symposium.

We do not mean to imply that the case studies in this volume are the very best ever done. We think only that this collection reflects a broad sample of successful problem-oriented policing projects across a wide variety of problem types and places.

With this brief description of the origins of the book completed, we can move on to the more substantive issues covered in this introduction—an overview of the case studies and the criteria for their inclusion, our definition of success, and the main lessons of the case studies.

BOX 1.1 GOLDSTEIN'S (2001) SUMMARY OF PROBLEM-ORIENTED POLICING

Problem-oriented policing (POP) is an approach to policing in which (1) discrete pieces of police business (each consisting of a cluster of similar incidents, whether crimes or acts of disorder, that the police are expected to handle) are subject to (2) microscopic examination (drawing on the especially honed skills of crime analysts and the accumulated experience of operating field personnel) in hope that what is freshly learned about each problem will lead to discovering a (3) new and more effective strategy for dealing with it. POP places a high value on new responses that are (4) preventive in nature, that are (5) not dependent on the use of the criminal justice system, and that (6) engage other public agencies, the community and the private sector when their involvement has the potential for significantly contributing to the reduction of the problem. POP carries a commitment to (7) implementing the new strategy, (8) rigorously evaluating its effectiveness, and, subsequently, (9) reporting the results in ways that will benefit other police agencies and that will ultimately contribute to (10) building a body of knowledge that supports the further professionalization of the police.

The 23 case studies included in this volume

The case studies included deal with a range of policing problems which fell into five general problem types: (1) gang violence, (2) violence against women, (3) vulnerable people, (4) disorderly places, and (5) theft, robbery and burglary, a set of problem types much smaller than the 18 general types listed on the website of the Center for Problem-Oriented Policing.[2]

Most of these case studies had been judged as finalists or winners in the years they were submitted for the Herman Goldstein Award for Excellence in Problem-Oriented Policing and, while the award is open to submissions from any country, most have been submitted by police agencies from the English-speaking countries of the United States, the United Kingdom, Canada, New Zealand, and Australia. In some but not all cases, the authors of these case studies had played some part in the original submission for the Goldstein Award. Where this was not the case, authors chose to write about the project because it illustrated some general themes that they were interested to discuss.

In order to bring some consistency of approach we asked the case study authors to organize their chapters roughly as follows: (1) summarize the project—including how the problem was identified, analyzed, addressed, and assessed (the SARA model)[3]—drawing from the police agency's original project report; (2) follow up with the police agency to learn what became of the problem in the years after the project was closed; and (3) discuss any aspect of the project that might be of interest to a wider audience of scholars and practitioners. To assist authors in meeting our charge, we sent them an exemplar case study.

Defining "successful"

We mentioned earlier that several systematic reviews of published evaluations of problem-oriented policing had found it to be effective. Several of the systematic reviews used the Maryland criteria (Sherman et al., 1997; Welsh & Farrington, 2002; Weisburd et al., 2010) to judge effectiveness, but in fact, these criteria are biased against problem-oriented policing. This is because their top scores are reserved for projects that utilize randomized controlled trials, which have very rarely been used in evaluating problem-oriented policing projects; in fact, most such evaluations make use of before-and-after comparisons or simple time series with or without controls. These are deemed weak designs under the Maryland criteria, and while some of these reviews concluded that problem-oriented policing is effective, this was at "promising," the lowest level of effectiveness.

In fact, unlike treatments to which people can be allocated randomly, such as counseling or enhanced care for juveniles, assigning problem-oriented policing interventions randomly is very difficult. One important reason is that while problem-oriented policing projects are led by police, they are frequently implemented with assistance from other local agencies, which are likely to be even less persuaded of the need for rigorous evaluation than the police might be. They would probably regard evaluation as an academic luxury and would argue that if there were any real doubt that the changes would be effective, why go to all the trouble of making them. They would also generally prefer to focus interventions where they were most needed rather than where dictated by random assignment. Thus, the randomization requirement would multiply many times the usual difficulties of obtaining cooperation and consent to an evaluation.

Even in the rare cases when it might be possible to use random assignment, doing so under the "double-blind" conditions that make these designs so useful in evaluating new drugs would be impossible. (Double-blind studies control for the "halo" effects of a new treatment by ensuring that the clinicians and those treated do not know who has received the drug and who the placebo.) Problem-oriented policing interventions would be much harder to conceal. For example, in a project where improved street lighting was randomly allocated between different neighborhoods, this would be immediately obvious to those who received the improved lighting and to those who did not. Another important reason why random allocation could never serve routinely as the preferred evaluative strategy for problem-oriented policing interventions is the much greater cost of prospectively undertaking random allocation studies compared with retrospective quasi-experimental designs. Testing the effectiveness of problem-oriented policing projects using what are widely regarded as the most rigorous of scientific standards and methods is impractical in all but rare instances. Moreover, some long-held assumptions about what constitutes an appropriately rigorous standard have been challenged of late, the seemingly bedrock principle of "statistical significance" being one. Challengers have called for a more nuanced and gradated interpretation of statistical significance in lieu of a binary one (Amrhein, Greenland & McShane, 2019).

Fortunately, the drops in crime and disorder achieved by problem-oriented policing initiatives are often so precipitous that simple time-series analysis leaves no doubt the interventions have been effective. Ross (2013: p. 129) has called these "cliff edge" effects, (see also Perry et al., 2017) of which there are two main kinds: (1) where an ongoing high rate of crime or disorder suddenly falls after an intervention and (2) those where a specific form of crime that has quickly risen drops precipitously after the intervention. As argued by Nagin and Weisburd (2013), drops of these kinds would require no detailed statistical treatment of the data. In commenting on drafts of the case studies for this volume, we asked authors to provide any data they could that might indicate a precipitous drop in the problems addressed in the case study. In half the case studies, the assessment of impact revealed what can fairly be deemed "cliff-edge" reductions in the incidence or harms caused by the problem.[4] Whether or not they yielded "cliff-edge drops" in the problem, all of our case studies demonstrated measurable improvements in the targeted problem that were plausibly caused by the problem-oriented policing intervention and to a degree that satisfied key stakeholders in the problem.

We had also asked authors to check in the course of their follow-up inquiries with the responsible police departments whether the same problems had subsequently reverted to their previous levels. Among the case studies included in this volume, there were at least four where this did occur. The most likely reason is that police agencies often fail to institutionalize problem monitoring so that when the key personnel responsible for successfully addressing a problem move on—as they inevitably will—no formal process exists to transfer responsibility for maintaining the conditions that led to initial success. Unfortunately, readdressing a problem once it has again become intolerable is often harder than it would have been to intervene early in its reversion cycle.

Few successes in crime and disorder reduction last forever. The police are seldom in the position of being able to claim that they have discovered and implemented the "once-and-for-all" solution to the problem. Their objectives are far more modest: to bring about noticeable improvements in the problem for a reasonable period in the jurisdiction in which they are being experienced. Changing conditions in communities, including when problem solvers move on to other priorities and diminish their oversight of the initial problem, can result in a resurgence of the problem; displacement of it to other locations, times, and targets; or unintended facilitation of new problems.

The relevant standards of success in highly complex and inherently political environments such as policing do and should differ from those of academia. Whether any problem-oriented policing intervention can be deemed "successful" entails a blended assessment of statistical evidence, cost–benefit calculations, political values, and judgments about the reasonableness of expectations. To adjudge problem-oriented policing as either successful or not by any single metric is to fail to understand the complexity of the policing task and the environment in which it occurs.

Few approaches that lead to success in one place will necessarily yield similar success in all places. The particular conditions that cause problems in one jurisdiction might be different in other jurisdictions experiencing a similar problem, and the particular interventions adopted in one jurisdiction might be deemed prohibitive—for legal, financial, or political reasons—elsewhere.

More fundamentally, whether the problem-oriented approach to policing is effective and whether a particular problem-oriented policing project is effective are separate questions. The systematic reviews referenced all seek to answer the former question by looking for examples of the latter. But, as Sherman et al. (1997: pp. 8–30) correctly noted, problem-oriented policing is, in essence, an applied scientific method, and accordingly, they wrote: "Evaluations of the scientific method, paradoxically, are not readily susceptible to the scientific method—except in gross comparison to **un**scientific methods." Thus, this book aims at answering the latter question—whether problem-oriented policing, faithfully applied, can yield effective results. And we show that it can.

Lessons of the case studies

In compiling these case studies, our intention was to let them speak for themselves. Readers will, of course, draw out their own lessons from the case studies, and the author of one of them, Professor David Kennedy, creator of the highly influential focused-deterrence approach, provides his own extended commentary in the volume's concluding chapter. In any event, we wanted to highlight four of the volume's important lessons: (1) that police are frequently successful in shifting and sharing responsibility with others for addressing many public-safety problems; (2) that distant corporate entities can thwart local problem-solving efforts; (3) that professional researchers are playing a vital role in problem-oriented policing practice, including by refining the standards and methods for measuring success; and (4) that monitoring problems is essential for preventing a reversion of the problem to its former or worse state.

Shifting and sharing responsibility

All the case studies illustrate some form of a central tenet of problem-oriented policing: that police should not bear sole responsibility for addressing a persistent and complex public-safety problem. Goldstein frames this issue as one of "shifting and sharing responsibility" (Scott & Goldstein, 2005). In short, once police determine that entities outside the police are acting (or failing to act) in ways that materially contribute to the creation of a public-safety problem, they should then try in various ways to encourage, persuade, or compel those entities to take measures that will help abate the problem.

Examples from these case studies include bringing a civil action (Oakland motel project), engaging existing service agencies (Lancashire vulnerable callers project), pressing for the creation of a new organization (Glendale, California day laborer project; Austin neighborhood revitalization project), pressing for legislative mandates (Chula Vista motels and hotels project), making a straightforward request (Houston convenience store project), educating others (London illegal taxis project), and making a targeted (sometimes confrontational) request (Lancashire broken glass project; Chula Vista domestic violence project).

Local problem solving can be thwarted by distant corporate entities

Oftentimes, the key stakeholder is a large corporation headquartered at a considerable distance from the business that is the focus of a problem-oriented policing project. As in the case of the Oakland Airport Motel, these stakeholders may even be based overseas. In fact, the motel was owned by a European corporation with hundreds of motels throughout the United States. Far distant stakeholders such as these are likely to be even less amenable to police pressure to alter their business practices than is a local business. A similar example comes from White and Katz's (2013) problem-oriented study of convenience store thefts in Glendale, Arizona. They found that these thefts were disproportionately occurring at Circle K convenience stores. Circle K stores are owned by a multinational corporation headquartered in Montreal, Canada, and, according to a Wikipedia estimate, have 15,000 convenience stores worldwide. In Glendale, the 15 Circle K stores, comprising 23% of the convenience stores in the city, accounted in 2010 for 79% of all convenience-store calls for service (White & Katz, 2013). Some of the Circle K stores called for police service more than 500 times per year.

The Glendale police targeted the top six call-generating Circle K stores and sought cooperation from the Circle K management to reduce the thefts. The management was cooperative when it came to introducing low-cost interventions, such as removing beer from the floors at a few stores and posting trespassing signs, but other management changes that required larger financial commitment were often ignored. "After initial meetings, Circle K leadership lost interest in addressing crime and disorder problems at their stores and reduced their communications (with the police)" (White & Katz, 2013: p. 9). In the course of their study, White and Katz discovered that Circle K stores were also magnets for crime in the nearby cities of Phoenix, Tempe, and Mesa. This led them to argue that "in addition to crime-prone people (repeat offenders) and places (hot spots) there may also be crime-prone corporations" (White & Katz, 2013: p. 14).

One implication is that local police would benefit from assistance from state or national governments in applying leverage to influence those larger entities—dubbed "super controllers" (Sampson, Eck & Dunham, 2010)—to employ preventive practices. In fact, Sampson et al. took a beneficent view of super controllers and did not consider that their influence might be toxic. However, our two examples show that the "super controllers" involved seemed to want to extract as much money as they could from their individual facilities with no regard to the crime-control costs that were passed on to the local police. In fact, it took extraordinary efforts by the police to bring them to the table and force them to cooperate to some degree.

More generally, criminal justice authorities have paid too little attention to toxic super controllers. Their frequently global nature, jurisdictional legal issues and the impenetrability of corporate law all help to explain why these toxic super controllers have escaped the attention of the law. Criminologists could draw attention to their failings by undertaking comparisons of the crime rates of such facilities as motels, malls, and large retailers, owned or not by corporate bodies or as between different corporations, such as between Walmart and Target.

The role of researchers in problem-oriented policing

In its original conceptualization, Goldstein envisioned problem-oriented policing being put into practice principally through partnerships between professionally trained researchers and police administrators (Goldstein & Susmilch, 1981). The earliest efforts largely followed this model, but police practitioners eventually began undertaking some problem-oriented initiatives—mostly smaller-scale ones—on their own, without the assistance of trained researchers. Sometimes they drew upon the assistance of in-house crime analysts who commonly represented an intermediate level of expertise in research methodology and statistics.

There is a similar pattern in this collection of 23 case studies: about half (13) of them had professional researchers (typically, doctoral-level academics) deeply engaged in various aspects of the project, usually guiding and/or conducting some of the analysis and assessment but often also being involved in developing the new response plan. Another four of the projects were led or strongly influenced by key in-house personnel (either sworn police officers or civilian analysts) with especially advanced training in research methodology and statistics, several of whom either possessed or subsequently earned their scientific doctorates. In the remaining 7 of the 23 projects, there is no indication of the direct involvement of professionally trained researchers, meaning that all analytical and conceptual work was undertaken by police officials and crime analysts who lacked advanced-level training in research methodology or statistics.

This collection of case studies shows therefore both that police are capable of undertaking high-quality problem-oriented policing without access to professionally trained researchers *and* that such assistance can also be enormously beneficial in refining the project—by improving an understanding of existing research on the problem, by establishing baseline measures of the problem, by focusing new responses on those most likely to be effective, and by designing and conducting reasonably rigorous impact evaluations.

The need for monitoring problems in the longer term

In several of the case studies, follow-up queries by the authors revealed that the problem that was successfully addressed subsequently reverted to an unacceptable state largely attributable to failures on the part of the agencies involved in the project to monitor conditions and to take quick remedial action. It is commonly the case that a key factor in the success of a problem-oriented policing project is the extraordinary dedication that one or more police officers have toward addressing the problem. The countervailing factor is that when these dedicated officers move on—through transfer, promotion, or retirement—as they inevitably must, absent an organizational system for monitoring problems, the conditions that gave rise to the problem in the first instance can easily prevail again, leading to the problem's recurrence. Because many police agencies find themselves overwhelmed by many critical incidents and political crises, in addition to the chronic crime and disorder problems that eventually become intolerable, the time and attention of police personnel can easily be drawn away from those problems deemed having been "solved." Learning how to sustain success for the longer term is seemingly as critical as learning how to achieve it in the short term.

Summing up

Kurt Lewin, one of the founders of social psychology, is often quoted for his maxim: "There is nothing so practical as a good theory" (Lewin, 1951). If one conceives of Herman Goldstein's conception of problem-oriented policing as a theory, this volume provides ample proof of its practicality. Together with some other well-evaluated projects (e.g., Hope, 1994 [drug houses in St. Louis]; Clifton, 1987 [convenience store robbery in Gainesville, Florida]; Eck & Spelman, 1987 [prostitution-related robbery and apartment burglaries in Newport News, Virginia]; Clarke & Goldstein, 2003a, 2003b [construction-site thefts and thefts from vehicles in Charlotte, North Carolina]), they demonstrate that problem-oriented policing is effective when properly applied. Moreover, it has been demonstrated to work in tackling a wide range of policing problems. It is not limited to working only on certain types of problems, whether "quality-of-life" nuisances, serious violent crime, accidental injury, or others. Because problem-oriented policing is a framework, or methodology, for addressing policing problems and not an intervention strategy *per se*, there is no reason why it cannot be effective for all policing problems. This said, there remains—and no doubt always will remain—room for further refinement of both the concept and its practice. Goldstein never intended it to be a fixed concept, only a push to move police in the direction of becoming more systematically effective and, simultaneously, more equitable in how they carry out their duties. That police ought always to work toward becoming increasingly effective and fair should be self-evident for, as Goldstein noted even before conceiving of problem-oriented policing, "[t]he strength of a democracy and the quality of life enjoyed by its citizens are determined in large measure by the ability of the police to discharge their duties" (Goldstein, 1977: p. 1). We hope that this volume will further widen interest in his approach to improving policing and will stimulate yet further refinement of its practice.

Notes

1 These include the Herman Goldstein Award for Excellence in Problem-Oriented Policing, the Tilley Award, and the New Zealand Evidence-Based Problem-Oriented Policing Awards.
2 The 18 overlapping problem types currently used on the POP Center website are alcohol & drug, animal, burglary & theft, business, disorder & nuisance, elderly, endangerment, frauds, gang, misuse of police resources, robbery, school & college, sex, traffic, vehicle, violence, wilderness, and youth/juvenile.
3 The SARA model was originally developed in the early test of problem-oriented policing in Newport News, Virginia (Eck & Spelman, 1987).
4 The case studies from Aurora, Boston, California Highway Patrol, Charlotte-Mecklenburg, Chula Vista, Cincinnati, High Point, Houston, Lancashire (Morecambe Bay), Vestfold, Oakland, and Winnipeg all reported cliff-edge declines.

References

Amrhein, V., Greenland, S. & McShane, B. (2019) 'Retire statistical significance', *Nature*, 567: 305–307.

Braga, A.A. (2010) *Problem-Oriented Policing and Crime Prevention*, Boulder, CO: Lynne Rienner Publishers.

Bullock, K. & Tilley, N. (2003) *Crime Reduction and Problem-Oriented Policing*, Cullompton, UK: Willan Publishing.

Bullock, K., Erol, R. & Tilley, N. (2006) *Problem-Oriented Policing and Partnerships: Implementing an Evidence-Based Approach to Crime Reduction*, Cullompton, UK: Willan Publishing.

Clarke, R.V. (2002) 'Problem-oriented policing and the potential contribution of criminology', Retrieved from www.popcenter.org

Clarke, R.V. & Goldstein, H. (2003a) *Reducing Theft at Construction Sites: Lessons from a Problem-Oriented Project*, Washington, DC: US Department of Justice, Office of Community Oriented Policing Services.

Clarke, R.V. & Goldstein, H. (2003b) *Thefts from Cars in Center City Parking Facilities: A Case Study*, Washington, DC: US Department of Justice, Office of Community Oriented Policing Services.

Clifton, W. (1987) *Convenience Store Robberies in Gainesville, Florida: An Intervention Strategy by the Gainesville Police Department*, Photocopy of Gainesville Police Department Internal Report.

Eck, J.E. & Spelman, W. (1987) *Problem Solving: Problem-Oriented Policing in Newport News*, Washington, DC: Police Executive Research Forum.

Goldstein, H. (1977) *Policing a Free Society*, Cambridge, MA: Ballinger.

Goldstein, H. (1979) 'Improving policing: A problem-oriented approach', *Crime & Delinquency*, 25: 236–258.

Goldstein, H. (1990) *Problem-Oriented Policing*, New York: McGraw-Hill.

Goldstein, H. (2001) *Problem-Oriented Policing in a Nutshell*, Presented at the International Problem-Oriented Policing Conference, San Diego, December.

Goldstein, H. & Susmilch, C.E. (1981) *The Problem-Oriented Approach to Improving Police Service: A Description of the Project and an Elaboration of the Concept*, Development of Problem-Oriented Policing Series, Vol. 1, Madison, WI: University of Wisconsin-Madison.

Hope, T. (1994) 'Problem-Oriented Policing and Drug-Market Locations: Three Case Studies', in R.V. Clarke (ed.), *Crime Prevention Studies*, Vol. 2, Monsey, NY: Criminal Justice Press.

Lewin, K. (1951) *Field Theory in Social Science: Selected Theoretical Papers* (D. Cartwright, ed.), Oxford, UK: Harpers.

Nagin, D. & Weisburd, D. (2013) 'Evidence and public policy: The example of evaluation research in policing', *Criminology and Public Policy*, 12(4): 651–679.

National Research Council (2004) *Fairness and Effectiveness in Policing: The Evidence* (W. Skogan & K. Frydl, eds.), Washington, DC: The National Academies Press.

Perry, S., Apel, R., Newman, G.R. & Clarke, R.V. (2017) 'The situational prevention of terrorism: An evaluation of the Israeli West Bank barrier', *Journal of Quantitative Criminology*, 33(4): 727–751.

Ross, N. (2013) *Crime: How to Solve It-and Why So Much of What We're Told Is Wrong*, London: Biteback Publishing Ltd.

Sampson, R., Eck, J.E. & Dunham, J. (2010) 'Super controllers and crime prevention: A routine activity explanation of crime prevention success and failure', *Security Journal*, 23(1): 37–51.

Scott, M.S. (2000) *Problem-Oriented Policing: Reflections on the First Twenty Years*, Washington, DC: US Department of Justice, Office of Community Oriented Policing Services.

Scott, M.S., Eck, J.E., Knutsson, J. & Goldstein, H. (2017) 'Problem-oriented policing', in R. Wortley & M. Townsley (eds.), *Environmental Criminology and Crime Analysis* (2nd ed.), London: Routledge.

Scott, M.S. & Goldstein, H. (2005) *Shifting and Sharing Responsibility for Public-Safety Problems*, Problem-Oriented Guides for Police, Response Guide Series No. 3, Washington, DC: US Department of Justice, Office of Community Oriented Policing Services.

Scott, M.S. & Goldstein, H. (2012) 'Ron Clarke's contribution to improving policing: A diffusion of benefits', in N. Tilley & G. Farrell (eds.), *The Reasoning Criminologist: Essays in Honour of Ronald V. Clarke*, Abingdon, Oxon: Routledge.

Sherman, L., Gottfredson, D., MacKenzie, D., Eck, J.E., Reuter, P. & Bushway, S. (1997) *Preventing Crime: What Works, What Doesn't, What's Promising*, Washington, DC: US Department of Justice, Office of Justice Programs.

Telep, C.W. & Weisburd, D. (2012) 'What is known about the effectiveness of police practices in reducing crime and disorder?', *Police Quarterly*, 15(4): 331–357.

Weisburd, D., Eck, J.E., Hinkle, J.C. & Telep, C.W. (2010) 'Is problem-oriented policing effective in reducing crime and disorder? Findings from a Campbell systematic review', *Criminology & Public Policy*, 9(1): 139–172.

Welsh, B.C. & Farrington, D.P. (2002) 'Conclusion: What works, what doesn't, what's promising, and future directions', in L.W. Sherman, D.P. Farrington, B.C. Welsh & D.L. MacKenzie (eds.), *Evidence-Based Crime Prevention*, London & New York: Routledge.

White, M.D. & Katz, C.M. (2013) 'Policing convenience store crime: Lessons from the Glendale, Arizona Smart Policing Initiative', *Police Quarterly*, 16(3): 305–355.

PART I
Gang violence

2

YOUTH GANG GUN VIOLENCE IN BOSTON, MASSACHUSETTS

Anthony A. Braga

Introduction

Focused-deterrence strategies have been found to be effective in reducing serious violence committed by gangs and criminally active groups (Braga, Weisburd & Turchan, 2018). The focused-deterrence approach developed from a well-known problem-oriented policing project that launched the "Operation Ceasefire" strategy to control an epidemic of gang violence in Boston during the early to mid-1990s (Kennedy, Piehl & Braga, 1996). Briefly, the goal of focused-deterrence strategies is to modify offender behavior by understanding underlying crime-producing dynamics and conditions that sustain recurring crime problems and by implementing an appropriately focused strategy of law enforcement, community mobilization, and social-service actions (Kennedy, 2011). Defining characteristics of focused-deterrence programs include direct communications of increased enforcement risks and the availability of social-service assistance to targeted groups and individuals.

The Boston Police Department (BPD) and their criminal justice, social service, and community-based partners received national acclaim for their innovative response to gang violence. For instance, Operation Ceasefire was the 1998 Herman Goldstein problem-oriented policing award winner among other impressive honors. Unfortunately, the Ceasefire strategy was discontinued in 2000 and, by the mid-2000s, youth homicide reemerged as a citywide crisis in Boston. The BPD eventually implemented a revitalized Ceasefire focused-deterrence strategy in 2007 after a problem analysis revealed that, once again, gang violence was driving citywide youth homicides. The focused-deterrence intervention subsequently reduced shootings by targeted gangs and these gun-violence-reduction impacts diffused to non-targeted gangs that were socially connected via rivalries and alliances with the targeted gangs (Braga, Hureau & Papachristos, 2014; Braga, Apel & Welsh, 2013).

This case study examines the implementation of Ceasefire during the 1990s and its revitalization during the mid-2000s in response to a resurgence of gang violence in Boston. It focuses on the vital role that problem analysis played in the revitalization of Ceasefire and the institutionalization of focused deterrence as the BPD's main response to outbreaks of serious gang violence. Police departments must make strong commitments to conduct ongoing analyses of crime problems to launch effective crime-prevention programs.

Problem-oriented policing, focused deterrence, and gang violence in Boston

The development of Operation Ceasefire during the 1990s

Like many American cities, Boston experienced a dramatic increase in serious violence after crack-cocaine first arrived on the streets in 1986 (Kennedy, Piehl & Braga, 1996). Boston youth gangs became involved in the lucrative street-level drug trade and used guns to settle disputes in drug-market settings. After street crack-cocaine markets stabilized, drug-related violence decreased in Boston. Unfortunately, serious gun violence had become "decoupled" from the crack trade. Guns were used by Boston youth to settle disputes that were once dealt with by fists, sticks, and knives. Figure 2.1 shows that Boston averaged roughly 28 youth homicides per year between 1980 and 1988; Boston youth homicides then surged to 40 victims in 1989 and reached a high of 73 victims in 1990. While the number of youth homicides declined, Boston youth homicides remained high at nearly 45 victims per year between 1991 and 1995.

The BPD collaborated with Harvard University researchers to launch the Boston Gun Project, a problem-oriented policing initiative intended to reduce the city's youth homicide problem (Kennedy, Piehl & Braga, 1996). An interagency working group comprising criminal justice, social service, and community-based partners was convened to develop policy-relevant insights on the nature of serious youth violence in Boston and advance an innovative response to the underlying dynamics driving the city's homicide problem. The problem-analysis research revealed that Boston youth homicide was highly concentrated among a small number of gang-involved youth who were caught up in ongoing cycles of violent retaliation against rival gangs (Kennedy, Braga & Piehl, 1997). A majority of gang violence occurred in the disadvantaged, mostly minority neighborhoods of Roxbury, Dorchester, and Mattapan. Youth-homicide victims and youth-homicide offenders tended to have extensive criminal records involving a wide range of offenses and were often under some form of criminal justice system control such as active probation supervision.

The interagency working group used the problem-analysis research to frame the "Operation Ceasefire" gang-violence-reduction strategy (Braga et al., 2001). The Ceasefire focused-deterrence strategy involved direct communications to gangs via call-ins and street conversations that violence would no longer be tolerated,

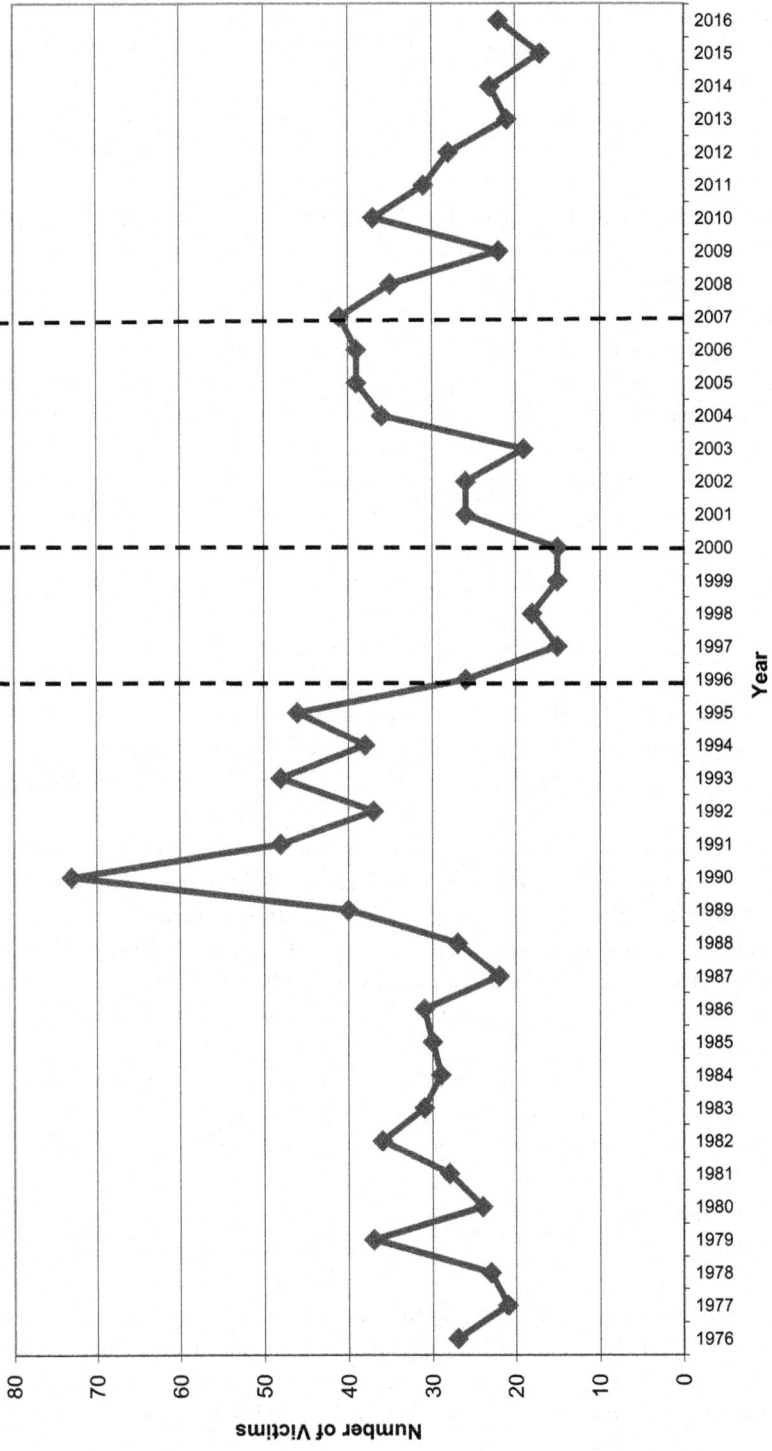

FIGURE 2.1 Youth homicides in Boston, 1976–2016

Source: Author.

enforcement responses customized to the chronic offending behaviors and criminal-justice vulnerabilities of targeted gangs and offers of opportunities and services to gang members who wanted them. The implementation of the Ceasefire intervention was supported by a robust "network of capacity" that was well positioned to launch an effective response to youth violence because criminal-justice agencies, community groups, and social-service agencies coordinated and combined their efforts in ways that could magnify their separate effects (Braga & Winship, 2006). Equally important, the inclusion of community partners, such as an influential black clergy group (known as the Ten-Point Coalition), allowed the BPD and their criminal-justice partners to develop a mechanism for transparency and accountability that was very desirable to Boston's minority community. Through these relationships, the BPD created the political support, or "umbrella of legitimacy," that it needed to pursue more focused and perhaps more aggressive intervention than would have been possible otherwise (Winship & Berrien, 1999).

Focused-deterrence programs seek to change the behaviors of targeted offenders by increasing the swiftness and certainty of sanctions and amplify these increased risks to offending populations through direct communications and advertising (Kennedy, 2011). Moreover, "carrot-and-stick approaches" that creatively use positive incentives, such as social services and job opportunities, to reward compliance and facilitate nonviolent behavior have been shown to generate crime-prevention impacts (Durlauf & Nagin, 2011). There are other crime-prevention mechanisms that seem to be at work in focused-deterrence programs. For instance, some observers have suggested that the procedural fairness inherent in giving offenders the choice to take advantage of social services rather than facing increased punishment risks could increase compliance with the law (Papachristos, Meares & Fagan, 2007). Community involvement in focused-deterrence programs could increase local informal-social-control capacities to reduce gang violence and better mobilize "intimate handlers" (such as clergy or street outreach workers) who can control violent offending by particular gang members (Kennedy, Kleiman & Braga, 2017). Indeed, the problem-oriented interventions applied to reduce gang violence in focused-deterrence strategies seem likely to draw upon multiple violence-prevention mechanisms.

Figure 2.1 shows that Boston experienced a large reduction in the yearly number of youth homicides following the mid-1996 implementation of Operation Ceasefire. A US Department of Justice (DOJ)–sponsored evaluation of Operation Ceasefire revealed that the intervention was associated with a 63 percent decrease in the monthly number of Boston youth homicides and significant decreases in nonfatal gun violence (Braga et al., 2001). The evaluation also suggested that the post-Ceasefire youth-homicide reductions observed in Boston were notably different from youth-homicide trends in most major US and New England cities during the late 1990s (Braga et al., 2001). The national media called these remarkable reductions "The Boston Miracle" (in part due to the involvement of clergy in the strategy), and the Ceasefire strategy was recognized as an important innovation in controlling serious youth violence.

The resurgence of gang violence and revitalization of Operation Ceasefire during the 2000s

Despite the national attention to its innovative gang-violence-reduction strategy, the BPD discontinued the Ceasefire intervention in January 2000 (see Braga & Winship, 2006). In its place, the BPD developed a broader slate of violence-prevention programs, such as a jail reentry program to facilitate the transition of violent offenders into the community, an initiative to enhance investigations of unsolved shootings, and an effort to coordinate services to criminogenic families in high-violence neighborhoods. Unfortunately, these new programs were not directly focused on preventing outbreaks of gang violence and instead diffused the capacity of the BPD and its partners to control citywide youth homicides. As revealed in Figure 2.1, the yearly number of youth homicides rose from 15 victims in 2000 to 41 victims in 2007.

The BPD did not engage in strategic analyses of its emerging youth-violence problem during this period (Braga, Hureau & Winship, 2008). In the absence of a clear description of the underlying dynamics driving the youth-homicide increase, the BPD was not well positioned to mount a meaningful problem-oriented response to the crisis. Indeed, then commissioner Kathleen O'Toole attributed the youth-homicide increase to an increasing juvenile population and prisoner-reentry issues (Johnson, 2006). There was also considerable internal dysfunction within the BPD between 2004 and 2006 that prevented the implementation of a unified response (Braga, Hureau & Winship, 2008).

In December 2006, Boston's then mayor Thomas Menino appointed Edward Davis as the new BPD commissioner. Davis immediately asked Harvard researchers to conduct a fresh problem analysis of the city's youth-homicide problem. The research found that the yearly number of youth-gang homicides increased sevenfold between 1999 and 2006 (Braga, Hureau & Winship, 2008). Gang-related motives were evident in more than two-thirds of youth homicides in 2006 and gang members were involved as either a victim, offender, or both in 70 percent of nonfatal shootings in 2006. Shootings were highly concentrated in and around gang-turf areas in Roxbury, Dorchester, and Mattapan. At the time of the problem analysis, Boston had 65 active street gangs with an estimated total membership of 1,422 youth, which represented only slightly more than 1 percent youth aged 15 to 24 in Boston. Certain gangs were much more involved in gun violence than others. The ten most violent gangs generated one third of the shootings in Boston in 2006.

The parallels between serious youth violence in the mid-1990s and mid-2000s were striking. In essence, the same kinds of gang conflicts drove the city's youth homicide problem during both periods. Commissioner Davis soon announced that Operation Ceasefire would be reinstated as the BPD's primary citywide, interagency response to ongoing gang violence in Boston. A revitalized Ceasefire intervention was formally implemented in January 2007; the interagency working group subjected 19 Boston gangs to the focused-deterrence strategy through December 2010. As Figure 2.1 reveals, Boston youth homicide decreased markedly following the second implementation of Operation Ceasefire. Between 2007 and 2016, the yearly number of youth-homicide victims fell by slightly more than 46 percent from 41 victims to 21 victims.

The first gang selected for post-2007 Ceasefire intervention was the very violent Lucerne Street Doggz, a loosely organized group of some 50 members based on Lucerne Street in a highly disadvantaged area of Mattapan (Braga, Hureau & Papachristos, 2014). In 2006, the Doggz had ongoing violent disputes with eight rival gangs, were the suspected offenders in 30 shootings, and were the victims of seven shootings. This one gang was involved in almost 10 percent of the 377 total shootings in Boston in 2006. The BPD's Youth Violence Strike Force (YVSF) started regular meetings of the Ceasefire interagency working group and the formal planning for a Ceasefire intervention focused on the Lucerne Street Doggz commenced in January 2007. Nevertheless, by the end of May 2017, the Doggz had generated another 21 shootings, and its members were the victims of six more shootings. The Ceasefire working group recognized that it was critical to reestablish the credibility of its antiviolence message on the streets of Boston by launching a strong response to the persistent gun violence perpetrated by the Doggz.

The YVSF collaborated on a focused investigation of the Lucerne Street Doggz with the BPD Drug Control Unit and District B-3 personnel, the US Attorney's Office, the Suffolk County District Attorney's Office, the Drug Enforcement Administration, and the Bureau of Alcohol, Tobacco, Firearms, and Explosives. On May 24, 2007, 25 Lucerne Street Doggz gang members were taken into custody and charged with federal and state drug and firearms offenses. The Ceasefire working group directly communicated with the remaining Doggz and the members of their eight rival gangs via a series of group call-ins and individual communications that further shootings would be addressed with an immediate focused-law-enforcement response. Ten-Point Coalition clergy, youth-outreach workers, and local Mattapan-based community groups informed these gangs that the community supported the law-enforcement action to keep their neighborhoods safe from gun violence and encouraged them to take advantage of the social services and opportunities being offered by Boston Centers for Youth and Families, Youth Opportunity Unlimited, and others.

Figure 2.2 shows that the impact of the Ceasefire focused-deterrence strategy on the shooting behaviors of the Lucerne Street Doggz was immediate and large. The Doggz averaged nearly 34 total shootings per year in 2006 and 2007. Between 2008 and 2010, the yearly average total number of shootings by the Doggz plunged by about 88 percent to slightly more than 4 per year. This highly successful Ceasefire intervention was subsequently used by the working group in its communications to other violent Boston gangs that a credible enforcement response would follow outbreaks of gang shootings. A rigorous quasi-experimental evaluation of the reconstituted Boston Ceasefire intervention found that total shootings involving treated gangs decreased by 31 percent relative to total shootings involving matched comparison gangs (Braga, Hureau & Papachristos, 2014).

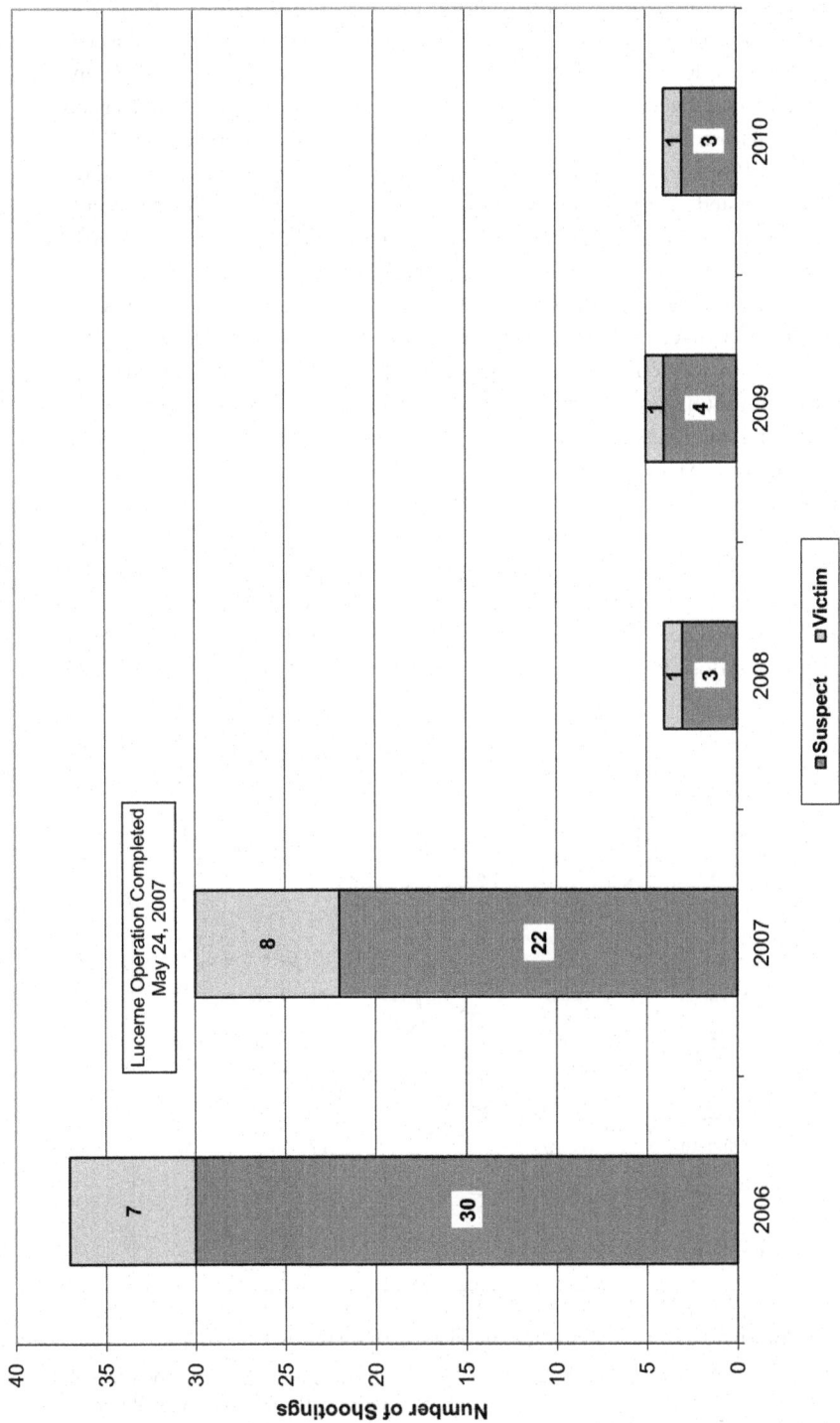

FIGURE 2.2 Lucerne Street Doggz shootings, 2006–2010

It is important to note that focused-deterrence strategies are explicitly designed to deter violent behavior by gangs and criminally active groups not directly subjected to the intervention. Kennedy, Piehl, and Braga (1996) note that the communications strategy implemented during the 1990s' Ceasefire intervention was intended to create spillover violence-reduction effects onto untreated gangs and neighborhoods. Ronald V. Clarke (1989) previously reported that situational crime prevention measures sometimes generated sizable crime control among gangs in areas that did not receive the intervention. Clarke and Weisburd (1994) later termed these unexpected crime-control gains as "diffusion of benefits" or the opposite of crime-displacement effects.

As suggested earlier, the reconstituted Boston Ceasefire program attempted to generate diffusion-of-crime-control benefits via direct communications with other gangs that were socially connected to targeted gangs through rivalries and alliances. A variety of communication methods were used to deliver these messages to socially connected gang members such as group call-ins, individual meetings with gang members under probation supervision, and street conversations among gang members, BPD officers, and street-outreach workers. A supplemental quasi-experimental evaluation showed that total shootings involving these "vicariously treated" gangs were also reduced by 27 percent relative to untreated gangs that were not socially connected to directly treated Ceasefire gangs (Braga, Apel & Welsh, 2013).

Figure 2.3 shows how a diffusion effect was transmitted by illustrating the social relations among Boston gangs that directly received the Ceasefire program and

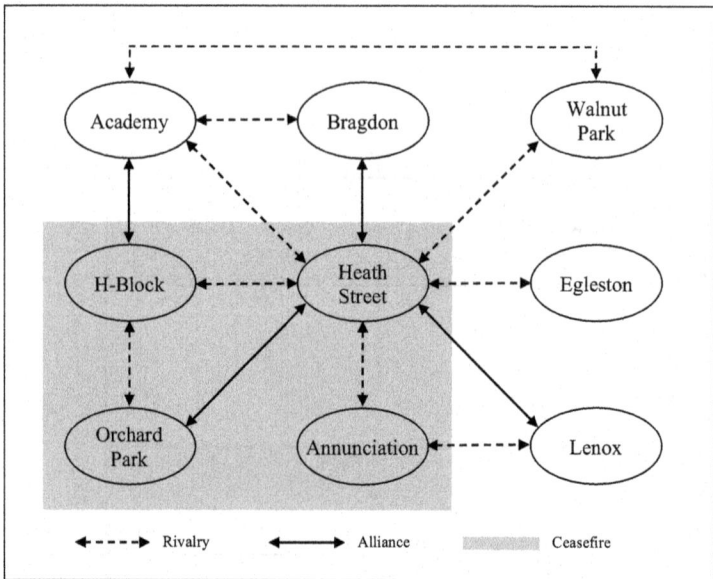

FIGURE 2.3 Heath Street first-order clique of alliances and rivalries

Source: Braga, A.A., Apel, R. & Welsh, B. (2013) 'The spillover effects of focused deterrence on gang violence', *Evaluation Review*, 37 (3–4) p. 325, copyright © 2013 by SAGE Publications, Inc. Reprinted by permission of SAGE Publications, Inc.

socially connected gangs that received vicarious focused-deterrence treatment (Braga, Apel & Welsh, 2013). Heath Street, H-Block, Annunciation Road, and Orchard Park gangs were directly subjected to the Ceasefire intervention by virtue of their violent behaviors. Academy, Bragdon, Walnut Park, Egleston, and Lenox Street gangs were not subjected to the Ceasefire intervention but connected to the treated gangs via rivalries and alliances. In essence, the evaluation evidence suggests that the Ceasefire treatment generated a significant spillover gun-violence-reduction impact on these vicariously treated gangs via knowledge of what happened to their rivals and allies.

Discussion: improving the implementation of focused deterrence in Boston and elsewhere

This case study highlights two key factors that contributed to the resurgence of gang violence in Boston—the *lack of ongoing problem analysis* to identify underlying conditions driving youth homicide and the *discontinuance of an effective program that was not institutionalized* as the primary response to gang violence in Boston. It is worth noting here that this parsimonious description neglects other relevant factors associated with the cessation of the Ceasefire program in 2000 such as the turnover of key personnel in the partnering agencies and a diminished sense of urgency and focus among partner agencies when youth homicide abated in Boston. Interested readers should consult the existing literature to get a full account of the varied and complex factors not covered here (Braga & Winship, 2006; Braga, Hureau & Winship, 2008). Nevertheless, there is a growing body of literature suggesting that it is very difficult in practice to sustain these focused-deterrence initiatives over an extended time period. Beyond Boston, replication programs in Baltimore and Minneapolis unraveled rapidly after some encouraging initial crime-control success stories (see Kennedy, 2011). Clearly, jurisdictions interested in implementing focused-deterrence strategies need to understand how to keep these programs on track for the long term (Scott, 2017).

As focused-deterrence programs have gained increasing prominence as a key component of a balanced portfolio of interventions to prevent urban violence, there have been systematic efforts to promote the proper implementation of these strategies. Most notably, the National Network for Safe Communities (NNSC) at the John Jay College of Criminal Justice has developed a variety of practitioner-oriented resources that structure program activities to ensure treatment integrity in focused-deterrence strategies. The NNSC (2016) outlined two ways that program sustainability and accountability could be enhanced: (1) establishing a governing structure that extends beyond the working group and (2) creating a performance maintenance system for intelligence gathering and analysis as well as continually keeping partners engaged in the project.

The most comprehensive approach to address sustainability concerns through establishing a formal multilevel governance structure was undertaken by the Cincinnati Initiative to Reduce Violence (CIRV). Three tiers made up the CIRV organizational structure (Engel, Tillyer & Corsaro, 2013). At the top was a *Governing Board* comprising high-ranking city officials who were responsible for overseeing the project, providing resources, and overcoming obstacles encountered during implementation. Reporting to the Governing Board was a *Strategy and Implementation Team* comprising spokespersons, heads of individual strategy teams, consultants, and an executive director, and this body was responsible for daily operations, strategy development, and monitoring results. There were four *Individual Strategy Teams* that were responsible for carrying out particular aspects of the intervention and these included a law-enforcement team, a social-services team, a community-engagement team, and a systems team. In this tiered organizational structure, the governing board offers a stabilizing presence when there is personnel turnover among team leaders, consultants, and members of individual strategy teams.

While the BPD did not follow this ideal citywide governance structure, it did take definite steps to better institutionalize the Ceasefire program within its own organization during the post-2007 implementation through ongoing problem analysis. The Boston Regional Intelligence Center (BRIC) supported the implementation of Ceasefire by developing a more refined understanding of ongoing gang-violence problems in Boston, ensuring that scarce enforcement resources were centered on the most violent gangs, and measuring the performance of implemented interventions in reducing gun violence by particular gangs (Braga, Hureau & Grossman, 2014). BRIC crime analysts and detectives worked with Harvard researchers to develop a systematic-review process to collect detailed information on fatal and nonfatal shootings. The BPD command staff immediately recognized the value of the enhanced shooting data in supporting their decision making. BRIC then adopted shooting reviews as part of its routine crime data and intelligence gathering and analysis process.

Shooting scorecards were included in biweekly Compstat crime-strategy management sessions and Ceasefire working-group meetings. The inclusion of shooting scorecards in the Compstat meetings ensured that the full BPD command staff was knowledgeable about the role gangs were playing in citywide gun violence and was involved in the decisions about how to handle particularly violent groups. Figure 2.4 presents an example of a shooting scorecard used by the BPD in 2010). It shows that the number of shootings committed by the CVO/Homes Avenue, H-Block, Orchard Park, Greenwood, Lenox, Hitfam, Morse, and Franklin Field gangs decreased between 2009 and 2010. While any implemented violence intervention clearly warrants more careful evaluation, this simple year-to-year comparison suggests that shootings committed by these gangs were in short-term decline. In contrast, shootings by the DSP and Mission gangs increased between 2009 and 2010. This suggests that BPD needed to reassess existing violence interventions focused on these groups; alternatively, if BPD was not focusing violence interventions directly on these groups, it needed to implement a strategic response immediately.

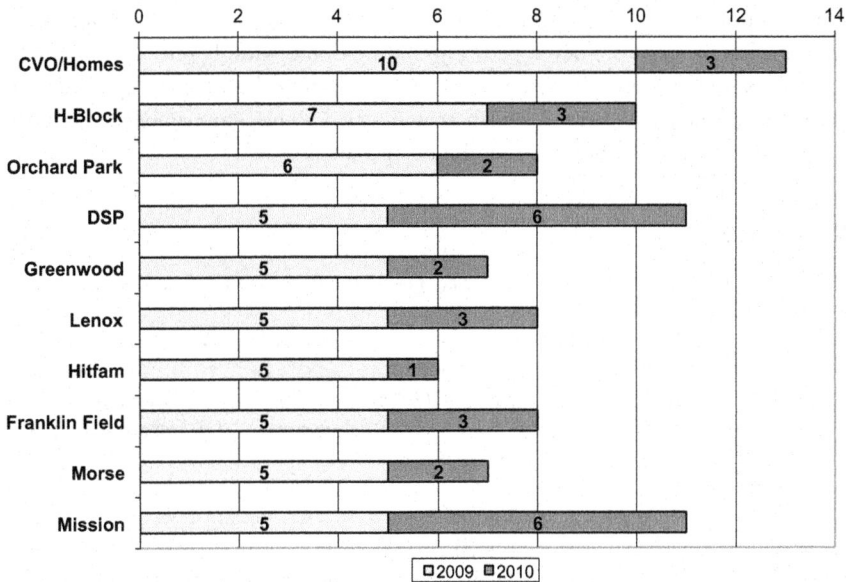

FIGURE 2.4 Number of shootings the 2009 most frequent shooter gangs committed in 2010

Source: Braga, Hureau, and Grossman (2014: p. 23).

Final thoughts

The Boston experience suggests that problem-oriented policing effectively reduced its youth-homicide problem in the 1990s and then again in the 2000s. The available evaluation evidence suggests that the Boston focused-deterrence strategy not only reduced violence by gangs directly targeted by the Operation Ceasefire intervention but also generated diffusion-of-violence-reduction benefits to those gangs not directly subjected to the intervention. Unfortunately, focused-deterrence strategies can be difficult to implement and sustain over time. A commitment to ongoing problem analysis can ensure that gang-violence problems do not reemerge and that police departments and their partners remain focused on implementing strategies that are well positioned to address the underlying dynamics and conditions that influence conflicts among gangs.

The key lesson to be learned from this case study is that developing and maintaining a strong analytical capacity within police departments is clearly essential to problem-oriented policing (White, 2008). A focused approach to crime reduction requires identifying high-risk situations, people, and places (Braga, 2008). It also requires developing an understanding of the underlying conditions that cause these identifiable risks to persist. Measuring whether implemented crime-prevention strategies seem to be generating the desired crime-reduction impacts is also important so that ineffective police strategies can be discontinued and more appropriate interventions developed. This orientation obviously puts a premium on data collection and analysis systems and on developing the human capital within police departments to carry out such analytic work. These investments are clearly worthwhile in keeping neighborhoods safe and secure.

References

Braga, A.A. (2008) *Problem-Oriented Policing and Crime Prevention* (2nd ed.), Boulder, CO: Lynne Rienner Publishers.

Braga, A.A., Apel, R. & Welsh, B. (2013) 'The spillover effects of focused deterrence on gang violence', *Evaluation Review*, 37(3–4): 314–342.

Braga, A.A., Hureau, D.M. & Grossman, L.S. (2014) *Managing the Group Violence Intervention: Using Shooting Scorecards to Track Group Violence*, Washington, DC: US Department of Justice, Community Oriented Policing Services.

Braga, A.A., Hureau, D.M. & Papachristos, A.V. (2014) 'Deterring gang-involved gun violence: Measuring the impact of Boston's Operation Ceasefire on street gang behavior', *Journal of Quantitative Criminology*, 30(1): 113–139.

Braga, A.A., Hureau, D.M. & Winship, C. (2008) 'Losing faith? Police, black churches, and the resurgence of youth violence in Boston', *Ohio State Journal of Criminal Law*, 6(1): 141–172.

Braga, A.A., Kennedy, D., Waring, E. & Piehl, A. (2001) 'Problem-oriented policing, deterrence, and youth violence: An evaluation of Boston's Operation Ceasefire', *Journal of Research in Crime and Delinquency*, 38(3): 195–225.

Braga, A.A., Weisburd, D. & Turchan, B. (2018) 'Focused deterrence strategies and crime control: An updated systematic review and meta-analysis of the empirical evidence', *Criminology & Public Policy*, 17(1): 205–250.

Braga, A.A. & Winship, C. (2006) 'Partnership, accountability, and innovation: Clarifying Boston's experience with pulling levers', in D. Weisburd & A. Braga (eds.), *Police Innovation: Contrasting Perspectives*, New York: Cambridge University Press.

Clarke, R.V. (1989) 'Theoretical background to Crime Prevention through Environmental Design (CPTED) and situational prevention', in S. Geason & P. Wilson (eds.), *Designing Out Crime: The Conference Papers*, Canberra, Australia: Australian Institute of Criminology.

Clarke, R.V. & Weisburd, D. (1994) 'Diffusion of crime control benefits: Observations on the reverse of displacement', *Crime Prevention Studies*, 2: 165–184.

Durlauf, S. & Nagin, D. (2011) 'Imprisonment and crime: Can both be reduced?', *Criminology & Public Policy*, 10(1): 13–54.

Engel, R., Tillyer, M. & Corsaro, N. (2013) 'Reducing gang violence using focused deterrence: Evaluating the Cincinnati Initiative to Reduce Violence (CIRV)', *Justice Quarterly*, 30(3): 403–439.

Johnson, O. (2006) 'Program seen as a prevention tool', *The Boston Herald*, April 8, p. 2.

Kennedy, D. (2011) *Don't Shoot*, New York: Bloomsbury.

Kennedy, D., Braga, A. & Piehl, A. (1997) 'The (un)known universe: Mapping gangs and gang violence in Boston', in D. Weisburd & J. McEwen (eds.), *Crime Mapping and Crime Prevention*, Monsey, NY: Criminal Justice Press.

Kennedy, D., Kleiman, M. & Braga, A. (2017) 'Beyond deterrence: Strategies of focus and fairness', in N. Tilley & A. Sidebottom (eds.), *Handbook of Crime Prevention and Community Safety* (2nd ed.), New York: Routledge.

Kennedy, D., Piehl, A. & Braga, A. (1996) 'Youth violence in Boston: Gun markets, serious offenders, and a use-reduction strategy', *Law and Contemporary Problems*, 59(1): 147–196.

National Network for Safe Communities (2016) *Group Violence Intervention: An Implementation Guide*, Washington, DC: US Department of Justice, Office of Community Oriented Policing Services.

Scott, M.S. (2017) *Focused Deterrence of High-Risk Individuals*, Problem-Oriented Guides for Police, Response Guide No. 13, Washington, DC: US Department of Justice, Bureau of Justice Assistance.

Papachristos, A., Meares, T. & Fagan, J. (2007) 'Attention felons: Evaluating project safe neighborhoods in Chicago', *Journal of Empirical Legal Studies*, 4(2): 223–272.

White, M. (2008) *Enhancing the Problem-Solving Capacity of Crime Analysis Units*, Problem-Oriented Guides for Police, Problem-Solving Tools Guide No. 9, Washington, DC: US Department of Justice, Office of Community Oriented Policing Services.

Winship, C. & Berrien, J. (1999) 'Boston cops and black churches', *The Public Interest*, 136 (Summer): 52–68.

3

GUN VIOLENCE IN CINCINNATI, OHIO

Tamara D. Herold and John E. Eck

Introduction

Sergeant Maris Herold, working as a Neighborhood Unit supervisor for the Cincinnati Police Department (CPD) in 2004, attempted to disrupt a violent open-air drug market by altering traffic flow into a disadvantaged residential neighborhood adjacent to an interstate off-ramp (a common problem; see, e.g., Zanin, Shane & Clarke, 2004). Sergeant Herold employed the basic tenets of problem-oriented policing, as advocated by Herman Goldstein 25 years prior to her efforts (Goldstein, 1979). She identified gun violence as a specific and harmful problem, she collected information and garnered support from neighborhood residents, she leveraged other city department resources to erect a traffic barricade, and she partnered with academics (including the authors of this case study) to evaluate her intervention (Madensen & Morgan, 2005).

There was an immediate and almost complete elimination of gun violence and drug sales along the targeted street segment. However, as Sergeant Herold attempted to expand the project to address nearby displacement and further enhance the intervention's effectiveness, the city council ordered the barricade's removal due to pressure from a local business owner (News Briefs, 2005). Violence and drug sales swiftly returned, and neighborhood crime eventually exceeded pre-barricade levels.

Many lessons were learned from this and other problem-solving projects conducted by the CPD in the years that followed. The CPD had adopted community problem-oriented policing as the department's primary crime reduction strategy. This strategy was mandated as part of the historic "collaborative agreement" (*In re Cincinnati Policing*, 2002) between the Cincinnati Black United Front, the American Civil Liberties Union, the City of Cincinnati, and the Fraternal Order of Police, which was drafted to settle a civil suit in federal court. As part of the collaborative agreement, the CPD engaged in and monitored the outcomes of hundreds of problem-solving projects across the city.

The CPD's community problem-oriented policing projects proved highly useful in reducing a wide variety of crimes and related harms. These projects sometimes encountered obstacles, as the barricade project illustrates, but the vast majority generated notable crime reductions and offered effective alternatives to traditional law enforcement and arrest strategies (Eck, 2014). The principal limitation of the CPD problem-solving projects was the inability to sustain crime reductions over time. Most problem-solving projects dramatically reduced crime post-intervention, but the effects of the projects were short-lived. In many cases, crime at targeted locations eventually returned to previous levels or exceeded previous levels. In 2015, a CPD police officer was shot and killed in the line of duty while the city experienced dramatic spikes in levels of violence and shootings. Undesirable national attention and community pressure prompted city officials to look for new solutions. It was within this context that Herold, by then a captain, was asked to accept a specialized assignment and develop a citywide violence-reduction strategy. This strategy, known as PIVOT (Place-based Investigations of Violent Offender Territories), earned the CPD the 2017 Herman Goldstein Award for Excellence in Problem-Oriented Policing and is the focus of this case study.

Development and implementation of PIVOT

Captain Herold assembled a strategy-development team including officers, analysts, and academic partners to examine gun-violence incidents throughout the city. The team framed their discussions and activities around general crime-science principles (see Clarke, 2010). Their work was grounded in the understanding that crime is not random; crime is concentrated across offenders, victims, and—most important for the early stages of the PIVOT project—places (Spelman & Eck, 1989).

During the **scanning** phase, analyses revealed that a disproportionate amount of gun violence was concentrated within 23 micro-locations[1] across the city. Analyses also determined that these locations had been chronically violent for a long time. Although many of the identified micro-locations had been targets of previous problem-solving projects, violence had been concentrated in these locations for several decades.

Additional analyses and a resident survey helped to confirm that gun violence in these locations met each of the six required elements necessary to define a problem, as outlined by the CHEERS criteria (Eck & Clarke, 2003):

- **Community**—Over 25 percent of residents planned to move out in the near future due to neighborhood conditions.
- **Harm**—In addition to the physical consequences of gun violence, fear of crime was rampant with over 81 percent of residents reporting concern over child safety.
- **Expectation**—Over 73 percent of residents gave specific examples of what they thought the police could do, or do better, to prevent crime (e.g., community partnerships, foot patrols, talk with residents).

- **Events**—Cincinnati crime data revealed that more than 42 percent of all shootings occurred in these micro-locations.
- **Recurring**—The 23 identified micro-locations make up only 1.4 percent of the city's landmass, yet they accounted for a disproportionate amount of crime and shootings (Figure 3.1).
- **Similar**—All of the incidents examined involved violent gun-related crimes: shooting victimizations, shots fired, robberies, and gun offenses.

Initial analyses discovered that the 23 violent micro-locations also posed a threat to officer safety. Officers were more likely to be injured or experience high-risk interactions in these locations. Specifically, 14.6 percent of officer injuries (67 of 460) and 24 percent of noncompliant behaviors (1,516 of 6,315 obstruction of official business, resisting arrest, and assault on a police officer charges—behaviors that increase risk of officer injury) occurred in the identified micro-locations between 2012 and 2015 (Figure 3.1).

Three objectives guided the **analysis** project phase: (1) develop a policing strategy to address systemically violent micro-locations, (2) select an initial project site, and (3) analyze data/gather intelligence to create a tailored response. To address the sustainability issue encountered by previous CPD problem-solving projects, the PIVOT team drew on recent advances in crime science research and theory. These advances led the team to hypothesize that, much like offenders and victims, crime places are networked.

Crime place networks provide the "infrastructure" necessary for offenders to operate illicit markets and promote violence interactions. These place networks extend

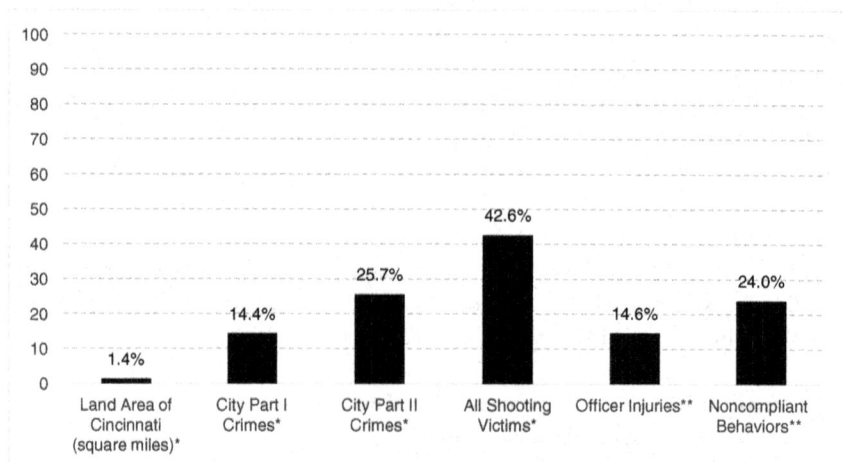

FIGURE 3.1 Involvement with violent micro-locations in Cincinnati

Source: Cincinnati Police Department

* 2015
** 2012–2015

beyond locations where crime is reported and can include four types of places (Felson, 2003; Hammer, 2011; Madensen & Eck, 2013):

- Crime sites—specific places where crime occurs
- Convergent settings—public places where offenders routinely meet
- Comfort spaces—private meeting, staging, and supplying locations
- Corrupting spots—places that encourage criminal activity in other locations

A persistently violent apartment complex with an open-air drug market (crime site) could be supported by a larger crime place network. This network might include a nearby neighborhood market and public park (convergent settings) used by offenders as an observation location to supervise drug market activities and warn dealers before police patrols arrive at the complex. The crime place network might also include nearby private residences (comfort spaces) used by offenders to stage crimes and stash weapons and drugs. A business (corrupting spot) that purchases stolen goods from those seeking to buy drugs at the open-air market or regularly offers concealment to offenders seeking to avoid police detection might also contribute to crime at the complex.

Crime sites regularly come to the attention of police through crime reports. The other three locations in crime place networks often remain hidden in the absence of focused police investigation. If left unidentified and unaddressed, new (or returning) offenders will continue to use these place networks to engage in criminal activity (Madensen et al., 2017).

A wide variety of investigative techniques can be used to uncover crime place networks. For example, interviews with patrol officers, detectives, specialized units (e.g., violent crime, gang, vice, homicide), crime analysts, city department personnel, and community members and service personnel (e.g., postal service workers) can be used to identify key places and offenders who are engaged in harmful conduct. The specific connections between people and places can be further investigated through various surveillance activities (e.g., temporary surveillance cameras, site observations, undercover officers) that reveal how other places (convergent settings, comfort spaces, and corrupting spots) are connected to identified crime sites. To build civil and criminal cases against place owners, managers, and serious offenders, investigations might involve the use of additional sources of information (e.g., security personnel, management personnel, labor contractors) and confidential informants.

A new strategy based on the idea of place networks was developed to disrupt crime in Cincinnati's systemically violent locations. Place-based Investigations of Violent Offender Territories (more commonly called PIVOT) uses investigative techniques, including those mentioned earlier, to identify the convergent settings, comfort spaces, and corrupting spots of the crime place networks.

Once locations within a crime place network are identified, a citywide PIVOT Investigative Board, made up of representatives from various city departments and community agencies, reviews CPD investigation findings, physically observes the violent location, provides additional intelligence about the location (using historical data from their respective departments/organizations), and offers recommendations and resources to dismantle the identified crime place network. The investigative board can dismantle the place network through various means, including the use of legal remedies to revoke business licenses, require new management practices, mandate employee training, order owners into court-mandated receivership, require changes to the physical design of a building, or, ultimately, order complete property abatement. The board can also prioritize city resources to impact crime-facilitating places (e.g., schedule buildings for demolition, reroute traffic patterns, initiate redevelopment projects). Table 3.1 provides examples of agencies and organizations that contribute to the PIVOT Investigative Board and the types of resources that can be leveraged to disrupt crime place networks.

An initial project site was selected and the PIVOT team, along with community partners, conducted investigations to identify the site's crime place network. Their location analyses uncovered eight key locations in the crime place network that included businesses, public spaces, private residences, and public parking locations.

TABLE 3.1 PIVOT investigative board and resources

City Department	Disruption Techniques
Fire	• Eliminate hazards (e.g., remove illegal scrapyard) • Fire code violations fines/arrests
Traffic/Engineering	• Street redesign (e.g., traffic calming, closures) • Adding/removing signage
Community Improvement Organizations	• Private property consultations (e.g., graffiti removal) • Adding fencing or public space definition markers
Buildings	• Parking spaces, dumpster placement/organization • Execute vacate orders
Health	• Removal of illegal kitchens or vendors • Address lead paint in buildings
Port Authority	• Building demolitions • Initiate large-scale redevelopment projects
Treasury	• Permit revocation (e.g., illegal dance halls) • Citations for nonlicensed activities (e.g., gaming)
Parks & Recreation	• Redesign or development of park spaces • Removal of dilapidated playground equipment
Non-profit Redevelopment Groups	• Purchase vacated properties • Help community leaders secure low-income housing
Public Services	• Foliage removal, community cleanup efforts • Altering trash pickup schedules
Human Relations Commission	• Advocacy and offender desistance outreach • Job and social services messaging

Source: Adapted from Madensen et al. (2017).

The PIVOT team identified six major gun-violence facilitators at networked places, including unregulated parking that provided cover during drive-by shootings, a lack of place management that allowed residences to be used as drug distribution centers, unsecured structures that concealed criminal activities, illegal vending activities that provided access to drug paraphernalia, inadequate lighting that concealed offender movement and activities, and blighted/abandoned properties used for crime staging. Ultimately, locations identified as part of the crime place network were connected through a group of offenders involved in drug trafficking.

Beginning in June 2016, the **response** phase was initiated. The PIVOT investigations team worked with more than 20 public/private partners to disrupt the crime place network. These partners, with community input and support, modified or eliminated the identified violence facilitators. Responses included, but were not limited to, permanent on-street parking restrictions, obtaining compliance from rental property owners, code enforcement and commercial/retail property owner partnerships, directed patrols, lighting, property demolition, and developing a community park and walking trail.

In the final **assessment** phase, the PIVOT team determined that the number of shooting victims fell from a high of 18 victims in 2015 to only one victim during the first half of 2017 Figure 3.2). In addition, a violence score metric was used to provide "real-time" information about changes in gun-related violence levels.[2] The violence score fell from a high of 172.4 to 28.6 at the time of the CPD Goldstein submission (Cincinnati Police Department, 2017). Observable blight at this location also decreased by over 29 percent. There was little to no evidence of crime

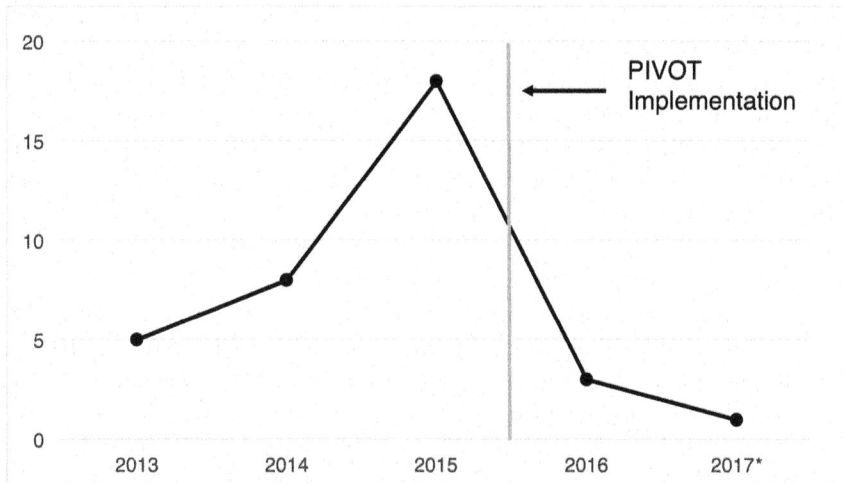

FIGURE 3.2 Yearly shooting victims at initial PIVOT site

Source: Cincinnati Police Department

* Approximately June 2017.

displacement, but analyses suggested a possible diffusion of crime control benefits to nearby locations.

Discussion

The PIVOT violence reduction strategy is *similar* to other Goldstein-winning problem-oriented policing projects in at least three ways. First, like most successful problem-solving efforts, PIVOT focuses police attention on a specific problem (i.e., shootings) and calls for the systematic analysis of opportunity structures that facilitate similar harmful events (see Clarke & Eck, 2005). Second, PIVOT focuses attention on specific places. Research consistently demonstrates that a small number of risky facilities (Clarke & Eck, 2007; Eck, Clarke & Guerette, 2007) or individual crime generators and attractors (Brantingham & Brantingham, 1995) account for the vast majority of crime events in any given area. PIVOT also promotes the "shifting and sharing of responsibility" (Scott & Goldstein, 2005; Scott, 2005) for solving crime problems by holding place managers accountable for incidents that occur on their properties, as well as shifting responsibility to "super-controllers" (Sampson, Eck & Dunham, 2010) who control local government resources. The success of this project, like many others, requires strong leadership and participation on the part of local government (see Plant & Scott, 2009). The success of Cincinnati's PIVOT strategy was in large part driven by a talented city attorney, Mark Manning, who aggressively targeted those ultimately responsible for places involved in the crime network. Manning worked directly with the PIVOT team to assess places identified as part of the crime network, direct police investigative activities to build criminal cases against place owners, and litigate state and city nuisance abatement laws.

PIVOT also *differs* from traditional policing strategies in at least three ways. First, PIVOT acknowledges the dangers associated with repeatedly sending police officers into violent micro-locations to respond to incidents. Failing to address chronic violent hot spots puts both residents and officers who serve these communities at risk. Police commanders should be aware of the trauma officers experience when continually dispatched into violent hot spots. The PIVOT evaluation suggests that overreliance on reactive policing tactics might unnecessarily place officers in harm's way.

Second, PIVOT focuses on crime place networks. Crime scientists have long encouraged police to focus on places that generate the most crime (crime sites), but PIVOT suggests that this approach, while often effective in the short-term (Braga, Papachristos & Hureau, 2014), fails to produce sustainable crime reductions. The key to long-term crime reduction is to identify and dismantle the entire physical infrastructure used by offenders. Investigators must be trained to uncover the connected network of offender-used places that are not brought to police attention through calls for service. These places include public and private locations used by offenders to plan and carry out crime (convergent settings and comfort spaces), as well as businesses that facilitate crime markets (corrupting spots). These locations are identified by learning about offender crime scripts (Cornish, 1994) that naturally highlight the way in which offenders move between and use places. A focus on place networks, rather than individual crime sites, roots out the larger infrastructure offenders retreat to and then reemerge from once police resources are deployed elsewhere.

Third, PIVOT is an all-city approach to reducing gun-related violence. The overall objective must be supported and driven by someone (e.g., the city manager) who controls resources beyond those available to police. PIVOT interventions block crime activities by changing the way in which places are managed and used. Interventions might involve altering parking restrictions or traffic patterns along a road commonly used in drive-by shootings or seizing and repurposing a corner store laundering money for a violent drug market. As it turns out, other city departments are often much better suited to design and implement crime prevention interventions than are police.

Follow-up

PIVOT is still a relatively new strategy, but enough time has passed to suggest that this approach has the potential to generate the sustainable crime reductions it was designed to achieve. The initial PIVOT site did not experience another shooting victim in 2017. During 2018, three shootings occurred in the location. Violence has not been eliminated, yet it appears that the strategy has produced violent crime reductions that are greater and last longer than the traditional three- to six-month reductions historically achieved by Cincinnati problem-solving projects that focus strictly on observable crime sites. It remains to be seen whether "maintenance" investigations and interventions are necessary to prevent offenders from rebuilding crime place networks in the same locations.

Led by Lieutenant Matthew Hammer and his team of investigators, PIVOT has now been implemented in a total of nine violent micro-locations across Cincinnati. All have experienced reductions in shootings and gun-related violent crime. Lieutenant Hammer plans to conduct a comprehensive evaluation of PIVOT's impact at each site as part of his doctoral dissertation being completed at the University of Cincinnati.

The PIVOT strategy was directly referenced in the 2018 Innovations in Community-Based Crime Reduction Program competitive grant solicitation, which provides jurisdictions across the United States with financial and technical resources to implement promising crime reduction strategies. Those who developed PIVOT in Cincinnati are serving as part of an expert panel that will provide technical assistance to the grant awardees. Additionally, the research center of the International Association of Chiefs of Police—the Center for Police Research and Policy—is conducting a formal process and outcome evaluation of the PIVOT strategy as implemented by the Las Vegas Metropolitan Police Department in 2018. Preliminary analyses suggest that PIVOT is responsible for the absence of violence (over 180 days) in a site that has historically been one of the most violent locations in Las Vegas, Nevada.

Summary and conclusion

Professor Jerry Ratcliffe recorded a podcast[3] about the Cincinnati PIVOT project with one of this case study's authors (Herold). He made a keen observation during our discussion about the origins of the project. PIVOT, like many creative policing strategies, was developed under conditions that spark innovation: historical struggle, pressing political crisis, diminishing resources, and a fortunate series of interactions between people who have a fortuitous combination of ideas and experience. Lessons learned from this project have contributed to our understanding of crime. It provides a new direction for crime science theory and research, as well as future police problem-solving efforts.

PIVOT has changed the way that Cincinnati addresses its most critical violent hot spots. More time must pass before we can assess the long-term success and influence of this project, both in Cincinnati and elsewhere. However, our follow-up to the Cincinnati project finds that PIVOT has served as an impetus for both organic and large-scale neighborhood improvements. In the absence of chronic violence, once-problematic properties are being reorganized, repurposed, and redeveloped. Cincinnati's Neighborhood Enhancement Program personnel served alongside CPD investigators to gather, organize, and direct resources in PIVOT locations to promote neighborhood redevelopment. PIVOT suggests that positive economic and quality-of-life changes can be fostered by prioritizing the distribution of city resources with the goal of reducing violent victimization.

Final thoughts

This summary neglects the challenges associated with implementing the PIVOT strategy. There are many. PIVOT not only requires new thinking and direction on the part of police administrators; it also relies on the support and direct involvement of other city officials—many of whom may not believe that they should be involved in crime-reduction efforts. PIVOT also involves sophisticated investigations. Crime place networks can vary extensively in design and scope. A small theft ring at a single crime site adjacent to one corrupting spot and comfort space will be very different from the place network associated with an international human trafficking ring. Relatedly, sophisticated investigations take resources and time. Police administrators looking for immediate solutions to long-sustained violence issues will likely be frustrated by the complexity, dedication, and leadership necessary to successfully execute the PIVOT strategy.

Despite implementation obstacles, there appear to be several benefits to using PIVOT as a crime-reduction strategy. PIVOT is grounded in evidence-based crime-science principles and, thus, rejects an overreliance on traditional police suppression tactics. While frequently effective in driving down crime, reactive tactics continually put officers at risk, offer short-lived crime reductions, and often harm police–community relations. PIVOT complements offender-based strategies. Place investigations can focus criminal-justice resources on impactful, targeted arrests by uncovering "hidden" locations where high-level players in violent offender networks operate. Furthermore, PIVOT, as implemented in Cincinnati, did not call for new resources. It simply asked officers to investigate (something that police do well) and required city leaders to better organize and reprioritize existing resources.

We end by offering two matters for future consideration. First, the PIVOT project outcomes suggest that crime place networks might offer a new and highly plausible explanation for the "diffusion of benefits" phenomenon. Researchers have sought to explain why crime is often more likely to decrease, rather than displace to, areas close to police intervention (see Clarke & Weisburd, 1994; Guerette & Bowers, 2009). However, if places are networked, then interventions affecting places in one part of the network might produce changes in places connected to those initially targeted. A partially disrupted crime place network might render the entire network less conducive for criminal activity. This is a potential direction for future theoretical development and study. Second, framing problem solving as "investigations" could hold great promise for promoting proactive police activity to address crime and disorder problems. Maris Herold, the person tasked with developing PIVOT, is now a police chief engaged in police reform in the University of Cincinnati Police Division. In building on the work of others who seek to institutionalize problem solving in police agencies (Boba & Santos, 2015), Chief Herold has developed a Tactical and Strategic Investigations policy. This policy directs investigators to lead both short-term and long-term problem-solving projects to address issues identified by analysts, officers, and the community. While police may or may not be more likely to embrace problem solving if framed as investigations, presenting problem solving as an investigative tool allows departments to harness the skills of criminal investigators to engage in the more productive and effective work of crime prevention and problem solving.

Acknowledgments

We thank Woodburn Brewery in Cincinnati for their creative space and Michael Scott and Ronald V. Clarke for their supportive and highly useful comments on our initial drafts.

Notes

1 A micro-location represented an area of approximately two square blocks that encompassed a violent hot spot.
2 Information on how to calculate the violence score metric, developed by Blake Christenson, can be found on the CPD's PIVOT website: www.cincinnati-oh.gov/police/community-involvement/pivot/.
3 See Podcast #5 on the Reducing Crime website: www.reducingcrime.com/podcast.

References

Boba, R. & Santos, R. (2015) *A Police Organizational Model for Crime Reduction: Institutionalizing Problems-Solving, Analysis, and Accountability*, Washington, DC: US Department of Justice, Office of Community Oriented Policing Services.

Braga, A.A., Papachristos, A.V. & Hureau, D.M. (2014) 'The effects of hot spots policing on crime: An updated systematic review and meta-analysis', *Justice Quarterly*, 31(4): 633–663.

Brantingham, P. & Brantingham, P. (1995) 'Criminality of place: Crime generators and crime attractors', *European Journal on Criminal Policy and Research*, 3(3): 1–26.

Cincinnati Police Department (2017) 'PIVOT: Place-based investigations of Violent Offender Territories', Winner, Herman Goldstein Award for Excellence in Problem-Oriented Policing, Center for Problem-Oriented Policing, Arizona State University, Phoenix, AZ.

Clarke, R.V. (2010) 'Crime science', in E. McLaughlin & T. Newburn (eds.), *The SAGE Handbook of Criminological Theory*, Thousand Oaks, CA: SAGE, pp. 271–283.

Clarke, R.V. & Eck, J. (2005) *Crime Analysis for Problem Solvers: In 60 Small Steps*, Washington, DC: US Department of Justice, Office of Community Oriented Policing Services.

Clarke, R.V. & Eck, J. (2007) *Understanding Risky Facilities*, Problem-Oriented Guides for Police, Problem-Solving Tools Guide No. 6, Washington, DC: US Department of Justice, Office of Community Oriented Policing.

Clarke, R.V. & Weisburd, D. (1994) 'Diffusion of crime control benefits: Observations on the reverse of displacement', in R.V. Clarke (ed.), *Crime Prevention Studies*, Vol. 2, Monsey, NY: Criminal Justice Press, pp. 165–183.

Cornish, D.B. (1994) 'The procedural analysis of offending and its relevance for situational prevention', in R.V Clarke (ed.), *Crime Prevention Studies*, Vol. 3, Monsey, NY: Criminal Justice Press, pp. 151–196.

Eck, J.E. (2014) *The Status of Collaborative Problem Solving and Community Problem-Oriented Policing in Cincinnati*, Cincinnati, OH: University of Cincinnati, School of Criminal Justice.

Eck, J.E. & Clarke, R.V. (2003) 'Classifying common police problems: A routine activity theory approach', in M.J. Smith & D.B. Cornish (eds.), *Theory for Practice in Situational Crime Prevention*, Crime Prevention Studies, Vol. 16, Monsey, NY: Criminal Justice Press, pp. 7–39.

Eck, J.E., Clarke, R.V. & Guerette, R.T. (2007) 'Risky facilities: Crime concentration in homogeneous sets of establishments and facilities', in G. Farrell, K.J. Bowers, S.D. Johnson & M. Townsley (eds.), *Imagination for Crime Prevention: Essays in Honour of Ken Pease*, Crime Prevention Studies, Vol. 21, Monsey, NY: Criminal Justice Press, pp. 225–264.

Felson, M. (2003) 'The process of co-offending', in M.J. Smith & D.B. Cornish (eds.), *Theory for Practice in Situational Crime Prevention*, Crime Prevention Studies, Vol. 21, Monsey, NY: Criminal Justice Press, pp. 149–168.

Goldstein, H. (1979) 'Improving policing: A problem-oriented approach', *Crime & Delinquency*, 25(2): 236–258.

Guerette, R.T. & Bowers, K.J. (2009) 'Assessing the extent of crime displacement and diffusion of benefits: A review of situational crime prevention evaluations', *Criminology*, 47(4): 1331–1368.

Hammer, M. (2011) 'Crime places of comfort', Unpublished M.S. demonstration project paper, Cincinnati, OH: University of Cincinnati, School of Criminal Justice.

In re Cincinnati Policing, 209 F.R.D. 395, 397 (S.D. Ohio 2002); *Tyehimba v. City of Cincinnati*, No. C-1-99-317, 2001 WL 1842470 (S.D. Ohio May 3, 2001).

Madensen, T.D. & Eck, J.E. (2013) 'Crime places and place management', in F.T. Cullen & P. Wilcox (eds.), *The Oxford Handbook of Criminological Theory*, New York: Oxford University Press, pp. 554–578.

Madensen, T.D., Herold, M., Hammer, M.G. & Christenson, B.R. (2017) 'Research in brief: Place-based investigations to disrupt crime place networks', *Police Chief Magazine*, 84(4): 14–15.

Madensen, T.D. & Morgan, D.G. (2005) *Evaluation of Traffic Barricade Impact on Crime in Pendleton: Cincinnati, Ohio*, Unpublished report submitted to the Cincinnati Police Department, Cincinnati, OH: Division of Criminal Justice, University of Cincinnati.

News Briefs (2005) 'Pendleton street barricade has been removed', *Cincinnati Enquirer*, April 16, p. B1.

Plant, J.B. & Scott, M.S. (2009) *Effective Policing and Crime Prevention: A Problem-Oriented Guide for Mayors, City Managers, and County Executives*, Washington, DC: US Department of Justice, Office of Community Oriented Policing.

Sampson, R., Eck, J.E. & Dunham, J. (2010) 'Super controllers and crime prevention: A routine activity explanation of crime prevention success and failure', *Security Journal*, 23(1): 37–51.

Scott, M.S. (2005) 'Shifting and Sharing Police Responsibility to Address Public Safety Problems', in N. Tilley (ed.), *Handbook of Crime Prevention and Community Safety*, Portland, OR: Willan Publishing, pp. 385–410.

Scott, M.S. & Goldstein, H. (2005) *Shifting and Sharing Responsibility for Public Safety Problems*, Problem-Oriented Guides for Police, Response Guide No. 3, Washington, DC: US Department of Justice, Office of Community Oriented Policing Services.

Spelman, W. & Eck, J.E. (1989) 'Sitting ducks, ravenous wolves, and helping hands: New approaches to urban policing', *Public Affairs Comment*, 35(2): 1–9.

Zanin, N., Shane, J.M. & Clarke, R.V. (2004) *Reducing Drug Dealing in Private Apartment Complexes*, Final report to the US Department of Justice, Office of Community Oriented Policing Services on the Field Applications of the Problem-Oriented Guides for Police Project, Washington, DC: US Department of Justice, Office of Community Oriented Policing Services.

4

GANG VIOLENCE IN ENFIELD, LONDON

Lisa Tompson and Kate Bowers

Introduction

The proliferation of mobile phones in circulation from the turn of the millennium, and their ever-increasing technological sophistication, created an archetypal 'hot product' (Clarke, 1999) for thieves to target. They were concealable, removable, available, valuable, enjoyable, and desirable, fulfilling all of Clarke's (1999) CRAVED criteria. Within the youth population, mobile phones were commonly believed to act as 'status symbols', with only the wealthiest able to afford them. It is little wonder then that they contributed to a reverse in the UK acquisitive-crime statistics that had been on the decline in the 1990s. Whilst possession of a mobile phone (indeed of a fairly high-end smartphone) has proliferated in the contemporary youth population and in-built anti-theft measures have improved, lessons learnt from early attempts to stem the tide of youth robbery are still relevant today.

This case study reports the problem-solving efforts of a multi-agency team to reduce youth robbery in the London Borough of Enfield in the United Kingdom (Enfield Community Safety Partnership, 2013). As we recount, Enfield had a large youth population and an associated robbery and violence problem affecting this age group. The analysts who spearheaded the Goldstein Award submission—Sandeep Broca and Iain Agar—had attended a number of courses at the Jill Dando Institute of Crime Science at University College London, where they learned of, and applied, environmental criminology theory and concepts to their work on a regular basis.

The precipitous rise of antisocial behaviour and crime involving youths from 2000 onwards had become a source of concern for many in Enfield. Residents were alarmed, naming youth crime as their top priority in a survey; politicians were making statements of condemnation in the press; and the Enfield youth population were especially anxious about becoming a crime victim. By 2008, declines were being experienced in most categories of youth crime, with the notable exception of robbery and violence, which had both risen by more than 20 per cent in the past year (Figure 4.1 shows trends for street robbery and other youth crimes in Enfield between 2007/08 and 2009/10).

Street robbery was of particular concern at this time, due to the link with 'gang' activities. Interviews and engagement with victims and offenders identified that street robbery was an offence that was instrumental in building reputation and status to gain social capital and acceptance, protection or recognition from gang members. The perceived disrespect associated with being robbed, particularly if this was witnessed by many people, resulted in victims feeling pressure and expectation to react in accordance with the 'street norms'—which would be retaliation, either robbing or assaulting the offender or one of their associates. Robbery was therefore identified as often preceding violent retaliatory attacks. These findings were mirrored in independent research with young people in Enfield (Hallsworth & Young, 2009).[1]

Robbery more broadly was a strategic priority for Enfield's Community Safety Partnership, since the borough was ranked the 16th-highest area nationally for robbery in 2010. Over four in ten robberies involved a victim aged 10 to 17. Robbery and violence accounted for 74 per cent of all youth crime in Enfield, prompting a coordinated multi-agency response. At the time in the United Kingdom, it was common practice for partnerships to express goals as numeric targets in terms of crime reduction. This practice arose from guidelines on the expected content of crime and disorder audits—the production of which was a shared statutory responsibility of stakeholders in community safety partnerships (including local authorities

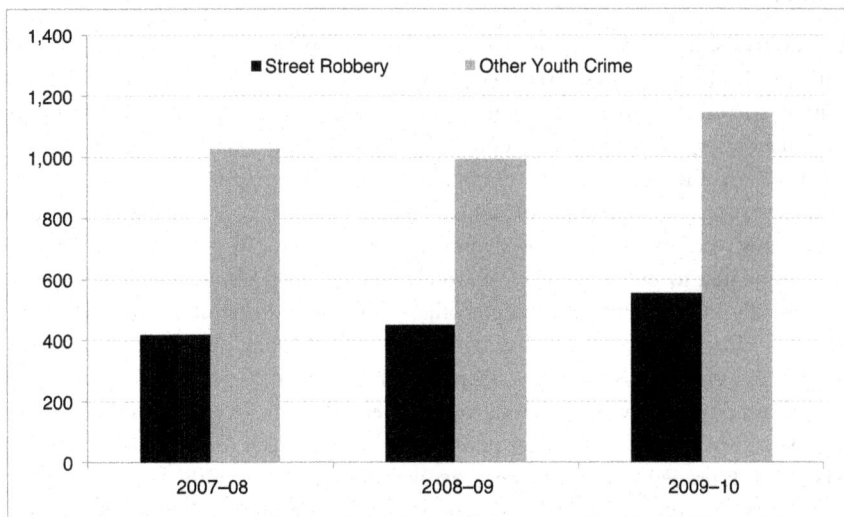

FIGURE 4.1 Street robbery and other youth crimes in Enfield between 2007/08 and 2009/10

and the police as a minimum) as laid out in the 1998 Crime and Disorder Act (e.g., Bowers, Jennings & Hirschfield, 2002). A target was therefore set in 2009/10 to reduce total street robbery by 7.5 per cent in each fiscal year, with an eventual decline in frequency of just over 20 per cent in 2012/13.

The SARA process

Scanning

More than 18,000 pupils were being educated across the 24 high schools in Enfield, which was the second-highest volume across the London boroughs. Young people— defined as 10- to 17-year-olds—were found to be disproportionately represented in the crime figures during the project **scanning** phase. Whilst they composed 10 per cent of the resident population, people from this age group were present in 44 per cent of all street-robbery offences recorded in the area between 2007/08 and 2009/10.

Research commissioned from London Metropolitan University on youth crime in Enfield found that more than half of the 100 participants who were interviewed felt under threat of being bullied or having their possessions stolen as they travelled to and from school. The qualitative analysis from this research further revealed that retaliatory violence often followed robbery, thereby perpetuating the violence problem in the Borough. Victimisation can have a heavy psychological impact on the victim, which may subsequently lead to days off school and a drop in attainment levels. It became obvious that addressing the safety of young people in the area should become a priority.

Analysis

The **analysis** phase used a wide range of partnership intelligence and was aligned with the Problem Analysis Triangle (Eck, 2003). For example, sources of information included Enfield Council, the Youth Offending Service, the London Ambulance Service, Social Care, schools, Enfield Retail Association and many more besides. Useful information was derived from police recorded-crime data, survey/interview data with young people and academic research.

Victims were found to be concentrated in the 12- to 16-years-old age cohort, which equated to 80 per cent of all youth victims. The ethnic profile of victims was broadly in line with the ethnic profile of the borough (which was particularly diverse). More than eight in ten victims were male. Mobile phones were stolen in 69 per cent of youth-on-youth robberies, with a further 26 per cent involving the loss of cash or currency. There was a very low recovery rate for stolen phones, meaning that it was unknown whether phones were being stolen for personal use or for selling on. Interviews with offenders revealed that 'rich'- or 'posh'-looking victims were being targeted, presumably because of the assumption that they would be carrying phones and/or cash. Victims were believed by the criminal justice agencies to be unwilling to support the prosecution process due to fear of reprisals from offenders who they might encounter again during their commute to and from school.

Offenders were found to be overwhelmingly male (96 per cent), with offending concentrating within the 15- to 17-years-old age cohort. Many were from low-income households. A significant proportion had been truant or excluded from school at the time of the offence. About one in ten offenders reported to their youth workers that they habitually used cannabis. These offenders typically offended in groups and/or repeatedly offended.

Co-offending was common, with more than three-quarters of offences involving two or more suspects. School rivalries were believed to play a part in the offender-victim relationship and robbery was seen as an escalation of bullying events common between pupils from different schools. Pupils in the school year below the offenders were often targeted, and particularly when there were multiple offenders, victims tended to acquiesce and hand over their possessions. In just under a third of offences, a knife was threatened or insinuated. The classic characteristics of intimidation were thus present in the profile of the youth robbery offences in Enfield.

Wider London-centric research by the Youth Justice Board had found that robbery offenders often came from lone-parent families and households where no adults were in employment. Their motivations for offending were inferred to be acquiring the luxury goods their parents could not provide but for which their peer groups valued as status symbols. Since a third of Enfield's resident youths were living in deprived households, this was taken to be a credible working hypothesis by the practitioners involved in the project.

Youth robberies were found to cluster in space and time in line with the routine activities of school pupils. They occurred almost exclusively in school-term times and were most concentrated in the 3–6 p.m. time window after high schools finished for the day. Hot spots closely aligned with schools and routes used by pupils to commute via transport hubs. The most intense hot spots were in locations where schools with very different pupil profiles—with respect to socio-economic backgrounds and attainment levels—were in close proximity to each other. One in five youth robberies occurred on weekdays, within half a mile of a high school, during the 3–6 p.m. time window.

The analysts involved in the project hypothesised that schools were acting as *crime generators* (Brantingham & Brantingham, 1995) in the school day—drawing pupils to them for legitimate activities whilst at the same time providing plentiful opportunities for motivated offenders to opportunistically commit robbery. However, before and after school, whilst pupils were commuting to and from school, these same schools transformed into *crime attractors*, where a particular victim profile was sought out (younger, wealthy-looking pupils who could be intimidated to giving up their possessions) by the motivated offenders (young males from deprived backgrounds).

Response

The police-led **response** phase of the project in 2010 drew from many different organisations to deliver a coordinated approach to simultaneously enhance controls on the victims, offenders and locations. This approach drew from best practice in tackling street robbery (Monk et al., 2010) and tapped into the 25 techniques of situational crime prevention (Cornish & Clarke, 2003).

Victims

In 2009/10, before joining high school, 4,000 pupils in Enfield were given personal safety lessons which raised awareness on victimisation and emphasised keeping their possessions out of view. In the first few weeks of being at high school, the same pupils received follow-up lessons which sought to encourage them to take sensible precautions when commuting to and from school, how to deal with online and offline bullying, and how to register their phones with 'Immobilise'. Set up in 2003, the free Immobilise property registration scheme has the support of the central government, the mobile phone industry and the police. The online checking service associated with Immobilise is widely used by UK police forces to identify stolen property and to reunite it with their owners.

Robbery and the theft of phones were also covered by Enfield's Anti-Bullying scheme, which makes it clear to both pupils and parents that these are crimes that will not be condoned. To disrupt local goods markets, Trading Standards (a statutory partner under the Crime and Disorder Act 1998) worked with local pawn shops to reduce disposal points for stolen mobile phones. Another prong of the response strategy targeted at victims was the introduction of a Victim Support Worker, who was employed by a charity and co-located in the Community Safety team, which helped navigate victims through the criminal justice process once they had reported an offence.

Offenders

Various controls were exerted on offenders. To reduce weapon carrying by pupils the 'Sharp System' (School Help Advice Reporting Page)—suggested by youths who participated in research in Enfield—was introduced. This provided a means of anonymously reporting information on pupils suspected of carrying weapons. To complement this, weapon 'sweeps' would be undertaken by the police to recover weapons from locations where it was believed they might be secreted (e.g. flower-beds in places where groups of youths loitered). Knife-arches, similar to airport security screening, were also used in robbery hot-spot locations which might serve as 'exit routes' for offenders (e.g. at transport hubs). Individuals seen to be avoiding the knife-arches would raise suspicion and would subsequently be stopped and searched by police. Test purchase operations were carried out by Trading Standards in stores suspected of selling knives to youths to reduce the availability of weapons.

To discourage potential offenders from coming into contact with victims, Dispersal Zones, which are authorised under the Anti-Social Behaviour Act 2003, were initiated, which allowed the police to move groups of two or more youths from a particular area for preventative purposes.

To identify a greater proportion of offenders, a robbery 'Q-car' was deployed for 12 hours a day, specifically in the hours after schools closed when robberies were concentrated. This police sleeper vehicle was located in identified hot spots and was dedicated to driving robbery victims around the local area in the immediate aftermath of a robbery to identify their offender(s).

Once identified, a variety of legal levers were levelled at offenders. For example, 16 repeat offenders were subjected to Anti-Social Behaviour Orders (ASBOs), mandating that they abide by certain conditions such as not associating with deviant peers, exclusion from particular areas and sometimes a home curfew. Breaches of these rules could result in a custodial sentence.

Targeted truancy work was carried out by a range of agencies. This involved close monitoring of truancy levels, with some 200 youths and parents visited when an individual's truancy reached a 'trigger level'. In particular cases, pupils would be referred to mentoring via community groups. For pupils at risk of suspension from school and/or offending, the charitable organisation Enfield Youth Engagement Panel provided peer-to-peer mentoring which uses credible messengers, such as ex-offenders and ex-gang members, to deliver a range of support programmes to youths. In addition, the high schools changed their exclusion policies so that offenders who were suspended from school were removed to a supervised area within the school rather than spending their time on suspension at home in an unsupervised environment.

Places

To disrupt the opportunity for motivated offenders coming into contact with suitable targets, staggered school closing times were introduced, which reduced the concentration of pupils travelling the same routes home from school at the same times. Further to this, on routes between schools and transport hubs that were identified as being high risk, a 'Community Help Point Scheme' was created, which involved local businesses that would provide safe havens to youths in times of vulnerability. Youth travel cards, which are government-subsidised passes for use on London buses, were withdrawn for offenders who carried out their offending on public transport to restrict access to future potential victims.

Both formal and informal surveillance was enhanced. High-visibility patrols, consisting of police and community groups, were deployed in hot spots at hot times. These aimed to provide a reassuring presence, engage young people and provide information on positive diversionary schemes. Funding won from the central and regional governments helped set up a mobile youth bus along with youth outreach teams, and existing youth centres were redeveloped to attract new attendees.

Informal surveillance was improved by cutting back trees and shrubbery in hot-spot areas, and formal surveillance benefited from direct communication between staff in the closed-circuit television (CCTV) centre and frontline staff in the organisations responsible for policing the transportation system (Transport for London and British Transport Police). In addition to the existing cameras,

14 portable 'Domehawk' CCTV cameras were deployed in emerging hot spots. These were damage resistant, high-definition, spherical 360-rotation cameras with advanced zoom functionality that could be controlled remotely. A local school-uniform database was provided to Enfield CCTV Control Centre to assist in the identification of offenders. The footage was reviewed by 'Safer Schools' officers who were designated to a specific school and therefore had extensive local knowledge of the pupils.

The ample response actions that were taken in this project have been mapped onto the 25 techniques of situational crime prevention (Clarke, 1995; Wortley, 1998) in Table 4.1.

Assessment

The **assessment** of the results of the robbery-reduction activities showed a resounding success, with the reduction target exceeded (total reduction of 21.5 per cent in street robbery by 2012/13). Remarkably, the frequency of youth robbery decreased by 59.2 per cent (from 537 down to 219) in the period between 2009/10, when the project started, and 2012/13, which had a large influence on the overall robbery figures. The reduction in youth robberies may also have contributed to the stunning reductions in youth violent crime over the period (77 per cent, from 634 to 353). The analysts utilised as many available data sources as they could access to explain these figures.

There was a 256 per cent *increase* in the number of street robberies that were captured on CCTV across Enfield during the project (from 97 to 346). Associated with this, there was an 83 per cent increase in the number of persons arrested at the scene with the aid of CCTV (from 54 to 99). The Domehawk cameras played a large role in these outcomes; they could be rapidly deployed to emergent hot spots and effectively filled 'CCTV blackspots' and allow for the flexible coverage that had

TABLE 4.1 Response activities mapped onto the 25 techniques of situational crime prevention

Increase the effort	Increase the risks	Reduce the rewards	Reduce provocations	Remove excuses
Harden targets	Extend guardianship	Conceal targets	Reduce frustration and stress	Set rules
Personal safety lessons provided to pupils before arriving at high school	Police vehicle (Q-car) instantly deployed to drive victims around the local area to identify the perpetrator	Youths encouraged to keep phones out of view	Refer truanting pupils to community groups for mentoring intervention	Antisocial behaviour orders (ASBOs) issued which contain rules that an offender must abide by

Increase the effort	Increase the risks	Reduce the rewards	Reduce provocations	Remove excuses
Control access to facilities	*Assist natural surveillance*	*Remove targets*	*Avoid disputes*	*Control drugs and alcohol*
Knife arch operations in schools in hot-spot areas	'Sharp system' introduced to encourage anonymous reporting of pupils carrying knives.	'Community Help Point Scheme' provided a safe haven to youths at risk	Stagger the school closing times	Offenders referred to local Substance Misuse Group Work Programme for youths to reduce dependency
	Trees and shrubbery trimmed to improve sightlines.			
	14 portable 'Domehawk' CCTV cameras deployed in emerging hot spots			
Screen exits	*Reduce anonymity*	*Identify property*	*Reduce emotional arousal*	
Youth travel cards withdrawn for offenders to restrict access to public transport and exits from offences	CCTV footage examined alongside school uniform database by 'Safer Schools' office to identify perpetrators	Pupils encouraged to register their mobile phones with Immobilise	Bullying policy implemented	
Deflect offenders	*Strengthen formal surveillance*	*Disrupt markets*	*Neutralise peer pressure*	
Suspended pupils confined to supervised area in school.	Victim Support Worker employed to assist youth victims through the Criminal Justice System process	Trading Standards team check records of local pawn shops for stolen property	Peer-to-peer mentoring delivered to youth perpetrators	
Dispersal orders used to disperse groups of potential offenders				
Control tools/ weapons				
Test purchase operations carried out in stores suspected of selling knives to youths				

not previously been possible. They also allowed the police to follow suspects and guide officers in the Q-car where to stop and/or arrest them. These cameras also provided good resolution facial images that could be shared with youth workers with the purposes of identifying the suspects. The wider provision of CCTV cameras also increased across Enfield during the course of the project and staff within the CCTV centre were provided with robbery hot spots and hot times and modus operandi information, with the express purpose of aiding proactive identification of offenders.

The 'Community Help Point Scheme', which sought to provide a safe haven to youths at risk signed up 220 local businesses. In the 12 months prior to the project concluding, these locations were used by 581 young people.

The proportion of robberies involving the use or threat of a knife, however, remained stable at about 30 per cent. The analysts intimated that this may indicate that the activities targeted at reducing weapon availability and use were not effective. In a related vein, the proportion of robberies involving mobile phones being stolen (about two-thirds) was unchanged over the lifetime of the project.

The numbers of offenders on Youth Offending Service orders increased during the project, and the length of the restraints in the interventions delivered by this organisation also increased, which was done with the intention of exerting controls on the offenders during the identified peak ages of offending (15–17). Sixteen offenders were placed on ASBOs. Whilst half of these breached their ASBO conditions on associating with particular peers and entering exclusion zones, none committed further robberies. There was some evidence of crime displacement, however, with prolific offenders turning instead to drug dealing and minor theft offences.

Half of the 22 offenders who were referred to the Substance Misuse Group Work programme did not commit further robbery offences. Twenty-seven per cent were recorded as having reduced cannabis use, and 18 per cent were reported to be free from dependency in the time of the project.

Youth street robberies in targeted hot spot areas at hot times declined by 19 per cent when compared with non-targeted areas. Responses targeted around schools with historical robbery problems were seen to significantly decrease over the project. No spatial displacement of offences was found in the analysis; in fact, robbery was found to decrease in the buffer areas as well as the targeted hot-spot areas, proof of some diffusion of benefits. This is in line with systematic research which suggests that evidence of diffusion of benefit is as commonly found as that of displacement in place-based crime prevention interventions (see Bowers et al., 2011; Guerette, 2009, for more information on how to measure displacement and diffusion).

The views of project partners were solicited when assessing the impact of the robbery reduction activities. Feedback indicated that the staggered closing times controlled the flow and volume of youths passing through routes and enabled the frontline officers (including police and transport workers) to manage the transport hubs more effectively. The views of the public also improved over the project, with far fewer reporting youth crime and antisocial behaviour was a problem in the Residents' Survey for Enfield.

With respect to a cost-effectiveness assessment, the analysts reported that the total costs expended on the project were £765,000/US$1 million. This was offset by a cost-saving of £2,916,110/US$3.8 million, based on the Home Office (2011) estimates of a robbery costing £8,810/US$11,500. Therefore, a saving of £2,151,110/US$2.8 million was estimated to have been made through this project. Whilst the resources were not expected to be available to support the continuation of all the activities reported here, this was still viewed as a decidedly successful project.

Figure 4.2 gives a diagrammatic representation of the various elements of response in the Enfield youth robbery project. The analysts who submitted the Goldstein Award application noted that it is difficult to pinpoint which of the activities had the biggest impact on the reductions in youth robbery but stress that the results of the integrated offender management produced appreciable reductions in reoffending and that the spatio-temporal targeting of places changed the space-time signatures of the robbery problem.

Discussion

As is true with other exemplary problem-oriented-policing projects, the Enfield robbery project had a few ingredients that contributed to its great success. First was a definable problem. The extraordinary problem that a particular place (Enfield) had with a particular, rather specific, type of crime (youth robbery) meant that focus could be cast on it. It was an issue which, by common agreement (by the media, community, police and many other stakeholders), needed addressing. This meant key stakeholders were primed to act. There are certainly other situations where preconditions are less conducive to support from the community and other stakeholders. Youth robbery is an emotive subject, and the opportunity to curb a trend—arguably caused, in part, by a 'crime harvest' (Ekblom, 1997) resulting from new mobile phones—was likely to reap the benefit.

Such benefit, of course, is not a given, which leads on to the second ingredient: strong analysis and an evidence-informed response strategy. The analysis was what might be termed '360 degrees', or comprehensive and from multiple perspectives. Resulting evidence did not just rely on one source or one perspective. For example, administrative data were used creatively to examine trends (such as the importance of areas where adolescents from different schools were likely to encounter each other), but surveys with the young people of Enfield provided another perspective in terms of attitudes and feelings. Crime scripting (see Cornish, 1994) was used to examine likely offender motivations. It is also evident that analysis was used not only to plan the response but also to assist at the implementation and assessment stages. Hence, the response was targeted at the offenders with the highest levels of truancy, and mobile CCTV was deployed at the most relevant times and places. Similarly, the analysis underpinning the assessment phase of the project drilled down into specific high schools with historic robbery problems to gain a more precise understanding of the impact that had been realised. Finally, the analysis was multi-faceted and intentionally included all aspects of the crime analysis triangle. The phrase 'paralysis by analysis' is well recognised, but in this case, there was a strong justification for the analysis undertaken—it was actually *used* in the response planning.

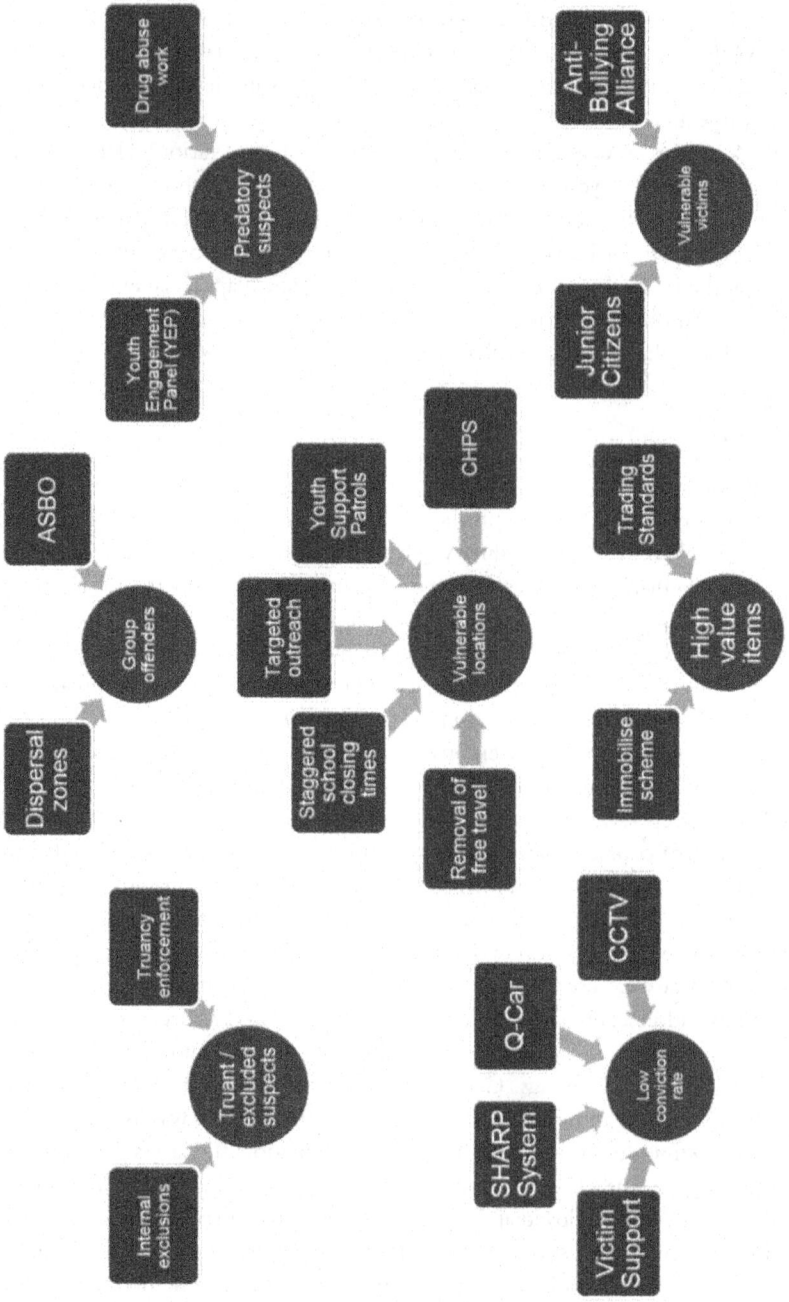

FIGURE 4.2 The responses organised with respect to the identified problem

A further ingredient—which perhaps is both a blessing and a curse of many successful problem-oriented-policing projects that is also evident here—is a multi-pronged response strategy. Figure 4.2 illustrates the extent of the activity which is, on first look, rather dizzying to behold. Interestingly, however, all the responses are carefully justified by the preceding analysis. This thorough strategy might well be one of the reasons for the resulting effectiveness of the initiative. However, it causes two issues for any potential future replicators. The first is that such approaches are necessarily *resource-intensive*—something that might be possible in the buzz of a pilot initiative but not so easy to address in subsequent incarnations. The second is that it makes it much harder to decipher which are the most effective or essential elements necessary to provoke the desired change (Tompson, 2012). In the modern era of evidence-based 'austerity' policing it is likely that there will be time or resource for only the most viable approach.

It is easy to conclude from these reflections that problem-oriented policing is a pipe-dream and was only possible in the 'golden age' of policing when there were extra resources for analysts and responses. However, in his recent acceptance speech for the 2018 Stockholm Prize for Criminology, Herman Goldstein lays out his vision for why problem-oriented policing is fully compatible with a modern policing approach by identifying four features inherent in the concept. These are (1) that problem-oriented policing is principled, (2) that it is holistic, (3) that it is built on being better informed and (4) that it is a continuing process (Goldstein, 2018). These concepts, in fact, fall in line well with what the modern public expect: an efficient, evidence-informed and compassionate police service that is not afraid of organisational change as and when this is necessary.

Follow-up

The analysts were able to establish that the reduction in robbery was seen to persist for four consecutive years after the project concluded. This suggests that the project might have demonstrated sustainable reductions for some time. However, it appeared that by 2017/18, robbery levels had returned to the volumes experienced in 2011/12. Unfortunately, critically assessing why the robbery problem remerged is difficult, in part, because the analysts had moved to positions elsewhere in the interim. As a general observation, for many crime reduction evaluations, it appears difficult to resource analysis of project effects in the longer term. Whilst understandable given the scarcity of resources, this means that reasons for the sustainability (or otherwise) of effects are still little understood. This would be a fruitful area for further research—but would depend, in part, on a general policing commitment to the exploration of this as part of Goldstein's 'continuing process' vision for modern problem-oriented policing approaches.

Note

1 See Enfield Scrutiny Commission (2009) for the broader summary report into which this research fed.

References

Bowers, K.J., Jennings, J. & Hirschfield, A. (2002) 'The crime and disorder audit process: A post-mortem on the first round', *Crime Prevention and Community Safety: An International Journal*, 4(3): 19–32.

Bowers, K.J., Johnson, S.D., Guerette, R., Summers, L. & Poynton, S. (2011) 'Do geographically focussed police initiatives displace crime or diffuse benefits? A systematic review', *Journal of Experimental Criminology*, 7(4): 347–374.

Brantingham, P.L. & Brantingham, P.J. (1995) 'Criminality of place', *European Journal on Criminal Policy and Research*, 3(3): 5–26.

Clarke, R.V. (1995) 'Situational crime prevention', in M. Tonry & D. Farrington (eds.), *Building a Safer Society: Strategic Approaches to Crime Prevention*, Crime and Justice: A Review of Research, Vol. 19, Chicago: University of Chicago Press, pp. 91–150.

Clarke, R.V. (1999) *Hot Products: Understanding, Anticipating, and Reducing Demand for Stolen Goods*, Police Research Series, London: Home Office.

Cornish, D.B. (1994) 'The procedural analysis of offending and its relevance for situational prevention', in R.V. Clarke (ed.), *Crime Prevention Studies*, Vol. 3, Monsey, NY: Criminal Justice Press, pp. 151–196.

Cornish, D.B. & Clarke, R.V. (2003) 'Opportunities, precipitators and criminal decisions: A reply to Wortley's critique of situational crime prevention', in M. Smith & D. Cornish (eds.), *Theory for Practice in Situational Crime Prevention*, Crime Prevention Studies, Vol. 16, Boulder, CO: Lynne Rienner Publishers.

Eck, J.E. (2003) 'Police problems: The complexity of problem theory, research, and evaluation', in J. Knuttson (ed.), *Problem-Oriented Policing: From Innovation to Mainstream*, Crime Prevention Studies, Vol. 15, Monsey, NY: Criminal Justice Press.

Ekblom, P. (1997) 'Gearing up against crime: A dynamic framework to help designers keep up with the adaptive criminal in a changing world', *International Journal of Risk, Security and Crime Prevention*, 2(4): 249–265.

Enfield Community Safety Partnership (2013) *The Robbery of School-Age Victims in Enfield*, Submission to the Herman Goldstein Award for Excellence in Problem-Oriented Policing, Center for Problem-Oriented Policing, Arizona State University, Phoenix, AZ.

Enfield Scrutiny Commission (2009) *Improving Life Opportunities for Young People in Enfield*, London: Enfield Council.

Goldstein, H. (2018) 'On problem-oriented policing: The Stockholm lecture', *Crime Science*, 7: 13. doi:10.1186/s40163-018-0087-3

Guerette, R.T. (2009) *Analyzing Crime Displacement and Diffusion*, Problem-Oriented Guides for Police, Problem-Solving Tools Guide No. 10, Washington, DC: US Department of Justice, Office of Community Oriented Policing Services.

Hallsworth, S. & Young, T. (2009) *Improving Life Opportunities for Young People in Enfield*, London, England: London Metropolitan University.

Home Office (2011) *Revisions Made to the Multipliers and Unit Costs of Crime Used in the Integrated Offender Management Value for Money Toolkit*, London: Home Office.

Monk, K., Heinonen, J. & Eck, J.E. (2010) *Street Robbery*, Problem-Oriented Guides for Police, Problem-Specific Guide No. 59, Washington, DC: US Department of Justice, Office of Community Oriented Policing Services.

Tompson, L. (2012) *Street Robbery*, JDiBrief Series, London: UCL Jill Dando Institute of Security and Crime Science.

Wortley, R. (1998) 'A two-stage model of situational crime prevention', *Studies on Crime and Crime Prevention*, 7(2): 173–188.

5

GANG VIOLENCE AND STREET DISORDER IN PORTLAND, OREGON

Greg Stewart and Kris Henning

Introduction

In 1996, one of us (Stewart) was a probationary police officer assigned to the Portland Police Bureau's (PPB) Northeast Precinct. The precinct was among the most diverse in the city and had more homicides (16) than any other precinct. In addition to leading the city in homicides, Northeast Precinct accounted for the vast majority of the city's gang violence. Rates for most other crimes were also well above the citywide average. Within this broader area, the intersection of NE Albina Avenue and NE Killingsworth Street stood out as a particularly dangerous location.

Despite having grown up in greater Portland, I found patrolling this intersection akin to visiting a foreign country. I can remember working my first missions as an officer, focusing on drug dealing and prostitution at this intersection. Working the afternoon shift, I had to drive through the intersection at the end of my shift on my way home. Senior officers advised me to avoid the area entirely or, if I chose to go through the intersection, to avoid stopping regardless of traffic control devices.

I returned to the Northeast Precinct as a newly promoted sergeant a decade later. Like most other large cities in the country, crime in Portland had dropped considerably in the intervening years. Citywide homicides declined from 46 in 1996 to 29 in 2004, and the rate of violent offenses had declined from 16 per 1,000 population to 7. Despite improvements in these citywide crime statistics, the area immediately surrounding the Albina–Killingsworth intersection remained resistant to change. Shootings, gang violence, and drug dealing were endemic.

Several attempts had been made to improve the area but the limited successes we achieved were always short-lived. These attempts generally centered on short-term missions, focusing on enforcement and increased visibility. They might improve the area in the near-term, but inevitably the area regressed at the end of the mission. It seemed that this area would remain problematic, even as the city as a whole benefited from a massive drop in crime.

Taking a problem-oriented approach

Five years later I was running the bureau's newly formed Crime Analysis Unit (CAU) and was contacted by North Precinct Commander Mike Leloff and Sergeant Mark Friedman.[1] Sergeant Freidman had been assigned responsibility for improving public safety in and around the Albina–Killingsworth intersection. Interested in adopting a problem-oriented-policing approach, he hoped to obtain additional data about crime and calls for service to the area as part of his **scanning** process (**SARA**).

Scanning

The CAU was already well aware of the issues facing the Albina–Killingsworth intersection, having recently conducted several in-depth reviews that were shared with Sgt. Friedman. For example, analyses for a separate gun violence initiative had revealed the broader area to be a hot spot for shooting incidents, including homicides and aggravated assaults. This had led to the city designating the location as a "Firearm Free Zone." The designation was intended to prevent individuals with certain firearms-related convictions from loitering in sections of the city known for gun violence.

While incident reports and calls-for-service data painted a grim picture of the area, Sergeant Friedman identified a number of local strengths that were not apparent in the official records management systems available to the CAU. Chief among these strengths was a diverse group of organizations and community members committed to improving public safety in the Albina–Killingsworth area. This included the Albina Killingsworth Safe Neighborhood Commission (AKSNC), the Humboldt Neighborhood Association, Portland Community College, Rosemary Anderson High School, Jefferson High School, the 11:45 initiative (a coalition of churches that organize community outreach and mentoring, often focused on gang activity), the Oregon Liquor Control Commission (OLCC), the Multnomah County District Attorney's Office, and the City of Portland's Office of Neighborhood Involvement (ONI). These organizations joined with Sergeant Friedman and the PPB to form the Albina-Killingsworth Collaboration.

Analysis

The collaboration spent several months in the **analysis phase** (SARA), pooling resources and information to develop a better understanding of the problems at the intersection. One of the primary goals was to identify environmental and social factors that were contributing to the area's crime and disorder. Key findings from this work included the following:

1   A low concrete wall that provided chronic drinkers and drug users a place to congregate. This contributed to an atmosphere of lawlessness, which, in the opinion of collaboration partners, provided cover for and facilitated other illegal activity.

2   A telephone booth enabled narcotics traffickers to conduct business without leaving evidence on their cell phones.
3   Adjacent businesses with poor lighting and/or other features either failed to discourage criminal activity or, in the case of street drinking, actively encouraged it.
4   Poor access control at nearby schools resulted in students exiting the premises unobserved and unauthorized entry into the building by others.
5   Local businesses with a profit model built on the sale of malt liquor, fortified wines, and other low-cost intoxicants attracted street drinkers.
6   A "norm" of behavior for the area that accepted street drinking, narcotics use, and drug distribution. This allowed gang members to actively recruit and operate in the area.

Discussions among the collaboration partners and local community members also highlighted concerns about the possible tactics that might be deployed to address crime and disorder at the intersection. A primary consideration was the fact that young minority males accounted for a disproportionate number of the people frequenting the area. Community members, along with the collaborating organizations, wanted to avoid to the extent possible further exacerbation of existing racial/ethnic disparities in criminal justice caseloads. Likewise, the Police Bureau was facing concurrent pressure to improve police–community relations and reduce use-of-force incidents. This led to the development of several "ground rules" for intervening in the target area:

1   The police would prioritize the enforcement of observable offenses. Actions based on reasonable suspicion alone would be avoided (e.g., "stop and frisk").
2   Intensive police tactics would be short-term and conducted in a manner that limited the likelihood of use of force and citizen complaints.
3   Environmental (e.g., crime prevention through environmental design [CPTED]) and regulatory changes would be made to address the underlying factors contributing to crime in the area.
4   The collaboration as a whole, rather than any single organization or person, would assume responsibility (and blame in the case of adverse outcomes) for the intervention.

Response

The collaboration's eventual **response** (SARA) adhered closely to these ground rules and was conducted over a period of nine months. Provided in the following is a summary of the changes that were made as part of this effort.

Environmental design

The collaboration facilitated several design changes in and around the Albina–Killingsworth intersection that sought to deter criminal activity. First, the public phone booth was removed, and the wall that previously served as a hangout was redesigned to discourage loitering and improve natural surveillance.

Second, nearby bus kiosks were redesigned to deter criminal behavior. This included changes to the types of seating available and rotating the kiosks to face the street. These modifications resulted in better natural surveillance and made it easier for local patrol officers to observe and respond to illegal transactions.

Third, the collaboration worked with the area schools to improve physical security and ensure that entrances and exits were better controlled.[2] This helped improve the security of the schools and prevent truancy in the secondary schools. An example of this strategy was closing off the side doors to one of the area high schools.

Fourth, the collaboration partnered with the Portland Development Commission to address miscellaneous CPTED issues with local businesses. Low-interest loans were provided to improve lighting, deter graffiti by planting "green walls," and make physical improvements, such as adding fencing and/or gates.

Regulatory efforts

Officers worked with the OLCC and local business owners to develop abatement agreements preventing the sales of certain types of fortified wines and malt liquors popular with street drinkers due to their low price and relatively high alcohol content. These agreements helped reduce street drinking, a chronic problem and community concern.

This also helped reduce the general sense of disorder that plagued the neighborhood. It was hoped that improvement to the area would increase business traffic and help mitigate the financial impact caused by the reduced sales of these kinds of products. This appeared to be the case as the area started to become a destination for shopping, dining, and other activities.

Community outreach

Steps were taken to change the social norms in the target area, promote legitimacy of the collaboration, and address the needs of at-risk youth. For example, the police and Multnomah County District Attorney's Office partnered with 11:45, a local religious group. They mentored youth and walked the intersection to discourage substance use.

Surveillance and guardianship

Efforts were taken to increase the perceived risk to would-be offenders by increasing formal surveillance and guardianship in the target area. To accomplish this the police worked with a number of partners in taking the following measures:

- Portland Community College (PCC) Security provided a daily presence in the area. They communicated with police officers on emerging issues and provided a uniformed presence when police officers were unavailable. PCC also provided video surveillance cameras that allowed police officers to develop probable cause for arrests. This was essential as the neighborhood wanted to avoid the use of more arbitrary methods, such as high levels of police stops.

- Portland Public Schools (PPS) Security also worked closely with police. With two high schools in the area and a large number of youth, PPS security was able to provide additional guardianship, especially where the students in the area were concerned.
- Police enhanced foot patrols in the area, drawing on both regular patrol officers and officers specially assigned to Sergeant Freidman's team.
- Police parked unoccupied police cars ("ghost cars") in a parking spot that had been designated for police cars as part of the project. The use of video surveillance prevented random vandalism to the cars. In combination with video surveillance, the presence of the cars made it difficult for potential offenders to know when they were being observed.

These tactics provided additional guardianship and helped curtail unwanted behaviors.

Police enforcement

Finally, the police significantly increased enforcement in the target area for the first four months of 2012. The number of arrests in those months rose from 32 in 2011 to 205 in 2012, more than a sixfold increase. The nature of the arrests was consistent with issues of concern identified by the collaboration. More than one-half were for alcohol-related offenses, and roughly one-quarter were for drug-related crimes. The bulk of the remaining arrests were for outstanding warrants, theft, assault, and weapon-related offenses. Also consistent with the collaboration's ground rules, the intensive-enforcement campaign was largely short term (see Figure 5.1).

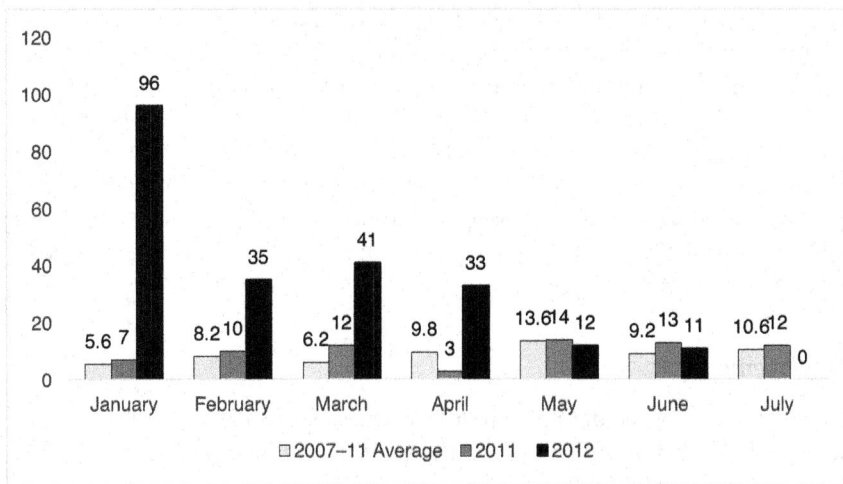

FIGURE 5.1 Arrests within 500 feet of NE Albina Avenue and NE Killingsworth Street

Assessment

The **assessment** (SARA) of the collaboration's efforts was focused on both traditional measures of crime and disorder, such as criminal offenses and calls for service, and on nontraditional measures, such as complaints and whether force was used by police when making arrests. This reflected the collaboration's concern with police tactics.

Criminal offenses

Criminal offenses generally considered to be serious—murder, rape, aggravated assault, robbery, burglary, larceny, motor vehicle theft, and arson reported as occurring within 500 feet of the intersection of N. Albina Ave and N. Killingsworth St. between January and July 2012[3] decreased 16.1% compared with 2011; and decreased 27.4% compared with a five-year average (2007 to 2011). In contrast, citywide crimes of these same types were up 9% at the time of this evaluation.

Radio calls

Consistent with other indicators there was a marked reduction in calls for service over the course of the collaboration. While initially high due to increased police presence, the number had fallen to about one-third of the historic average by July. Calls for service decreased 8.8% compared with 2011, decreased 15.3% compared with the five-year average (2007 to 2011), and decreased to 22 in July (compared with 58 calls in 2011 and 66 calls being the five-year average).

Use of force

The use of force by the police was very rare before, during, and after the collaboration's efforts. Between 2008 (when the PPB adopted the use-of-force reporting policy in effect at the time of the collaboration's efforts) until 2012, there were 11 incidents where force was used in the targeted area. This makes drawing conclusions about the collaboration's impact on officers' behavior difficult to assess. With that limitation in mind, there was a reduction in the percentage of arrests involving force[4] (see Figure 5.2).

There were no citizen complaints generated during the months of January to July. As with the use of force, citizen complaints are very rare. Their absence was important but also not abnormal. The important point was that efforts did not seem to increase complaints.

Displacement

Displacement of crime did not appear to be an issue. Crime and calls for service were examined for an area within 500 feet of the intersection, and a separate analysis examined crime and calls for service out to one-quarter of a mile. The benefits of the intervention appeared to dissipate with distance but there was a noticeable reduction in calls for service (15%) out to one-quarter of a mile. This suggests there may have been some diffusion of benefits.

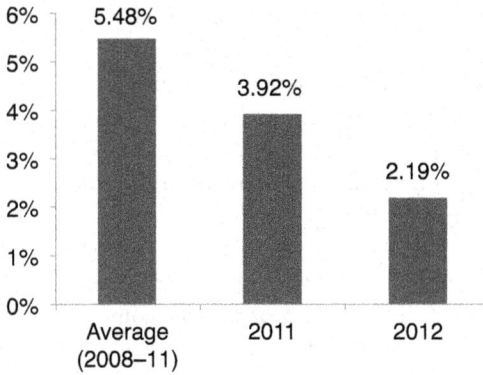

FIGURE 5.2 Percentage of arrests involving use of force

Long-term Impact

Finally, the benefits remained two years later. As of 2013, calls for service near the intersection were down 65%, while citywide, they had increased by 4.3%. Violent crime was down 50%, compared with a citywide reduction of 1%. Overall, reported crime in the targeted area was down by just over 1%. While this overall reduction was not substantial, for the most part, violent crime appeared to have been replaced with property crimes, and calls for service fell dramatically. The area had been transformed from a place to be avoided to a destination for students and residents to socialize and shop.

Discussion

A key component of this intervention was the development of the collaboration itself. The identification and recruitment of community partners during the scanning and analysis phases provided a level of support for police efforts not seen in other interventions. The long list of community partners included neighborhood and business associations, religious groups, and high school and junior college educators (along with security resources for these institutions). Once the police had helped restore order to the area, the same resources were also able to take over and maintain an adequate level of guardianship to prevent the area from backsliding.

An important aspect of the collaboration was the shared vision of its members. This vision guided the intervention. The police intervention was guided by the collaboration's philosophy and adhering to it was essential in maintaining support both during and after enforcement efforts. The police agreed to the following:

- Work with community members to identify acceptable behavior for the area surrounding N Albina Avenue and Killingsworth Street.
- Make probable-cause arrests to discourage behaviors deemed problematic by the community.

- Engage in intensive problem solving in partnership with community members to reduce the need for ongoing law enforcement.
- Maintain ongoing partnerships with the community to ensure continued improvements in the area.

Additionally, the vision for police involvement in the collaboration precluded the following activities or assumptions:

- The program is not a "stop and frisk" model. It emphasizes probable-cause arrests of problem behaviors identified by the community.
- The program is not a limited duration "operation/mission": it emphasizes ongoing partnerships.
- The program is not police-directed: community partnerships direct the actions.

The police conducted analyses and provided data to collaboration partners to demonstrate their commitment to the philosophy. This included analyses examining the age of those arrested, demographic analyses, examining the use of force, and tracking complaints. This level of transparency helped provide legitimacy to the police efforts.

Additionally, while the collaboration utilized data from a variety of sources, the scanning and analysis were largely conducted by Sergeant Friedman and the other collaboration members. They gathered existing analyses, reviewed historic meeting minutes, and reviewed preexisting community surveys. These efforts provided important information and context that were incorporated into the response phase. This initiative was a bottom-up effort where those most impacted by the area's problems took the lead in both scanning and analyzing the issues they faced. This is important in terms of replicability.

The scan and analysis were supplemented by the CAU, but the lion's share of the work was conducted by the collaboration. For instance, a survey conducted by PCC provided important perspectives on public safety issues facing students and staff. This effort occurred independent of police data collection but proved valuable for the project. Other important contributions to public safety included the leadership and resources provided by the AKSNC, PCC Security, and PPS. Security for PCC and PPS had intimate knowledge of the area's problems. The ability of both organizations to share information and then act as guardians significantly reduced demands on the police. The initiative was occurring during the aftermath of the "Great Recession," and these extra resources were invaluable.

Follow-up

But what of the intersection itself? Did the cessation of intensive law enforcement and the inevitable shift in police focus to other problem locations result in a return to its previous condition?

The PPB switched from reporting its crime to the federal government via the Uniform Crime Reports system to the new National Incident-Based Reporting System part way through 2015. This change was accompanied by the implementation of a new internal police records management system. These changes make it difficult to assess the long-term benefits of the intervention in terms of reported crime. However, it can be said with confidence that the intersection remains vibrant and is no longer among the most violent in Portland.

Additionally, despite having two high schools, a community college, a shopping area, and two libraries in the vicinity, the call-for-service load remains low. The intersection had 58 calls for service in 2017, only 31 as of the end of November 2018, and the calls that do come in tend to be for low-level incidents (e.g., minor theft, nuisance behavior, and conditions) as opposed to the shootings and other serious calls seen prior to the intervention.

Conclusion

The efforts of the collaboration provided a benefit to those who lived, worked, attended school, or otherwise frequented the area around N. Albina Ave and Killingsworth St. Beyond this, those efforts provided a template for other interventions in North Precinct. These efforts continue to this day.

Notable follow-up projects include an intervention on a group of businesses that provided gaming (lottery-style games are legal in Oregon), a problem mobile home park, and another problematic intersection where a lottery, a bar, and a hotel created a highly criminogenic environment. By providing a blueprint as to process, the Albina-Killingsworth Collaboration continued to deliver dividends at other locations.

Police involvement in the collaboration was spearheaded by Sergeant Friedman and officers assigned to him. The team was freed from taking radio calls and told to focus on the intersection. They were successful and then moved on to have several other successful interventions in other parts of the precinct.

Conversations with those involved highlight their belief that having the freedom to work on the issues, without having to continually monitor the radio and respond reactively to calls for service, was essential to their success. This should not be surprising. It is a lot to ask of a patrol officer to engage in high-level problem solving and simultaneously respond to calls for service and attend community meetings without frustrating co-workers, community members and him- or herself. A simple problem-solving activity can be integrated with other routine patrol duties, but high-level problem solving of the sort described in this case study demands considerable amounts of time to dedicate to the project.

An initiative of this magnitude also demands higher-level managerial support such as that provided in this project by Commander Leloff. He built partnerships at a strategic level with local religious groups, the District Attorney's Office, the Mayor's Office, and other key players. He met weekly with Sergeant Friedman and the team to set and reaffirm the strategic vision for the project but then allowed them to design the tactics needed to implement that vision. This resulted in oversight without micromanagement.

This case study at NE Albina Avenue and NE Killingsworth Street in Portland, Oregon, thus provides useful lessons for others not only about how long-standing violent-crime areas can be brought under sustainable community control but also about the internal police managerial structures that can help bring about such results.

Notes

1 In 2007–2008, the City of Portland reduced the number of precincts from five to three, resulting in the Northeast Precinct being reassigned to North.
2 This included both physical alterations as well as the redeployment of existing security personnel. Police-only parking, located at the intersection, was also included to help facilitate additional police presence in the area.
3 Reported as of August 4, 2012.
4 Although this was not the case in total force cases. There were two uses of force in 2011 and three in 2012.

6

GANG VIOLENCE IN AURORA, ILLINOIS

Brandon R. Kooi

Introduction

In 2007, I was an assistant professor at Aurora University and preparing to move my family to Aurora, Illinois. During this time, I met with the Aurora Police Department about the city's gangs and gun-violence problems. The officers spoke of retaliatory shootings, gang turf wars, and their inability to solve murders. While searching for housing, our real estate agent made a comment that stuck with me: "Don't tell anyone I said so, but look for housing east of Highway 59 so your kids will be in Naperville schools and not Aurora schools." This comment convinced us to buy a home in Naperville, but I also learned that Aurora had a lot to offer beyond its reputation for gangs and gun violence.

This case study describes a problem-oriented policing initiative by the Aurora Police Department, dubbed "Finding Typhoid Mary: Ganging up on Gang Violence," which was recognized as a finalist for the 2013 Herman Goldstein Award for Excellence in Problem-Oriented Policing. Project leaders chose this title while assessing the impact of the initiative; they came to think of chronic gun-violence offenders as the functional equivalent of disease spreaders—or Typhoid Marys after the 19th-century New York City woman who knowingly spread incurable typhoid fever.

Aurora lies 40 miles west of Chicago and encompasses portions of four counties. The population grew considerably over the past two decades and is now over 200,000, nearly two-and-a-half times its population in the 1980s, with an estimated 30,000 undocumented, mostly Hispanic residents. Aurora has the largest Hispanic population in Illinois outside of Chicago. From 2000 to 2010, the percentage of Caucasian residents dropped 8% while the Hispanic population increased 8%. The community today is 42% Hispanic, 39% Caucasian, 10% African American, 7% Asian, and 2% mixed.

Downtown Aurora has a number of vacant businesses and is dominated by a large casino on the banks of the Fox River. Many local shops and grocery stores cater to a Hispanic clientele. Almost a quarter of Aurora's population was not born in the United States, and as a consequence, gangs often try to recruit new immigrants and first-generation American youth.

Beginning around 2007, local police leaders were increasingly being tasked with devising more immediate and sustainable results to help business investors, real estate companies, and elected officials revitalize Aurora's downtown. At the same time, the police department experienced major budget and staffing cuts. In 2008, Greg Thomas was appointed police chief and he pressed his staff to practice problem-oriented policing.

Limited effectiveness of prior responses to youth gun violence in Aurora

Prior responses to Aurora's gun-violence problem that had limited effectiveness included zero-tolerance strategies, gun buybacks, and a version of a program known as Operation Ceasefire.

Zero tolerance was a routine practice, prior to 2007, for how Aurora officers dealt with suspected and known gang members who were frequently questioned, frisked, and watched by officers, yet these practices were often unfocused and not driven by analysis. When shootings occurred, the stop-and-question strategies intensified for days afterward. The process was expensive, led to numerous low-level arrests, and did little to enhance police legitimacy. In 2002, the city tied a previous record of 26 murders and 251 shootings, causing the police to question their zero-tolerance policing strategy that seemed to be doing more harm than good.

Aurora tried gun buybacks in the past but ultimately concluded that they had little impact on gang violence, a conclusion confirmed by other evaluations (Phillips, Kim & Sobol, 2013). The police sponsored gun buybacks as early as 1994, purchasing 256 weapons for $50 each and then destroying the weapons. In 2003, the International Gun Safety Council sponsored an event to buy guns independently to be used for parts and profitable resale. In both instances, the gun buybacks consisted mainly of people cleaning out their closets and turning in inoperable or antique firearms. Gang members were certainly not lining up to turn in their guns.

Aurora received a grant in late 2004 to implement a variation of Operation Ceasefire that originated in Boston in the late 1990s (Kennedy, Braga & Piehl, 2001) but one that sought to reduce violence via a public-health approach rather than through the focused-deterrence approach used in Boston. Aurora's program entailed community marketing and violence interrupters who tried to mediate interpersonal disputes. Whether due to flaws in the conflict-mediation theory, implementation errors, or grant-management problems, Aurora abandoned its Ceasefire initiative in 2007.

Concomitant with Aurora police's decisions to abandon both zero-tolerance policing, gun buybacks, and violence interrupters was a commitment to targeting those offenders who were influencing infectious violence (Zeoli et al., 2014).

Applying a problem-oriented approach

Police leaders committed themselves to reanalyzing the problem, building relationships with key community stakeholders, and improving collaborative responses. In essence, they went back to the drawing board having learned much about what was not working.

Using the SARA process as a framework, the Aurora gun-violence initiative is described in detail in the following four sections.

Scanning

The scanning phase began by looking at the number of shootings and murders from 2002 to 2007. In 2002, the city was faced with 26 murders and 251 shootings. This number mirrored 1996 numbers when the city had a then record-high 26 murders and 357 shootings. While the rest of the country experienced significant declines in violent crime in the aftermath of the 1990s, Aurora still saw 116 shootings and 13 murders as late as 2007. This persistent violence was undermining business reinvestment, neighborhood revitalization, and property values.

From 1980 to 1989, the city had a 10% population increase and 53 murders (an annual average of 5.3 and a rate of 6.52 per 100,000). From 1990 to 1999, there was a 23% population growth, and murders tripled to 163 (averaged 14 annually) or a rate of 14 per 100,000. In our 2000–2007 scan, we found the city still averaged more than one murder every month and was on track for repeating the 1990s' numbers. The debilitating reputation for gang violence was continuing to affect the city's ability to gentrify successfully. See Figure 6.1.

Analysis

Police leaders hypothesized that a relatively small number of individuals drove most of the violence in the city but that suppressing those individuals would result in short-term results if further gang recruitment mechanisms were not challenged

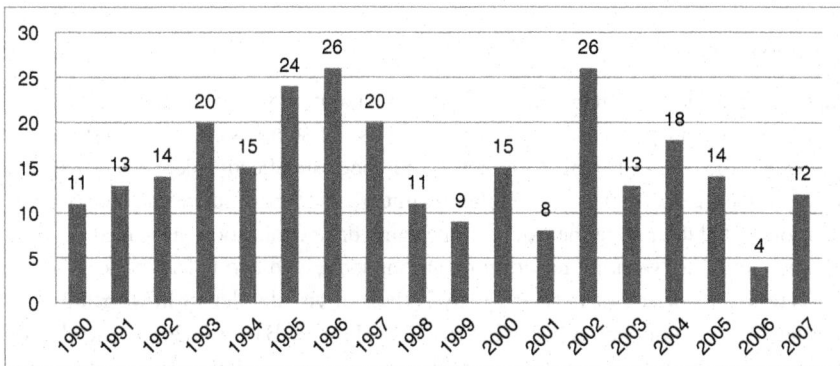

FIGURE 6.1 Number of murders in Aurora, Illinois, 1990–2007

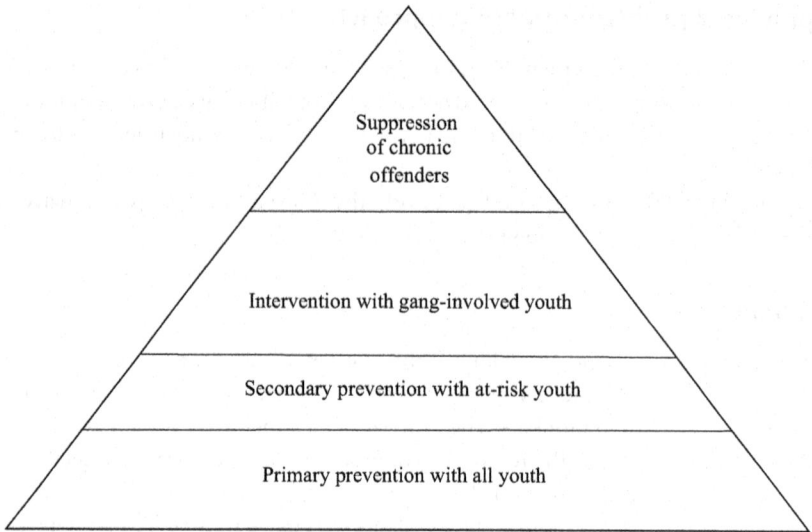

FIGURE 6.2 Comprehensive gang prevention strategies
Source: Adapted from Wyrick (2006).

by the wider community. The analysis followed a three-prong comprehensive approach. First, the analytical focus was directed toward determining who to target for suppression strategies through arrest, prosecution, and other coercive methods. Second, the problem was analyzed from the perspective of determining which targeted neighborhoods were risky facilities (Clarke & Eck, 2007) and in need of intervention that did not include arrest. Last, the problem was analyzed from the perspective of community-wide prevention to determine additional modes of mobilization. Wyrick's (2006) model for comprehensive gang-reduction strategies (Figure 6.2) is useful for understanding this comprehensive strategic plan and, retrospectively, fits what occurred in Aurora over the past decade.

Suppression

Suppression is the most frequently used gang-intervention strategy (Decker & Pyrooz, 2015) and Aurora police had made extensive use of suppression tactics historically. Ultimately, the extent to which suppression methods are effective depends heavily on how offenders perceive them. The offender interviews Aurora police and federal partners conducted to analyze the extent of the gang–drug connection persuaded them of the need for better working relationships among local, state, and federal police.

As police made use of network analysis tools to visually depict how groups and individuals were connected (Papachristos, 2006; Huff & Barrows, 2015), they better understood who was susceptible to retaliatory violence following a shooting and where to target resources to prevent it.

Intervention

Crime analysts and gang investigators analyzed neighborhood conditions to determine what interventions to employ, and where. They concluded that intervening in gang recruitment was critical in the targeted neighborhoods and that youth who lacked self-esteem were particularly susceptible to recruitment (Vigil, 2002). A major challenge, however, is that police relationships with at-risk youth and those who influence them are themselves often strained. But, given that research suggests gang membership is often short-lived (Decker & Van Winkle, 1996) and young members are generally amenable to disengagement (Roman, Decker & Pyrooz, 2017), intervention efforts are important.

An environmental analysis of the targeted Aurora neighborhoods revealed that there was also gang graffiti present and that its cleanup was not timely. Additionally, the analysis concluded that some landlords were leasing housing to problematic tenants.

Analysis of the violence problem also led to the conclusion that some gang-suppression tactics were ultimately counterproductive in that they discouraged some key community stakeholders—particularly recent immigrants—from cooperating with police in controlling conditions and conduct that contributed to the violence problem (Simons et al., 2005; Maxson, Matsuda & Hennigan, 2011). The analysis indicated intervention with gang-involved youth would be compromised if police legitimacy was questioned.

Prevention

A key component of a gang-reduction strategy is that targeted intervention be paired with broader community-based prevention strategies and with the building of social capital (Scott, 2002). The outlook for secondary prevention sought to increase mentoring available for at-risk youth throughout the city. There was also the need for wider primary prevention programs that were directed toward all youth through various educational institutions.

Response

The Aurora gun-violence initiative sought a comprehensive integration of suppression, intervention, and prevention approaches.

Suppression

Rather than focusing suppression measures against guns, they were focused on those gun-violence perpetrators who most incited gang violence in the city. Part of this effort required addressing some limitations on local police investigations. By collaborating with state and federal law enforcement—who could bring more resources, better surveillance capabilities (including wiretaps), and stronger sentencing rules to the investigations—in what would be called "Operation First Degree Burn,"

Aurora police gained a better understanding of local gang structures; secured much longer prison sentences of gang leaders, who typically directed much of the violence; realized greater cooperation from targeted offenders, some of whom became valuable informants against more-influential offenders; facilitated prosecutions for related offenses such as drug crimes; discouraged gun trafficking; helped solve cold murder cases; and disrupted gang loyalty.

A five-year-long investigation culminated in 2007 with the identification of the main Typhoid Marys; the arrest of 31 members of a major gang who were implicated in 22 murders over nearly 20 years; the arrests of a dozen other suspects for murders and shootings; and the infiltration of a major rival gang that was explicitly recruiting Aurora youth.

Intervention

The goal of targeted intervention responses was to educate the community about anti-gang messages and push for capacity building (Renauer, Duffee & Scott, 2003). Using the public-health analogy, whereas suppression efforts targeted disease spreaders, targeted neighborhood intervention sought to inoculate future disease spreaders through early intervention, rather than threats of punishment. Police deemed it critical to overcome immigrants' fears of the police in order to secure their assistance intervening with at-risk youth.

Intervention was targeted at neighborhoods and households at risk for gang activity. Within this part of the response, Aurora police officers gave out their cell phone numbers to block captains within the targeted intervention areas to help build crucial relationships. Officers also went door to door to speak with parents of children suspected of being in or susceptible to joining a gang. This intervention helped police develop working hypotheses about gang recruitment. For example, they concluded that gang leaders could effectively control their members by depersonalizing them, much like the military does, so that groupthink and collective experiences create perceptions of anonymity (Hennigan & Spanovic, 2012) and a greater willingness to participate in crimes that benefit the group (Decker & Pyrooz, 2015; McGloin & Decker, 2010; Venkatesh & Levitt, 2000).

In implementing their intervention responses, police did not publicize the prosecution and sentencing of gang leaders as might be done in a focused-deterrence strategy (Kennedy, 2006) but instead focused on teaching key community members how to recognize the signs of youth gang involvement. The police department produced an educational film about gangs that was shown in schools and on local television and conducted presentations to inform students about the realities of affiliating with gangs.

Police also persuaded the city council to enact a "crime-free housing" city ordinance in 2008. The ordinance increased penalties on landlords who rent property where criminal activity is occurring or who call the police excessively, a measure supported by research (Payne, 2017). Under this ordinance, if a nuisance report is filed on a property, the police chief can order the owner to abate the problem, suspend or revoke the owner's rental license, or recoup the costs to the city for having to correct the violations. The ordinance further required rental property owners to attend landlord training that included crime-prevention measures.

Prevention

Community-based prevention initiatives rounded out the overall strategy by providing targeted youth with positive individual attention to counter the group-esteem attraction of gang culture. While the police may not have explicitly initiated these prevention efforts toward youth, their problem-oriented initiatives did help to mobilize the community to rethink its role in preventing youth gang/gun violence. Community mobilization toward wider prevention efforts is a critical supplement for suppression and intervention strategies (Spergel, Wa & Sosa, 2006).

East Aurora High provides an excellent example of a primary community prevention response boasting the largest naval Junior Reserve Officer Training Corps (JROTC) program in the nation with about 17% of the student body enrolled. The student population is 96% minority, primarily Latino (87%), and has a low 57% graduation rate. Mentoring these populations is a critical supplement to suppression and targeted intervention. In 2008, police and city leaders targeted middle school students as most amenable to primary prevention efforts. In response, Aurora University's Institute for Collaboration formed a partnership with four school districts to create an after-school program that was titled MyTime. The program is free of charge and targets middle school preadolescent students with positive activities and role models. Aurora University students are bused to area middle schools to assist with academics, constructive use of time, support, help with communication, development of social competency, and positive self-esteem. Since its inception, the program has grown to include nine middle schools throughout the city. Attempts were made to evaluate the effectiveness of MyTime through juvenile self-reports, but issues with institutional review boards circumvented acquiring the data.

One of the most prominent community-based gang-prevention programs in Aurora that targets minority at-risk youth is Boys to Men. The program was created by an Aurora community member, Clayton Muhammad, who ran the program out of the mayor's office. The mission was to recruit at-risk youth who vowed to not become part of the gang culture and to defy stereotypes that existed for young minority men. The program emphasized professional attire and demeanor and positive attitudes toward academic success. The aim was to replace contagious violence with contagious peace, ironically, using some of the same methods as gang recruiters. The program encouraged Latino and African American young men to focus on their commonalities and redefine what it means to be a man of color in Aurora.

Assessment

A 10-year assessment of shooting/murder data compared the 2003–2007 period with the 2008–2012 period. A five-year update to those numbers is also presented.

Figure 6.3 shows the annual number of shootings recorded by police from 2003 to 2012. In the five-year period from 2003 to 2007, the city averaged 156 shootings per year. In the following five-year period from 2008 to 2012, the city averaged 79 shootings per year, a 49% decrease.

Figure 6.4 shows the annual number of murders in Aurora recorded by the police from 2003 to 2012. In the five-year period from 2003 to 2007, the city averaged 12.2 murders per year. In the following five-year period from 2008 to 2012, the city averaged 2.6 murders per year, a 78% decrease. The decrease from 2007 to 2008, along with the decrease from one five-year period to the next represent what Clarke (2018) calls a cliff-edge decline (see also Perry et al., 2017). The zero murders in 2012 had last been experienced in Aurora in 1946.

Suppression

While Operation First Degree Burn alone did not cause the reductions in shootings and murders in the city, collaborative efforts to suppress chronic offenders have appeared to change the city's overall gang structure. Aurora gangs now

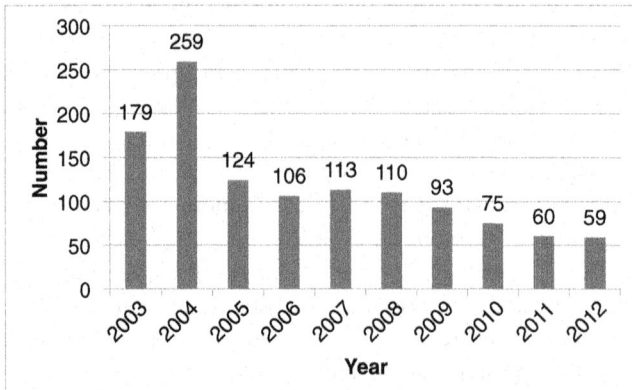

FIGURE 6.3 Number of shootings recorded by police in Aurora, Illinois, 2003–2012

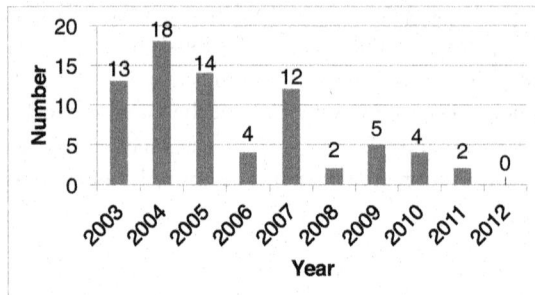

FIGURE 6.4 Number of murders in Aurora, Illinois, 2003–2012

appear to be less formal, less violent, and not nearly as motivated by territorial rivalries with other gangs. Reportedly, members of different street gangs often play basketball with one another and hang out socially, something that was unheard of in the past. In 2007, gang investigators estimated there to be 773 active gang members in the city. Gangs were also more likely to be cohesive. Investigators estimated only 357 active members in 2012. By impacting gang cohesion and perceived social identities, gang violence was reduced. In the period of 2003 to 2007, 78% of murders were gang-related; in the 2008–2012 period, only 21% were linked to gangs. Murders in Aurora today are much less likely to be related to gangs.

Intervention

A police officer in a town adjacent to Aurora who grew up in Aurora and who had some family members in gangs reported to the project team that whereas he was afraid to walk into some Aurora neighborhoods prior to 2008, today, Latino Aurora youth are not as likely to have the same fears or face the same threats of violence. By countering the gang culture and increasing police legitimacy in targeted neighborhoods through knock and talks, education, and media campaigns, police were able to empower key stakeholders to themselves counter the gang culture. Aurora youth now have a variety of community groups—other than gangs—with which to identify.

Prevention

While there has not been a direct assessment linking the East Aurora High School Naval JROTC program to a reduction in city shootings/murders, the timing of the increase in the high school participants is correlated with the significant five-year reduction in city violence. No evaluation of the impact of the MyTime after-school program on juvenile offending has yet been conducted.

From 2008 to 2012, an estimated 200 youth, mostly from Aurora high schools, went through the Boys to Men program. During the five-year evaluation period, 100% of consistently attending members graduated from high school, 92% attended college, and 5% joined the military. Boys to Men graduation ceremonies are attended by hundreds of community members, and the program has received extensive positive media coverage from national, state, and local outlets. Aurora-area police leaders believe the group has helped reduced criminal offending.

Follow-up

In the years following 2013 when this project report was written, Aurora's shooting and murder trends have reversed course. From 2008 to 2012, Aurora experienced 13 murders. From 2013 to 2017, the city experienced 34 murders. While this is still only about half of the 61 murders occurring between 2003 and 2007, it is nonetheless

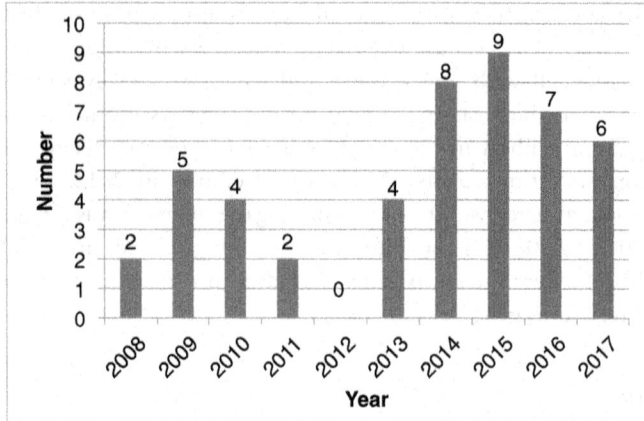

FIGURE 6.5 Number of murders in Aurora, Illinois, 2008–2017

a sharp increase from the 13 occurring during the Finding Typhoid Mary project assessment years. Also, there were 599 shootings from 2013 to 2017 compared to 397 shootings from 2008 to 2012, a similar reversal of trend. Anecdotally, Aurora police officers believe the rise in shootings and murders is connected to gangs, uncooperative victims, and intimidation via social media. Figure 6.5 depicts the upward trend in murders over the past five years indicating problems with sustainability.

Observations

Like many initiatives, long-term sustainable "cliff-edge" results are difficult to sustain and the need for consistent reanalysis is vital. Aurora was successful at creating a comprehensive long-term strategic plan for reducing gang violence. However, maintaining these reductions may require revisiting past strategies. These strategies have to focus on community assessments that are directed toward specific neighborhoods where shootings are concentrated. Choosing strategic neighborhood intervention can be supplemented with data on locations of students who have been expelled, suspended, or are otherwise not regularly attending high school. Intervention through mentorship and social support within these stressed neighborhoods will be needed. These efforts will also help to build legitimacy for inevitable suppression efforts by law enforcement.

The integration of broad community prevention, targeted intervention, and legitimized suppression has to include collaborative partnerships. Aurora, like many cities struggling with youth violence, should set lofty reduction goals that are shared with the public and media. Collaboration should be publicized with the intent of showing a new norm for shared policing efforts and increased accountability.

References

Clarke, R.V. (2018) 'The theory and practice of situational crime prevention', in *Oxford Research Encyclopedia, Criminology and Criminal Justice*, Oxford: Oxford University Press.

Clarke, R.V. & Eck, J. (2007) *Understanding Risky Facilities*, Problem-Oriented Guides for Police, Problem-Solving Tools Series, Guide. No. 6, Washington, DC: Office of Community Oriented Policing, US Department of Justice.

Decker, S. & Pyrooz, D. (2015) *The Handbook of Gangs*, West Sussex, UK: John Wiley & Sons, Ltd.

Decker, S. & Van Winkle, B. (1996) *Life in the Gang: Family, Friends, and Violence*, New York: Cambridge University Press.

Hennigan, K. & Spanovic, M. (2012) 'Gang dynamics through the lens of social identity theory', in F.A. Esbensen & C. Maxson (eds.), *Youth Gangs in International Perspective*, New York: Springer.

Huff, C. & Barrows, J. (2015) 'Documenting gang activity: Intelligence databases', in S. Decker & D. Pyrooz (eds.), *The Handbook of Gangs*, West Sussex, UK: John Wiley & Sons, Ltd., pp. 59–77.

Kennedy, D. (2006) 'Old Wine in New Bottles: Policing and the Lessons of Pulling Levers', in D. Weisburd & A. Braga (eds.), *Police Innovation: Contrasting Perspectives*, Cambridge, UK: Cambridge University Press, pp. 155–170.

Kennedy, D., Braga, A. & Piehl, A. (2001) *Reducing Gun Violence: The Boston Gun Project's Operation Ceasefire, Research Report*, Washington, DC: US Department of Justice, Office of Justice Programs, National Institute of Justice.

Maxson, C., Matsuda, K. & Hennigan, K. (2011) '"Deterrability" among gang and non-gang juvenile offenders: Are gang members more (or less) deterrable than other juvenile offenders?', *Crime & Delinquency*, 57(4): 516–543.

McGloin, J. & Decker, S. (2010) 'Theories of gang behavior and public policy', in H. Barrow & S. Decker (eds.), *Criminology and Public Policy: Putting Theory to Work*, Philadelphia: Temple University Press, pp. 150–165.

Papachristos, A. (2006) 'Social network analysis and gang research: Theory and methods', in J. Short, Jr. & L. Hughes (eds.), *Studying Youth Gangs*, Oxford, UK: Rowman & Littlefield Publishers, Inc., pp. 99–116.

Payne, T. (2017) 'Reducing excessive police incidents: Do notices to owners work?', *Security Journal*, 30: 922–939.

Perry, S., Apel, R., Newman, G.R. & Clarke, R.V. (2017) 'The situational prevention of terrorism: An evaluation of the Israeli West Bank barrier', *Journal of Quantitative Criminology*, 33(4): 727–751.

Phillips, S., Kim, D. & Sobol, J. (2013) 'An evaluation of a multiyear gun buy-back programme: Re-examining the impact on violent crimes', *International Journal of Police Science and Management*, 15(3): 246–261.

Renauer, B., Duffee, D. & Scott, J. (2003) 'Measuring police-community co-production trade-offs in two observational approaches', *Policing: An International Journal of Police Strategies & Management*, 26(1): 9–28.

Roman, C., Decker, S. & Pyrooz, D. (2017) 'Leveraging the pushes and pulls of gang disengagement to improve gang intervention: Findings from three multi-site studies and a review of relevant gang programs', *Journal of Crime and Justice*, 40(3): 316–336.

Scott, J. (2002) 'Assessing the relationship between police-community co-production and neighborhood-level social capital', *Journal of Contemporary Criminal Justice*, 18(2): 147–166.

Simons, R., Simons, L., Burt, C., Brody, G., & Cutrona, C. (2005) 'Collective efficacy, authoritative parenting and delinquency: A longitudinal test of a model integrating community- and family-level processes', *Criminology*, 43(4): 989–1029.

Spergel, I., Wa, K. & Sosa, R. (2006) 'The comprehensive, community-wide, gang program model: Success and failure', in J.F. Short & L.A. Hughes (eds.), Studying Youth Gangs, Lanham, MD: AltaMira Press, pp. 203–224.

Venkatesh, S.A. & Levitt, S. (2000) '"Are we a family or a business?" History and disjuncture in the urban American street gang', *Theory and Society*, 29: 427–462.

Vigil, J. (2002) *A Rainbow of Gangs: Street Cultures in the Mega-City*, Austin, TX: University of Texas Press.

Wyrick, P. (2006) 'Gang prevention: How to make the "front end" of your anti-gang effort work', *United States Attorneys' Bulletin*, 54: 52–60.

Zeoli, A., Pizarro, J., Grady, S. & Melde, C. (2014) 'Homicide as infectious disease: Using public health methods to investigate the diffusion of homicide', *Justice Quarterly*, 31(3): 609–632.

PART II

Violence against women

7

DOMESTIC VIOLENCE IN HIGH POINT, NORTH CAROLINA

David M. Kennedy

Mapping a problem-oriented approach on to domestic violence

Some five years after the initial implementation of the Boston Gun Project's Operation Ceasefire in 1996, and with the recognition that it represented a different way of thinking about and addressing violence, program officers from the Family Violence Prevention Fund, with support from the William and Flora Hewlett Foundation, asked me to produce a paper on whether those lessons held any implications for addressing domestic violence, one of a series it was commissioning (Rosewater, n.d.). I knew next to nothing about domestic violence, but a review of the domestic violence literature, and some quick but fascinating consultations with public safety professionals working on domestic violence, suggested that the answer might well be "yes." That was a surprise to me; it turned out to be more than, or worse than, a surprise to quite a lot of other people. This chapter is a meditation on that experience.

Operation Ceasefire and the "focused deterrence" approach that emerged from it were based on the finding that homicide in Boston was heavily concentrated amongst a small, identifiable number of extremely active groups, comprised largely of high-rate criminal offenders with high rates of violence victimization and representing a very small fraction—about one-quarter of 1 percent—of the city. Direct communication to these groups by a partnership of law enforcement, service providers, and community figures and spelling out the carefully developed and focused formal consequences that would fall on groups for continued violence, community standards against violence, and opportunities for support and services rapidly and dramatically reduced homicide and gun violence. On the face of it, there was little similarity between that violence and domestic violence. The former involved group members and group dynamics, was tightly linked to drug dealing and other economic crimes, was more or less public, was concentrated in poor urban minority neighborhoods, occurred among individuals who often had weak and even no personal relationships, and was overwhelmingly gun violence. Domestic violence involved largely individuals, was not directly connected to economic offending, was largely private, was relatively rarely gun violence, involved individuals who overwhelmingly knew each other and often had sustained relationships, and was broadly distributed among men without a connection to chronic offending, economic status, or place.

Or so was the conventional and advocacy wisdom and much of the public policy discussion. As I did my literature review, I found to my surprise that the research strongly suggested otherwise: the literature largely presented a fact pattern of concentration of particularly the most serious violent domestic abuse by race, ethnicity, and neighborhood, with victimization concentrated among poor women of color and with the most serious offenders displaying not only repeat domestic offending with the same and serial victims but also chronic offending across a wide range of offense categories. It is worth quoting at length from a paper reporting the findings (citations omitted):

> We should begin by recognizing that the dominant perception of domestic violence offenders as "anyone"—as distinct from other violent offenders and from their patterns and dynamics—is often, and perhaps largely, wrong. Domestic violence offenders tend to be serial offenders in two ways. As is well-known, they tend to commit multiple acts of domestic violence within a given relationship and across multiple relationships. But beyond that, despite the widespread belief that domestic violence offenders are uniquely "specialized" and that domestic violence is evenly distributed across society, research suggests that offenders tend to have robust criminal histories including a wide range of both domestic violence and non-domestic violence offenses, and that domestic violence homicide victims are quite disproportionately poor and minority. A review of individuals arrested for assault in Lowell, Massachusetts, found that "domestic offenders are commonly thought to be 'specialists' who do not pose a threat to the community at large. Our data indicate that this is not the case. The domestic offenders [studied] were just as likely as the non-domestic offenders to have committed non-domestic offenses in the five years prior (46 percent of each group had been arraigned for nondomestic offenses). Additionally, the two groups had statistically equal proportions of high-rate offenders."
>
> Similarly, a study of more than 18,000 Massachusetts men with restraining orders found that three-quarters had some sort of prior criminal history: nearly half had an arraignment or conviction for a violent crime, more than 40 percent for a property crime, more than 20 percent for a drug offense, one-quarter for driving under the influence, and nearly half for other offenses. Qualitative work gives similar results. Unpublished research on the Quincy, Massachusetts, Probation Project, based on victim interviews, found that

55 percent of batterers had prior criminal records of which the victim was aware. Another study that examined reports from 270 women in intervention programs found that nearly half of spouse abusers had previously been arrested for violent crimes and that those who had been arrested for violence against strangers were more frequently and severely violent at home.

Additional research shows other parallels. Violent and chronic offending tends to be concentrated among poor and minority populations. This is also true with domestic violence. One study found that "marital violence is found across all social classes, but rates are higher in lower socioeconomic status, blue-collar families, especially those marked by underemployment and unemployment"; a study cited in the article shows a two-to-one proportion of lower to higher economic status among offenders who commit family violence. One study of female victims of domestic homicide in New York City between 1990 and 1997 found that victims were disproportionately black: half of all victims were black, relative to about a quarter of the population. Victims were also somewhat disproportionately Latina and came primarily from the poorer boroughs of Brooklyn, the Bronx, and Queens.

(Kennedy, 2004)

All of that was in the available literature. As compelling was the knowledge of frontline practitioners. One of the most important aspects of the violence the Boston Gun Project had addressed was that it was very well understood by the police officers, probationers, outreach workers, and the like who dealt with it every day. They knew what was going on, including who the most violent groups and group members were and often when they were likely to act. I put together a meeting in Boston of police department domestic violence investigators, victim services providers from prosecutors' offices and outside agencies, advocates, shelter operators, and the like. As part of it I asked them, "Do you know who the most dangerous [domestic violence] offenders in Boston are, and to which victims?" The room said no. "We've tried to predict it," they said. "We've looked at criminal records, violations of restraining orders, all kinds of things. We don't know how." "That's not what I asked," I said. "This is what you do every day. Do you know?" The room said yes. "We deal with the most threatened, frightened women every day, and the guys who do this to them. Mostly, yes, we do know."

Framing a different kind of domestic violence strategy out of those facts was remarkably easy. Put together a partnership of law enforcement, advocates, service providers, and community figures. Make a concerted effort to address the most dangerous men, whom we can designate our "A" offenders. When necessary incapacitate them by any legal means, including by "pulling levers": using their nondomestic legal exposures—an outstanding warrant, a drug case, a gun charge, an assault-on-a-stranger case—when indicated. Market that back to the next round of likely prospective violent offenders, whom we will call our "B" offenders, through direct communication. Organize the system actors to ensure meaningful consequences for the most dangerous offenders and focus with particular care on services for and the safety of their victims. The latter was a very serious concern; this was a problem of people in sustained contact, and taking the wrong kind of action with abusers could get people killed, so very close monitoring of victim safety and sentiment would have to be an essential part of any intervention.

There was more to it than that, but the strategic outline was clear. There were even some field experiences to draw on; authorities in several Massachusetts cities were pursuing trial programs that focused on the most dangerous offenders, put them on notice, and maintained a high degree of contact with both offenders and victims. The results were apparently good. And there was a paper on an action-research project in Killingbeck, England, inspired by criminology's repeat victimization framework, that came remarkably close to what I was thinking about (Hanmer, Griffiths & Jerwood, 1999). It reported that most offenders were much more easily deterred than had been thought; that when put on notice, they greatly overestimated the actual capacities of the authorities; and that victims welcomed the new approach. Evaluation found that early intervention with abusers reduced repeat victimization, putting abusers on notice reduced recidivism, those who did reoffend took longer to do so, and that the process both identified and reduced the number of chronic offenders, encouraged victims and those supporting them to ask for assistance, and identified risk factors for repeat victimization and repeat police visits. Something like this seemed worth working out and trying.

Moltke's maxim and the Kennedy corollary: the impossibility of achieving policy consensus for innovative public-safety interventions

I got nowhere. The domestic violence world hated my idea. The Family Violence Prevention Fund held a meeting of domestic violence scholars and advocates to review their commissioned papers; mine was almost universally panned. It was the same in city after city for years on end, as both the domestic violence prevention world and the domestic violence enforcement world heard me out and shut me down. Advocates had lots of reasons not to like it: it focused efforts primarily on those cases known to the criminal justice system and not those unknown, which meant it also focused attention disproportionately on poor women of color and not on better-off white women; it risked putting victims at further risk; it focused on serious violence and not on the larger range of abusive and controlling behavior that comprises domestic abuse; it focused on offenders and preventing offending and threatened to take attention away from victims and their needs; it failed to address patriarchy and the toxic nature of men (one of the advocates at the Family Violence Prevention Fund session ended the meeting by saying, "I don't think we'll get anywhere on this until we can change how men *are*"). Many people felt, and said, that they did not think police or communities would go along with it. This would require police and community actors to say domestic violence was wrong, and they will not do it, many advocates thought; police and community think domestic violence in *normal* and *right* (they are wrong about that, but their own awful experiences made it dreadfully plausible). Over it all hung what seemed to me a sense of disproportion my notion triggered: domestic violence was *huge*, enveloping, cultural, and this idea was so *small*, so technical, so . . . inadequate. It could not possibly work.

Law enforcement's stance was largely simpler. They—police and prosecutors in particular—were overwhelmed, exhausted, frustrated, and hopeless. They were drowning in calls. Nobody was happy to see them when they arrived. They knew what they had to offer did not work, and so did the people they offered them to. They went to the same addresses and saw the same people over and over and over. Victims, mostly women, were back with the abusers, mostly men, the next day or the day after; would not help with cases; and would not come to court. Abusers sweet-talked or threatened them out of cooperating, were not afraid of the police, were not afraid of the courts, and knew nothing would happen. They had done it before, with this woman and others; they would keep doing it, with this woman and others. Law enforcement could not imagine anything that would work, could not imagine working any harder. I peddled the idea in city after city; I got no traction whatsoever.

This was a special case of a general phenomenon that anybody working to address public-safety issues in innovative and unexpected ways has experienced. Helmuth von Moltke, a 19th-century Prussian field marshal, coined one of the pithiest and most-honored maxims in military theory: "no strategy," he is said to have said, "survives first contact with the enemy."[1] The public-safety corollary—as certain in practice as the military one—is that no idea for preventing violence and enhancing public safety survives first contact with anything like a representative sample of practitioners and the public. It does not matter how well-thought-through it is, how grounded in analysis, how "evidence-based." Consultation will kill it, and the more quickly and the more definitively the more it colors outside the lines of the conventional.

This is partly because of the two main ways of thinking about crime and public safety. One habit of mind, and one camp, believes in individual accountability, the criminal justice system, and rules and sanctions for breaking those rules. One habit of mind, and the other camp, believes in collective accountability, root causes, and community, family, and individual support (I draw these distinctions out further in another essay in this volume). In practice, this means that for nearly any given idea, one side, the other, or both will hate it. It will seem too harsh to the supportive camp and too weak to the accountability camp. If it mixes accountability and support more or less equally, it is as or more likely to draw the enmity of all as it is their endorsement. The theoretical implication is that if one employs a consultative process that perfectly represents these tendencies in the underlying population, it will produce consensus on exactly nothing. In practice, that is about what happens.

It then gets worse, because both sides are essentially determinists. Individual accountability folks believe that crime and violence are caused by settled aspects of character, that those aspects are fiercely resistant to change, and that tendencies toward bad behavior are therefore essentially immutable. That leads to the belief that nothing that does not effectively deter or incapacitate—in practice, mostly the latter—can matter very much (and if deterrence is suggested, the discourse moves inexorably to displacement and the near-theological conviction that "they'll just move"). Collective accountability folks believe that crime and violence are caused by the deep structures of societies and communities and that the outcomes of those structures are essentially immutable. That leads to the belief that nothing that does not alter those tectonic forces can matter very much (and then to the theological devotion to addressing "root causes" and superficially "progressive" but, in fact, deeply insulting and demeaning notions like "we have to get to the boys before they're eight, because after that it's too late"). Since in practice no actual public-safety strategy can guarantee incapacitation, on one hand, or general social transformation, on the other, once again nothing can survive scrutiny.

It then gets worse, because the search for effective leverage on each side inevitably leads each camp to bigger, broader, more ambitious, and less practicable programs. A kind of Gresham's Law—bad money drives out good money (Encyclopaedia Brittanica, 2019)—operates for public safety: consideration of things that cannot be done drive out consideration of things that can be done. A group will gather to address, say, domestic violence. "Women don't report," someone will say; "we need to get women to report." "They don't like the police response," someone will say; "we need to change the way the police behave." "It's more than the police," someone will say; "we need to get the hospitals on board." "It's more than the hospitals," someone will say; "we really need to educate boys in elementary school, before it's too late." "It's more than the schools," someone will say; "this is really about changing the men in the community; they all need to get on board." "We need to organize all the churches," someone will say. And the conversation will go on until "what we have to do" is so enormous that it cannot possibly be done—certainly not by the people in the room—and everybody goes home having accomplished exactly nothing and with no plan for doing so.

And, finally, it gets worse because these are all issues soaked in norms and values—properly so—and ideas and positions that speak to deeply held beliefs almost invariably, in practice, trump more practical but cooler and more pragmatic approaches. I remember being a panelist in front of an open public meeting on youth violence called by the police chief in New Haven, Connecticut. I laid out the approach that had evolved from Boston Ceasefire—how it worked, why it worked, the considerable and positive evaluation record. The room barely reacted. A community activist on the panel said, "I just really believe we should love our kids more." The room exploded in applause. (The city implemented the Boston approach and cut homicide nearly 60 percent and shootings nearly 80 percent over several years (Caniglia, 2016; Sierra-Arevalo, Charette & Papachristos, 2017)). In a different room, with different folks, calling for flogging would have gotten the same response. People *know what they think* about these issues—about guns, about drugs, about families, about communities, about police, about race and racism, about deeply held notions of right and wrong—and what and how they think is overwhelmingly what and how they keep on thinking.

Making progress

In practice, what one needs to get beyond all this is a setting and partners who are willing to go beyond the usual positions and habits of mind, take the outline of a new approach, work out what it would actually mean to implement it, and see if it works. For the intimate partner violence work, it finally clicked in High Point, North Carolina, for no better reason than that they were willing to try. I had had a long, wonderful working relationship with High Point going back to the late 1990s. We had worked together on gun violence, overt drug markets, robbery, group-related violence, an iterative process that had been so successful that ten years after it began domestic violence was overwhelmingly the city's most serious remaining violent crime problem. I dusted my paper off and shared it. The police department was initially no more enthusiastic than anywhere else, but Jim Fealy, the chief, commissioned an internal domestic homicide review that showed a situation so awful it shocked them into optimism.

The review showed that every domestic violence homicide in the city going back years fit the chronic- and repeat-offender profile; that the offender and often the victim and situation had been reported to the police; that there had been ample opportunities to intervene in what just a little attention would have revealed to be dire and worsening situations; and that it was largely women of color in the city's poor neighborhoods who were being killed. It also showed thoroughgoing internal and interagency dysfunction. The High Point Police Department had a mandatory arrest policy that was overwhelmingly not being followed. Its record management system did not distinguish between domestic violence, which could be a father and a son getting into it over a football game, and intimate partner violence, which tended to be much deeper and more dangerous and destructive. What Fealy and the rest cared about was intimate partner violence, but they could not even tell how much of that they had. Police did a lousy job of letting prosecutors know which people and cases mattered; prosecutors did a lousy job of letting judges know. Law enforcement agencies had no systematic relationships with advocates, service providers, and shelters. In a surreal marker of just how bad it all was, the review uncovered the fact that one of the probation departments covering High Point had a special intensive supervision program for extreme domestic violence offenders: and if, as such an offender, your reaction to being placed in it was to *never even show up and meet your probation officer*, eventually the department declared you "inactive"—and did not tell the court.

Fealy, Deputy Chief Marty Sumner, and his top people took this all in. We had a big meeting to chew on the findings; Sumner remembers me sitting in the back of the room and asking, "Are they resisting our best efforts?" Clearly they were not; clearly we can do better than this.

Beginning in 2009, the better part of ten years after first framing the notion, we formed up to try. Fealy assembled a team from the police department; local and federal prosecutors; probation and parole; domestic violence service providers and advocates; community partners; researchers from the University of North Carolina,

Greensboro (UNCG); national domestic violence expert Susan Herman; and me. Recognizing that the special class of known—to criminal justice actors, advocates, shelter providers, and the like—extremely serious violent abusers and their targets had not been getting anything like the attention they deserved, the team made an immediate priority of assertively looking for those offenders, victims, and situations and taking immediate action to stop those offenders and protect those victims. Domestic homicides in High Point began falling at that point, marking reductions that began before the entire strategy was even designed (I refer elsewhere in this volume to the murder of Tabitha Birdsong; there is reason to believe that had she lived in High Point, she would be alive today).

The UNCG researchers took a deep look at years of domestic violence calls, charges, offenders, and incidents, further illuminating and confirming what the department's initial review had sketched. Domestic violence calls came from all over the city, but homicide was hugely concentrated in minority and low-income victims and neighborhoods. Homicide offenders were 86 percent minority; 93 percent unemployed and virtually all low income; and averaged almost 11 prior arrests, with assault as the predominant charge; all of them had an offense history beyond intimate partner violence incidents. Going beyond homicide, over a ten-year period going back to 2000, 1,033 people had been charged with a domestic-related offense in High Point, totaling 10,328 distinct charges, most of them had lengthy nonspecialist criminal histories and frequent contact with criminal justice agencies (Sechrist & Weil, 2014). The basic idea that had driven our thinking—there was a special class of particularly vulnerable victims at particular risk from particularly chronic offenders—was confirmed.

Over the next two years, the group put together the intervention design (see Figure 7.1). The original notion of two classes of offenders—an "A" group that would be incapacitated by any legal means available, and a "B" group to which that would be marketed—was replaced by a four-level structure. With the express aim of intervening as early as possible and communicating clear formal commitment to preventing domestic abuse, a "D" group was identified as needing notification prior even to a domestic violence call or charge, as when, for example, officers responded to a non–domestic violence call but saw what they thought might be domestic violence that did not rise to the level of an arrest. "C" offenders had one domestic violence–related charge; "B" offenders had two or more or had violated prior notifications to stop; "A" offenders needed immediate incapacitation, based on criminal histories or their known behavior. Steps for classifying and engaging with those levels were worked out carefully. Victim services and safety planning were matched to each level, with targets of "B" and "A" offenders getting particularly intense support.

The basic logic and structure were not particularly difficult to sort out. The group was intensely conscious of the risk of putting victims in harm's way,

Offender Categories

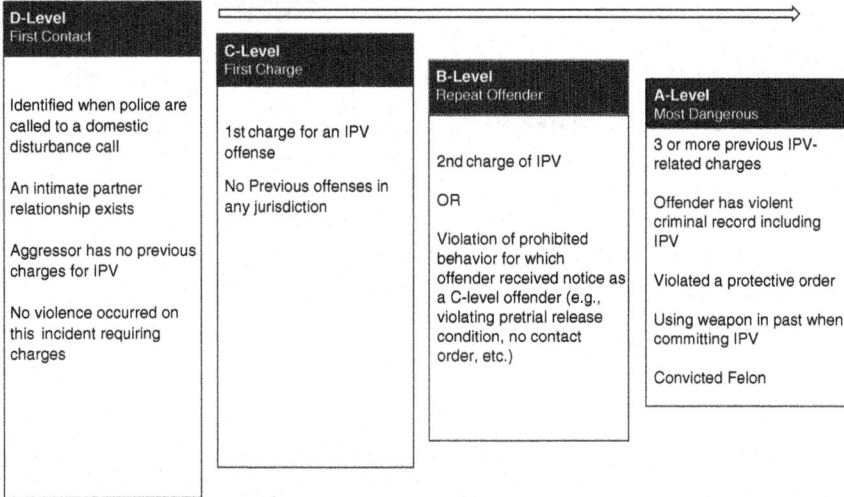

D-Level
First Contact

Identified when police are called to a domestic disturbance call

An intimate partner relationship exists

Aggressor has no previous charges for IPV

No violence occurred on this incident requiring charges

C-Level
First Charge

1st charge for an IPV offense

No Previous offenses in any jurisdiction

B-Level
Repeat Offender

2nd charge of IPV

OR

Violation of prohibited behavior for which offender received notice as a C-level offender (e.g., violating pretrial release condition, no contact order, etc.)

A-Level
Most Dangerous

3 or more previous IPV-related charges

Offender has violent criminal record including IPV

Violated a protective order

Using weapon in past when committing IPV

Convicted Felon

Notification Type by Offender Category

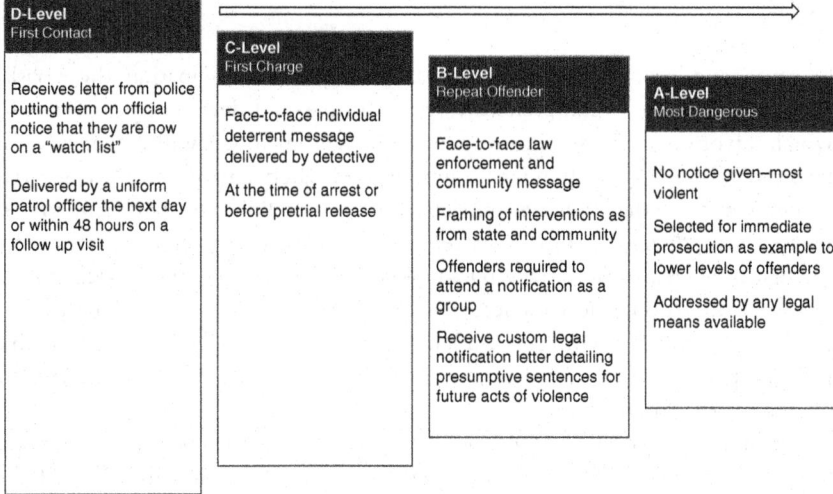

D-Level
First Contact

Receives letter from police putting them on official notice that they are now on a "watch list"

Delivered by a uniform patrol officer the next day or within 48 hours on a follow up visit

C-Level
First Charge

Face-to-face individual deterrent message delivered by detective

At the time of arrest or before pretrial release

B-Level
Repeat Offender

Face-to-face law enforcement and community message

Framing of interventions as from state and community

Offenders required to attend a notification as a group

Receive custom legal notification letter detailing presumptive sentences for future acts of violence

A-Level
Most Dangerous

No notice given—most violent

Selected for immediate prosecution as example to lower levels of offenders

Addressed by any legal means available

FIGURE 7.1 Offender categories

Source: National Network for Safe Communities (2016). *Intimate partner violence intervention (IPVI): High Point Police Department.* Submission to the Herman Goldstein Award for Excellence in Problem-Oriented Policing.

Victims Services & Contact by Offender Category

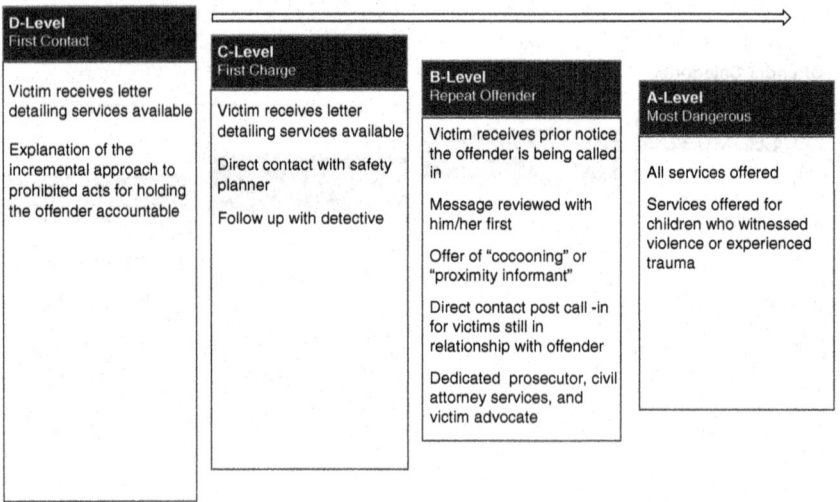

D-Level First Contact	C-Level First Charge	B-Level Repeat Offender	A-Level Most Dangerous
Victim receives letter detailing services available Explanation of the incremental approach to prohibited acts for holding the offender accountable	Victim receives letter detailing services available Direct contact with safety planner Follow up with detective	Victim receives prior notice the offender is being called in Message reviewed with him/her first Offer of "cocooning" or "proximity informant" Direct contact post call-in for victims still in relationship with offender Dedicated prosecutor, civil attorney services, and victim advocate	All services offered Services offered for children who witnessed violence or experienced trauma

Based on: Lave, T., & Miller, E. (Eds.). (2019). *The Cambridge Handbook of Policing in the United States* (Cambridge Law Handbooks). Cambridge: Cambridge University Press. doi:10.1017/9781108354721

FIGURE 7.1 (Continued)

however, and proceeded with granular attention to anticipating those risks, attending to them as comprehensively as possible, and developing measures by which advocates and law enforcement could stay in touch with, especially, the targets of "B" and "A" offenders to support their safety and identify any negative consequences of the intervention. The High Point Police Department implemented a fundamental shift in its reporting processes and records systems, for the first time creating and tracking a new set of "intimate partner" categories, as distinct from "domestic violence," and retrained all of its officers. The process took about two years, with full implementation underway by 2011, and the first intimate partner violence call-in held in early 2012 (National Network for Safe Communities, 2016).

The impact was immediate and dramatic. High Point had experienced seventeen intimate partner violence homicides in the five years prior to the initial 2009 focus on "A" offenders; in the more than seven years leading up to High Point's submission for the 2016 Goldstein Award, there was one, of a couple passing through the city and staying in a motel. Calls for service dropped by a fifth, while calls with injuries fell from nearly 70 percent to less than 50 percent (National Network for Safe Communities, 2016). Recidivism rates for intimate partner violence present methodological difficulties, with results affected by what is considered intimate partner violence (as opposed to domestic violence more generally), standards for defining reoffending, and the temporal period under review, but studies tend to find ranges from about 50 percent up to 60 percent and higher over several years; a recent review of High Point's intimate partner violence recidivism rate going back to 2011 showed it to be less than 18 percent (National Network for Safe Communities, n.d.).

The core High Point partnership meets monthly in a large group, often as many as forty or fifty people, to keep the intervention on track, address intervention and system issues, and give intense scrutiny and strategizing to offenders and situations that present particular risks. I have seen a single such case—a given known offender representing a serious danger to a known victim—get an hour's focused attention from that partnership, with granular attention to what was going on and how the abuser could be stopped and the victim protected. Early replications in other sites are also showing promise, and my organization, the National Network for Safe Communities, is working with the US Department of Justice's Office for Violence Against Women on a multisite replication and evaluation.

I argue elsewhere in this volume that public safety practitioners should take a problem-oriented approach that consciously sets aside "criminal justice system" and "prevention" frameworks in favor of more focused and practical thinking and operations. That is not the world we live in today. In this world, it is the common experience that making a case for the most well-justified departures from conventional thinking and practice get one nowhere. The best antidote to the failure of talk, I find, is not more talk. In our original Boston work, we had taken a lot of time to understand that high-risk group members were more traumatized than predatory, did not much like the violence, respected lots of people in the community, did not understand their own legal risks, and therefore might well be influenced by respectful engagement with the Ceasefire partnership. We did not know ourselves that it would work until we tried it. Before it did work, the prospect that we could convince anybody that the way to address homicide was to find the most dangerous men in the city, gather them together, and tell them exactly what your law enforcement plans were was beyond ludicrous. After, it had a chance.

For now, the best antidote to the failure of talk is new facts on the ground. Get something done, make it real, point at it, and change thinking and discourse. In public safety, for some decades now, there has been no better engine of new public-safety facts on the ground than Herman Goldstein's notion of problem-oriented policing. The Goldstein Award winners are among the very best of those. It is among my greatest sources of professional and personal satisfaction and of pride in belonging to an extraordinary community of thought and action, that the High Point Offender-Focused Domestic Violence Intervention is one of them.

Note

1 His actual words were longer but to the same effect (see Keyes, 2006).

References

Caniglia, J. (2016) 'What cities can learn from New Haven's fight to rein in gang violence', *Cleveland Plain Dealer*, March 24.

Encyclopaedia Brittanica (2019) *Gresham's Law*. Retrieved from brittanica.com

Hanmer, J., Griffiths, S. & Jerwood, D. (1999) *Arresting Evidence: Domestic Violence and Repeat Victimisation*, Police Research Series, Paper 104, London: Home Office Policing and Reducing Crime Unit, Research and Statistics Directorate.

Kennedy, D.M. (2004) 'Rethinking law enforcement strategies to prevent domestic violence', *Networks, National Center for Victims of Crime*, 19(2–3): 8–15.

Keyes, R. (2006) 'The quote verifier', *The Antioch Review*, 64(2): 256–266.

National Network for Safe Communities (2016) *Intimate Partner Violence Intervention (IPVI): High Point Police Department*. Submission to the Herman Goldstein Award for Excellence in Problem-Oriented Policing, Arizona State University Center for Problem-Oriented Policing, Phoenix, AZ.

National Network for Safe Communities (n.d.) *Intimate Partner Violence Issue Brief*, New York: National Network for Safe Communities at John Jay College.

Rosewater, A. (n.d.) *Promoting Prevention, Targeting Teens: An Emerging Agenda to Reduce Domestic Violence*, San Francisco, CA: Family Violence Prevention Fund.

Sechrist, S.M. & Weil, J.D. (2014) 'The High Point OFDVI: Preliminary evaluation results', in D.M. Kennedy (chair), *Using Focused Deterrence to Combat Domestic Violence*. Symposium presented at the John Jay College of Criminal Justice International Conference, The Rule of Law in an Era of Change: Security, Social Justice, and Inclusive Governance, Athens, Greece.

Sierra-Arevalo, M., Charette, Y. & Papachristos, A.V. (2017) 'Evaluating the effect of project longevity on group-involved shootings and homicides in New Haven, Connecticut', *Crime & Delinquency*, 63(4): 446–467.

8

DOMESTIC VIOLENCE IN CHULA VISTA, CALIFORNIA

*Karin Schmerler, Deborah Lamm Weisel,
and Julie Wartell*

Project summary

Domestic violence (DV) is one of the most common problems facing law enforcement agencies. In Chula Vista, California, a diverse border city of 270,000 located seven miles south of San Diego and seven miles north of Mexico, police officers were frequently dispatched to domestic violence and domestic dispute calls for service—often repeatedly to the same addresses—to sort out interpersonal disputes between intimate partners or to respond to physical violence between them. (In this chapter, unless otherwise specified, "DV" refers to both non-criminal domestic disputes, such as loud verbal arguments, and criminal incidents between intimate partners, including assaults, violations of restraining orders, vandalism, and sex crimes). While DV victims may have felt helpless, police officers also had a sense of futility because of the recurrent pattern of DV and concern that offenders were rarely held accountable. The Chula Vista Police Department (CVPD) developed a solution to DV that included a structured message delivered at the initial DV incident, as well as follow-up contacts with victims, suspects, and "subjects" (individuals involved in non-crime disputes).

Scanning

In 2013, domestic violence was the second most common type of call for police service in Chula Vista, exceeded only by false burglar alarms. Chula Vista is not a high-crime city, but like many communities across the United States, DV dominates the police call workload. In 2013, there were more DV calls to police in Chula Vista than the combined total of all robbery, residential burglary, vehicle theft, and vehicle burglary calls.

Citywide, there were about 4,000 DV calls each year in Chula Vista. This number remained steady from 2007 to 2014 while calls other than DV dropped 10%. Although CVPD had partnered with victim advocates for more than 15 years to provide around-the-clock, on-scene services to DV victims, there had been no reduction in DV calls. The recurring nature of DV continued to have a negative effect on DV victims, as well as any children who were present, other family members and neighbors. The high volume of DV calls and crimes also affected police officers, victim advocates, prosecutors, and others.

Analysis

Prior research

CVPD conducted an extensive review of research on police problem-solving efforts relating to DV. While there were evidence-based practices to guide police on reducing DV crime—particularly the most serious DV crimes—there was a dearth of police responses to the broader spectrum of DV (see Sherman, 1992; Sampson, 2007). Scant research on DV included responses to non-crime calls such as disputes between intimate partners or DV crimes other than assaults. In Chula Vista, DV disputes and varied types of DV crimes seemed closely related.

The research identified three police initiatives that had focused on the range of DV calls and police responses and measurably reduced DV or its severity: Fremont, California; West Yorkshire, England; and High Point, North Carolina. In the mid-1990s, Fremont patrol officers began conducting unannounced follow-up visits with couples at chronic DV addresses. Fremont was able to reduce repeat calls to these locations by 67% (Fremont Police Department, 1997). In the late 1990s, West Yorkshire officers implemented a tiered response to DV couples based on whether officers had been dispatched to their address once, twice, or three times or more in the past. The West Yorkshire response reduced the number of couples who "graduated" to higher levels due to repeat incidents (Hanmer, Griffiths & Jerwood, 1999). Finally, in 2009, High Point began using a focused-deterrence model, mixed with some elements of West Yorkshire's tiered-response initiative, to reduce DV. The High Point project reduced DV calls, injuries, and homicides (Sechrist & Weil, 2018; Sechrist, Weil & Shelton, 2016).

Focus groups and surveys of officers

As part of CVPD's analysis, focus groups were conducted with patrol officers and a department-wide survey was conducted in 2014. Eighty-seven percent of officer respondents expressed frustration with responding repeatedly to the same couples involved in non-crime intimate partner disturbances. And a large segment of officers were skeptical about traditional criminal justice responses to DV. Approximately 70% said they did not think restraining orders or mandatory treatment for batterers was effective; almost 50% said arresting DV suspects seldom prevented future DV.

Call and crime data

To identify DV patterns, a team of three CVPD analysts examined more than 10,000 DV-related calls for service received by the police department between January 2012 and June 2014. (While a portion of DV calls are also crimes, CVPD documents non-crime verbal disputes between intimate partners in the agency's computer-aided dispatch system differently from DV crime calls.) The analysts found that more than 70% of DV calls did not result in a crime report because the incidents were "verbal-only" disturbances involving intimate partners.

The analysis also showed that repeat DV was a substantial problem—just as the officers had described. Just 6% of unique residential DV addresses in one area— only 23 unique residential addresses—accounted for 19% of unique residential DV calls for service (CFS) in that area over a six-month period. Although most residential addresses did not experience repeat DV calls, when repeat calls did occur, the vast majority (86%) reoccurred at least three days after the initial call.

An analysis of a sample of 2,612 DV crime cases (including assaults, restraining order violations, and other crimes such as robbery, burglary, and vandalism designated as DV-related in the records management system) during the 30-month period from 2012 to mid-2014 revealed the following:

- More than half of all couples (56%) had children under 18, and children were present during one-third of DV crimes.
- DV victims and suspects were relatively young—more than 75% were aged 40 or under.
- DV suspects were not exclusively male—about 25% of DV suspects were female.

In addition, few DV suspects were held accountable through the criminal justice system:

- In about half of DV crimes, suspects fled the scene and were never arrested due to limited patrol resources. (Most DV crimes were misdemeanor batteries such as a slap or push with no evidence of injury.)
- When DV suspects were arrested, they were detained pretrial for a relatively short period. Overall, 42% of suspects bailed out of jail, and 80% were released within 24 hours.
- About half of DV arrests were not prosecuted by the district attorney due to a lack of independent corroboration—that is, sufficient evidence to convince a jury of guilt.
- Among DV crimes that were prosecuted, the vast majority resulted in guilty dispositions; however, fewer than 2% of all DV suspects were arrested, convicted, and incarcerated.

Because few DV offenders were held accountable for their crimes—as officers had also reported—it was clear Chula Vista needed to focus the bulk of its efforts on

Chula Vista, California
01/01/2012 to 06/30/2014

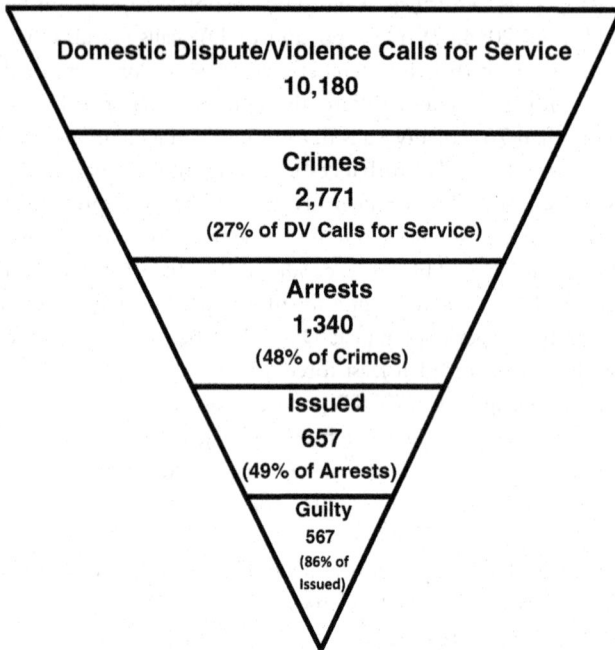

Domestic Dispute/Violence Calls for Service
10,180

Crimes
2,771
(27% of DV Calls for Service)

Arrests
1,340
(48% of Crimes)

Issued
657
(49% of Arrests)

Guilty
567
(86% of
Issued)

FIGURE 8.1 Domestic violence incident funnel

the front end of the criminal justice system—the police response—to reduce and prevent future DV (see Figure 8.1).

Partner perspectives

To shape the response, CVPD sought the perspectives of partner organizations: victim advocates who routinely provided on-scene services for DV victims, Child Welfare Services (CWS), Probation, and the District Attorney's Office (local prosecutor). The perspectives of the partner organizations were informative. For example, CWS personnel educated police that that loud arguments (not just physical assaults) between adult intimate partners are damaging to children. The youngest children are the most vulnerable to fear and trauma related to intense arguments because their brains are still in critical stages of development.

Response

Based on the problem analysis findings, a tiered response model was developed that drew on prior initiatives identified. Specifically, CVPD developed a graduated response protocol for DV incidents based on the type of DV that had occurred—a non-crime DV call, an initial DV crime, or multiple DV incidents. The goal of the follow-up response model was to reduce DV by changing social norms and behavior—without relying on traditional criminal justice interventions—unless repeated, customized, and increasingly intensive police contacts were not effective.[1] While police were concerned about the volume of DV calls, their focus was reducing DV crimes and not discouraging people from calling the police about DV.

In late 2015, CVPD launched a quasi-experimental research design to carry out the problem-solving effort. The initiative was implemented in one geographic area of the city; a matched comparison area was selected that had a similar population, demographic composition, and volume of DV calls and crimes. Both areas had between 50,000 and 69,000 people and were about 70% Hispanic. The two areas had almost identical trends in the number of DV calls and DV crimes during the 15-year period before the problem-solving effort was launched.

Educational message for subjects in non-crime DV calls

In the experimental area, officers responding to a "verbal-only" disturbance call provided both subjects with a consistent verbal message and an educational brochure. Since there were no "victims" or "suspects" in non-crime disputes, officers told both subjects that police took these disturbances seriously. Officers explained that everyone had disagreements but not disagreements so loud that police were called for help. The messaging included an explanation of the harm to children, and this seemed to resonate with subjects. Officers also explained that police would be back to check on everyone's welfare. A civilian police employee later sent both subjects a follow-up text with a link to a short survey to make sure they were okay. For example, the first survey question read: "Police were recently called to help with a domestic issue. Since police responded, have things: gotten worse; stayed the same; gotten better." The personalized text contacts were novel and appropriate for relatively youthful subjects.

Warnings to DV suspects

When officers made an arrest at a DV crime, they delivered a stern warning to the suspect. Officers told suspects they could expect future unannounced visits from police and would receive a great deal of attention from a special task force if they did not stop the abuse. Officers stressed that this new approach was being driven by police, not the victim. Officers asked suspects to sign the warnings and gave the suspects and victims copies.

DV victims: three-day follow-up

Approximately three days after an initial DV crime occurred, officers conducted an in-person follow-up at the residence. If no one was home, officers left a card on the door that said: "We stopped by to check on your safety," along with their contact information. This card let the victim and suspect know the police were actively working to prevent problems at the home. In some cases, the cards were informative to other family members or neighbors who were aware of the issues. Most important, the in-person contact or follow-up card provided concrete evidence that police were following through on their promise to check on the welfare of victims. The contact also provided evidence that the police response was not activated by the victim calling the police.

Chronic suspects and ongoing verbal abuse

Finally, for those suspects who continued to abuse their partners, a customized problem-solving plan was developed by the police officer who served as the program coordinator. Sometimes the plan involved working with the District Attorney's Office to prioritize a suspect for prosecution or notifying the suspect's probation officer. In other situations, such as continued verbal abuse or crimes with little evidence, the project coordinator met with the victims, suspects, and people with influence over the offenders, such as parents and siblings, to try to stop the behavior. For example, the coordinator once worked with a severely disabled suspect who physically abused his wife even though he was confined to a wheelchair. To remind the suspect that police would continue to check on her safety until the violence stopped, his wife taped a project flyer to their bathroom wall with a note to that effect. The victim later told police that the situation eventually improved to the point that she was able to take the flyer down.

Assessment

The project was implemented over an 18-month period (from September 2015 to February 2017). During that time, officers administered more than 570 in-person educational messages to people involved in non-crime DV calls, gave formal warnings to 247 suspects, and made more than 280 three-day follow-up attempts. More than 60 customized problem-solving plans were carried out with victims, suspects, and subjects involved in repeat crimes or chronic verbal abuse situations. To assess the impact of the initiative, numerous outcome measures were tracked: DV crimes, DV calls, DV victim and subject views, and officer perspectives.

Crime impact

Changes in DV crime (only actual crime cases were included in this analysis, not non-crime domestic disputes) were measured based on weekly averages; the use of a weekly mean number of crimes smoothed out seasonal variations in the data. Weekly counts also permitted a large number of observations—more than 300 weekly observations were included in the impact evaluation.

8.2	**6.2**	**8.5**	**7.1**	**7.5**	**7.4**	
Phase 1	Phase 2	Phase 3	Phase 1	Phase 2	Phase 3	
Experimental Area			**Comparison Area**			

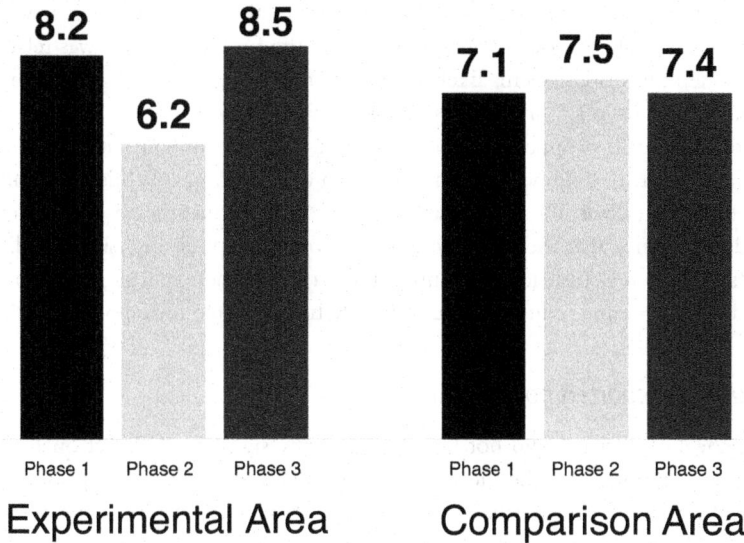

Phase 1 = baseline; Phase 2 = after response in place 1 year; Phase 3 = paused experiment

FIGURE 8.2 Crime impact: mean weekly number of DV crimes

The initiative did not show immediate results, but after the first full year, DV crime dropped 24% in the experimental area—a statistically significant drop—from a baseline period of 156 weeks. During the same period, DV crime increased 3% in the matched comparison area, but the increase was not statistically significant. After the experiment was concluded, the project was temporarily paused to allow for further evaluative work; crime subsequently returned to preproject levels (see Figure 8.2).

DV crimes initially increased in the experimental area before dropping. This is because the project was not implemented all at once but phased in over time, resulting in a cumulative effect on crime. Officers implementing the new DV protocol did so over a year, contacting new subjects, victims, and suspects only as each new call or crime occurred. It was noteworthy that the drop in DV crime in the experimental area did not contribute to an increase in DV crime in the comparison area. While crime displacement may occur for some crime types, it was not expected that DV would be easily displaced. Moreover, the steady volume of DV crime in the comparison area—before, during, and after the experiment—provided sound evidence that the experiment alone was responsible for the crime drop in the experimental area and there were no other explanations for the crime reduction.

Call impact

After the first year, DV calls dropped slightly (3%) in the experimental area and increased 10% in the comparison area. The drop in calls in the experimental area was not statistically significant, but the increase in the comparison area was significant ($p = .041$). It does not seem likely that the increase in calls was related to displacement; instead, it seems likely that calls in the experimental area might also have increased if the DV initiative had not been undertaken.

While DV calls dropped after the first year, calls had initially increased in the experimental area—following a similar pattern as DV crimes. While it was anticipated that DV calls in the experimental area would decline, the absence of a drop provided evidence that the initiative did not work by suppressing calls to police or reporting of crime. Instead, the continuity of calls in the experimental area confirmed the DV crime reduction could reliably be attributed to the police initiative.

DV subjects reported positive outcomes

While the DV initiative did not have a statistically significant impact on DV calls in the experimental area, the more important reduction in DV crime provides evidence of a reduction in the harm associated with calls. That interpretation is also supported by evidence from two additional sources of data—feedback from DV call subjects and DV victims.

As part of the initiative, subjects involved in non-crime DV disturbances were sent follow-up texts. Recipients were asked to complete a three-question online survey. Overall, 88% of subjects who responded said things had gotten better since the incident, and 81% said police had helped the problem. A relatively low percentage of subjects—8%—said they would not call police again for help. This provided more evidence that the DV initiative reduced DV crime and did not have the unintended consequence of suppressing calls to police.

Victims satisfied with police

Because the text survey was limited to DV subjects in the experimental area—and since the responses obtained from a solicitation by the police department may not have been candid—an independent survey was conducted with DV crime victims throughout the city. This survey also consisted of a limited number of questions administered by DV victim advocates. The survey questions were "add-ons" to the standard victim contacts made by victim advocates after DV crimes occurred. Overall, 97% of victims in the experimental area reported being "satisfied" with the police response compared to 81% of victims in the comparison area. While a limited number of surveys were completed, the administration of the surveys by DV advocates increased the validity associated with the findings.

Officers supportive

In late 2016, officers involved in the project completed a survey about their perceptions of the initiative. A large majority (77%) thought the project was effective in reducing repeat DV; 67% said the project should be expanded in patrol. Of note, the survey occurred before any impact results were reported to police. Anecdotally, however, several officers had already observed that DV crimes seemed to be down in the experimental area.

Discussion

Use of call data and focus on crime prevention

This problem-solving effort took a broad view of the problem of DV that included both non-crime DV calls to police as well as DV crimes. Non-crime DV calls were more common than DV crimes and provided a more complete picture of DV. These non-crime DV calls also provided an opportunity for crime prevention.

While Bland and Ariel (2015) found no evidence that DV crimes escalate or worsen among repeat offenders, police in Chula Vista believed that non-crime DV calls might be precursors to DV crimes and, since non-crime calls were a common point of contact with police, officers could use this opportunity to educate or caution subjects about the harms.

Using call data was valuable but not without problems. Call data revealed that police were unable to make contact with any of the primary parties in about 20% of the calls, since both subjects were gone when police arrived. In addition, call data did not typically include standardized name or person-specific data. Although call data was an imperfect proxy for crime data, it was nonetheless a valuable resource, since fewer than one-third of DV calls resulted in an official crime report.

Reliance on sworn personnel

Because of their frequency and repetitive nature, DV calls can be frustrating to patrol officers and some police administrators might designate specialized DV officers to respond to these calls. But CVPD administrators felt that because of the high volume of DV calls, a specialized initial response was not practical—these calls are so common that every officer must be able to handle them effectively.

The prevailing view in Chula Vista was that the initiative undertaken should be one that could be carried out by all patrol officers—supplemented by detectives—as part of their routine duties. Recognizing the key role of front-line officers, the problem analysis drew on information gleaned from focus groups and surveys of officers—the surveys were conducted pre- and post-project—as well as insights of sworn officers in other settings, such as training and protocol pilot test debriefs.

Most officers were exasperated with the repeat nature of DV and felt offenders were not held accountable. Early in the project, Agent Osvaldo Cruz suggested conducting in-person follow-ups with DV suspects to hold them accountable for their behavior. Cruz had done these types of follow-ups on his own initiative when he had worked patrol as a K-9 officer years earlier and had identified the temporal sequence of DV—the timing when offenders got back together with their partners—as typically being about three days. The problem analysis substantiated this timeline. Cruz indicated that DV suspects were not happy to see him at the door several days after a DV crime had occurred, since no one had called police. Suspects were unnerved by ongoing police interest in the violence, the victims, and themselves. Victims seemed to appreciate Cruz's unannounced follow-ups to check on their safety.

Cruz also suggested that a text follow-up contact with subjects would get their attention. During a training of officers, another detective suggested leaving the "We stopped by card" if officers were unable to locate victims and suspects on a three-day follow-up contact. These contributions were not part of the initial treatment design, but the ideas were key aspects of the response. Because they had a voice in the development of the initiative, officers were invested in the outcome. In addition, the specifics of the field response were both practical and more effective than if they had been developed based solely on prior research findings.

Built on previous problem-solving efforts

The initiative in Chula Vista was built on and informed by prior DV problem-solving efforts; a concerted effort was made to learn from earlier work carried out in Fremont, California: West Yorkshire, United Kingdom; Redlands, California; and High Point, North Carolina.

CVPD personnel contacted the Fremont Police Department, where police had focused on reducing DV calls to chronic addresses. CVPD inquired why the initiative was discontinued after it proved successful, but more than 15 years had passed since the effort had concluded, and it was unclear why it was not sustained. The short-term nature of the Fremont project underscored the importance of testing a sustainable response with broad buy-in from sworn personnel.

A former police detective from Redlands, California, was interviewed about their initiative in which police made follow-up contact with DV victims after an initial incident. CrimeSolutions.gov had rated this program as having "No effects" in reducing revictimization. Police in that effort did not tailor their response to the number of prior incidents and focused only on victims—not offenders (Davis, Weisburd & Hamilton, 2010).

The graded initiative in West Yorkshire was exclusively focused on incidents with male offenders and female victims, both of whom received tiered responses. Notably, West Yorkshire's tiered response was implemented for all DV calls, regardless of whether they were criminal in nature (Hanmer, Griffiths & Jerwood, 1999).

Efforts in the High Point (North Carolina) Police Department (HPPD) were also focused on both DV offenders and victims, but few non–crime DV disturbance calls resulted in a focused-deterrence response. To learn more about HPPD's effort, CVPD personnel made two separate site visits to High Point, spending time with police leaders, project managers, external partners, patrol officers, detectives, and an analyst. One CVPD crime analyst remained in close contact with HPPD. When HPPD was selected as the Herman Goldstein Problem-Oriented Policing Award

Winner in 2016 (National Network for Safer Communities, 2016) CVPD project personnel attended and met with HPPD to debrief.

Due in large part to review and adaptation of prior efforts, CVPD included suspects, victims, *and* non-crime DV subjects in the response and did not differentiate between males and females. CVPD also invested in a project database to address the challenges of using call data to monitor DV-related police contacts. The prior DV projects also influenced the evaluation design used to measure impact.

Use of quasi-experimental research design

Police in Chula Vista initially wanted to implement the DV initiative citywide. They agreed, however, to participate in a more rigorous quasi-experimental research design to produce "evidence-based" findings that met more stringent scientific standards used by CrimeSolutions.gov and the Campbell Collaboration.[2] There is no evidence that initiatives in West Yorkshire or Fremont used a rigorous design; this was also a limitation in High Point, where researchers conducted their pre-post evaluation *post hoc* (Sechrist & Weil, 2018).

A randomized control trial was ruled out because of resources, but CVPD agreed to a quasi-experiment in which the response was tested in one area of the city and matched in an equivalent area of the city. Police agreed to conduct the experiment for at least one year to provide sufficient sample sizes, and to track DV victims and suspects for an additional year to provide adequate follow-up periods to detect impact.

By limiting police efforts to one geographic area, the research project used fewer resources than a citywide effort would have. The results of the experiment—comparisons between two similar areas of the city—were easily understood by everyone, even by would-be skeptics in the police department. Most threats to validity were controlled by the research design, but there was likely some contamination. For example, DV victims, suspects, or subjects may have moved from the experimental area to the comparison area or vice versa, or victims may have lived in a different area than the suspects did. The design did cause some complaints by police supervisors, who could not rotate all patrol officers into the experimental area—only patrol officers who had volunteered to work on the project and received training could be deployed there.

Collaboration with external partners

The DV problem-solving effort was developed and led by police, but CVPD incorporated external partners throughout the process. While the contributions of the partners might appear minimal, they were of critical importance:

- CWS helped shape the messaging about the harmful effects of loud arguments on children.
- Victim advocates surveyed victims and signed off on text follow-ups.

- Probation assisted with recalcitrant offenders.
- The district attorney prioritized chronic cases.

While their roles were not resource-intensive, CVPD felt it was important to include these partners, keeping them updated and seeking their advice. Presented with the incontrovertible reduction in DV crime and the value of using data and analysis to drive decision making, the San Diego County District Attorney's Office (DA) in 2017 sought to take the focused-deterrence concept further. The DA's Office plans to identify suspects at high risk of committing repeat offenses and implement an initiative to systematically caution suspects who were not being prosecuted.[3]

Follow-up

After the Chula Vista experiment was completed, CVPD subsequently implemented a citywide protocol for responding to DV incidents. The new protocol is simply called CVPD's Domestic Violence Protocol and is not considered a special study or temporary experiment but the department's standard approach to DV calls and crimes.

Acknowledgments

The authors would like to thank CVPD Chief Roxana Kennedy for her leadership on the project—in particular her strong endorsement of a quasi-experimental evaluation design and expansion of the project to the entire city after the research project ended; Agent Xanthe Rosario, who served as the project coordinator, for her passion and dedication to ensuring the experiment was successfully implemented; Agent Norene Andersen for her steadfast support; Agent Osvaldo Cruz (Ret.) for his vision and commitment to reducing domestic violence; and the more than 60 Chula Vista Police Department patrol officers and detectives who participated in the effort.

Notes

1 In this way, Chula Vista's approach was substantially different from second-responder programs that emphasize providing follow-up services to DV victims after the initial police response (see Davis, Weisburd & Hamilton, 2010). Victim advocates in Chula Vista were already providing these services.
2 Evidence-based standards are available at www.crimesolutions.gov and www.campbell collaboration.org.
3 The development of this cautionary messaging was underway in early 2019.

References

Bland, M. & Ariel, B. (2015) 'Targeting escalation in reported domestic abuse: Evidence from 36,000 callouts', *International Criminal Justice Review*, 25(1): 30–53.

Davis, R.C., Weisburd, D. & Hamilton, E.E. (2010) 'Preventing repeat incidents of family violence: A randomized field test of a second responder program', *Journal of Experimental Criminology*, 6: 397–418.

Fremont Police Department (1997) *Domestic Violence Revictimization Prevention: Improving Police Response to Repeat Calls of Domestic Violence.* Submission for the Herman Goldstein Award for Excellence in Problem-Oriented Policing, Arizona State University Center for Problem-Oriented Policing, Phoenix, AZ.

Hanmer, J., Griffiths, S. & Jerwood, D. (1999) *Arresting Evidence: Domestic Violence and Repeat Victimisation*, Police Research Series Paper 104, London: Home Office, Policing and Reducing Crime Unit.

National Network for Safer Communities (2016) *Intimate Partner Violence Initiative.* Submission for the Herman Goldstein Award for Excellence in Problem-Oriented Policing, Arizona State University Center for Problem-Oriented Policing, Phoenix, AZ.

Sampson, R. (2007) *Domestic Violence*, Problem-Oriented Guides for Police, Problem-Specific Guide No. 45, Washington, DC: U.S. Department of Justice, Office of Community-Oriented Policing Services.

Sechrist, S.M. & Weil, J.D. (2018) 'Assessing the impact of a focused deterrence strategy to combat intimate partner domestic violence', *Violence against Women*, 24(3): 243–265.

Sechrist, S.M., Weil, J.D & Shelton, T. (2016) *Evaluation of the Offender-Focused Domestic Violence Initiative (OFDVI) in High Point, NC and Replication in Lexington, NC*, Washington, DC: US Department of Justice, Office of Community Oriented Policing Services.

Sherman, L.W. (1992) *Policing Domestic Violence: Experiments and Dilemmas*, New York: Free Press.

9

SEXUAL ASSAULT OF WOMEN BY ILLEGAL-MINICAB DRIVERS IN LONDON

Steve Burton[1], Mandy McGregor, and Gloria Laycock

Introduction

The 2006 winner of the Herman Goldstein Award for Excellence in Problem-Oriented Policing was a project submitted by Steve Burton, then deputy director of the Transport Policing and Enforcement Directorate which was part of Transport for London (TfL).[2] The project involved a collaboration among TfL, the then mayor of London/Greater London Authority (GLA),[3] and the Metropolitan Police Service (MPS).[4] London is one of the most cosmopolitan, vibrant and energetic cities in the world and in 2006 was increasingly becoming a 24-hour city. Over half a million people regularly went 'clubbing' at the weekend, with many more visiting pubs and theatres and enjoying other activities in the evening. While London was and continues to be safe for most people travelling at night, there were major concerns over the number of sexual attacks and the dangers for women travelling in illegal minicabs.

The problem (scanning and analysis)

It is an offence for private-hire vehicles (PHV), also known as minicabs, to ply for hire in the street in the United Kingdom under the Criminal Justice and Public Order Act 1994. Those arrested and charged with 'taxi touting'[5] are also charged with having no valid insurance. Drivers who tout for business are commonly referred to as taxi touts or illegal-minicab drivers.

Analysis by the MPS showed that 212 sexual offences were committed by illegal-minicab drivers between October 2001 and September 2002; 54 of these women were raped. The number of sexual offences in illegal minicabs was rising and formed a substantial proportion of those sexual offences in London committed by offenders not previously known to the victim. This was a serious problem affecting Londoners and visitors to London.

A contributing factor to this growing issue was the endemic problem of touting in Central London. Illegal minicabs provided a cover for some of the most serious crimes in London, including sexual attacks on women. Local isolated responses were having limited effect, and a coordinated, systematic and broader approach was needed to address the underlying conditions that were contributing to the problem. To this end, the Safer Travel at Night (STaN) partnership was created to undertake further analysis, develop a response and implement any actions identified.

Further scanning of the problem, coordinated by the STaN Project Board, highlighted the problems with touting more generally. Although the government and the police were aware that it was widespread across London, it was not until the problem of sexual offences in illegal minicabs was highlighted that attention was focused on the extent and seriousness of the problem. Furthermore, touting was being dealt with as a minor traffic offence and not as an issue that could act as a gateway to serious crime.

Touting was a particular problem in the West End, which although geographically small, is London's main entertainment district. The combination of no significant legal deterrent to touting, their availability and relatively low price in comparison to London's licensed black taxis, together with a lack of awareness amongst the public regarding the laws surrounding minicabs and of the potential risks to passengers, allowed the illegal-minicab market to thrive. Touting provided an ideal cover for sexual predators.

The police expected that the number of attacks on women would rise in what appeared to be a growing illegal-minicab trade operating in the city. Numbers of sexual offences (rape and sexual assault)[6] in illegal minicabs had risen to more than 200 reported over a year compared with 66 in 1997. The police acknowledged that the numbers were likely to be far higher given the considerable under-reporting of sexual offences across society in general. Women travelling in illegal minicabs were at serious risk. In 2002, the *Times* newspaper reported that minicab touts were one of the most underrated and fastest-rising dangers of city nightlife.

The MPS undertook a detailed analysis of these predatory crimes to test the hypothesis that a large percentage of stranger rapes and sexual assaults were committed by sexual offenders purporting to be minicab drivers. The analysis confirmed this. Further spatial and temporal analysis was undertaken, and trends identified. Patterns were identified in the three major components of the problem analysis triangle—the victim, offender and location (Eck, 2003).

The police recognised that the details provided by victims were sometimes hazy or incomplete, as victims were often intoxicated at the time of the incident. However, the majority of victims were able to confirm that they had got into a minicab in the West End after leaving a late-night venue. Analysis of the crime data showed that approximately 80% of the sexual offences in illegal minicabs over this year originated with a pick up in the West End. These attacks were being committed by illegal-minicab drivers—the journeys were not pre-booked through a licensed minicab office.

The targets were young women who were travelling alone. The analysis found that in nearly 50% of cases the victims were aged 24 or under and 91% of victims aged 35 or under.

This full crime-analysis exercise was supplemented by an in-depth analysis of touting activity and market usage of late-night transport services undertaken by TfL. This helped the key stakeholders to better understand the touting problem and aid the evaluation of anti-touting initiatives. Surveys were also commissioned to gain a better understanding of the night-time travel patterns of Londoners, including the use of minicabs and other late-night travel options.

Baseline survey results showed that that the overwhelming majority of minicab users in the West End picked up one in the street or outside the venue, rather than booking it from a minicab office, giving illegal minicabs a 14% total market share in the West End area prior to STaN initiatives being implemented.

A number of significant contributory factors were identified as part of the analysis stage:

- lack of public awareness of the laws surrounding minicabs,
- lack of public awareness of the potential risks associated with illegal minicabs,
- an active illegal-minicab trade that was operating in a largely unregulated market with little enforcement and with no real legal deterrent and
- limited legitimate travel options at night and public unawareness of how to access them.

Local borough police (Basic Operational Command Units, or BOCUs)[7] had been adopting different local approaches to tackling the problems of sexual offences and illegal-minicab touting. These offender-based strategies were not effective in reducing the number of sexual offences on women in illegal minicabs.

The multi-agency project board, with the support of the mayor of London (then Ken Livingstone), signed up to the following objectives:

- reduce the number of sexual offences (rape and sexual assault) committed by illegal-minicab drivers,
- raise awareness amongst Londoners and visitors to London of the risks of using illegal-minicab drivers and
- reduce the demand for and the availability of illegal minicabs.

The response

The responses to the problem followed the principles of situational crime prevention (Clarke, 1997) by increasing the effort of offenders through target hardening, increasing the risks for offenders and reducing the rewards by disrupting the illegal-minicab market. The strategy adopted had four main elements that were implemented as part of a coordinated package. These include three demand reduction activities focused on victims and a supply reduction area focused on offenders and locations:

- raising public awareness—informing the public of the dangers of using illegal minicabs,
- delivery of improved late-night travel services,
- providing the public with enhanced travel information and better access to safe travel options and
- improving safety through greater regulation of the PHV industry, enforcement and safety measures.

Each element involved a programme of integrated activities that evolved in response to feedback and evaluation.

Raising public awareness

The aim of the multimedia awareness campaign was to persuade the public (women in particular) to choose what they perceived to be a less convenient form of transport at a time when they are least likely to make a rational decision. The primary target audience for the campaign was women aged 16 to 35 going for or returning from a night out in London. The campaign was focused on hard-hitting images and messages to highlight the risks associated with illegal minicabs. It was called the "Know what you're getting into" campaign and was launched in October 2002 as a poster campaign utilising sites on bus shelters and Underground (subway) stations across London and at pubs, clubs and other late-night venues in Central London. The campaign material was regularly updated and continued to be used, with posters and postcards distributed at major London events and festivals, to universities and to late-night venues.

The campaign was further strengthened by a chilling cinema and television advertisement that was directed by acclaimed British director Mike Leigh. By 2006, the campaign had already won two prestigious national advertising awards for successfully alerting women to the dangers of using illegal minicabs. The cinema advert showed a harmless-looking middle-aged man talking as he drives. He says that he has been in and out of trouble over the years and how hard it is to get a proper job with a criminal record. A conviction for sexual assault has not stopped him from picking up women, however—far from it. We see him stop the car and lean out to talk to a young woman on the pavement—'Minicab, love?' he says.

Delivering improved late-night travel services

A key component of TfL's transport strategy was and continues to be to encourage the use of legitimate public transport services such as night buses and underground and rail services as well as *licensed* taxis and licensed, legally booked minicabs. TfL provided better late-night transport options, including more night-time buses than ever before. The 100th night-time bus route was introduced in June 2006. The response delivered easier, safer and more reliable night-time travel options, including improvements to the frequency and capacity of bus services and hence shortened passenger waiting times. In 2005 there were 34 million passengers travelling by night bus, and this figure continued to rise. Furthermore, the entire London bus fleet which consists of more than 8,000 vehicles was fitted with closed-circuit television (CCTV) cameras.

TfL also introduced changes to the operation of black taxis to encourage greater provision of these services. Higher night tariffs for taxi fares were introduced in order to encourage more licensed taxi drivers to work unsociable hours to increase their availability at key times. Black cabs were also mandated to accept all journeys of up to 12 miles which was double the old limit of 6 miles. In support of this TfL set up a marshalled taxi rank (stand) on Friday and Saturday evenings near Leicester Square tube (subway) station in London's West End. Marshals provided a reassuring presence to passengers and coordinated taxi travellers with taxi drivers heading to similar destinations. The rank was covered by CCTV and patrolled regularly by police. Marshalled taxi ranks were then rolled out to various locations across London and formed an important and increasing part of the STaN campaign at the time.

Late-night travel was also made safer with the launch of the Transport Operational Command Unit (TOCU), a unique partnership between TfL and the MPS, in 2002. With some 1,300 staff, including over 600 police and 400 police community support officers, the TOCU provided a dedicated police capability to focus on reducing crime and the fear of crime on London's bus network, enforcing the law relating to taxis and PHVs and dealing with critical congestion across London. The TfL/MPS partnership was highly effective in reassuring passengers and staff by providing a visible, uniformed presence across the surface transport network and, for the first time, providing focused policing for the bus, taxi and private hire networks.

Further TfL improvements at the time included

- the extension of running hours of the London Underground on Friday and Saturday nights and
- the Dockland Light Railway's Last Mile Home initiative, which focused on improving public safety on the final leg of the journey from station to home.

Enhancing travel information

Another key part of the STaN strategy was informing people of the safer travel options that were available to help them make the right choice when travelling late at night. STaN aimed to encourage and to make it easier for people to pre-plan their journeys. A number of initiatives have been introduced to provide people with better access to safe travel options through enhanced travel information.

TfL's travel information line and internet journey planner played a major role in providing travel information with the number and website address used in all publicity and information material. The journey planner is a tool designed to help people plan trips in London. Women were able to use this facility to find licensed female drivers.

In September 2005, the UK's first text service aimed at reducing sexual offences in illegal minicabs was launched as part of the STaN initiative. The new service meant that people could text 'Home' to 60835 and receive the numbers of licensed minicab and taxi firms in the area they were texting from.

Travel information and access to information was improved in a variety of other ways including

- freefones (toll-free telephones) to licensed minicab offices installed at a number of student unions across London,
- localised travel information boards at clubs and bars,
- a single number booking system that allowed easy access to taxis from different taxi operators,
- local transport maps distributed at late-night venues and displayed at bus shelters and underground stations and
- closer collaboration between TfL and local authorities to provide localised travel information that meets the needs of those living and visiting the area.

Improving safety through industry regulation, enforcement and safety measures

The final element of the STaN initiative aimed to increase the risks for offenders in a number of ways. The introduction of PHV licensing by TfL reduced the anonymity of taxi touts and was supported by targeted police enforcement as a deterrent to potential offenders. The STaN agencies also lobbied for legislative change to increase the risks of detection and the consequential penalties.

Since October 2001, as part of a mayoral-driven initiative, it has been illegal to operate as a PHV operator or driver without a licence from TfL. TfL's team of dedicated compliance officers visited licensed operators to ensure that they and their drivers were complying with regulations. This regulation gave passengers using a licensed minicab operator confidence that they were dealing with an honest, professional organisation with reliable drivers and safe vehicles. It gave them additional reassurance in that there was a record of the journey and vehicle should there be any problems.

Driver licensing was regarded as the most important part of this process and was completed in late 2006 with a range of rigorous checks on drivers aimed at improving safety. More than 2,260 operators, 40,000 vehicles and 30,000 drivers were licensed during this period. All licensed minicabs were fitted with a distinctive disc to the front and rear windscreens (windshields) to indicate that the car is licensed and has met strict safety standards.

The dedicated pan-London police Cab Enforcement Unit, funded by TfL, was responsible for enforcing the law relating to taxis and PHVs in London. The unit was effective in targeting PHV drivers that touted illegally, as well as clamping down on unsafe vehicles and other taxi and private hire offences. The majority of its efforts were focused towards anti-touting activities at key hot spots in and around Central London and developing enforcement expertise and tactics to ensure maximum impact. Tactics included high-visibility patrols and covert operations informed by intelligence and associated analysis, including female officers dressed in formal wear exiting from hotels or from bars and clubs in touting hot spots.

More than 2,750 arrests were made for cab-related offences including touting in the first four years of its operation. The unit carried out hundreds of operations, both overt and covert, to deter and apprehend taxi touts.

In December 2003, following strong lobbying from the STaN partners, touting was made a nationally recordable offence, allowing police to take DNA samples, fingerprints and photographs from all offenders. The benefits included tracking persistent offenders, identifying those unlawfully at large, improved opportunities to detect perpetrators of sexual offences and the ability to build offender history at a national level to inform licensing decision making. It was recognised that DNA collected from touts would be a powerful tool in identifying the perpetrators of these crimes and ultimately reducing the number of rapes and sexual assaults.

TfL and the mayor of London also raised concerns with the Home Office about the inconsistency and leniency of penalties being imposed for touting. The average fines were not high enough to be seen as a deterrent. As a result, the maximum fines for touting and the linked offence of no insurance were increased. The inconsistency of penalties continued to be an issue at the time but was being addressed in a variety of ways including magistrate briefings and sentencing guidelines. The MPS Cab Enforcement Unit sought to address this issue by arranging all of its cases to be heard by a single court, which was valuable in ensuring that the penalties were both consistent and appropriate for the offence.

The STaN agencies worked with bars, clubs and other late-night venues to ensure the safety of customers and staff once they have left the premises. The GLA, TfL and the MPS worked with licensing authorities and local authorities to sign up to and follow 'best practice' guidelines. In many cases, door staff at clubs were being utilised as place managers to help prevent sexual attacks on women. Door staff were directing patrons to legitimate modes of travel and providing police with valuable intelligence.

Did this work? Results

STaN was highly successful in achieving its primary objective of reducing the number of sexual offences (rape and sexual assault) by illegal-minicab drivers. Sexual offences fell each year from 2002 to 2006. In the first 12 months of the initiative, sexual offences by illegal minicabs fell by 27% to 155, with rapes falling by 22% to 42. The number of reported offences fell to 140 the following year; 32 of these

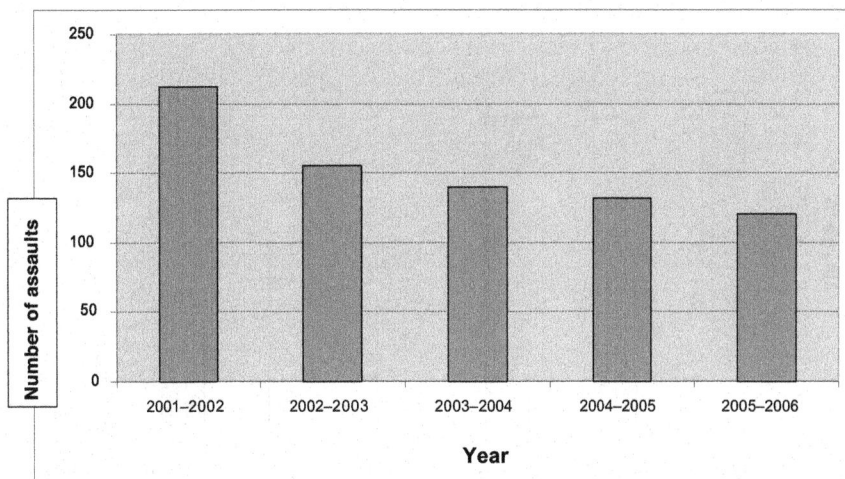

FIGURE 9.1 Reported sexual assaults in illegal minicabs

were rapes. By 2006, the MPS reported that this number had fallen to ten offences per month. See Figure 9.1.

TfL commissioned an independent agency to provide an ongoing market-share measure of the night transport services in the West End, including the share of journeys taken with illegal minicabs. The research was carried out twice a year—prior to and after the media campaign. It provided

- a baseline measure of market share prior to the launch of the anti-touting initiatives and further monitoring to assess changes over time,
- explanations for the market share of each transport mode and assessment of the extent to which these changed over time and
- feedback on the awareness of the complementary measures such as marketing and communications campaigns and public relations activity and assessment of their impact on the perceptions of illegal minicabs versus other forms of transport.

Results from the research undertaken in February 2006 (Wave 7) again highlighted the positive impact of the STaN initiative in the West End. The research showed that STaN had been successful in changing attitudes to illegal-minicab usage. Usage has fallen from 14% in Wave 1 (September 2003) to only 4% in Wave 7 (see Figure 9.2). A diffusion of benefits also occurred with illegal-minicab usage falling from 18% to 11% in areas other than the West End.

The research also showed that fewer females were making journeys in illegal minicabs. Females were previously more likely to use illegal minicabs than were males (18% vs. 10% in Wave 1). The proportion of males using this mode of transport over the period has remained steady, but the proportion of females using an

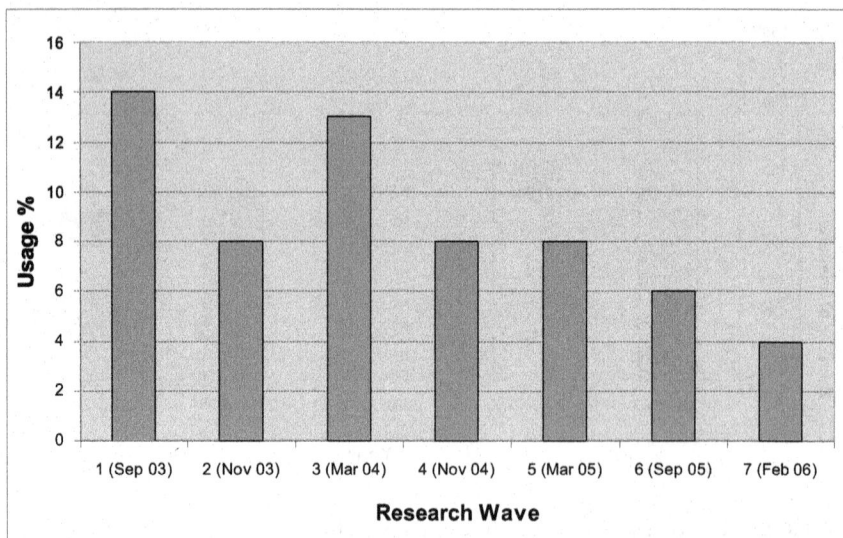

FIGURE 9.2 Illegal minicab usage

illegal minicab had dropped significantly (18% in Wave 1 to 7% in Wave 7). This demonstrated that the anti-touting initiatives had been most successful with this key demographic group as originally planned. This interpretation was also supported by the fact that females had a much worse perception of the safety of illegal minicabs than was the case with males. Results in 2006 showed the following:

- The incidence of touting fell steadily from the start of the anti-touting initiatives and, by Wave 7, was significantly lower than in Wave 1.
- The main reasons for regarding illegal minicabs as the least-preferred option related to safety and risk. Women were significantly more likely than men to choose an illegal minicab as their least-preferred choice. The proportions mentioning illegality of minicabs rose significantly in the West End.
- The preferred late-night transport modes were the night bus or black cabs.
- Respondents were also specifically prompted as to whether they had seen any of the "Know What You're Getting Into" adverts. In total, 59% could recall seeing these adverts—a very high figure for this type of campaign.

Research undertaken after the first media campaign highlighted the fact that the marketing campaign needed to be stronger to achieve the desired income. Taking this into account the campaign was relaunched to include more hard-hitting images and a cinema advert.

Posters and radio adverts used shock value to raise awareness of this issue and remind people that ten women a month were still sexually assaulted or raped by illegal-minicab drivers in London.

In Wave 7, 55% of West End respondents recalled seeing or hearing advertising or communications relating to STaN compared with only 24% in Wave 1. In Wave 7, 22% of respondents recall advertising messages with stories about attacks/rapes in illegal minicabs compared with 6% in Wave 1.

The results from a number of research waves showed an altered pattern of touting activity and highlighted the increase in more 'passive touting'—unlawful plying for hire—which suggested that the touts were becoming aware of how to avoid police detection/arrest. The police identified that these offenders were beyond the reach of the police's traditional covert approaches and police tactics had to change in response to changing touting methods. The tactics used by the Cab Enforcement Unit were revised in response to this although the apprehension and prosecution of touts continued to be an integral part of the overall approach.

Follow-up

Ongoing analysis of taxi- and private-hire journey-related sexual offences and illegal-minicab activity shows a sustained reduction in both the levels of touting and sexual offending in illegal minicabs. This is a result of the ongoing efforts of TfL and the police to improve the safety and security of travelling by taxi and private hire as well as some significant changes to transport provision and usage in London. These include the following:

- The number of licensed PHV has greatly increased primarily because of the growth in app-based services including Uber (there are currently about 114,000 licensed PHV drivers in London, over three times as many as seen in 2006).
- The launch of the night Tube and cheaper minicab rides has dramatically changed weekend travel patterns.
- The type of residual touting has changed—as noted above, touts no longer approach people but sit in cars waiting for passengers to approach them. This is known as unlawful plying for hire.
- Traditional hard hitting STAN messaging about the dangers of unbooked minicabs has become less relevant, less effective and more complicated due to the structural changes in the sector and the significant reduction in the usage of unbooked cabs.
- TfL has actively encouraged victims to come forward and report offences so that action can be taken against offenders. It has also started following up passenger complaints to minicab operators and comments posted on social media. This would have an effect on the overall figures but it has not been quantitatively measured.

Nevertheless, the picture does not look as bad as might have been expected given such dramatic increases in PHVs. Figure 9.3 shows the *number* of recorded offences from 2002 to 2016 together with the moving three-year average.

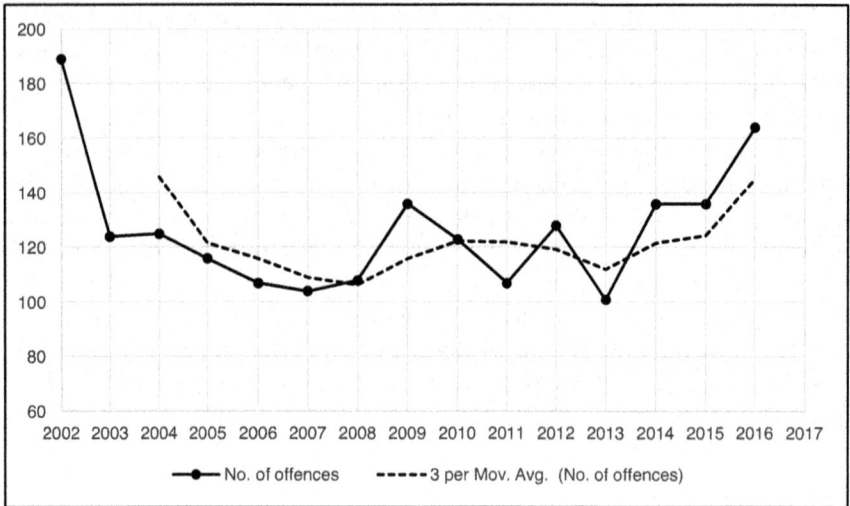

FIGURE 9.3 Recorded sex offences in taxis/private-hire vehicles in Greater London

The recent upturn coincides with increases in police-recorded crime more generally in London and the United Kingdom (ONS, 2018). These numbers, it should be remembered, are not rates. Over the last 12 years, in addition to the increase in safer travel options, there has been a significant increase in the number of people using PHVs, particularly via Uber and other app-based operators.

Summary and conclusion

The evidence suggests that the STaN initiative was a successful problem-solving initiative and achieved the outcomes set for it. The reduction in sexual offences involving illegal minicabs has been sustained. The initiative highlights the benefits that can be achieved through strong collaboration, partnership and pooling of resources between city agencies in the problem-solving process. Evaluation via measures other than simply reported crime (user surveys, etc.) provided a richer picture during the analysis and assessment phases. The emphasis on strong partnership working throughout the entire SARA process also contributed to making it a more effective initiative and provided the resources and expertise needed to change earlier existing social norms in relation to night time travel in London.

Since 2006, the private-hire sector in London has radically changed, and a new but related problem has manifested itself. The majority of PHV users are doing what was asked of them in booking their minicabs in advance and completing their journey safely, but there has been an increasing proportion of offences taking place in licensed and legally booked minicabs. The latest available figures for 2016 indicate that of those drivers charged with an offence, approximately 70% were licensed and legally booked. Although it is a challenging problem work is now underway to address this, with planned policy changes and refreshed operational tactics. For example, all customer complaints of a suspected sexual or other criminal nature to PHV operators are to be reported to the police, which will mean that offenders may come to police attention earlier, and new signage being considered for insertion in vehicles will advise customers to report complaints to TfL or call 999 in case of emergency. This is likely to increase reporting in the short to medium term but will also support further problem-oriented work.

Notes

1　At the time the original work was carried out Steve Burton was the STaN project sponsor and a senior executive with Transport for London.
2　TfL is the integrated body responsible for the capital's transport system. Its role is to implement the mayor's Transport Strategy for London and manage the transport services across the capital for which the mayor has responsibility. TfL manages London's buses, London Underground, the Docklands Light Railway and London Trams. It also runs London River Services, Victoria Coach Station and London's Transport Museum. As well as running the central London congestion charging scheme, TfL manages a 580-km network of main roads, all of London's 4,600 traffic lights and regulates taxis and the private hire trade.
3　The GLA is a unique form of strategic citywide government for London. It is made up of a directly elected mayor – the mayor of London – and a separately elected assembly – the London Assembly. The GLA's main areas of responsibility include transport, policing, fire and emergency planning, economic development, planning, culture, environment and health.
4　The MPS is by far the largest of the police services that operate in Greater London (the others include the City of London Police and the British Transport Police). At the time of the project, the MPS employed 31,141 officers, 13,661 police staff, 414 traffic wardens and 2,106 Police Community Support Officers and covered an area of 620 square miles and a population of 7.2 million.
5　Touting implies an annoying, aggressive, bold – or in this case, illegal – form of advertising.
6　The definition of sexual or indecent assault in the United Kingdom is an act of physical, psychological or emotional violation in the form of a sexual act, inflicted on someone without their consent. It can also involve forcing or manipulating someone to witness or participate in any sexual acts. In the context of touting, it would include groping/fondling passenger against their will.
7　The basic street-level policing of London was carried out by 33 BOCUs.

References

Clarke, R.V. (1997) 'Introduction', in R.V. Clarke (ed.), *Situational Crime Prevention: Successful Case Studies* (2nd ed.), Guilderland, NY: Harrow and Heston Publishers, pp. 2–43.

Eck, J. (2003) 'Police problems: The complexity of problem theory, research and evaluation', in J. Knutsson (ed.), *Problem-Oriented Policing: From Innovation to Mainstream*, Crime Prevention Studies, Vol. 15, Monsey, NY: Criminal Justice Press (and Willan Publishing, UK).

Office for National Statistics (2018) *Crime in England and Wales: Year Ending March 2018*, London: Office for National Statistics.

10

SEXUAL ASSAULT OF WOMEN BY ILLEGAL-TAXICAB DRIVERS IN TØNSBERG, NORWAY

Johannes Knutsson

Introduction

In 2003, at a national conference about problem–oriented policing, I proposed to Norwegian police commissioners to get in touch with me if they had a policing problem for which I could be of assistance. The police commissioner of Vestfold Police District reacted positively. The problem consisted of illegal taxi cabs that operated at night on Saturday and Sunday in the city of Tønsberg, a small Norwegian coastal town of 36,000 inhabitants. The passengers and drivers of these unlicensed cabs sometimes got into fights, and there were allegations of drivers assaulting and robbing passengers and raping female passengers. A police enforcement crackdown had not helped, and they were blamed for their inability to get rid of the problem.

Organizing and safeguarding the project

In offering my services to this local police force to help it apply a problem–oriented policing approach properly, I had the following goals:

- To assist in solving a concrete problem
- To provide the police first–hand experience of conducting problem–oriented policing
- To check the robustness of the concept
- To produce a case study illustrating problem–oriented policing for educational purposes

To initiate the project and to safeguard its integrity the following steps were taken, all in agreement with the Vestfold police commissioner.

Meeting with the chief of the uniformed police

The problem was described as a 'fleet' of illegal taxis that operated in the downtown area Saturday and Sunday nights. The police believed that the drivers were political asylum seekers staying in temporary residential facilities and that the illegal taxi service was organized with an informal dispatch centre. However, the description was diffuse and largely based on impressions and rumours.

Informing the police district's senior leaders about problem-oriented policing

In a leader-team conference, I informed senior police officials about problem-oriented policing principles and methods. I also let them know that the project could call for their spending some fiscal and personnel resources.

Visiting the problem area with the commander of uniformed police and accompanying patrols during two night shifts

The first night I went on patrol with the commander so he could show me the downtown area where the illegal taxi cabs operated and how the operators carried out their illegal services and criminal acts. The second night was spent with ordinary uniformed patrol officers to get familiar with the site and how they policed it.

Visiting the problem area with the project manager

The commissioner appointed a promising young uniformed police officer to be the project manager. His time was freed to allow him to work as much time on the project as needed. He was also authorized to use members of his shift to engage in the project. We spent two night shifts planning the project, intermittently in the field and in the police station. We formulated a number of solution-oriented hypotheses and figured out the type of data needed to answer them and how these data could be attained.

Informing all middle-rank police leaders about problem-oriented policing principles and methods

I wanted all district police leaders to know me and my purpose and to understand what a problem-oriented policing project entails.

Setting up a steering group

The commissioner set up a steering group with him as chairperson. The project manager and the local commander were included in the group. It had a budget for running the project and followed its progress. All important decisions were taken by the group.

Altogether I made five site visits during the whole project period. Most of the communication with the project manager was carried out by e-mail and phone. I also had regular contacts with the commissioner.

Location of the problem

The illegal activities were concentrated in the downtown area of Tønsberg that had become a vivid night-time entertainment centre for the province, attracting great crowds from the surrounding communities There are 30 licensed premises—restaurants, pubs and other places of public entertainment—in this area, which is bisected by a national highway. Because many revellers on weekend nights cross this highway back and forth in a more or less inebriated state, thereby creating a traffic hazard, traffic is diverted from this part of the city on weekend nights by means of a pair of barriers (see Figure 10.1). The barriers are controlled by the police, who close off this section of the highway on Friday and Saturday evenings and open it again on Saturday and Sunday mornings. Some of the area's parking lots are not available for parking at these times, but taxi cabs and buses are permitted to use this temporarily closed section of road.

Scanning

Particular care was made to get a thorough identification and description of the problem, since this would constitute the foundation for subsequent phases. All data collection and primary compilations were carried out by police officers, mainly by the project manager who produced memos summarizing information from the different phases of the process; memos that were used as 'raw material' for report writing purposes.

For the scanning, we formulated the following questions:

- From where were the illegal-cab operations carried out?
- How, precisely, were they carried out?
- At what times?
- By whom?
- How many taxi cabs were involved?
- What kind of cars were used as taxi cabs?
- What was known about the passengers?
- What were the passengers' experiences?
- How much money was involved?
- How many and what specific crimes against the person were committed?

Rich data was available from the crackdown—information available in complaints and investigations about cars used, suspected drivers and passengers. However, in order to answer all the questions, additional methods had to be used (see Table 10.1). Because these methods are also used by police for purposes of criminal investigation, they were easily adapted for purposes of problem analysis.

TABLE 10.1 Problem analysis topics and methods used in the scanning phase

Topic	Method
To establish the number of cars used, from where, how and at what times	Systematic direct observation via police stakeouts
Information about drivers operating illegal cabs, their cars and crimes they committed	Obtaining information from police records of complaints and investigations about cars, suspected drivers and crimes
Costs for journeys and illegal-cab passengers' experiences	Telephone interviews (names and phone numbers obtained from complaints and investigations)
Illegal cab drivers' experiences and opinions	Field interviews with persons affiliated with illegal cab drivers
Legal-cab drivers' experiences and opinions of illegal-cab driving	Focused interviews with local cab drivers

Systematic observations

Night-time observations were carried out on three weekends at three specific locations that were of central importance. The observations made from concealed positions revealed that two parking lots to the north-west of the downtown area, as well as a section of a street at the other end, were used as pick-up points for illegal taxis (see Figure 10.1).

The location of the suspected informal and illegal dispatch centre (a kiosk at a corner of a parking lot) was observed particularly intensely, but there were no signs that persons in the kiosk made phone calls, subsequent to which illegal cabs came to pick up passengers.

Passenger interviews

For the vast majority of passengers, the ready availability of illegal taxi cabs constituted the decisive reason for travelling by them: they were so much easier to get hold of than legal taxis and the cost was about the same.

Interviews with affiliates to illegal drivers

Some persons moved around in the downtown area and interacted with the illegal cab drivers; they communicated with them, handed over drinks and fast food and assisted interested passengers. On one weekend night, three of these affiliates were interviewed by a female officer in civilian clothes (it was decided not to interview active drivers because of potential legal problems). She identified herself as a police officer and asked if they were willing to talk to her. The answers can be summarized as follows: An active illegal driver could earn more than the equivalent of 100

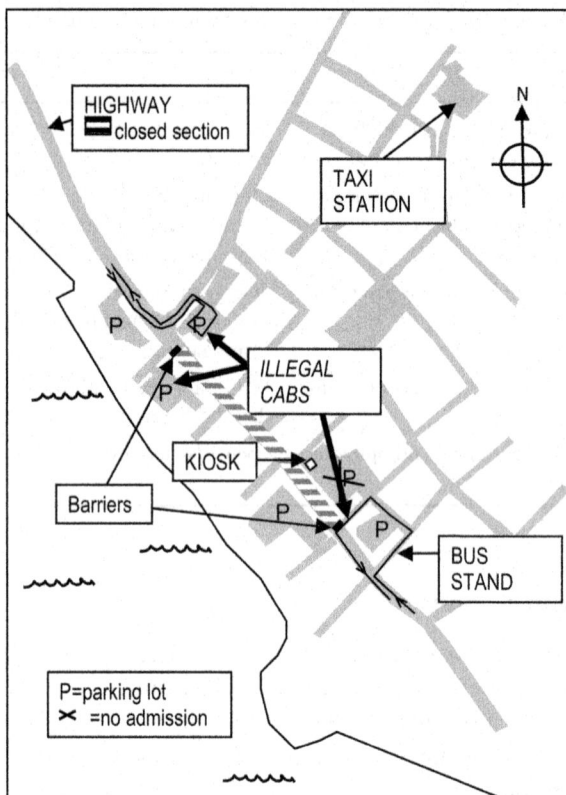

FIGURE 10.1 Downtown Tønsberg prior to the introduction of the measures

GBP/130 USD/1,000 NOK per night. Some had regular jobs, and others lived on social welfare. The drivers often hung around the kiosk, picking up customers. Besides being motivated by economic gain, a few drivers also wanted to meet people and to relax. For some, it was a means of making contact with women, and they sometimes took advantage of intoxicated females who had lost some ability to protect themselves.

Records checks of illegal drivers and cars

Most drivers were of Middle Eastern origin, particularly from Iraq. Of the checked 36 illegal-taxi drivers four lacked a driver's licence. The majority lived in communities near Tønsberg, and only one stayed in an immigrant residential facility.

The cars were on average 16 years old, which means that, compared to legal cabs all with newer models, they were much less safe.

Crimes committed during illegal-cab journeys

Record checks were conducted of all complaints relating to assault, robbery and rape reported during the 15-month period prior to the onset of the project. One case of aggravated assault had taken place in the centre of Tønsberg following an argument over prices. Two rapes had also been committed. In one case, the perpetrator was a man accompanying the driver, and in the other, it was the driver himself. Two illegal-cab drivers, both with prior criminal records, were reported for having robbed their passengers.

Meeting with the Tønsberg Taxi Association

The project manager invited the legal taxi cab drivers to a meeting to discuss the situation. About 40 attended the meeting which is a huge turn-out considering that there are only about 50 licensed cabs in Tønsberg. They criticized the police for neglecting to take care of the problem. A central complaint was that the drivers had to work harder to produce the same net income because illegal-cab drivers did not pay any taxes. They had also come to dominate the best pick-up locations and had intimidated legal drivers in this location.

Analysis

Scanning suggested that the root of the problem was a temporary imbalance in the local supply and demand for means of transport. Following additional analysis, five causal factors associated with the illegal cab operations were identified:

- A temporary shortage in the supply of legal transportation. Many of the revellers were from places away from Tønsberg and needed transport to return home. After closing hour, there was a huge crowd queuing for means of transportation.
- Easy availability of illegal cabs. They had more or less taken over the area close to where most restaurants, discos and pubs were located.
- A simple means of earning money. Technically only a car was needed, and the earnings went straight into the pocket.
- The relatively inconvenient location of pick-up areas for legal means of transportation. Night buses operated in the Tønsberg area as a means of legal transportation in the early hours of the morning to Sundays in order to help people from surrounding communities to get back home. The stand used by the night buses was located some distance from the downtown area in a place that was difficult to find. More important, however, was the location of the taxi stand, which lay at a considerable distance from the downtown area where the illegal cabs operated (see Figure 10.1).

• A lack of awareness among customers of the potential consequences of using illegal taxi-services. It is not an offence to use illegal-taxi services. That it might be dangerous to do so is probably not something that most passengers think about, despite their placing themselves at considerable risk of victimization. This is particularly true for women travelling by themselves, many of whom may be unaware of the risk to their personal safety.

Response

The proposed measures were all suggested by the police, with no interference from me, the researcher. The negotiations in the response phase were carried out by the project manager, on occasion supported by a senior manager. These discussions were conducted with partners representing local, regional and national organizations:

• National Road Authority
• County government
• City administration
• Local taxi association
• Bus companies
• Enterprises in charge of parking lots

The measures introduced to solve the problem were chosen principally to correct the imbalance in the availability and supply of legal means of transportation by comparison with the illegal alternative, partly by making legal transportation more available and illegal transportation less so.

Blocking off pick-up areas for illegal cabs

A long section of the highway running through the area was closed in order to block access to two of the parking lots and to the street used by illegal-cab drivers to pick up passengers. Two parking lots located outside this area were also closed off during the critical hours to stop illegal-cab drivers from relocating to new pick-up areas (see Figure 10.2).

Making buses and legal taxis more accessible

By moving the bus stand to a more central location, and providing a new taxi stand closer to the downtown area, buses and legal cabs were made more easily accessible. The local drivers also accepted taxis licensed from other towns to pick up passengers at the new taxi stand.

Stiffer penalties for persons caught driving illegal cabs

The Occupational Transport Act[1] authorizes the police to impose immediate and tougher sanctions than those previously in place. Besides the usual fine (equivalent to

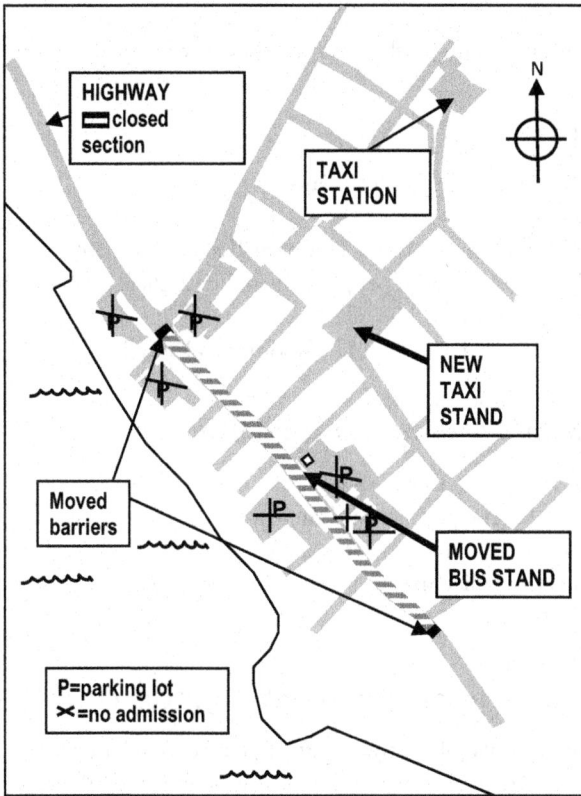

FIGURE 10.2 Downtown Tønsberg following implementation of the measures

1,100 GBP/1,450 USD/12,000 NOK), use of a car for illegal-taxi service could be prohibited for three months, and it was decided to put this particular regulation into use.

Informing suspected illegal-cab drivers about consequences

A decision was taken to produce informational leaflets: one for suspected illegal cab drivers and another for actual or potential customers. In the leaflets—which were to be handed to suspected illegal taxi drivers who were stopped by police officers— the possible consequences of the offence were explained. The leaflet was printed in Norwegian, Arabic, Kurdish and Albanian, the languages commonly spoken among the illegal-taxi drivers.

Informing the public about risks and the legal alternatives

The leaflet for passengers in suspected illegal taxis stopped by the police contained information about the risks associated with travelling in illegal cabs. It also contained details of the night bus service and phone numbers for legal taxis. Additionally, posters were produced and displayed in the downtown area during the weekends.

Assessment

The assessment consisted of four elements:

1 A follow-up meeting with the Tønsberg Taxi Association
2 Follow-up interviews with people affiliated with illegal-cab drivers
3 Repeat observations
4 A check of recorded acts of public disorder and assaults

Meeting with the Tønsberg Taxi Association

The vast majority of the about 40 legal cab drivers who attended the follow-up meeting claimed that the problem had improved considerably, and some even stated that it had disappeared. The project manager perceived a change from feelings of hostility towards the police in the prior meeting to appreciative of what the police had accomplished.

Interviews with persons affiliated with illegal cab drivers

There were simply no illegal-cab-driver affiliates to be found. Interviews with the staff at hotels and other establishments in the local area confirmed the changed situation. Even if some drivers were still active, this activity was not as open and blatant as before.

Observations

The post-intervention observations were carried out over the course of two weekends. Prior to these, observations had been carried out during one weekend to detect possible displacement areas where new locations were used by illegal cabs. It was found that a few illegal taxis were still around, although their activities were much less intense and obvious than before. Unfortunately, the systematic observations were not carried out as rigorously as intended, partly because the police leaders believed they were not necessary—the improvement was clearly evident and quantifying it would be a waste of resources. The results of the observations, however, taken on their face value, did not indicate as clear-cut a result as the leaders assumed, considering the number of illegal cabs operating. However, it is clear that the problem had vanished from the most affected downtown area.

The public order situation

Theoretically, one possible unintended negative effect of the intervention might have been an increase in public disorder and violence in the downtown area. If the overall capacity to evacuate people from the area decreased, more persons would remain in the area and for a longer time, possibly resulting in more disorder and conflict. An analysis of reported cases of assaults and disorderly conduct, however, did not indicate any such effect.

Fulfilment of project goals

This problem-oriented policing project had four goals. The first was to solve the problem, and even though there are some uncertainties in the observation data, there are good reasons to believe that the measures introduced to deal with the illegal-cab problem were effective. Where conventional police activities for the cost of the equivalent of 35,000 GBP/46,000 USD/380,000 NOK had failed, a problem-oriented policing project costing less than one-third that amount was successful.

The second goal was to give the police first-hand experience of conducting proper problem-oriented policing. One confirmation that this goal was achieved was that the project was recognized as a finalist in the 2004 Herman Goldstein Award for Excellence in Problem-Oriented Policing (Vestfold Police District, 2004).

As for the robustness of this application of problem-oriented policing—the third goal—I only gave police direct instructions in certain crucial stages of the project—primarily in the use of methods in the scanning and assessment phases—but otherwise adopted a passive supervising and supporting role. Once the initial preparations for the project were made, it took around five months from the start of scanning until the measures were in place, with results from evaluation being available four months later. Thus, it was possible for the police, with some external assistance, to carry out a high-quality problem-oriented policing project.

Last, the fourth goal of producing a case study illustrating problem-oriented policing for educational purposes was also fulfilled. A booklet was published in Norwegian and Swedish for educational purposes and is still in use in both Norway and Sweden (Knutsson & Søvik, 2005a, 2005b).

The follow-up study

Since the project was completed unexpectedly swiftly, smoothly and successfully, I decided to do a follow-up study, in which key persons were interviewed about the project (Knutsson, 2006). These interviews took place almost two years after the project was carried out.

The police commissioner

In the police commissioner's opinion, important project success factors were the appointment of the project manager, the guidance provided by the senior researcher (the author of this chapter), the establishment of a project steering group, the formulation of a project budget and the use of follow-up checks to ensure project tasks were completed. Contacts with the local government administration, which, in the commissioner's opinion, constitute a prerequisite for projects of this type, were good to begin with and improved over time.

The project manager

The project manager had been led to believe from his introduction to problem-oriented policing in the police academy that it was simple to follow the SARA model. Unexpected was the time, rigour and effort it took to collect data in the scanning phase. Formulating possible response measures was not difficult, but negotiating them with the partners was more demanding and time-consuming than he anticipated.

Chairman of the city council

The chairman had some prior knowledge about the illegal-cab operations but had not considered them harmful. However, he accepted the description of the problem conveyed to him by the police such that he came to support even the most drastic measure—that of temporarily closing off part of the city from car traffic.

The National Road Authority agent

There were some internal discussions as to whether the National Road Authority should take part in the initiative since the suggested measure was outside of the authority's usual concern. However, the presentation of the problem and the measures suggested were convincing, and decreasing illegal cab activities would serve to increase the overall road safety.

The bus company agent

The problem was greater and more severe than the agent had realized. He was impressed by the thoroughness of the work and responded favourably to the suggestions of involving the bus company in the solution to the problem.

Chairman of the local taxi drivers association

The problem had been present for a considerable period and had worsened over the last few years. The thoroughness of the problem description, and the ensuing analysis, was impressive. Following the implementation of the measures, the situation improved dramatically.

Discussion

Early assessments of problem-oriented policing in the United States and the United Kingdom indicated that its implementation was weak (for the United States, see Scott, 2000; Clarke, 1998). The UK experience can be summarized as follows: the projects were often conducted by community police officers, with short time frames on ordinary policing priorities, where the analysis was weak, and with inadequate

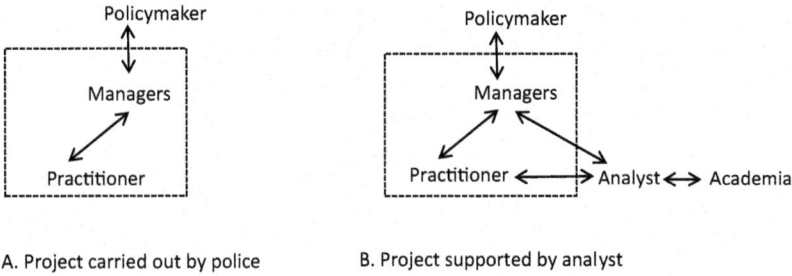

A. Project carried out by police   B. Project supported by analyst

FIGURE 10.3 Configurations of problem-oriented policing practice

Source: Adapted from Knutsson (2012).

evaluations of the projects' effectiveness (Leigh, Read & Tilley, 1996, 1998; Read & Tilley, 2000).

One explanation for this poor state of affairs can be found in the way practice was structured. Configuration A in Figure 10.3 schematically demonstrates a common pattern. For illustrative purposes only, a few actors at different levels, with interacting roles, are included: policymakers, police managers, practitioners and supporting analysts (see Knutsson, 2012).

Policymakers from a department of justice (or its equivalent), or from the upper police bureaucracy, instruct the police to perform problem-oriented policing as part of their crime prevention task. Managers comply by stating goals in their plans and assign officers to carry out problem-oriented policing projects. Two obvious vulnerabilities follow: (1) the lack of competencies necessary to properly practice problem-oriented policing and (2) a susceptibility to pressure to produce 'positive' results (Knutsson, 2012). This is especially problematic under so-called new public management regimes, where police managers must show goal fulfilment to their higher administrative bureaucracies, requiring their officers to deliver the wished-for results, thereby incentivizing manipulations of findings (see e.g. Eterno & Silverman, 2012).

In configuration B, by contrast, an analyst supports the practice of problem-oriented policing. A properly trained analyst provides the requisite competencies and will interact with managers to safeguard the project, advise practitioners and take an active part in the endeavour, especially in the more demanding elements of the process like the assessment (Knutsson, 2009, 2012). Analysts, even if internal, identify more with academic norms than with those of the police organization. This makes them less vulnerable to social pressures to produce 'positive' results. A configuration that incorporates researchers and analysts is more in line with Goldstein's original vision of problem-oriented policing (Goldstein, 1979, 2003).

How projects are configured will have consequences for the style of the problem-oriented policing practice. It might be useful to divide the practice into two modes: instrumental and conceptual (see Cherney, 2009). Instrumental use often signifies a simplified utilization of evidence relating to a specific problem, where the SARA process is applied superficially, lacking rigorous problem identification and analysis, and with an overemphasis on implementing a preferred response, that might even have been selected in advance of the analysis. This mode is commonly associated with configuration A. To be sure, there have been some award-winning problem-oriented policing projects that were undertaken solely by police officers, but this is not the rule.

Conceptual practice, by contrast, is characterized by depth and openness. To create a foundation for the most appropriate ways of solving the problem, hypotheses are checked in the process of defining and analysing the problem. There is an understanding of the core theoretical concepts underpinning the suggested responses (Cherney, 2009: pp. 246–247). It is more demanding, requiring a higher level of competence of those involved in the project than is customarily the case in a pure instrumental mode. Configuration B can create conditions for practising problem-oriented policing according to the conceptual mode.

When starting the project, I was confident that in one way or another we would solve the problem by applying the action-research model of problem-oriented policing. My intention was to contribute with competencies that police normally lack, ensuring that the project would be carried out in an open conceptual mode. A significant step toward realizing this intention was in the very first collaboration with the project manager during which we formulated the solution-oriented hypotheses that guided the project's scanning phase. The thoroughness of scanning set a standard for rigour for all the later phases.

Post-script

In the summer of 2018—about 15 years after the formal conclusion of the project—I returned to Tønsberg. The barriers were still in use, although they had a nicer design, and the taxicab stand was now more conveniently located beside a closed parking lot in the downtown area and thus was even more accessible than before. The uniformed-police commander informed me that the illegal-taxi problem remained noticeably much improved all those years later.

Note

1 Lov om yrkestransport 21. Juni 2002 nr 45.

References

Cherney, A. (2009) 'Exploring the concept of research utilization: Implications for evidence-based crime prevention', *Crime Prevention and Community Safety*, 11(4): 243–257.

Clarke, R.V. (1998) 'Defining police strategies: Problem-solving, problem-oriented policing and community-oriented policing', in T.S. O'Connor & A.C. Grant (eds.), *Problem-Oriented Policing: Crime-Specific Problems, Critical Issues and Making Problem-Oriented Policing Work*, Washington, DC: Police Executive Research Forum.

Eterno, J. & Silverman, E. (2012) *The Crime Numbers Game: Management by Manipulation*, Boca Raton, FL: CRC Press.

Goldstein, H. (1979) 'Improving policing: A problem-oriented approach', *Crime and Delinquency*, 25(2): 234–258.

Goldstein, H. (2003) 'On further developing problem-oriented policing: The most critical need, the major impediments and a proposal', in J. Knutsson (ed.), *Problem-Oriented Policing: From Innovation to Mainstream*, Crime Prevention Studies, Monsey, NY: Criminal Justice Press, pp. 13–47.

Knutsson, J. (2006) 'What is there to gain? Implementing without self-interest: A case study', in J. Knutsson & R.V. Clarke (eds.), *Putting Theory to Work: Implementing Situational Prevention and Problem-Oriented Policing*, Crime Prevention Studies, Vol. 20, Monsey, NY: Criminal Justice Press, pp. 89–109.

Knutsson, J. (2009) 'Standard of evaluations in problem-oriented policing-projects: Good enough?', in J. Knutsson & N. Tilley (eds.), *Evaluating Crime Reduction Initiatives*, Crime Prevention Studies, Vol. 24, Monsey, NY: Criminal Justice Press, pp. 29–58.

Knutsson, J. (2012) 'Vulnerability of evaluators of problem-oriented policing projects', in N. Tilley & G. Farrell (eds.), *The Reasoning Criminologist: Essays in Honour of Ronald V. Clarke*, London: Routledge, pp. 108–118.

Knutsson, J. & Søvik, K.-E. (2005a) *Problemorienterat polisarbete i teori och praktik*, Rapport 2005:1, Solna: Polishögskolan.

Knutsson, J. & Søvik, K.-E. (2005b) *Problemorientert politiarbeid i teori og praksis*, PHS-Forskning 2005:1, Oslo: Politihøgskolen.

Leigh, A., Read, T. & Tilley, N. (1996) *Problem-Oriented Policing: Brit Pop*, Crime Detection and Prevention Series, Paper 75, London: Home Office.

Leigh, A., Read, T. & Tilley, N. (1998) *Brit pop II: Problem: Oriented Policing in Practice*, Police Research Series Paper 93, London: Home Office.

Read, T. & Tilley, N. (2000) *Not Rocket Science? Problem-Solving and Crime Reduction*, Crime Reduction Research Series Paper 6, London, UK: Home Office, Police Research Group.

Scott, M.S. (2000) *Problem-Oriented Policing: Reflections on the First 20 Years*, Washington, DC: US Department of Justice, Office of Community Oriented Policing Services.

Vestfold Police District (2004) *Gypsy Cabs in Tønsberg: A Case for Problem Oriented Policing*. Submission to the Herman Goldstein Award for Excellence in Problem-Oriented Policing, Center for Problem-Oriented Policing, Arizona State University, Phoenix, AZ.

11

ASSAULTS WITH GLASSES IN BARS AND CLUBS IN LANCASHIRE, ENGLAND

Ronald V. Clarke

Introduction

I clearly remember being sickened by the best-selling account of Japanese atrocities in World War II (Russell, 1958), which I read at age 17. The book was on the shelves of a local town's bookstore where I went for driving lessons and where I read it standing up on my successive visits. Whether the book triggered dormant emotions or was simply a vehicle for their expression, I do not know. It was less the violence and cruelty that revolted me but the physical mutilation of living people.

I had the same reaction on recently reading Natarajan's account of deliberate acid and kerosene burns inflicted on young brides by their husbands' families, dissatisfied with dowry arrangements (Natarajan, 2014). These attacks destroy the young women's appearance and their sense of being worthwhile human beings. Many never recover and soon die.

"Glassing" attacks committed in UK pubs and in those of other beer-drinking cultures provoke the same powerful emotions in me, especially when the victims are young women. Glassing is the use of glasses and bottles deliberately broken to use as jagged weapons, which are then thrust into the victim's face.

Glassings are more impulsive and may be less cruelly premeditated than the Japanese war crimes or the deliberate burns inflicted on young brides in India, but they can also result in disfigurements that devastate the lives of the victims, especially if they are women. Young men, like dueling students in 19th-century Germany, might wear their scars with bravado, but for young women, a scarred face would be a ruinous calamity. This is why I chose to write about the Lancashire Constabulary's successful project to reduce glassings submitted for a Goldstein Award in 2007.

The winning team consisted of Acting Inspector Richard Hurt and Temporary Sergeant Steven Hardman, both of the Lancashire Constabulary (hereinafter "the police" or "Constabulary") and David Rigby—Sector Manager of the North

West Ambulance Service. The submission had three notable features: (1) it sought to implement a proven situational crime prevention measure (replacement of the regular glasses used in local pubs by "hardened" polycarbonate glasses), (2) strong partnerships formed with other local agencies and (3) an evaluation commissioned from a local university—John Moores Liverpool University (JMLU).

This remarkably clear and comprehensive evaluation is in many ways the submission's most remarkable component. It goes far beyond most problem-oriented policing partnerships with university researchers, who might undertake a post hoc assessment of the project but whose role in other respects is mostly advisory. In this case, the police brought LJMU into the project at an early stage, and the university designed the intervention in ways that would permit a reliable assessment to be undertaken. JMLU's preliminary report was made available for the submission and was later published in full (Anderson et al., 2009).

When the police decided to take tackle glass-related injuries in the Constabulary's Western Division, it was natural that they would turn to JMLU for assistance. In fact, JMLU's involvement with the police preceded the glassing project. Its Centre for Public Health is well regarded for its expertise on alcohol matters, and the police had previously called upon it to advise on ways to make Blackpool, the Constabulary's seaside resort in its Western Division, a safer and more attractive city for visitors and residents alike.

During the year 2006/7, the Western Division had experienced 41 glass-related injuries in its pubs, nightclubs and other licensed venues. These injuries were generally reported in the media and were consistently identified by local agencies as a significant issue that needed addressing, along with other crime issues. Apart from the undesirable publicity, the injuries were often serious, and the costs of their treatment were considerable. For the 41 incidents in 2006/7, the medical costs were estimated to be £7.54 million, and the subsequent criminal justice investigatory costs and processing were estimated to be an additional £1.46 million, for a total cost of £9 million, roughly equivalent to US$16 million at that time.

The police decided that the solution to this problem would be to replace ordinary glasses with polycarbonate glassware, which is virtually unbreakable. This decision followed the lead of other police forces and Licensing Authorities that had purchased these glasses and insisted the licensed premises should use them. However, the Constabulary first made inquiries to see if the introduction elsewhere of polycarbonates had been successful.

Polycarbonate glasses look the same as ordinary ones used in pubs, bars and nightclubs (e.g. pint, half pint and mixer glasses). They are very difficult to break, making them safer than ordinary glass that can shatter into splinters and shards and cause significant injury. They are hard-wearing, reducing replacement costs, and manufacturers claim that they are more environmentally friendly, using one-ninth of the energy in production compared with standard glasses.

In fact, the use of polycarbonate glasses had been widely advocated in the UK's media as a means of reducing glass-related injuries in pubs, and indeed, they had been quite widely adopted in some parts of the country. This widespread support was in large measure due to an extensive program of research (reviewed in the LJMU report) demonstrating the benefits of polycarbonate glasses. Professor Jonathan Shepherd (1998) is credited with stimulating this program for which he was rewarded with the Stockholm Prize, generally considered criminology's premier honor.

The police and the JMLU researchers together devised an implementation plan that would facilitate an assessment of the effectiveness of the polycarbonate glassware. In three towns in Lancashire, the police recruited between three and five licensed venues (polycarbonate glassware [PCG] venues), identified by local officers, to replace standard glassware with polycarbonate glasses for a three-month period. These towns were chosen to represent the different types of nightlife areas in Lancashire. The police provided each PCG venue with enough hardened glasses to replace their entire glassware stock, and provisions were made to provide additional polycarbonate glasses during the trial if required. The police obtained funds for this purpose from National Health Service through BSafe Blackpool and the Cumbria and Lancashire Alcohol Network. For each PCG venue, the police recruited a similar non-PCG venue from the area to act as a comparison site. In total, 22 venues were included in the project.

The police undertook several key tasks in addition to those mentioned earlier. They recruited a number of other local agencies with a stake in reducing glassings to serve as partners in the project; they worked together with JMLU researchers to check that PCG venues were in compliance with the arrangements made on being recruited; and they employed the Problem Analysis Triangle (see Clarke & Eck, 2005, step 8) to assist in the analysis of glassings and unfavorable perceptions of polycarbonate glasses among customers and venue managers, which included that they were unpleasant to drink from and were costly.

A range of measures were used to assess the impact of using polycarbonate glasses, including the following:

1 Customer surveys conducted in each participating venue before and after the trial
2 Observational research in each participating venue
3 Venue-collected data including the number of glass injuries among staff and customers, the number of broken bottles and glasses, incidents (e.g. fights) and weekly sales figures.
4 Interviews with licensees/managers from all PCG venues
5 Collection of police and accident and emergency department data

As might be expected, this raft of measures produced a wide range of results described in the evaluation report. Despite the careful evaluation plan, certain contingencies limited the conclusions that could be drawn from the results (more on this later). Thus, some of the venues that were initially included dropped out of the project and some PCG venues did not always comply with instructions to which they had initially agreed (e.g. by giving regular clients the ordinary glasses they wanted).

In addition, despite the project's broad coverage, numbers were still too small to show any consistent differences between PCG and other venues in some important variables. Thus, police data showed no significant changes in the number of glass-related incidents occurring in study towns during the trial period compared with the same period in the previous year—a not-unexpected result of the low numbers of violent incidents recorded by participating venues pre- and post-trial.

Even so, a number of results were reported attesting to the project's success. These were as follows:

1   In venues that consistently used polycarbonate glasses throughout the trial, glass breakages decreased from an average of 17 per venue per week before the trial to none during the trial. No reductions in glass breakages were seen in non-PCG venues.
2   The proportion of customers in PCG venues reporting having cut themselves on broken glass over the last three months decreased from 11% pre-trial to 6% post-trial.
3   The proportion of customers in PCG venues reporting that they would be more likely to visit a bar if it used polycarbonate glasses increased significantly from 11% to 27%, an increase not seen in non-PCG venues.
4   Managers and licensees had generally been skeptical about introducing polycarbonate glasses, fearing negative customer reactions and consequently negative effects on trade. Upon receiving the glasses, however, they were impressed with their quality and happy to introduce them.
5   At the interview, all licensees and managers in PCG venues stated that polycarbonate glasses were much safer than standard glassware and many reported that the introduction of these glasses had increased feelings of safety among their staff. Some mentioned that their staff who collect empty glasses felt much safer going into a crowd when the venue was packed.
6   All those introducing polycarbonate glasses as part of the trial stated that they would continue to use them for the foreseeable future, due to the reduced costs and increased safety they bring to their businesses.
7   Analyses of weekly sales figures showed no significant differences between pre-trial sales and sales during the trial in either PCG or non-PCG venues.

Because I was convinced of the benefits of polycarbonate glasses even before the Lancashire trial, I need to be aware of the dangers of "cherry-picking" the favorable results, but only two criticisms were made of these glasses. First, some drinkers complained that the glasses felt too light when they had finished their beers, which is a problem that perhaps could be corrected at manufacture. Second, some drinkers resented the government treating them like children and dictating how they should drink their beer. Both these problems seem relatively minor, and the JMLU evaluators concluded that "[d]espite the limitations of the study, the overall findings are positive" (p. 6).

Discussion

The choice of response—the introduction of polycarbonate glasses—for the Lancashire Constabulary's (2010) Goldstein Award finalist submission might be considered obvious in the light of the considerable publicity touting the benefits of such glasses. The response also focused on the most significant harm resulting from pub violence. Even so, many other interventions have been proposed for reducing violence in pubs and clubs (Graham et al., 2004; Scott & Dedel, 2006) which might have had greater appeal to local partners. Most important of these might be attempting to deal with motivational variables for assault and, indeed, in its final paragraphs the JMLU evaluation report makes this case.

The introduction of polycarbonate glasses must have seemed fraught with difficulty, but here again, the Constabulary was well served by JMLU, which drew up a remarkable implementation plan which, among its other benefits, was designed to facilitate the assessment. Nonetheless, the university acknowledged some limitations of the assessment. Those listed in its report were the following:

1   The number of participating venues (22) was limited by the resources available for the research. Of 22 originally recruited, two closed during the trial period and two changed management, with new managers choosing not to participate.
2   Four further venues failed to collect data continuously during the study.
3   Two PCG venues did not use these glasses consistently, and most PCG venues continued to serve ordinary glass bottles.
4   No bar staff responded to the post-trial survey, despite repeated attempts to encourage participation.
5   Injury incidents occurring in venues were low, hampering identification of impacts, and police and health data could not be linked to individual venues.

Criminologists more used to evaluating situational interventions might also question whether the JMLU design would have been adequate to detecting displacement, diffusion of benefits or anticipatory benefits following the introduction of polycarbonate glasses (e.g. see Clarke, 2018). Despite these uncertainties, as concluded earlier, the Liverpool team assembled convincing data that the response was effective, although it would have been helpful to have more data on the degree to which it actually resulted in a decline of criminal assaults.

Follow-up

The Goldstein Award submission's report on the effectiveness of the polycarbonate glasses presented data for only one year after their introduction in 2007/8. To see whether the reported reductions in glassings were sustained, further data were sought from Professor Stuart Kirby, who was a senior commander of the Lancashire Constabulary when the submission was made. In his present university position, Professor Kirby maintains his links with the Constabulary, and he has also authored a chapter in this volume. Rather than asking for information about the full range of positive results reported by the submission's university partners, his help was sought for just one measure: the total numbers of glass-related injuries in the Western Division for as many years as possible after the intervention. These numbers could be compared with the 41 incidents of glass-related injuries in the Western Division reported in the submission for the year prior to the intervention.

Professor Kirby noted some problems with this plan, the most important being that Western Division no longer exists. However, he thought it should be possible to reconstruct its 2007 boundaries. He also said that access to the help of crime analysts was more difficult following recent budget cuts, but he would try an informal approach. Last, he said there was no marker in the crime data for glassings, and a manual search must have been done in 2007. Because this would be impossible to undertake for more than a year or two, he thought the best that could be done would be to try to pick up glassing events using a modus operandi search. However, when Scott Keay and Ellen Richardson of the Lancashire Police Corporate Analysis sought to follow this approach, they encountered further problems. They could not replicate the original numbers, and they could find no record of how these were produced or of the definition of "glassing" that was used. Accordingly, they ran a new search from scratch on crime data from 1 April 2006 through 31 March 2018. This search produced the data for "wounding and other crimes endangering life" recorded in Table 11.1, after some corrections, including removal of incidents in home addresses.[1]

For 2006/7, the year prior to the intervention, the number of "crimes" (150) recorded in the table is more than three-and-a-half times the number of glassing incidents (41) recorded in the original submission. In 2007/08, the year of the intervention, the table shows there was a marked 19% fall in crimes (122), which decreased even more (92) in the following year and continued to fall thereafter until there was an unexplained rise in 2014/15, with a rapid return to low numbers in subsequent years. Despite their imperfections, the pattern of these figures is largely consistent with a marked and enduring decline in glassings resulting from

TABLE 11.1 Number of wounding and other crimes endangering life recorded in non-residential settings in the Lancashire Constabulary Western Division, 2006–2012

Year	No. Crimes	Year	No. Crimes
2006/07	150	2012/13	44
2007/08	122	2014/15	85
2008/09	92	2015/16	32
2009/10	79	2016/17	40
2010/11	52	2017/18	47
2011/12	39	**Total**	**767**

the intervention—the introduction of polycarbonate glasses—and they are consistent with other evaluations (e.g., Warburton & Shepherd, 2000; Graham et al., 2004; Ker & Chinnock, 2006; Forsyth, 2008). There can be no doubt that wider adoption of these glasses would lead to reduced risks of egregious injuries, which can have enduring emotional consequences for victims, especially for women, who composed 167 of the victims compared with 481 men (in a further 119 cases, the sex of the victim was not recorded).

Summary and conclusion

The unusually active role played by the university partners in the submission was mentioned earlier. They had been brought in as partners from the beginning of the intervention and, in effect, they designed the implementation of the response. This is quite different from the advisory role of most university partners in problem-oriented policing projects, even when they undertake a *post hoc* assessment. Knutsson (2012) explains the benefits for police of allowing research partners a much stronger hand in guiding the project and this volume includes other case studies, akin to that of the present submission, where university researchers played such a role. In the 1990s, Kennedy, Piehl and Braga (1996) from Harvard University worked directly with the Boston Police Department in developing the Ceasefire model, and subsequently, Braga, who was a member of the original Ceasefire team, worked to revitalize that approach when gang violence re-emerged (see Chapter 2, this volume). In 2016, Kennedy, this time working from John Jay College, worked with the High Point, North Carolina, Police Department to apply a focused-deterrence response to domestic violence (see Chapter 7, this volume). Madensen and Herold in Cincinnati developed the theoretical underpinnings for PIVOT—Place-based Investigations of Violent Offender Territories that won the Goldstein Award in 2017 (see Chapter 3, this volume). In these interventions, the researchers' role was much more than post-intervention evaluation, although they did that too.

Final thoughts

Some customers in the PCG venues complained that they did not want to be told by the government (i.e., the "Nanny State") what kind of glasses they should use for drinking beer. This kind of complaint is regularly made whenever governments curtail individual freedoms for the greater good. The history of introducing seat belts, helmet laws, drunk-driving laws, smoke-free venues and compulsory vaccinations will be familiar to most readers. I have difficulty taking these complaints seriously, and in general, I believe that governments often fail to take strong action when the facts dictate that they should. In particular, it was very frustrating for me that governments refused for so many years to compel motor manufacturers to make their vehicles harder to steal (Newman, 2004), and there are many other examples of government failure to act in the public interest (see Clarke & Newman, 2005). Indeed, one example we cited in that publication was the failure of governments in the United Kingdom to promote the use of toughened glasses in pubs.

This case study also brought home to me the importance of having good data for problem-oriented policing. This was not just because of the trials and tribulations of measuring glassings recounted earlier. It was also because I had tried unsuccessfully during the follow-up to obtain some reliable data on the proportions of pubs and clubs in the United Kingdom that use hardened glasses. This information would have been helpful in assessing the overall contribution of hardened and polycarbonate glasses to pub safety. I had imagined that this information would be routinely available, but this was not the case as I discovered after scouring the internet, and making exhaustive inquiries of expert groups and individuals, including the Home Office, the Portman Group and Professor Johnathan Shepherd himself. However, Professor Kirby mentioned that the "continental" approach to licensed premises which makes use of more seating outside has made the use of polycarbonate glasses more commonplace since ordinary glasses are not allowed outside the premises. In fact, it became clear to me that to obtain what would probably be at best crude estimates of the use of hardened glasses in pubs and clubs would require a major research effort of its own, out of proportion to the value of that information for present purposes.

Given the very wide range of problem-oriented policing projects, it is hard to anticipate what data might be needed for any single project and hard to see how these data might be made routinely available. In fact, the question is so difficult as to be hardly worth thinking about. Perhaps one can only hope that the enormous advances being made in artificial intelligence and that the digital world will produce new sources of data that will likely benefit policing as much as any other sphere of social activity.

Acknowledgments

The following generously helped me with information and comments: Zara Quigg (née Anderson), Professor Jonathan Shepherd and Professor Stuart Kirby, who at the time of the glassing submission for the Goldstein Award was a senior commander of the Lancashire Constabulary. I am particularly indebted to Scott Keay and Ellen Richardson of the Lancashire Constabulary Corporate Analysis unit, who took great care to ensure that for the follow-up the number of "glassings" could be compared for 2006 to 2018.

Note

1 Despite my "final thoughts" about the importance of good data for problem-oriented policing, I do not believe that publishing the complex details of this method would serve any useful purpose. Those who doubt the validity of the conclusions reached here could undertake their own search of the Lancashire data.

References

Anderson, Z., Whelan, G., Hughes, K. & Bellis, M.A. (2009) *Evaluation of the Lancashire Polycarbonate Glass Pilot Project*, Liverpool, England: Centre for Public Health, Liverpool John Moores University.

Clarke, R.V. (2018) 'The theory and practice of situational crime prevention', in H. Pontell (ed.), *Oxford Research Encyclopedia of Criminology and Criminal Justice*, New York: Oxford University Press.

Clarke, R.V. & Eck, J.E. (2005) *Crime Analysis for Problem Solvers: In 60 Small Steps*, Washington, DC: US Department of Justice, Office of Community Oriented Policing Services.

Clarke, R.V. & Newman, G. (2005) 'Modifying criminogenic products: What role for government?', in R.V. Clarke & G. Newman (eds.), *Designing Out Crime from Products and Systems*, Crime Prevention Studies, Vol. 18, Monsey, NY: Criminal Justice Press.

Forsyth, A.J.M. (2008) 'Banning glassware from nightclubs in Glasgow (Scotland): Observed impacts, compliance and patrons' views', *Alcohol & Alcoholism*, 43(1): 111–117.

Graham, K., Osgood, D.W., Zibrowski, E., Purcell, J., Gliksman, L., Leonard, K., Pernanen, K., Saltz, R.F. & Toomey, T.L. (2004) 'The effect of the *Safer Bars* programme on physical aggression in bars: Results of a randomized controlled trial', *Drug and Alcohol Review*, 23(1): 31–41.

Kennedy, D., Piehl, A. & Braga, A.A. (1996) 'Youth violence in Boston: Gun markets, serious offenders, and a use-reduction strategy', *Law and Contemporary Problems*, 59(1): 147–196.

Ker, K. & Chinnock, P. (2006) 'Interventions in the alcohol server setting for preventing injuries (Review)', *The Cochrane Database of Systematic Reviews*, (2).

Knutsson, J. (2012) 'Vulnerability of evaluators of problem-oriented policing projects', in N. Tilley & G. Farrell (eds.), *The Reasoning Criminologist: Essays in Honour of Ronald V. Clarke*, London: Routledge, pp. 108–118.

Lancashire Constabulary, Western Division (2010) *Smashing Time: Or Not?* Submission for the Herman Goldstein Award for Excellence in Problem-oriented Policing, Center for Problem-Oriented Policing, Arizona State University, Phoenix, AZ.

Natarajan, M. (2014) 'Differences between intentional and non-intentional burn injuries in India: Implications for prevention', *Burns*, 40: 1033–1039.

Newman, G.R. (2004) 'Car safety and car security: An historical comparison', in M.G. Maxfield & R.V. Clarke (eds.), *Understanding and Preventing Car Theft*, Crime Prevention Studies, Vol. 17, Monsey, NY: Criminal Justice Press.

Russell, E.F.L. (Lord Russell of Liverpool) (1958) *The Knights of Bushido: A Short History of Japanese War Crimes*, London: Cassell.

Scott, M.S. & Dedel, K. (2006) *Assaults in and Around Bars* (2nd ed.), Problem-Oriented Guides for Police, Problem-Specific Guide No. 1, Washington, DC: US Department of Justice, Office of Community Oriented Policing Services.

Shepherd, J. (1998) 'The circumstances and prevention of bar-glass injury, Editorial', *Addiction*, 93(1): 5–7.

Warburton, A.L. & Shepherd, J.P. (2000) 'Effectiveness of toughened glassware in terms of reducing injury in bars: A randomised controlled trial', *Injury Prevention*, 6: 36–40.

PART III

Vulnerable people

12

ACCIDENTAL DROWNINGS OF MIGRANT LABOURERS IN MORECAMBE BAY, ENGLAND[1]

Nick Tilley

Background

Cockles are, as the traditional Irish air 'Sweet Molly Malone' tells us, a traditional street food. Molly 'wheeled her wheelbarrow down streets broad and barrow, singing cockles and mussels alive alive oh . . . So were her mother and father before as they (too) wheeled their wheelbarrow through streets broad and narrow (again) singing cockles and mussels alive alive oh.' Cockles are on the menu of high-end restaurants around the world. In addition, many cockles are bottled. There is, thus, a substantial market for cockles.

Cockles are harvested in coastal regions, in particular in some sandy areas where there are large cockle beds. The price of cockles can fluctuate quite widely. One recent study found that at 2014 prices, between 1987 and 2014, the value of cockles per tonne in the United Kingdom had fluctuated between a low of £199 in 1990 and a high of £1,232 in 2003. The most recent figure given was for 2014 and stood at £400 (Murray & Tarrant, 2015: p. 49).

Morecambe Bay is a major site for cockle picking in North-West England. It covers a large area, where the beds are exposed and available for picking during intertidal periods. Commercial cockle picking in Morecambe Bay, as elsewhere, is hedged around with regulations covering health and safety, who can pick cockles at what times, where, of what size and using what methods. Pickers have to apply for and be granted a licence if they are to pick cockles legally. The main reason for much of the regulation relates to conservation. Cockle picking is simple but physically demanding. It involves riddling sand, raking out cockles, bagging them and transporting them to the shore for processing.

On 5 February 2004, 23 Chinese cockle pickers were drowned in Morecambe Bay, unable to beat the incoming tide (it advances at 5 mph). The police had, of course, to mount an investigation to determine if any crimes had been committed and, if so, who could be charged with and prosecuted for them. The investigation was complex and protracted. It involved producing some 2,900 statements and 2,500 exhibits, the analysis of 20,000 phone calls and the collation of 1.5 million pages of documentation. Evidence had to be collected in China as well as the United Kingdom. Documents had to be translated from Mandarin, Spanish and French. The investigation took about 18 months, and the trial that was eventually held lasted 7 months. In the end, three people were convicted and sentenced to serve 14 years, 4 years and 2 years 9 months in prison, respectively, for crimes including manslaughter, conspiracy to pervert the course of justice and immigration offences. Moreover, the presiding judge ordered the deportation of those convicted once their sentences were completed (Kirby & Penna, 2010: p. 206). Although important, tricky and painstaking, the efforts made by the police to detect the crime did not exhaust their interest in dealing with a range of problems that came to the surface in relation to cockle picking in Morecambe Bay. Operation SeaQuest[2] comprised the problem-solving initiative established in the wake of the tragedy.

The following problems were identified in the course of the work on SeaQuest.

Organised crime

Organised crime took the form of human trafficking. 'Gangmasters' charged up to £20,000 to bring illegal immigrants into the United Kingdom in the expectation that they could make a lot of money. The trafficked workers' debt was to be repaid through deductions from paltry pay for cockle picking—they were in 'debt bondage'. The migrants were put up in crowded multi-occupancy housing, often with no electricity or heating. The rental was deducted from their pay. Those involved in this organised crime were convicted in connection with the 23 deaths by drowning in February 2004. The trafficked workers were victims of what is now known as 'modern slavery', which is receiving increasing attention in England and Wales following the Modern Slavery Act of 2015. In 2004, the issue was given relatively little attention.

Illegal cockle picking

Many cockle pickers lacked relevant permits, and of those who had permits, many had obtained them fraudulently. Thus, within a workforce estimated to be more than 800, only 160 had permits, and of these 160, 48 had been obtained fraudulently. In October 2004, nearly 80 per cent of the 61 Chinese cockle pickers working illegally had permits which had been obtained fraudulently.

Breaches of health and safety regulations

Only 11 per cent of the cockle pickers carried lifejackets, GPS and flares while on the sands. Of the average 100 vehicles on the sands (carrying up to 400 cockle pickers), 79% were found to be un-roadworthy, overloaded or to be carrying multiple roof-riding passengers, putting them in obvious danger. The organised crime groups had little interest in the safety of their workers.

Fraud

The Department of Work and Pensions estimated that 29 per cent of the cockle pickers were fraudulently claiming benefits, resulting in losses to Her Majesty's Treasury. These were estimated at £1,216,800 between April 2003 and 2004.

Antisocial behaviour

The local community were unhappy at a situation in which many unknown workers came and went with little regard for the nuisances they produced, for example extensive littering and abandoned vehicles. There were 29 complaints in the summer of 2004. Door-to-door surveys of local residents confirmed complaints both from local residents and businesses.

Risky behaviour

The drowning of the 23 individuals in February 2004 was an isolated tragic event, but it reflected a pattern of risky behaviour that continued and threatened more loss of life. There had been 34 calls to the lifeboat service between April and September 2004, where cockle pickers were in difficulty on the sands, each callout costing around £300.

Understanding the problem

Morecambe Bay's cockle beds provide diverse crime temptations and opportunities. In some years the rewards from illicit cockle picking are high, as in 2003–2004 when prices were high, but when there was a glut in supply specifically in Morecambe Bay. Newspapers in Hong Kong reported in 2003 that a basket of cockles could fetch $37 and that sums of up to $2,000 per day could be earned from harvesting them. The regulatory regime then in place for cockle picking was hard to enforce. This is, in part, because cockle picking, notably in Morecambe Bay, takes place across a vast, featureless area of about 120 square miles, reaching as far as five miles beyond the shoreline, which can be accessed from many points. This means that the scope for surveillance and guardianship of the cockle beds themselves and of workers on them was low.

The periodic rich pickings explain why Morecambe Bay attracts casual labour and why it also attracted organised criminals making use of illegal migrants from China in 2004, when prices were especially high. The rights of the English to cockle picking evidently go back to 1215 where they were enshrined in the Magna Carta, which defined the sands as rights of way, providing for the common people of England to collect up to seven pounds of cockles for personal or commercial benefit! This has made direct control difficult.

There were many other cockle pickers alongside the Chinese migrants in Morecambe Bay. Up to 400 travelled daily to take part in cockle picking. Most were poor and already known to the police and other public bodies. They had evidently learned to be wary of those responsible for law enforcement and so avoided them. These casual internal economic migrants were often reckless in pursuing rich pickings from the cockle beds and indifferent to the interests of local people with whom they did not associate or identify.

Other cockle pickers, as well as Chinese migrants, were at serious risk of drowning given that the rapidity with which the tide comes in and the changing nature of the sandscape.

A variety of regulatory agencies had an interest in the cockle picking that was happening in Morecambe Bay in the early 2000s. These included the police, the Immigration Service, the local authority, the Health and Safety Executive, the Sea Fisheries Committee, the Maritime and Coastguard Agency, the Vehicle Operating Service Agency, the Department of Work and Pensions and the Department of Environment and Fisheries. They each had the responsibility to deal with at least one problem that emanated from the patterns of cockle picking taking place, but none had an overview of the situation and the pattern of inter-linkages between the individual problems. Hence, they worked largely independently of one another, with responses that were ad hoc and uncoordinated.

The response

As already indicated, the police investigation of the deaths of the Chinese Nationals was complex but ultimately successful. It brought into much sharper relief problems of modern slavery, how it was conducted, the conditions for its practice and the consequences for its victims, as well as the diverse range of other problems associated with cockle picking.

The preventive response introduced with SeaQuest involved the creation of a partnership between the several agencies with responsibilities for problems associated with cockle picking and the formulation and delivery of a coordinated strategy. The role of the police was to help kick-start the partnership as well as to help devise and deliver the strategy.

The Morecambe Bay Action Group (MBAG) was formed, with an inaugural meeting in November 2014. The first and primary concern of MBAG was with improving the safety of the cockle pickers themselves to prevent the risk of more tragic losses of life, in which all agencies had a major interest. MBAG aimed more generally to establish safer working practices. Members agreed to data-sharing protocols and to create a database of those employed to harvest cockles. Finally, they shared a concern to show they were working together as a means of reassuring the community that the issues concerning them related to cockle pickers were being addressed.

MBAG was also to contribute to the achievement of member agencies' particular concerns, for example compliance with local bye-laws (Sea Fisheries), removal of illegal immigrants working on the sands (Immigration Service), improved compliance with laws and regulations relating to vehicles and their use (Police, Vehicle Inspectorate, Health and Safety Executive, and Marine Coastguard Agency), reduced benefit fraud (Department of Work and Pensions), managed access and minimal coastal erosion (Environment Agency) and litter removal (Local Authority). Hence, MBAG was set up both to achieve pressing common objectives and to develop a concerted way of working that would help address problems falling within the remit of individual agencies.

The SeaQuest team identified a 'pinch-point'[3] for the suite of problems centred on cockle picking in Morecambe Bay. They all depended on the anonymity and ignorance of the cockle pickers, which was furnished by the wide area of featureless sands in which the cockle beds lay and the lack of formal or informal guardians within it. Modern slavery could thrive if no one noticed it and the harms associated with it. Risks of drowning were increased if the cockle pickers failed to understand tidal movements and if they failed to alert one another to imminent dangers from a fast-incoming tide. Health and safety were compromised where there was no one to notice or intervene in the event of unsafe practices and breaches of relevant regulations. Likewise, the fact that cockle pickers could enter and leave the cockle beds unnoticed meant that they were unlikely to be held accountable for a lack of permits, breaches of regulations covering what could be picked and when and fraudulent claims for benefits while they were working.

The team thought through how that anonymity could be reduced by increased surveillance, and at low cost. They lit on the idea of creating a 'muster point', where cockle pickers could obtain refreshments and shelter before entering and after leaving the sands, where at the same time they could be informed (or reminded) of the rules relating to cockle picking and to work, health and safety more generally. Mustering meant that cockle pickers would become known to one another and to agencies there to help (and check up on) them.

Creating the muster point posed its own challenges. The muster point eventually comprised a catering caravan (chuck wagon) that was allowed to park on the sands. It had operated from the promenade. The proprietor had to be persuaded that they would get more business by taking the caravan onto the sands. Permission had to be obtained for the caravan to operate on the sands themselves and required a change in the relevant local bye-law. The caravan provided shelter and refreshments for cockle pickers. It functioned as an outdoor community centre, an informal contact point for agencies (including, most important, the police) with responsibilities relating to the cockle beds and those working on them and a place where information, relating, for example, to safety as well as regulation, could be conveyed to pickers on a noticeboard. Pickers became visible to the police and to each other. They lost their anonymity and comprised guardians and handlers of one another. Risks to the cockle pickers as victims were reduced and risks of them as potential offenders were increased.

Gangmasters,[4] who supply and direct the workers, also valued the facility provided by the catering caravan, so much so that when threatened with its removal, they agreed to a daily litter collection and to cover the cost to the Local Authority of taking the collected litter away, through a small surcharge on the refreshments provided.

The impacts claimed for SeaQuest

There was an increase in the number of vetted pickers with permits working in the formal economy, leading to an estimated saving to the Treasury of £828,000 in the first year (Kirby & Penna, 2010: p. 208).

The number of unroadworthy vehicles on the sands fell by 84 per cent, and roof riding was almost eliminated.

Lifeboat deployments to cockle pickers went down from 34 in 2004 to 1 in 2005–6.

Continued offending became more difficult for organised criminals engaged in orchestrating cockle picking using slave labour as it became more and more difficult for them to operate anonymously and without legitimate permits.

The local community was reassured, as shown by a reduction in letters of complaint from 29 to 2 between 2004 and 2005.

The legacy of SeaQuest

Operation Seaquest has left a lasting legacy, both locally and nationally. It brought to the surface serious harms that had been overlooked and that called for attention. Sustained local and national impacts include the following.

Multi-agency cooperation

The multi-agency provisions for identifying and managing any emerging problems associated with the cockle beds in Morecambe Bay remain. These involve the Environment Agency, Local Authorities, Food Standards Agency, North West Inshore Fisheries and Conservation Authority (NWIFCA) and the police. The range of specific issues addressed relate to modern slavery (forced labour, illegal immigration), adherence to fishing regulations (use of required registration and permits, carriage of movement documents, respect for seasonal closure of beds, collection only of shellfish that reach minimum dimensions, use only of approved gathering methods) and accordance with food hygiene requirements (lab testing of shellfish).

Establishment of the NWIFCA

Regulation of the cockle beds was enhanced with the establishment of the NWIFCA in 2011, which has enforcement responsibilities for relevant local, national and international law. It adopts an approach to its responsibilities through consultation and partnership with interested parties, involving minimum burden on third parties. It produces bye-laws covering the use of cockle beds, but these are formulated in consultation with others, including those in the fisheries industry, who are invited to comment. Bye-law 3 (NWIFCA, 2012) at the time of writing sets out the main conditions that must be satisfied for cockle collection. The police are able to use this regulation, if necessary, in applying leverage to those they suspect of involvement in other crimes. Indeed, briefing to officers concerned with other criminal activity, notably relating to modern slavery, highlights Bye-law 3.

Legislative attention to modern slavery

The Morecambe Bay tragedy and the ensuing successful investigation were important in highlighting the seriousness of modern slavery, its association with organised crime and the need to take preventive action against it. This included the passage of the Modern Slavery Act in 2015, as well as the establishment of the Gangmasters and Labour Abuse Authority (GLA).

The Gangmasters and Labour Abuse Authority

The GLA was set up in 2005, as a result of the Gangmasters (Licensing) Act 2004, which was hastily passed in the wake of Morecambe Bay tragedy. The GLA was established to prevent debt bondage and forced labour of the sort exposed in Morecambe Bay and requires that those providing labour in gathering shellfish (and agriculture) be licenced. It created a range of offences surrounding the provision of such workforces. Licensees have to meet standards relating to health and safety, accommodation, pay and transport and training. GLA officers check that Gangmasters are fit to award a licence and also that all tax and National Insurance regulations are met. The approach to enforcement, as with the NWIFCA, is to encourage compliance in as consensual a way as possible. The GLA continues to employ three ex-Lancashire Constabulary detectives.

The significance of SeaQuest

SeaQuest was an interesting project, created out of a crisis. It was a worthy winner of the 2006 Tilley Award. As well as providing a great example of problem-oriented policing in practice, several specific issues for problem-oriented policing emerge from it, which may be important for others involved in problem-oriented policing at a strategic or tactical level.

First, Operation SeaQuest responded to a problem that had not hitherto been recognised. It was not developed to manage existing demand on the police. There was no reference to cockle beds, cockle picking, illegal workers and antisocial behaviour associated with cockle picking in the local prequel to SeaQuest, Operation Boswell. This suggests that problem-oriented policing may have a role not only in responding to high-harm problem patterns but also in unearthing them before they surface.

Here, problem-oriented policing would not be focused on reducing demands on the police but on fostering attention to important but hidden issues, calling for an investment of time and effort not just by the police but by other organisations also.

Second, SeaQuest reminds us of how sets of crime and disorder related problems, with diverse responsibilities across a range of agencies, may be interlinked in a hot spot and that finding a simple pinch point and a way of closing it in that location could have a substantial impact. The cockle beds provided a rich set of opportunities for criminal and nuisance behaviours for which no competent organisation had overall responsibilities. It took a partnership, led by the police, to work out what could be done and to implement measures that could be effective. The police alone could not run a refreshments caravan, agree to its operation on the sands, furnish the information circulated through the caravan as a mustering point and so on: a partnership was required.

Third, SeaQuest shows how local problems can be lodged in a global context but that effective local action can be taken by reducing the immediate opportunities to prevent or ameliorate the problems whilst wider attention may also be called for. The risks of modern slavery could be reduced by making cockle pickers less anonymous, the risks of harms to all cockle pickers reduced by informing cockle pickers of the dangers they face and by enforcing regulations relating to vehicle safety and the risks of damage to fisheries reduced by curbing opportunities to sidestep regulations relating to cockle picking. However, the NWIFCA, the GLA and the legislation relating to modern slavery enhance the motivation for and scope for preventing harms on a wider scale.

Fourth, SeaQuest occurred in a police service that was heavily invested in problem-oriented policing. There was strong central support for it in Lancashire and those involved had already developed a problem-oriented-policing mentality. This mentality was not about slavishly and mechanically following the familiar SARA (Scanning, Analysis, Response and Assessment) process. Rather, it was about having a habitual orientation to problem solving, whereby it was no longer assumed that the police operate in a silo in which they are mainly concerned with responding to obvious police enforcement priorities. Instead, the mentality was one in which the key focus was on harms that fell broadly within the police remit but could often most effectively be reduced by working with others. It is, perhaps, no coincidence, that Keith Collins, a multiple problem-oriented-policing award winner, was already in Morecambe, had co-developed some foundations for the approach taken in Sea-Quest in a previous project (Operation Boswell, Collins, 2004) and helped deliver the initiative.

Notes

1 Lorraine Ellwood and Stuart Kirby provided invaluable advice in the preparation of this chapter, supplementing the information provided in the Tilley Award entries.
2 "Operation Seaquest" was the name they gave to the problem-solving initiative they mounted in the wake of the tragedy (Collins, 2006).

3 A pinch point is 'a readily available site for a measure that will reduce or eliminate a problem' (Tilley, 2009: p. 153).
4 'Gangmasters' are defined in English law as those who supply workers in agriculture, gathering shellfish and processing or packaging produce from agricultural work or shellfish and shellfish products.

References

Collins, K. (2004) *The Invisible Menace: Operation Boswell.* Submission to the Tilley Award, Lancashire Constabulary, Center for Problem-Oriented Policing, Arizona State University, Phoenix, AZ.

Collins, K. (2006) *Operation SeaQuest.* Submission to the Tilley Award, Lancashire Constabulary, Center for Problem-Oriented Policing, Arizona State University, Phoenix, AZ.

Kirby, S. & Penna, S. (2010) 'Policing mobile criminality: Towards a situational crime prevention approach to organised crime', in K. Bullock, R. Clarke & N. Tilley (eds.), *Situational Prevention of Organised Crimes*, London: Routledge, pp. 193–212.

Murray, F. & Tarrant, P. (2015) *A Social and Economic Impact Assessment of Cockle Mortality in the Burry Inlet and Three Rivers Cockle Fisheries*, South Wales, UK: Maritek Worldwide, Ltd.

NWIFCA Byelaw 3 (2012) *Permit to Fish for Cockles (Cerastoderma Edule) and Mussels (Mytilus Edulis)*, Carnforth, England: North Western Inshore Fisheries and Conservation Authority.

Tilley, N. (2009) *Crime Prevention*, London: Routledge.

13

TRAFFIC INJURIES AND FATALITIES IN FARM-LABOR VEHICLES IN CALIFORNIA

Gary Cordner

Introduction

In the literature and research on modern police strategy, almost all the attention is on crime reduction. Intelligence-led policing, predictive policing, proactive policing, hot-spots policing, risk-terrain modeling, focused deterrence—all are aimed at reducing crime. Even community policing, which arose mainly as a strategy for improving relations with the public, is often touted as a method for better engaging citizens in the fight against crime.

What is often overlooked is that a lot of police work involves incidents and problems that are either unrelated to crime or only tangentially related. To put it another way, the police mission and the outcomes that police organizations exist to achieve (the policing "bottom line") are multi-dimensional (Moore & Braga, 2003). One of the great strengths of problem-oriented policing (POP) is that it acknowledges the wide range of problems that police are asked to tackle, providing a methodology for problem solving and a framework for capturing and sharing information about what works under what conditions.

A significant dimension of police performance relates to safety in public spaces. People want highways, roads, streets, sidewalks, parks, and other common areas to be safe, and the task of regulating behavior in those places is largely assigned to police. Of course, crime does represent one threat to people's safety when they are out and about, but another big threat comes from motor vehicles. And a big threat it is—for example, in the United States, in 2016 there were more than 37,000 traffic deaths compared to 17,000 criminal homicides (National Highway Traffic Safety Administration, 2017; Federal Bureau of Investigation, 2017).

The award-winning POP project described in this chapter was aimed at reducing a particular category of traffic fatalities, and it succeeded. The impetus was a horrific crash in California in 1999 in which 13 people died. Lest one think that such mass-casualty accidents are no longer a concern, recent news in 2018 reports a limousine crash in New York State resulting in 20 deaths (Ferré-Sadurní, 2018).

Farm labor transportation safety

The California Highway Patrol won the 2002 Herman Goldstein Award for Excellence in Problem-Oriented Policing based on actions taken following the aforementioned 1999 fatal crash.[1] The agency implemented a number of short- and long-term responses under the Safety and Farm Labor Vehicle Education (SAFE) Program, an initiative that continues to this day.

Scanning

The California fatal accident occurred just after 5:00 a.m. on August 9, 1999. A van carrying 15 farmworkers collided with a tractor trailer that was making a U-turn on a two-lane road. The farmworkers were being transported home after working all night during harvest season. Thirteen of the farmworkers died in the crash.

Although driver error was certainly a causal factor of the crash, the design features of the vehicle in which they were riding contributed to the severity of the consequences. The inside of the van behind the front seats was outfitted with flat benches on either side. Passengers sat on the benches or on the floor, without seatbelts or other safety restraints.

In the immediate aftermath of the tragic incident, the California Highway Patrol (CHP) sought to determine the frequency of farm-labor-vehicle crashes, injuries, and fatalities. A review of the past eight years in the Central Valley region where the crash occurred indicated an annual average of 48 farm-labor-vehicle collisions from 1992 to 1996, with an increased rate of 62 per year between 1997 and 1999. The numbers were not considered completely reliable, though, due to inconsistent application of the label "farm-labor vehicle." Subsequent analysis added hand searches of crashes with multiple victims in order to get a better measure of the seriousness of the problem.

Transporting farm workers to and from work is a common phenomenon in California, especially in the Central Valley farming region. It was estimated at the time that there were 300,000 farm-labor jobs in the region during peak harvest season (May–September) and 100,000 such jobs the rest of the year.[2] A large proportion of the jobs were filled by migrant farmworkers, many of whom did not have vehicles or licenses and therefore were dependent on transportation provided by employers or commercial transport services.

Prior to the 1999 crash, CHP was already providing traffic-safety education within the farmworker and migrant communities and reaching out to the Hispanic community with its El Protector program, established in 1987. However, the agency came to recognize that it might need to develop a stronger focus, specifically on farm-labor-vehicle safety.

Analysis

CHP's analysis focused mainly on accident data, statutory considerations, and cultural factors. Not surprisingly, review of Central Valley crash data indicated peaks during harvest season and during the early-morning and midafternoon farmworker rush hours. Closer analysis of motor-vehicle-accident reports revealed 10 crashes of farm-labor vehicles between 1993 and 1997 that each had 10 or more casualties (inclusive of injuries and deaths). There were 18 people killed and 127 people injured in those 10 mass-casualty crashes. At least seven of the drivers in the crashes lacked proper licenses (one driver fled the scene and was not identified).

An important factor highlighted by the analysis was that motor vehicles with nine or more passenger "seats" were exempt from California's mandatory seat-belt law. As a result, the most common van-type vehicles used to transport farmworkers did not have the kinds of safety equipment taken for granted in nearly all other types of passenger vehicles in 1999. A related consideration was that passenger-safety systems, when available, were designed to protect forward-facing and backward-facing passengers, not side-facing as was common in many farm-labor-transport vehicles.

As of 1999, CHP engaged in routine vehicle inspections and driver's license checks throughout the state, including occasional task-force operations during harvest season. But the agency did not have any inspection or enforcement initiatives applied systematically or specifically to farm-labor transportation.

A variety of relevant cultural factors were identified. Migrant workers, most of whom were from Mexico, often did not speak English, and some even spoke indigenous dialects rather than Spanish. Many of the workers were young and had left school early to begin earning money that could be sent home to their families. Few had driver's licenses of their own. Transportation in their home country was often substandard and unsafe, especially in agriculture, including riding in the backs of pickup trucks. Thus, the typical farm-labor vehicles and drivers they encountered in California did not seem particularly unusual or dangerous. Of course, their employment situation was such that they would have been unlikely to complain anyway.

A related cultural factor was distrust and fear of the police, based on conditions and experiences in Mexico. If migrant farmworkers had concerns about vehicle or driver safety, they would be hesitant to turn to the police based on what they knew of police from back home. In addition, workers with questionable immigration status would have been even less inclined to contact U.S. police for fear of being detained or deported.

Response

The response was quick and multi-faceted. In less than two months, with CHP support, the California legislature passed, and the governor signed, new laws with key safety provisions:

- Farm-labor vehicles were explicitly added to the legal definition of motor vehicles, requiring each passenger position to be equipped with a safety belt.

- Drivers were prohibited from operating farm-labor vehicles unless they and each passenger were properly restrained by safety belts.
- Owners of farm-labor vehicles were made responsible for obtaining and maintaining proper vehicle inspections and certifications.
- All farm-labor vehicles were required to display an "FLV" certification sticker listing their annual inspection date.
- Penalties for illegal operation of farm-labor vehicles were enhanced.
- CHP was mandated to implement a toll-free telephone number for the public to report any observed violations by farm-labor vehicles.
- CHP was funded for 10 additional positions for farm-labor-vehicle inspection and enforcement.
- CHP was mandated to implement, in cooperation with county and local farm bureaus, a program to educate growers, farmers, vehicle owners, and drivers about safety and certification requirements.

CHP then created the SAFE program and began implementing a comprehensive inspection regime, described as follows in the Goldstein Award submission:

> CHP officers conducted regularly scheduled, non-punitive inspection operations throughout the farming regions in order to annually certify farm labor vehicles. These operations also provided opportunities to ensure drivers were properly licensed, notify drivers about safety defects that needed correction, certify that corrections had been made, and if necessary, prevent unsafe vehicles and drivers from transporting passengers. The number of sites used by CHP Motor Carrier units was expanded from two to eight. This allowed more accessibility to inspections by limiting the driving time from any point in Central Division to no more than 30 to 45 minutes.
>
> *(California Highway Patrol, 2002: p. 6)*

Enforcement was increased and targeted during the harvest season and other peak times and locations. As necessary, citations were issued and vehicles were impounded, based on vehicle and driver safety violations. When vehicles were impounded, CHP provided safe transportation for workers to their destinations.

Public education and awareness were delivered with the assistance of a variety of stakeholders, including Hispanic civic groups, health care agencies, farm-labor contractors, growers, and others. A majority of the SAFE officers were bilingual, brochures and other materials were provided in Spanish as well as English, and all communication was provided in plain language. Routine inspections and certifications were scheduled, widely publicized, and conducted in a nonpunitive manner. CHP SAFE officers appeared regularly on radio and television, including Spanish-language media, achieving local celebrity status. They also provided safety education at all kinds of community events. A toll-free telephone line was established and publicized throughout the region.

TABLE 13.1 Enforcement and inspection activity during 2000

Activity	Number
Vehicles stopped	3,492
Vehicles inspected	3,060
Vehicles certified	1,274
Vehicles taken out of service	521
Registration violations	209
Driver's license violations	949
Seat-belt violations	346
Equipment violations	2,049
Citations issued	1,201
Warnings issued	66
Enforcement/inspection contacts	8,076

Assessment

Assessment of the CHP farm-labor-vehicle initiative showed that the chosen responses were systematically implemented and that crashes and fatalities decreased. Table 13.1 reports enforcement and inspections carried out in 2000. More than 3,000 farm-labor vehicles were inspected, and 1,274 were certified as meeting legal requirements. Citations were issued in only one-third of farm-labor-vehicle stops, indicating that the emphasis was more on compliance than punishment. More than 500 vehicles were taken out of service, that is, not permitted to transport farmworkers until they were brought into compliance with safety requirements.

With regard to public education and safety awareness, SAFE officers made 195 presentations at farming community events in 2000, directly reaching an estimated 38,000 farmworkers and area residents. In addition, CHP officers were featured in more than 80 radio and television interviews and programs explaining and discussing the importance of the new inspection and certification system. The constant theme was protecting the safety of farmworkers and everyone else involved.

Beginning in 2000, CHP was able to measure farm-labor-vehicle crashes, injuries, and fatalities more accurately. Comparison to previous years was somewhat constrained by the fact that the "farm-labor vehicle" code was not consistently used prior to the August 1999 crash. Nevertheless, the data indicated that crashes and casualties did immediately decline starting with the implementation of the SAFE initiative:

- There were no farm-labor-vehicle fatalities in 2000 or 2001. These were the first zero-fatality years since 1992.
- From 2000 to 2001, total farmworker injuries in crashes dropped from 48 to 12, a 75% reduction.

- In certified farm-labor vehicles, crash injuries dropped from 31 to 5, a reduction of 84%.
- Total farm-labor-vehicle collisions went from 63 in 1999 to 17 in 2000, a 73% reduction, with an additional decline the next year (final crash numbers for 2001 were not available when the POP project submission was written in early 2002).

Follow-up

The farm-labor-vehicle-safety program was recognized for its positive impact as early as 2001 by the California legislature. As noted, the legislature approved funding in October 1999 for 10 additional CHP positions to help support the SAFE program. Funding for the positions was not available until July 1, 2000, but CHP reassigned personnel in the meantime. After initial implementation in the Central Valley region, CHP expanded the program to its other field divisions and established a SAFE unit at headquarters to coordinate statewide efforts and represent the program in the state capital.

An important subsequent statutory development came in 2002 when side-facing bench seats were prohibited in farm-labor vehicles, even if they were outfitted with safety belts. Under the new state law, farm-labor vehicles were "required to have forward-facing seats, meeting original equipment manufacturer specifications, for all passengers" (California Highway Patrol, 2002: p. 10).

The program has continued to the present as explained by CHP (Kelly, 2018):[3]

> SAFE is an important component of the CHP's community outreach efforts. It has been embraced by the community and continues to foster positive working relationships with the agriculture industry. The program's officers and supervisors receive training related to the program's operation such as Spanish language, cultural sensitivity, cultural awareness, and public affairs. Furthermore, the officers receive additional specialized training in Level 1 North American Standard inspections and advanced training on FLV [farm labor vehicle] related laws and certification procedures.
>
> The CHP conducts a comprehensive training program in Fresno annually. At this training, CHP officers and the Department's motor carrier specialists from around the state are trained in FLV inspection procedures. The CHP's jurisdiction is statewide and FLVs are everywhere farm laborers are transported. These locations include the northernmost areas near Oregon where Christmas tree farms are cultivated to the southernmost areas in San Diego where turnips are harvested. The training program provides consistency in the CHP's enforcement efforts and allows for peer to peer networking and sharing of ideas.

The positive impact on farm-labor-vehicle crashes and casualties has been maintained since 2001. According to the agency, "no CHP inspected and certified FLV have been the cause of a fatal collision since the inception of the program" (Kelly, 2018). Examining a snapshot of recent data, since the start of 2015, there has been an average of 18 farm-labor-vehicle crashes per year, compared to 63 in the 1999 baseline year, and almost identical to the 17 in 2000 despite a nearly certain increase in the number of vehicles being operated. As another positive sign of occupant safety, over half of the crashes involving certified farm-labor vehicles over the last 3-plus years have been property damage only.

Discussion

Impact

The drop in farm-labor-vehicle crashes and casualties since 1999 has been dramatic. Lives were certainly saved. However, whether the new legislation and the initiatives implemented by the California Highway Patrol deserve the credit is not self-evident. Since the revised law and practices were not applied experimentally in treatment and control areas, it is possible that something else caused the decline in crashes, injuries, and fatalities.

While rival causes (hypotheses) cannot absolutely be rejected, there is no evidence that other explanations deserve any of the credit. The bottom did not fall out of California's agricultural economy in 2000—total migrant farmworkers continued to grow, estimated at more than 800,000 by 2014 (Martin et al., 2016). Migrant workers did not suddenly start bringing their own cars with them, reducing the need for farm-labor vehicles. CHP did not implement any other new programs or strategies likely to have affected the numbers.

Significantly, the decline in crashes and casualties began immediately in 2000, following the new legislation and SAFE program implementation by CHP. A legitimate statistical concern would be a regression to the mean—any really bad year might be expected to be followed by better years. However, while 1999 was an anomaly due to one crash with 13 deaths, the preceding five years had averaged at least five farm-labor-vehicle fatalities annually, which then dropped to zero and stayed there. In addition, total farm-labor-vehicle crashes, which had averaged 53 per year from 1992 to 1999, dropped immediately below 20 and stayed down. Therefore, it is reasonable to conclude that sustained levels in the range of 70% below those in the 1990s were not likely to have occurred naturally, by chance or by any cause other than the implementation of the SAFE program.

Exemplar of problem-oriented policing

As an example of POP, the CHP farm-labor-vehicle initiative had several interesting characteristics. POP projects can be categorized in terms of the crime triangle—they might primarily be location-focused, offender-focused, or victim-focused (Center for Problem-Oriented Policing, n.d.). The SAFE initiative was mainly victim-focused, and the responses largely concentrated on migrant workers' "guardians," namely, their employers and transporters, who both had a stake in workers' safety and could be held responsible for creating and maintaining safer conditions.

Another interesting feature of the CHP project is that it was targeted at an undeniably serious problem: traffic fatalities and injuries. With all the pressure on police to reduce crime, problems related to traffic, disorder, community relations, fear, and service quality sometimes get lower priority, understandably, but this project is a reminder that crime problems are not always the most serious.

Also interesting is that the initiative was instigated by a single incident. Because POP is generally conceived as a way of responding to a series or pattern of related incidents, scanning usually involves looking for interrelated events that might have the same underlying causes or conditions (Goldstein, 1990). In this case, that is the direction that scanning took but only after one tragic case brought the issue to public and CHP attention. At that point, scanning revealed that the problem was bigger than previously recognized, in part, because the involvement of farm-labor vehicles in crashes was not previously systematically flagged in the state's accident-reporting system.

Analysis of the problem was hampered by the past failure to utilize the farm-labor-vehicles label in accident reports, but hand searching for mass-casualty crashes over the previous decade revealed an average of at least one such crash a year involving farm-labor vehicles. At that point, it might have been easy to focus on driver error, since many of the drivers in those crashes were not properly licensed, which, in turn, might have given the initiative a heavy enforcement emphasis. A crucial insight, however, was the lack of safe passenger seating in farm-labor vehicles and the realization that current law allowed such unsafe conditions. This strongly informed subsequent responses, which did not ignore driving behavior and driver licensing but mainly concentrated on improving vehicle safety. In essence, CHP took a harm-focused approach more than an enforcement-focused one.

The adoption of new laws in response to the problem might seem contrary to POP principles, since a key element of problem solving is recognizing that the law is only one tool available to police. POP practitioners are taught that a common police tendency is to turn too quickly to legalistic remedies when other responses might be more effective. In this case, however, a type of vehicle had been allowed to "slip through the cracks" of the traffic code, resulting in the very type of unsafe conditions that traffic laws are meant to regulate and prevent. The new laws were not examples of overreach, nor did they result in overenforcement, but rather they applied existing safety regulations to a previously overlooked type of vehicle. Indeed, this is very much an example of the sort of problem-oriented regulation contemplated by POP (Goldstein, 1990: p. 127).

It would be naïve not to mention that allowing vehicles transporting migrant farmers to avoid bothersome safety regulations might have been more than just oversight. Migrant workers are not voters and they certainly have less political influence than growers, owners, and larger commercial interests. It may have been the case that it took a terrible tragedy to galvanize willingness to address the situation in a meaningful way. Motivation and historical apathy notwithstanding, credit is due to the California legislature for acting swiftly and responsibly following the 1999 crash.

Once the vehicle safety laws were revised, CHP showed creativity in devising a multi-faceted response plan and then followed through managerially to make sure the plan was carried out. The plan was balanced across inspection, enforcement, and public education. The agency avoided the temptation to go all-in on one response, a "silver bullet," recognizing that utilizing multiple responses is usually more effective. Especially in a big agency, however, implementing and coordinating several responses is a harder administrative challenge. CHP seems to have been up to the task, however.

The project report identifies farm-labor-vehicle inspections and certifications as one of the responses that got the most attention and probably had a substantial impact. Establishing an annual vehicle-inspection requirement and giving CHP the authority to take farm-labor vehicles out of service if they failed the inspection not only put teeth in the program but also set up a recurring process that became routine and predictable. An element of this process that deserves mention is the FLV inspection sticker. With that sticker prominently displayed (or absent), CHP officers could easily tell if a farm-labor vehicle was in compliance with the inspection regime. Also, farmworkers could recognize whether a vehicle in which they were about to be transported was legal or not. This simple visual indicator may have been one of the more crucial components of the SAFE initiative.

Finally, the strong outreach and public education effort undertaken by CHP was a nice complement to increased inspections and enforcement. Officers were able to explain to growers, owners, and transporters why the safety regulations had been adopted and give them plenty of opportunities to come into voluntary compliance. Officers were also able to explain to the farmworkers that the new measures were enacted for their safety, emphasizing CHP's role in protecting the public, even migrant workers.

Conclusion

The CHP used problem-oriented policing to address a serious yet previously unrecognized traffic-safety problem involving the transportation of farmworkers. The agency quickly identified several factors contributing to the problem, developed responses, systematically implemented the responses, and has maintained them ever since. The number of deaths, injuries, and crashes dropped immediately and has stayed at a much lower level for nearly 20 years.

Notes

1 This section describing the POP project draws heavily on the CHP submission for the Goldstein Award (California Highway Patrol, 2002).
2 The number of farm-labor jobs is calculated on the basis of a 40-hour workweek, but many of the laborers work less than full-time. Thus, the number of farm laborers was even higher than the number of jobs cited here (Martin et al., 2016.)
3 Former CHP commissioner Joe Farrow and Officer David Kelly assisted in obtaining up-to-date information on the SAFE program and farm-labor-vehicle crashes.

References

California Highway Patrol (2002) *SAFE: A Safety and Farm Vehicle Education Program*. Submission to the Herman Goldstein Award for Excellence in Problem-Oriented Policing, Center for Problem-Oriented Policing, Arizona State University, Phoenix, AZ.

Center for Problem-Oriented Policing (n.d.) *The Problem Analysis Triangle*, Phoenix, AZ: Center for Problem-Oriented Policing, Arizona State University

Federal Bureau of Investigation (2017) *Crime in the United States, 2016*, Washington, DC: US Department of Justice, Federal Bureau of Investigation.

Ferré-Sadurní, L. (2018) 'After limo crash that killed 20, a call for more regulation', *New York Times*, October 14.

Goldstein, H. (1990) *Problem-Oriented Policing*, New York: McGraw-Hill.

Kelly, D. (2018) *Personal Communication with Officer David Kelly, Commercial Vehicle Section*, Sacramento, CA: California Highway Patrol.

Martin, P.L., Hooker, B., Akhtar, M. & Stockton, M. (2016) 'How many workers are employed in California agriculture?', *California Agriculture*, 7(1): 30–34.

Moore, M. & Braga, A. (2003) *The Bottom Line of Policing: What Citizens Should Value (and Measure) in Police Performance*, Washington, DC: Police Executive Research Forum.

National Highway Traffic Safety Administration (2017) *USDOT Releases 2016 Fatal Traffic Crash Data*, Washington, DC: US Department of Transportation.

14

REPEAT CALLERS TO POLICE IN LANCASHIRE, ENGLAND

Stuart Kirby

Introduction

Whilst viewers of popular media may be fooled into thinking that police officers are constantly chasing offenders or pitting their wits against criminal masterminds, the general reality is much more mundane. Many citizens contact the police in times of crisis for a variety of welfare and safety needs, due to their immediate availability, which is free at the point of delivery. Indeed, contrary to popular opinion, studies show that only about 20% of calls to the police are associated with crime, with a recent UK study putting this figure at 17% (College of Policing, 2015). As such, researchers often highlight the quasi–social worker role of the police, with Herman Goldstein (1977: p. 35) once pointing out that a critical police objective was to, 'assist those who cannot care for themselves: the intoxicated, the addicted, the mentally ill, the physically disabled, the old, and the young'. This means it is vitally important that police pay more serious attention to non-criminal matters emanating from vulnerable citizens. The reasons for doing so are diverse: first, it is central to the police mission; second, if left unattended the situations can escalate further requiring even more resources; third, individual vulnerability can evolve into more serious crime (as victims or offenders).

This chapter describes a Goldstein Award finalist of 2017, implemented by the Lancashire Constabulary, to assist vulnerable people who create a high level of demand on the police and other public-sector agencies. The Lancashire Constabulary covers an area of 2000 square miles in the north-west of England, inhabited by approximately 1.5 million people. The agency employs 2,889 police officers and 1920 unsworn police staff, being the 11th largest of 43 police forces in England and Wales. It is also worthy of note that from 2010 onwards, all UK police forces suffered significant budget reductions (approximately 20%), which placed renewed emphasis on managing demand.

Jurisdiction-wide problem solving: the importance of infrastructure

For projects that extend across a police jurisdiction, it is useful to have a comprehensive infrastructure which helps prepare the ground upon which successful implementation can take place. This project was supported by a two-year government grant, which enabled the constabulary to put in place six *Early Action Teams* across Lancashire to act as small problem-solving units. Furthermore, as this multi-agency initiative required the support of many agencies, the chief officers of the Lancashire Constabulary met with leaders from other public-sector agencies to secure their commitment. Once completed a monitoring meeting took place every three months at police headquarters involving representatives from up to 17 different agencies. The agencies included the Office of the Police & Crime Commissioner (responsible for local police governance), local government services (including adult and child services), the Fire & Rescue Service, Ambulance Services, Health Services, volunteer schemes, the Youth Offending Team and Probation Service. Staff at the local university (University of Central Lancashire) were also asked to assist with the evaluation, and this decision introduced myself (and some of my colleagues) to the project from the outset. With all this in place, the project began in earnest.

The problem-solving process utilising the SARA format

During the **Scanning** phase, there were initial difficulties establishing how 'vulnerable' people should be identified. Whilst accepting that not all vulnerable people require police assistance (Keay & Kirby, 2017), one individual was found to be calling the police contact centre 94 times a month, with many others ringing over 50 times a month. These individuals were also calling other services, especially ambulance, social services and mental health services.

To systematically identify these individuals, a headquarters-based analyst started to identify high-frequency numbers from 101 (non-emergency) and 999 (emergency) phone lines, taking care to remove those numbers associated with businesses, care homes, hospitals and public telephones. From the initial trawl (1 April 2015 to 1 December 2016), a total of 1,546 repeat-caller numbers were identified and passed to the local *Early Action Teams* to conduct further research. This further research showed only 866 (56%) of the callers fitted the vulnerable-caller criteria, and these were spread disproportionately across Lancashire, with one of the 14 districts composing 23% of all callers. The analysis also showed that 87% of these callers had previously been flagged as vulnerable on police systems, but due to the lack of an effective action plan, they continued to call for help.

The **analysis** phase involved a personal visit to the caller. The purpose of this was to help understand the underlying cause of the vulnerability and the impact this generated as well as establish what support they needed. This visit provided really important social context, which could not be found on police information systems, with practitioners explaining observation of the home environment often allowed the unique circumstances of the case to be understood. One example was an alcoholic suffering from a severe personality disorder. She would frequently ring the police (and the mental health crisis team) threatening to commit suicide; however, when services attended, she would become aggressive and verbally abusive towards them. The analysis found her behaviour was linked to significant childhood trauma and required a longer-term approach, which was subsequently organised. Another example relates to a woman who had been repeatedly ringing the police over many years. She shared the house with her two sons (one of whom was disabled), her grandson, and one of her son's girlfriends. Both sons had an alcohol dependency, and the family suffered domestic abuse from her husband, who had been diagnosed with dementia. Again, the underlying causes had to be teased apart and dealt with.

As academics, we were interested in identifying any underlying patterns associated with these callers. To assist we used a database compiled by Lancashire police, incorporating a list of 15 factors observed across a sample of 1,352 vulnerable callers. We placed this data into a statistical software package known as *Smallest Space Analysis* (SSA; Shye, 2014). This software calculates the likelihood of any of the 15 characteristics co-occurring and illustrates this relationship in a graphic form. Put simply, those factors which are likely to co-occur with each other are shown close to each other on a graph, whilst those unlikely to co-occur are distanced from each other. So, by way of an obvious example, Figure 14.1 highlights that *Elderly* people

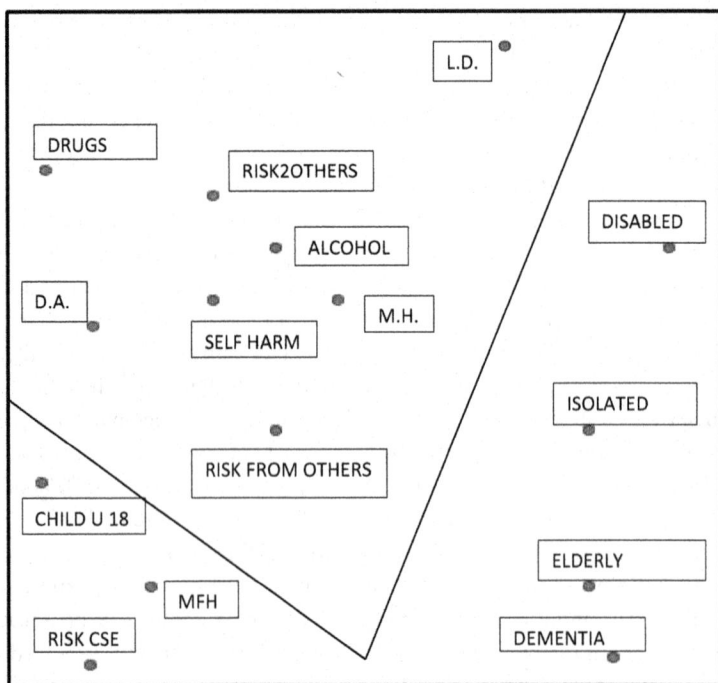

FIGURE 14.1 SSA of behavioural themes of vulnerable callers

are unlikely to be associated with suffering *Child Sexual Exploitation* (CSE), as these points are distant from each other. Conversely, *Alcohol* and *Self-harm* are likely to co-occur and are shown close to each other on the graph. Once these factors are plotted, the researcher (or practitioner) can interpret the findings to identify any patterns. We thought three themes were evident and have drawn lines on the plot to distinguish them. They comprise (a) youth-related factors (situated bottom left), (b) elderly-related factors (bottom right) and (c) vulnerable risk factors (centre). The frequency of each of these 15 factors occurring and an explanation of the abbreviations are shown in Table 14.1.

These results also show the most frequent reasons associated with repeat calls were *Mental Health* (23%), being *At Risk from Others* (20.9%) and *Domestic Abuse* (20.7%), which were all featured within the Vulnerable Risk Factor theme. This appeared to be a theme that was dominated by 'dynamic' risk factors generated through individual or situational factors, which could be changed through effective interventions (e.g. a reduction in alcohol consumption, medication, anger management). The Youth-related theme was associated with very specific issues: *Child Under 18* featured in 17% of all cases, with 3% showing *Risk from Child Sexual Exploitation*. Finally, the Elderly theme showed that 6.9% of incidents were associated with *isolation and loneliness*. This latter theme is of concern as the elderly population is predicted to grow exponentially. Age exists as a 'static' factor (i.e., we

TABLE 14.1 Frequency of factors relating to the three themes

Characteristic	*Theme*	*1352 subjects exhibiting 2105 behaviours*	*% of subjects showing behaviour*
Mental Health (MH)	Vulnerable risk factors	311	23%
At Risk from Others	Vulnerable risk factors	282	20.9%
Domestic Abuse (DA)	Vulnerable risk factors	280	20.7%
Alcohol	Vulnerable risk factors	190	14.1%
Risk to Others	Vulnerable risk factors	105	7.8%
Self-Harm	Vulnerable risk factors	100	7.4%
Drugs	Vulnerable risk factors	81	6%
Learning Disability (LD)	Vulnerable risk factors	59	4.4%
Child Under 18	Youth	230	17%
Missing from Home	Youth	103	7.6%
Risk from Child Sexual Exploitation (CSE)	Youth	41	3%
Elderly	Elderly	115	8.5%
Isolation & Loneliness	Elderly	93	6.9%
Alzheimer's & Dementia	Elderly	61	4.5%
Disabled	Elderly	54	4%

cannot get younger), and because the elderly are increasing as a proportion of society, the theme needs to be understood more fully. Overall, the police practitioners felt the analysis assisted in helping to understand the dominant themes across the repeat callers, which ultimately helped in implementing policy, as well as designing more effective interventions and training programmes.

Once the analysis had been completed the **response** phase was introduced. At the outset, the challenge of addressing the underlying challenges of vulnerable callers should be highlighted. For example, some of these individuals will have had long-standing mental illnesses, substance abuse, and ingrained personal habits and lifestyle choices. Initially, each of the 'vulnerable' individuals was assigned a lead professional (LP), who came from a variety of agencies. Members of the police *Early Action Team* provided the largest proportion of LPs (41%), whilst other police officers comprised a further 15%. Significant numbers also came from Adult and Child Social Care departments (6%) and Mental Health Services (5%). The rest came from other public-sector bodies or charitable/volunteer organisations (e.g., domestic violence advisors, Age UK—an organization to support the elderly). It was the role of the LP to meet with the frequent caller and negotiate a coordinated multi-agency response to reduce the person's vulnerability or increase his or her resilience to it. Ideally, this person would remain in the role for the duration of the intervention, but for some cases, this proved impossible.

The initial phase, when the vulnerable person made the call to the police, was critical. In the new system, these calls generated a flag which allowed the police operator to access a file note explaining the agreed action plan. This provided advice to the police operator on how to assist the caller, which often obviated the need of police or other public-sector agencies being deployed. Overall, many of the actions, either conducted by the contact centre or by the LP, were straightforward. For example, a significant number of callers (especially the elderly) were confused and called the police as a default mechanism, unable to think who else to contact. In some of these examples, the LP placed a prominent note by the caller's phone, reminding the person who to contact when becoming distressed (i.e., a friend/family member/care assistant). For others, the intervention was more complex and required referral to Mental Health Services or other professionals. It could also require applications for rehousing, or counselling over alcohol or drug use. In one example, an elderly gentleman regularly contacted the police, complaining that his neighbours were directing death threats towards him. A subsequent home visit found the individual lived in squalid conditions and was hearing voices. As a result, the allegations were dismissed, and the individual was helped to relocate to more suitable accommodation, with welfare support. Each month, all cases involving the vulnerable callers were discussed with local supervisors to generate ideas and provide support for the practitioners.

Two more case studies serve as useful examples to understand this tailored approach. The first involves a 61-year-old male, whose background was as a senior professional with a stable family life. However, following the breakdown of his marriage, he became a reclusive and homeless alcoholic who let his personal hygiene slip. Domestic-abuse incidents involving his ex-wife resulted in a court injunction to stay away from the family home. However, whilst drunk, he persistently contacted police or ambulance services and expressed violent and suicidal thoughts. This led to him being detained three times, under powers provided by the UK Mental Health Act. Following the introduction of an LP, he was found a place in a mental health facility. On his return, he was further supported by his LP, who arranged a six-month alcohol rehabilitation course. He also received weekly visits from his LP, who introduced him to additional support to assist with his depression and alcohol addiction, as well as helping him clean and decorate his home. Contact with his family was reinitiated and he remains sober. Whilst his involvement with the programme has now finished, he has worked as a volunteer to assist ex-addicts, recently released from prison, to rebuild their lives.

In a further case study, a 48-year-old male repeatedly called the police for no apparent reason (apart from saying he liked to listen to police radios). A home visit found he had recently become blind after cataract surgery and was wary of going outside. Mental health issues were also suspected. Over a six-month period, this man called the police unnecessarily 565 times (94 times a month), at an estimated cost of £33,867 ($44,470), as well as contacting other agencies. An LP from the *Early Action Team* began to work with this male, referring him to a third-sector organization who provided a mentor to assist him in socialising. He was also provided with details of volunteers who supported people with poor mental health or loneliness. In addition, the male was provided with a CB radio which allowed him to contact his brother and listen to the radio. At the time of assessment, his calls had reduced to nine times a month.

Whilst these case studies provide inspiring examples of success, we also saw the LPs experience frustration when the caller failed to keep appointments or follow the agreed action plan.

In an attempt to obtain a wider view during the **assessment** phase, we looked at four evaluation elements. The first element looked specifically at the frequency of *Calls for Service* and *Deployments*. In these we randomly identified a representative group of 259 callers, whose intervention allowed a six-month before-and-after assessment. These individuals made 11,123 calls to the police (via either the 999 or 101 telephone lines) in the six months prior to the intervention, and 8,231 calls in the six months after the intervention start date. This 26% reduction ($n = 2,892$) of calls to the police contact centre was found to be statistically significant, using a paired samples t-test, $t(258) = 3.466, p < .01$. Correspondingly, *police deployments* were reduced by 116 deployments (–6.2%), although a paired t-test indicated no statistical significance ($p > .05$). More information as to why these particular tests were used can be found in a range of sources (see Babinec & Stehlik-Barry, 2017).

Early Action Team practitioners suggested that different types of vulnerability created different levels of need and requirement from public services. To explore their hypothesis, we compared those who had been identified with a mental health issue (including dementia) with other vulnerable categories. Using a Mann–Whitney U analysis, it was established that those with identified mental health issues were significantly more likely to call at a higher rate to the police, compared with those who had no identified MH issue ($p < .05$). Furthermore, these showed the biggest reduction in calls following the intervention. Therefore, whilst MH-related callers made an average of 48 calls six months prior to intervention, these reduced to 38 in the six months post-intervention. This 21% reduction was statistically significant, $t(125) = 2.090$, $p < .05$, which indicated those with MH issues were a category most likely to benefit from an intervention.

Attempts were made to establish if the interventions actually benefitted the caller (rather than just diverting them from calling the police). This was explored using the Warwick-Edinburgh Mental Well-being Scale, often abbreviated as WEMWBS (Tennant et al., 2007). The purpose of the questionnaire is to allow the callers to report upon their well-being, before and after receiving support (examining levels of happiness, life satisfaction and psychological functioning). LPs from the *Early Action Team* officers were requested to complete this well-being questionnaire when meeting clients during their first visit and then again every three months. We received very few forms back, and in asking why this was the case, the officers reported being uncomfortable in completing them for two main reasons. First, they reported that the service users often had low self-esteem and that they felt the questionnaire would embed these negative feelings further. Second, they questioned whether filling out forms, and asking personal questions, would affect relationship building. This meant at the time of the evaluation only 47 questionnaires had been returned (13% of those expected), with only seven individuals completing the questionnaire on two occasions. Most of the individuals captured in this process were female, with age ranging from 36 to 81 years (average 58 years). Based on total scores, five service users ($n = 71\%$) indicated that their mental well-being had improved, whilst the mental well-being of two services users decreased (29%). More research was needed to generate robust conclusions.

Finally, we looked at whether there was any difference in the results across the LP groups, specifically comparing *Early Action Team* personnel with others. We divided a random sample of 259 vulnerable callers into one group of 155 callers (59%) who had been managed by the *Early Action Team* personnel and a group of 104 callers (41%) whose LP came from a specialist organization not connected with the police. These LPs could come from a wide variety of other public-sector organisations (e.g., Social Services) or third sector (e.g. volunteers working on behalf of a charity looking after the aged or those with mental illness). The analysis found the police *Early Action Team* were associated with a larger reduction in the average number of calls, post-intervention, than non-police LPs (29% to 21%; 12 calls compared with 9 calls per caller), although this difference was not statistically significant, $t(257) = -1.112$, $p > .05$. This trend was even more apparent in relation to deployments. Whilst there was a 16.5% reduction for clients with an *Early Action Team* LP, there was a 2.7% increase in deployments associated with other LPs. To put it another way, those individuals assisted by *Early Action Team* personnel show an average reduction of 8.6 deployments, whilst clients of other LPs are associated with an increase of 1.5 deployments. Although this is a clear trend, the sample was not large enough to be statistically significant, $t(344) = -1.385$, $p > .05$.

Follow-up

The funding behind this project finished following the evaluation and the dedicated headquarters-based support and partner meetings have also disappeared. However, the philosophy remains, with the approach to vulnerable people now mainstreamed. This means that high-intensity vulnerable callers are still identified, and action plans are put in place to assist them. Furthermore, there is an ongoing and ambitious project to integrate electronic information, from police and social services databases, to identify and assist vulnerable callers more effectively. However, no further monitoring is taking place, and as such, there is no further information as to longer-term actions and effects of the initiative.

Observations on the case study

In conclusion (when considered in its totality), there was a strong consensus from all involved that the project was successful. This was no doubt supported by the three themes associated with good project implementation (Rosenbaum, 1986). The project was founded on clear academic theory, which shows incidents occur disproportionately and that the instigation of a problem-solving approach can reduce their incidence. Also, the project was supported with sufficient resources and management, and finally the process was evaluated to establish whether it had indeed generated a change in calls, deployments and behaviour.

The project also generates further important points. First, non-crime calls are an increasing source of demand, and this trend persists over time and across different countries. The Elderly theme is of specific concern as this demographic will grow and generate further demand on public-sector agencies in coming years. When added with the many other characteristics of vulnerability highlighted by Goldstein more than 40 years ago, it appears that assisting the vulnerable is a major strategic issue. Very few police forces appear to take a systematic approach to this issue; however, the Lancashire Constabulary has shown that a measurable impact can be achieved if an explicit strategy is implemented based upon problem-oriented policing principles.

Second, it should be highlighted that individual-level success is not always guaranteed. Even when problem solving is theoretically possible it still needs effective implementation and requires committed practitioners. Many of the vulnerable callers had long-standing mental illnesses, substance abuse, ingrained personal habits, and lifestyle choices, which proved difficult to change. If vulnerable callers were not fully committed to change their condition (e.g. to reduce their alcohol or drug consumption or to avoid the individual they were in conflict with), it was unlikely to occur. Progress surrounding change was also inconsistent and set-backs were common. Ultimately (and this was supported by practitioner focus groups), success was aligned with five critical factors:

- Participation of a Vulnerable Caller who is motivated to change
- A skilled and committed practitioner who can engage effectively with the caller

- A clear definition of the underlying cause of the problem
- An action-oriented, evidence-based plan
- Effective implementation of the proposed solution

Third, and this appeared counter-intuitive at the time, the LPs from the *Early Action Teams* appeared to be associated with a greater impact, even though they had less experience and specialist skills than did LPs from specialist agencies. We explored this further in practitioner interviews and focus groups, and it appeared this had more to do with the police and the special role that they were able to play in addressing these complex cases. Their sense of discretion, coupled with their flexibility in addressing some of these problems, appeared to be much more developed. Whilst rarely using official powers to compel the assistance and coordination of others their willingness to accept responsibility and accountability, as well as their persistence and level of knowledge, was particularly effective. Police personnel appeared more likely to take a more pragmatic and problem-oriented approach, explaining (and we saw evidence of this) that they were less likely to be deflected by a procrastinating caller and more likely to persuade other agencies to assist in a timely fashion.

In contrast, other agencies appeared to lack this flexibility. Practitioners from other specialist agencies were often constrained by mandatory thresholds and treatment pathways. This meant they were unable to take specific action until the person's condition reached a specific intensive level, which was counter-intuitive as the philosophy of prevention requires early intervention. Furthermore, responses to particular conditions were often specifically designated, which generated specific treatments rather than a nuanced package which was specifically tailored to the caller.

Finally (and perhaps unsurprisingly), I would encourage practitioners to get academics on-board at an early stage. Whilst police officers are busy trying to solve operational challenges, an academic has the time and the skills to look at the evidence and reflect objectively on the findings. This means the researcher can find patterns and make sense of things that the officer has not the time or inclination to explore. Inviting an academic in at the start helps both parties establish the effectiveness of the project much more ably.

Acknowledgements

Special thanks to Inspector Christina Shorrock and Ms Christy Frampton (Lancashire Constabulary), who provided data, understanding and general support. Also, to Drs Sarah Shorrock, Rom Okeke, Michelle McManus Laura Boulton, Lauren Metcalfe and Rebecca Phythian (University of Central Lancashire), who all assisted with the evaluation of the project.

References

Babinec, A.J. & Stehlik-Barry, K. (2017) *Data Analysis for IBM SPSS Statistics*, Birmingham, UK: Packt Publishing.

College of Policing (2015) *College of Policing Analysis: Estimating Demand on the Police Service*, Ryton: College of Policing.

Goldstein, H. (1977) *Policing a Free Society*, Cambridge, MA: Ballinger. Republished as Goldstein, H. (1990) *Policing a Free Society*, Madison, WI: University of Wisconsin Law School.

Keay, S. & Kirby, S. (2017) 'Defining vulnerability: From the conceptual to the operational', *Policing: A Journal of Policy and Practice*. doi:10.1093/police/pax046

Rosenbaum, D.P. (1986) *Community Crime Prevention: Does It Work?*, Beverly Hills, CA: Sage Publishing.

Shye, S. (2014) 'Faceted smallest space analysis (Faceted SSA: FSSA)', in A.C. Michalos (ed.), *Encyclopedia of Quality of Life and Well-Being Research*, Dordrecht, Germany: Springer.

Tennant, R., Hiller, L., Fishwick, R., Platt, S., Joseph, S., Weich, S., Parkinson, J., Secker, J. & Stewart-Brown, S. (2007) 'Warwick-Edinburgh Mental Well-being Scale (WEMWBS): Development and UK validation', *Health and Quality of Life Outcomes*, 5(63): 1.

15

OPIOID ABUSE IN RENO, NEVADA

Emmanuel Barthe, Deena DeVore,
and Stacy Ward

Introduction

Prescription drug misuse has become a serious drug problem across the United States. The abuse of prescription drugs is now growing faster than any other drug problem in our country, and this epidemic is not only rampant but also deadly. The problem is multifaceted in that prescription drugs are easily obtained from medical professionals or taken from household medicine cabinets, their potency is quite high (especially dangerous when mixed with other drugs), and there is a perception that their pharmaceutical nature makes them safer than traditional illicit drugs bought on the street. All these factors explain the rapid spread of the prescription drug problem plaguing so many jurisdictions today. The Centers for Disease Control & Prevention (CDC) recently reported that one person dies from prescription drug abuse every 19 minutes in the United States (Centers for Disease Control & Prevention, 2012). Medications that were intended to alleviate suffering are being diverted, overused, and abused, and it is costing lives.

In 2016, 665 Nevadans died from a drug overdose. In Washoe County (northern Nevada) alone, prescription drug overdoses were responsible for 43 of the 110 drug overdose deaths in 2016 (Washoe County Medical Examiner Report, 2017). That number equates to 21.7 deaths per 100,000 residents, above the national average of 19.8, according to a recently released study by the CDC (NCHS, 2016).

In short, the national reliance on these dangerous pills for pain relief needs to be addressed from multiple angles, but primarily, two main things need to be examined: (1) Who is taking all of these medications, and (2) From whom are they getting them?

Description of the data

This problem-solving approach to prescription drug abuse was part of a Bureau of Justice Assistance grant designed to use the Nevada Board of Pharmacy's prescription drug monitoring program data to identify patients who engaged in doctor shopping and to identify doctors who appeared to prescribe opioid-based medications excessively.[1] For this project, the pharmacy board provided deidentified prescription records for seven years (2011–2017). During this time frame, there were more than 32 million controlled-substance prescriptions filled in the state of Nevada.

It was decided to exclude prescriptions that exceeded 30 pills per day, and prescriptions that exceeded 2,000 morphine milligram equivalents (MMEs) per day. According to the CDC, the recommended daily dosage should not exceed 90 MMEs. Therefore, these extreme cases were removed from the database, and the ongoing analysis focused on prescriptions that involved fewer than 30 pills per day and where MMEs were less than 2,000 per day.[2]

Overview of prescriptions in Nevada

Tables 15.1 and 15.2 depict the overall picture of prescriptions filled in Nevada. Between 2011 and 2017, physicians wrote more than 29 million prescriptions for all controlled drugs, 28 million of which dispensed only pills, and of those, over

TABLE 15.1 Prescription drug demographics in Nevada,* 2011–2017

	Prescriptions for all Drugs	All Drugs (pills only)	Prescriptions for all Controlled Drugs	Controlled Drugs (pills only)	Opioids (pills only)
Number of prescribers	16,559	16,423	16,238	16,062	14,488
Number of patients	2,462,989	2,294,847	2,320,083	2,168,180	1,852,679
Number of pharmacies	1,558	1,511	1,452	1,438	1,244
Number of prescriptions	29,856,708	28,340,615	28,050,379	26,940,099	14,316,422

* Values represent prescriptions filled in the state of Nevada.

TABLE 15.2 Prescriptions for all controlled drugs, Nevada cases,* 2011–2017

Drug Type	Number of Prescriptions	Percentage
Opioid	14,177,566	52.63
Stimulant	2,191,565	8.13
Barbiturate/Benzodiazepine	7,078,947	26.28
Opioid mix	14	0.00
Sedative/sleeping pill	3,492,007	12.96
Total	26,940,099	100.00

* Values represent prescriptions filled in the state of Nevada.

TABLE 15.3 Opioid prescriptions: pills only, Nevada cases,* 2011–2017

Opioid Type	Number of Pills	Number of Prescriptions
Hydrocodone	521,229,842	7,246,997
Oxycodone	372,664,733	4,145,612
Tramadol	80,105,926	1,029,511
Morphine	59,880,642	847,863
Methadone	45,543,368	346,900
Hydromorphone	17,110,754	190,877
Oxymorphone	8,013,151	119,194
Codeine	6,180,141	86,111
Tapentadol	3,703,921	51,740
Buprenorphine	2,494,262	81,144
Meperidine	664,690	12,779
Pentazocine	128,780	1,526
Levorphanol	37,163	262
Opium	5,746	289
Butorphanol	180	6
Total	1,117,763,300	14,160,811

* Values represent prescriptions filled in the state of Nevada, with 31-plus pills per day removed and 2000 plus daily MMEs removed.

14 million were opioid-based. Given that the state has a total population of 2.99 million residents, these are significant numbers. Table 15.2 indicates that over 52% of all controlled-substance prescriptions involved opioid-based medications, with barbiturates and benzodiazepines coming in second with 26.2%. Table 15.3 shows that doctors issued over 14 million prescriptions for opioids, totaling more than 1 billion pills collected by patients during the study period, with hydrocodone being the most prescribed opioid type. These numbers mirror national trends.

Applying the SARA model to the problem

Scanning

Scanning the prescription drug monitoring program data, the researchers quickly noticed that there were some prescriptions that stood out in terms of the dosage and quantity of the drugs prescribed. This led to the conclusion that the analysis should focus on patients, doctors, and pharmacies to identify "heavy hitters" and individuals responsible for potential drug-diversion practices.

As with physicians, identifying patients who engage in doctor shopping is important. Identifying problem patients is similar to identifying problem doctors.

For problem patients, it entails looking for outliers in the number of prescriptions received within a certain time frame, the number of opioid prescriptions, the number of doctors visited, and some of the additional indicators described below.

Analysis

Identification of problem physicians

Doctors can be considered as "high prescribing" if they exceed the average rate. Of course, some doctors (such as oncologists, end-of-life physicians, or long-term care professionals) legitimately exceed the average because of their patients' special medication needs.

During the research timeframe (2011–2017), there were 16,559 medical professionals who prescribed controlled drugs in Nevada. These included physicians, advanced-practice registered nurses, and physicians' assistants. The majority of these medical professionals will remain within normal boundaries when it comes to prescribing patterns. Physicians who overprescribe risk addiction (and possible fatal overdoses) for their patients, and they compromise the integrity of the medical profession. Hence, the emphasis of this research is to identify medical professionals who stand out in terms of the *nature* and *quantity* of pills they prescribe.

Type of prescriptions

An initial indicator of a doctor's proclivities toward opioid prescription is to look at the percentage of their controlled substance prescriptions that are opioid-based. Obviously, depending on the nature of the medical professional's specialty, these percentages will vary. For instance, an oncologist or pain-management specialist should have higher percentages of opioid prescriptions than should pediatricians or podiatrists. A simple sorting procedure can identify the top physicians who have exceptionally high rates of opioid-based prescriptions. Table 15.4 shows that for about one-quarter of the doctors who prescribed any opioids, opioids composed more than 94% of their total controlled substance prescriptions.

TABLE 15.4 Percentage of prescribers' total prescriptions that are opioids,* 2011–2017

Percentage of Opioid Prescriptions	Number of Prescribers	Percentage
0–40	3,652	25.20
41–73	3,674	25.40
74–93	3,600	24.80
94+	3,562	24.60
Total	14,488	100.00

* *Prescribers who have prescribed at least one opioid pill prescription.*
(N = 14,488 prescribers; mean = 64.75%; median = 73.00%)

Quantity of pills

Another facet of the analysis is to examine the sheer number of pills that are pre-scribed. The opioid abuse problem has grown because of "pill diversion". This is when legitimately prescribed pills are either stolen or sold for unintended purposes. An example would be if a patient goes in for a routine dental procedure, receives a prescription for 60 OxyContin pills, takes only three to help with the pain, and then forgets the rest in the medicine chest. A family member or friend then helps him- or herself to the remaining pills, either for personal use or for resale. The quantity of pills prescribed can also be a problem when patients simply take too many pills based on the prescription and develop an addiction to the pain-relieving and euphoric effects of the opioids.

The quantity of pills analysis is perhaps the simplest of all the analyses in that it examines solely the sheer number of pills prescribed. As mentioned earlier, prescrip-tions with a pill quantity greater than 30 per day were eliminated from the data set as the pharmacy board deemed these cases unlikely and probably errors. In order to identify the doctors who prescribed high numbers of pills, we collapsed the number of prescribed pills per day into three categories (1–10 pills, 11–20 pills, and 21–30 pills) and focused on all the doctors that fell into the third category. With a simple sorting procedure, Table 15.5 shows the top doctors with the greatest num-ber of pills prescribed during the research period. In terms of the number of pills, one doctor had 176 instances where he or she prescribed 21 to 30 pills per day per patient for a total of 111,668 pills. That is an average of 634 pills per prescription.

TABLE 15.5 Total number of pills for top Nevada prescribers, 2011–2017

Prescriber*	Total Pills Prescribed	Number of Prescriptions	Average Number of Pills by Prescription
Doc	111,668	176	634.48
Doc	81,680	136	600.59
Doc	69,011	199	346.79
Doc	63,980	165	387.76
Doc	62,506	149	419.5
Doc	54,939	79	695.43
Doc	37,780	111	340.36
Doc	32,546	56	581.18
Doc	31,278	46	679.96
Doc	30,680	82	374.15

* Out of the 14,488 Nevada prescribers who have prescribed at least one opioid pill prescription in the research time from (2011–2017), 1,132 prescribers have opioid prescriptions in the 21–30-pills-per-day range grouping. (N = 1,132 prescribers in 21–30 pills per day grouping; mean = 1,618.19 total pills prescribed; median = 180 total pills prescribed)

TABLE 15.6 Number of prescriptions for top prescribers, 2011–2017

Prescriber*	Number of Prescriptions
Doc	86,469
Doc	56,818
Doc	55,506
Doc	55,107
Doc	54,716
Doc	51,891
Doc	51,021
Doc	48,311
Doc	47,188
Doc	47,010

* Deidentified prescriber DEA number.
(N = 14,484 prescribers; mean = 977.69 prescriptions; median = 80.00 prescriptions)

While this doctor was not the highest offender in terms of the total pills pre-scribed, it is interesting to examine some of the potential signs of overprescribing: one doctor wrote 9,277 different prescriptions over the course of the seven years, had 762 patients, and prescribed over 1,000,000 opioid pills, 46% of which were hydrocodone. These numbers are deemed high when compared to the mean and the median of the other active physicians. For example, the analysis showed that the mean number of prescriptions was 977 per doctor and that the median number was 80. In terms of the number of patients, the mean was 328, and the median was 51. Numerous doctors had numbers well above these averages.

Tables 15.5 and 15.6 can also help identify questionable prescribers by showing the medical professionals with the highest number of prescriptions. For example, one physician wrote 86,469 prescriptions, with the second-highest writing 56,818.

Response

Publicity about a problem and education on possible harm-reduction techniques are effective to target specific crime problems such as this (Barthe, 2006). In an effort to limit the available supply of opioids and other commonly abused prescrip-tion drugs, such as benzodiazepines, a focused educational campaign was carried out targeting prescribers of these medications—physicians, nurse practitioners, and physicians' assistants. The presentation of information about questionable prescrib-ing practices was delivered by local doctors and a nationally recognized physician and expert in opioid addiction and chronic pain treatment. This communication approach served to establish legitimacy in two ways: (1) a face-to-face interac-tion motivates the participants and fosters relevant discussion and (2) the perceived professional background of the speaker lends credence to the training itself (Martin, Kolomitro & Lam, 2014). Local physician speakers help participants connect the educational content to their daily tasks. Having both types of speakers provides the audience both *context* (a nationally recognized speaker illustrates the topic as it unfolds in other areas) and *content* (local speakers illustrate the topic as it unfolds in their immediate environment). The speakers discussed laws regarding prescribing of controlled substances and how to ensure compliance, as well as the surprisingly low success rates in treating chronic pain with opioid medications, suggesting to the audience that prescribing them they may be doing patients more harm than good. The goal of these educational events was to raise awareness in the medical community on proper prescribing patterns. The hope was that after exposure to the information provided by the medical peers, prescribing rates of opioid medications would decrease.

Assessment

One particular educational event invited more than 200 medical professionals from the northern part of the state, with 192 attending. Of those 192 individuals, 163 were prescribing professionals, and others were medical administrators. In order to compare prescribing behaviors before and after the presentation, only doctors that had prescribed controlled substances in the three months before and after the training were selected for the assessment of the educational event.

Ultimately, there were 65 physicians who met the criteria. A comparison group of doctors that were matched on geographic region, prescribing patterns, and average–pills–per–day prescription rates were also monitored for the same periods.

Several measures were used to gauge the effectiveness of the educational campaigns: (1) levels of MMEs prescribed by physicians, (2) quantity of pills per prescription, and (3) overall number of prescriptions for opioid-based medications. For this particular chapter, we focus only on the number of pills prescribed, as this is the best indicator of prescribing patterns and the most salient since we are primarily concerned about the sheer number of pills released out into society.

As we can see from Table 15.7, the 65 prescribers were separated into three groups (low, medium, and high prescribers), and we compared the total number of pills they prescribed pre- and post-training. Table 15.8 shows the comparison group's prescribing patterns pre- and post-training. When it comes to the number of opioid pills dispensed, Table 15.7 shows that doctors who attended training and were in the low-prescribing category had an overall 24% decrease in the number of pills prescribed. The medium prescribers had a total of 12% decrease, and the high prescribers had a 29% decrease in the number of pills prescribed. Across all groups, doctors who attended the training prescribed 23% fewer pills than before the training. The comparison group only experienced a 3% decrease. When looking at individual drug types, hydrocodone experienced the largest decrease in prescriptions among doctors attending the training, with a 26% drop in the low prescribers, a 27% drop in the medium prescribers, and a 33% drop in high prescribers. The

TABLE 15.7 Number of opioid pills dispensed by training group ($N = 65*$) February 2017 to August 2017

Opioid Type	Pre-Training	Post-Training	Overall Percentage Difference
*Low Prescribers***			
Codeine	1,473	798	−46
Hydrocodone	44,434	32,807	−26
Hydromorphone	3,092	2,647	−14
Methadone	1,250	1,750	40
Morphine	24,036	14,413	−40
Oxycodone	37,184	28,137	−24
Oxymorphone	2,700	2,430	−10
Tramadol	17,394	17,542	1
Total	**133,577**	**102,139**	**−24**
*Medium Prescribers****			
Codeine	540	450	−17
Hydrocodone	45,258	33,073	−27
Hydromorphone	2,244	2,784	24
Methadone	4,816	5,208	8
Morphine	14,840	16,098	8
Oxycodone	44,222	40,159	−9
Oxymorphone	266	720	171
Tramadol	9,982	9,144	−8
Total	**122,708**	**108,086**	**−12**
*High Prescribers*****			
Codeine	440	640	45
Hydrocodone	92,834	62,617	−33
Hydromorphone	6,720	5,496	−18
Methadone	4,580	5,120	12
Morphine	3,240	2,500	−23
Oxycodone	86,755	60,971	−30
Oxymorphone	720	1,200	67
Tramadol	29,120	20,250	−30
Total	**224,409**	**158,794**	**−29**
Grand Total	480,694	369,019	−23

* Of the 163 prescribers who attended the May 2017 training, only 65 had written a pill prescription at least once during both the pre- and posttraining period.
** Prescribers in the 25th percentile grouping, between 0–60 pills prescribed overall.
*** Prescribers in the 50th percentile grouping, between 61–90 pills prescribed overall.
**** Prescribers in the 75th percentile grouping, between 91–120 pills prescribed overall/

TABLE 15.8 Number of opioid pills dispensed by comparison group ($N = 65*$) February 2017 to August 2017

Opioid Type	Pre-Training	Post-Training	Overall Percentage Difference
Codeine	1,045	1,300	24
Hydrocodone	96,630	93,164	−4
Hydromorphone	1,004	876	−13
Methadone	138	182	32
Morphine	2,295	1,935	−16
Oxycodone	5,030	4,078	−19
Oxymorphone	55,317	53,057	−4
Tramadol	60,126	60,937	1
Total	221,585	215,529	−3

* Of the 163 prescribers who attended the May 2017 training, only 65 had written a pill prescription at least once during both the pre- and posttraining period.

comparison group only experienced a 4% decrease in hydrocodone prescriptions (see Table 15.8). These tables clearly show that the educational event decreased the number of pills released into households and medicine cabinets.

Discussion

The educational component response positively affected prescribing behaviors. While the slight drop in the comparison group (−3%) probably reflects slow changes in behavior due to the media coverage of the opioid crisis, the importance of education is clearly shown in the 23% reduction of the "training" group. We are aware that there is a chance that the prescribers who attended the training did not do so out of pure concern of the overprescription problem: many simply attended to receive continuing education credits or for some other professional reason. Motive aside, the impact of sharing of relevant information with the prescribing community cannot be disputed and the reduction in prescribing patterns may be attributed to several factors.

First, from evaluation surveys collected after previous training, we noted that physicians routinely stated that they simply were not aware of the extent of the opioid addiction problem or that they did not know how to handle doctor shoppers effectively. There was a general feeling of isolation, with many physicians feeling lost in how to combat this problem. These educational sessions have the benefit of showing medical professionals that they are not alone in the fight against opioid diversion, and they also provided a forum where doctors and nurses can share experiences, effective practices, and general concerns when it comes to opioid addiction. This creation of a temporary "prescribing community" reduces the anonymity of individual prescribers and the audience members suddenly become active participants in addressing this problem.

Second, these educational sessions have the benefit of educating doctors about regulatory mechanisms by which their prescribing behaviors can be checked and monitored. Many physicians are aware of the prescription drug monitoring program, but many feel as though the regulatory agencies will focus on "the other guy". Having a fellow physician explain how questionable prescribing behaviors can be flagged by a simple query and the legal ramifications involved makes not only the problem but also the consequences less abstract. The opioid crisis is then made relevant to their everyday working lives. It is unignorable and shifts from passive knowledge (abstract and disconnected to daily tasks) to more active knowledge in the sense that the problem and consequences are concretely defined, and this knowledge is routinely used by the physician.

Third, training and educational events impact social norms. Like many very specialized professions, the medical community tends to be insular by nature and wary of outsiders criticizing their methods and means. By having a fellow physician discuss and share knowledge about the problem of opioid addiction, social norms of the profession are slowly changed by having the speakers address the desired behaviors, as opposed to having a speaker that merely chastises and threatens the audience with possible repercussions. Ultimately, a great majority of prescribing professionals want the best for their patients, and these educational moments allow them to be exposed to alternate paths to patient care. By discussing the desired social norms of the profession, these events paint a broad picture of the accepted practices of the field. Given the closed nature of the profession, few physicians will risk appearing as if they are out of the "common" circle and will most likely adopt the recommended guidelines of the broader profession. The increased use of prescriber report cards (easily manufactured reports of prescriber patterns) and the increased publicity about regulatory agencies monitoring the Prescription Drug Monitoring Program (PDMP) closely, adds to this professional peer pressure to not stand out and draw unwanted attention.

Obviously, these training sessions will not eradicate the opioid problem in the region, but they do reduce the harm by reducing the number of pills that are available for diversion. Reducing the number of local opioid pills by 100,000-plus three months after the training is a significant harm reduction strategy. While beneficial in reducing the number of available pills, these training sessions cannot be seen as the panacea when it comes to the opioid epidemic. A broader discussion about pain management and the reliance on pills to treat every ill needs to be fostered across all communities. When problem doctors or patients are identified through this type of research, law enforcement agencies should follow through and investigate those actors as they would conventional drug rings. In the end, this problem will become less of a social threat when health professionals, pain specialists, counselors, police officials, and concerned families all become part of a comprehensive strategy that addresses all aspects of this drug problem.

While only a small part of the overall solution, this research effort on physician education demonstrates that by bringing the medical community together and informing them of the pitfalls of opioid diversion, some success can be achieved.

Finally, an added benefit to this type of intervention is that in a single afternoon, or in a single two-hour session, several hundred physicians can be reached at a time (with relatively low cost), allowing important information to be disseminated within the medical community, hopefully reducing future opioid addictions.

Notes

1 These findings are the sole property of the listed project partners, and may not be shared, disseminated or sold without the express permission of the Reno Police Department. This project was supported by Grant No. 2015-PM-BX-K005 awarded by the Bureau of Justice Assistance. The Bureau of Justice Assistance is a component of the Department of Justice's Office of Justice Programs, which also includes the Bureau of Justice Statistics, the National Institute of Justice, the Office of Juvenile Justice and Delinquency Prevention, the Office for Victims of Crime, and the SMART Office. Points of view or opinions in this document are those of the author and do not necessarily represent the official position or policies of the U.S. Department of Justice.
2 Only prescriptions involving pills were considered, as those dealing with liquids, patches, ointments, and so on made some calculations difficult. Finally, only prescriptions written in the state of Nevada were included in this analysis and physician U.S. Drug Enforcement Agency numbers have been scrambled to protect their identity.

References

Barthe, E. (2006) *Crime Prevention Publicity Campaigns*, Problem-Oriented Guides for Police, Response Guide No. 5, Washington, DC: US Department of Justice, Office of Community Oriented Policing Services.

Centers for Disease Control and Prevention (2012) *Morbidity and Mortality Weekly Report*, January.

Centers for Disease Control and Prevention & National Center for Health Statistics (2016) *Drug Overdose Deaths*. Retrieved from www.cdc.gov/drugoverdose/data/statedeaths.html

Martin, B.O., Kolomitro, K. & Lam, T.C.M. (2014) 'Training methods: A review and analysis', *Human Resource Development Review*, 13(1), 11–35.

Washoe County Medical Examiner (2017) *Report*.

PART IV

Disorderly places

16

DISORDERLY DAY LABORERS IN GLENDALE, CALIFORNIA

Rob T. Guerette

Introduction

Few issues in the developed world are as pressing and contentious as those involving the management of illegal migration. The control of immigration, authorized or not, is squarely the responsibility of federal governments. Yet, because of the deeply rooted and differing views on what exactly should be done to address undocumented immigration, most actions by the US government over the last several decades have largely been symbolic and, for the most part, ineffective at curtailing the flow of migrants entering the country. These government efforts have mostly focused on enhanced border fortification and sequential judicial policy enactments which are marked by increasing punitiveness. Largely neglected has been any substantial increase in workplace enforcement within the US interior. The reason why the federal government has fallen short of achieving meaningful immigration reform is due to the lack of any majority consensus. Even within the prevailing political parties, considerable divisions exist.

While the quagmire of federal government efforts to curtail or assist in the management of undocumented migration continues, the problems that arise from uncontrolled immigration flows undoubtedly fall on many local jurisdictions across the country, particularly those along the southern border region. Local-jurisdiction concerns in dealing with migrant populations are often related to perceptions of increased crime; increased demands on governmental systems, particularly schools and hospitals; decreasing property values as migrants concentrate in specific neighborhoods; as well as greater disorder and disruption within communities where migrants attempt to find employment. Another concern is that their undocumented status also makes migrants more susceptible as crime victims since they may be less likely to call for police assistance for fear of deportation. Equally true is that immigrants provide benefits for many jurisdictions. Most notably they provide relatively cheap labor for an assortment of industries such as restaurants, hotels, farming, manufacturing, landscaping, and construction, among others. This circumstance allows many local businesses to prosper and sustain themselves when they otherwise could not.

This situation poses many challenges for local jurisdictions when confronted with trying to manage the tribulations associated with the presence of immigrants within their communities. In most cases, this has meant that the police have found themselves at the forefront of dealing with these problems. This chapter presents an overview of one early 1990s' problem-oriented policing project that tackled the problem of disorderly day laboring within a southern California community. The project was submitted for consideration of the Herman Goldstein Awards for Excellence in Problem-Oriented Policing in 1997 and was the overall winner for that year. The project is notable for several reasons, but mostly because it effectively dealt with a long-standing city problem in a holistic and comprehensive way; one which enlisted the assistance of multiple community groups and shifted much of the ownership of the problem to them and which resulted in improved community conditions and less police involvement over time.

Addressing the problem of day laboring

The city of Glendale, California, which borders northeast Los Angeles in the southern region of the state, suffered for 25 years from problems associated with migrants soliciting work along city roadways and intersections. It was so long-standing and pervasive that it was deemed by police and city administrators as an "unsolvable problem." This was the initial problem-solving project selected during the **scanning** process of the newly created Community Police Partnership (COPPS) unit within the Glendale Police Department. For sure, it was no small task, especially for a new unit that needed to prove itself to the department and the community. While it was an ambitious inaugural project, the two-officer team of Officers Javier Ruiz and Ron Gillman, were undaunted and committed to solving the problem.

Scanning

In the initial identification of the problem, several key features became immediately apparent. The first was that the problem was mostly related to blight and quality-of-life issues that affected many different community members including residents, business owners, and the laborers themselves. The second was that the problem was multifaceted. As the day laborers—those who solicit employment on a daily and temporary basis—searched for employers, they congregated along streets or sidewalks in commercial areas or in parking lots of home-improvement and paint-ing-supply stores. With only one or two laborers seeking work, there was no real problem. However, in large numbers their presence became problematic. In large numbers, competition became fierce, and many workers would "swarm" potential employers' vehicles, vying for selection. This occurred at busy intersections, which created traffic hazards and congestion within street and sidewalk areas. In addition, pedestrians complained of being harassed by day laborers and the laborers fought among themselves. The laborers also engaged in theft, property damage, littering, excessive noise, and public intoxication, urination, and defecation.

Analysis

While these overt symptoms of the problem were well understood, the project team sought to better identify the harms they were causing various community groups. The officers carried out their **analysis** through surveys and meetings with community members, business organizations, local residents, and day laborers themselves. They also gathered information and data from the government agencies that had repeatedly been called on to address issues surrounding day-laboring activities. In looking at records of government services, it became apparent that every year tens of thousands of public dollars were spent trying to manage day-labor activities and associated difficulties. Not only was this the case for police, but other city divisions such as fire and paramedic services, as well as code enforcement and sanitation, were also routinely deployed. County, state, and federal resources, largely from social service agencies, had also been heavily expended on this problem in previous years.

For businesses and residents, the primary concern related to the impediment of traffic as a result of workers swarming and scrambling toward arriving vehicles. They also complained of sidewalks being persistently blocked and pedestrians harassed as they attempted to pass by or enter local businesses. As migrants often congregated for long hours on street corners waiting to be hired, they would utilize nearby buildings and parking lots as public restrooms and would leave trash and litter on the streets, sidewalks, and surrounding areas. Community members were especially vocal about these problems to the policing team as the conditions began to spur neighborhood blight that negatively affected their home values and deteriorated the overall quality of life within the community. Area business owners also complained that the conditions were discouraging customers from patronizing their stores.

The project team also took great effort to understand and accommodate the circumstances from the day laborers' perspective. The officers met with them regularly to build a working relationship. In doing so, the officers learned several important things about the laborers:

- The laborers were mostly male immigrants and refugees from Central or South America, as well as Mexico. Some were former migrant farmworkers seeking a new economic alternative in an urban work environment. As such, many were not familiar with the United States or even urban ways of life and standards for appropriate public behavior.
- The majority of the laborers had honest intentions of finding labor to support themselves and their families.

- Many of the laborers spoke very little or no English and lacked formal educa-tion, and several had no legal documentation. Because of this, day laboring was their only option for gainful employment.
- Employment for day laborers was sporadic, and they were often underpaid or cheated out of compensation completely.
- As immigrants, many were fearful of police and distrustful of government rep-resentatives. Most were reluctant to sign any documents.

In the course of their analysis, a few other crucial matters became apparent to the officers. First, in order for the project to be successful, it was imperative that the officers had to have buy-in from the laborers themselves. Second, the activity of day laboring was very place-dependent: the workers selectively sought labor in areas immediately adjacent to building-supply and paint stores since that was where potential employers shopped. Indeed, the officers learned that past efforts to relocate day laboring to area churches failed since they were too far from where potential employers routinely visited. Third, previous attempts to address the prob-lem through enhanced patrol or enforcement crackdowns resulted in temporary and limited effects. Because there were no legal prohibitions against soliciting labor in public places, enforcement activities resulted in citations for various nuisance behaviors (i.e., jaywalking, littering, public intoxication) or the occasional arrest for assault or drug possession. Once enforcement activities were withdrawn, the problem quickly returned.

Response

With a better understanding of the particular dimensions of the problem, the COPPS team clarified their objectives and put together an action plan. The pri-mary objective was to establish a permanent facility to serve as a hiring site where prospective laborers could assemble and lawfully seek temporary employment without causing problems for the surrounding community. Beyond establish-ing such a site, the officers knew that they also had to find a way to effectively manage and operate the facility on an ongoing basis without police or other city resources.

The officers first began meeting with several local social service providers, which included the Salvation Army and Catholic Charities, to begin formulating plans for the type of facility that was envisioned. Once their willingness to participate was established, officers also visited other day-laboring centers in the area that had both successes and failures in their implementation. Armed with a better understanding of the issues surrounding the implementation of such a facility, a five-step plan was established:

1   *Locate a site for a facility.* Placement was key as it had to attract both laborers and employers. A railroad easement across the street from the Home Depot store where they already gathered was selected.

2   *Site development.* The site had to be constructed so that it would include a drive-up section for employers, offices for staff, a waiting area for laborers, access for disabled, and installation of telephones, benches and awnings, drink machines, water, restrooms, and trash bins.

3   *Facility staffing.* Facility staff would be provided by area charities on a full-time basis. They would establish a lottery system for workers and facilitate social services for the workers such as food, clothing, shelter, immigration services, English classes, legal services, and wage negotiation and monitoring, among other things. Staff would also keep records of who was hired, the wage amounts, and the contractors.

4   *Creation of a city ordinance that would require laborers and employers to use the site.* In order for the facility to be effective, other opportunities for soliciting work had to be eliminated. A new city ordinance prohibited both labors and employers from soliciting work on city streets.

5   *Establishment of an outreach program.* Volunteers were enlisted to educate both area contractors and laborers on the benefits and requirements of utilizing the facility.

With the implementation of this plan, a comprehensive, humane, and dignified solution would be established that would alleviate the harms on the community. Throughout the implementation phase, the officers met regularly with all community groups involved. A day-labor advisory board was created to ensure direction and oversight of the facility. The board membership included a paid political consultant, local business owners and residents, and representatives of Home Depot, the Glendale Community Development and Redevelopment agency, Catholic Charities, and the Salvation Army.

It was agreed that in order for the initiative to succeed, all involved parties had to contribute. Home Depot agreed to provide construction materials for this facility and one staff position for five years. The City of Glendale would provide ongoing support if there was significant private-sector involvement, including the social worker service provider to administer the program. Catholic Charities agreed to administer the facility if funding could be provided for the staff workers. The COPPS officers agreed that they would spearhead the implementation if all parties carried through on their commitments. Construction of the facility was estimated at $100,000, and the police officers secured two facility-development grants with supplemental funding from the City's Community Development Block Grant allocation. Home Depot's contribution in the form of building materials, an office trailer, and a paid staff worker with benefits amounted to another $50,000.

Assessment

One year after the center was established, the formerly unsolvable problem was solved. Although the project **assessment** did not provide hard data, it was reported that the activity of day laboring had become effectively managed in a way that eliminated the previous harms. The outreach program focused mostly on the laborers

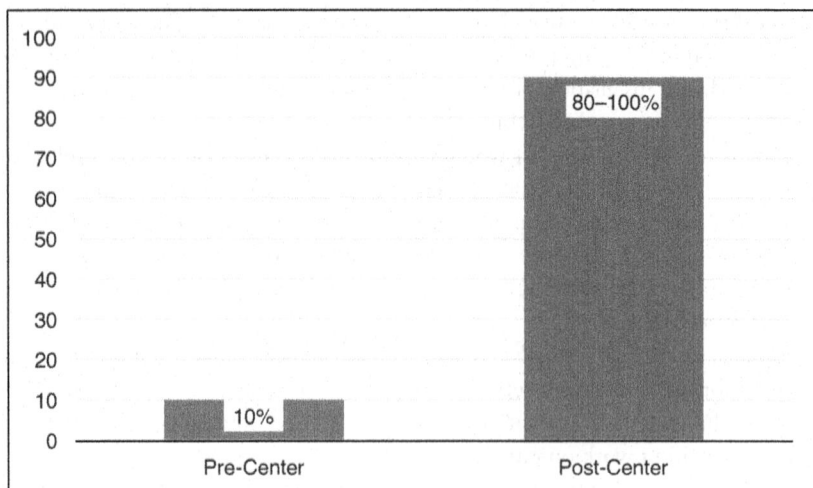

FIGURE 16.1 Average day-laborer hire rate

themselves which resulted in them using the day-labor facility exclusively. Surprisingly, as a result, officers did not have to enforce the no-solicitation zone ordinance, and no arrests for unlawful solicitation violations were made. Because the day-laboring activity was effectively managed at the facility, the demands on city service resources were curtailed since they were no longer being repeatedly called to the area. This saved the city tremendous amounts of money with only limited ongoing supportive action from the COPPS officers.

There was, however, some confusion regarding the use of the facility and the new city ordinance among contractors, businesses, and the overall community. In hindsight, the project team recognized that they should have made greater effort to market the program to those other entities. Despite this, day laborers who utilized the site were employed 80% to 100% of the time. This was a dramatic improvement over the 10% of laborers that were hired prior to the establishment of the facility (see Figure 16.1). While waiting for employment, laborers also took advantage of the many services provided at the facility. The most utilized services included English and computer classes and the sessions related to immigration processing. Equally important, it was reported that community members no longer had to run the gauntlet of disorderly laborers in order to patronize area businesses. There was little, if any, displacement as a result of the project that was believed to be the result of the comprehensive strategy and in particular the citywide no-solicitation ordinance.

Update

The new day-labor facility in Glendale continued to operate for 15 years. During that time, the city had earmarked $90,000 every year to help sustain the program. However, crippled by the economic recession of the late 2000s, the city was forced to cut that expenditure in an effort to close the city's $18 million budget deficit. Without this subsidy to help manage the facility, Catholic Charities was forced to close the day-labor center on July 1, 2011. Although the original project report did not provide firm cost data, it is highly likely that the $90,000 spent per year by the city in allocation was much less than the previous citywide resources that were spent incessantly responding to disorderly day laborers. Without this empirical assessment and the decade and a half of effectively managed day laboring to erase the community's memory of the past, it was much easier for the city to cut that expenditure when the budget shortfall came about.

Another factor contributing to the closing of the center was that the antisolicitation ordinance was declared unlawful by a court, which undermined much of the incentive for workers and employers to utilize the facility (Rocha & Hicken, 2011a, 2011b). While the project could not be sustained in Glendale, there continues to exist other day-labor facilities across the United States that were based on the Glendale model (see www.hireadaylaborer.org).

Discussion

The Glendale day-laboring project is noteworthy for many reasons. Not only did the project alleviate the repetitive harms caused to the community by disorderly day laborers, but it also established a model that could have been sustained longer had it not been for the unfortunate global economic recession. The successes were achieved with a small police detail of just two officers, which resulted in returns on the commitment that far exceeded the allocation of manpower. Beyond this, there are several distinct features of the project that are informative for future problem-solving efforts and that offer lessons well beyond those dealing with issues surrounding day laboring (see a summary in Table 16.1).

The first is that the project identified and focused on alleviating the harm caused by day-laboring activities, not by the mere legal status of those involved. It would have been easy for the project team to label this as an immigration problem and try to relegate it to federal responsibility. Whether they did not do that because they had already tried it in the past to no avail or they were adhering to principles of sound community-based problem solving is unclear, but whichever the case, not doing so allowed the project to set achievable objectives. It also made it easier for the community, including the city government, to accept responsibility for the problem and to recognize what needed to happen locally. By doing so, it shifted the perception of the problem from one of federal immigration to one of local disorder. This allowed the project team to develop responses directed at attenuating the conditions that were disruptive to the community.

Second, the project also established meaningful collaborations with multiple community groups. While collaborative work is a foundation of most problem- and community-based policing initiatives, this one is particularly noteworthy not only because of the multitude of community groups that they engaged but also because these groups were active agents in addressing the problem. As such, it

TABLE 16.1 Overview of day-laboring project's notable features

Notable Feature	What It Entailed	What It Required	What It Achieved
Harm-focused	• Identified and focused on alleviating the harms associated with soliciting labor, not on status of workers	• Acceptance of the problem by the community • Understanding and recognition of what could be acted on locally to address the community harms	• Allowed project efforts to attenuate the conditions that were disruptive to the community
Community partnerships	• Ongoing collaboration with multiple community stakeholders	• Organization and open communication • Accommodation of all parties' needs	• Facilitated community action to address problem
Shifted ownership of problem	• Community organizations took lead in daily management of the day-laboring problem	• Incentivizing groups to manage day laborers • Financial contributions from enlisted stakeholders	• Alleviated burden on police making their role supplementary rather than primary
Created new city ordinances	• New city ordinance prohibiting labor solicitation on roadways and street corners	• Lobbying of city officials to create a new city ordinance	• Gave tool for police to incentivize use of day-laboring center
Acted in face of legal ambiguity	• Establishment of facility and regulations to incentivize day labor center use and operation	• Leadership and persistence to act and follow through on project plans	• A new model for managing day-laboring activity

required the COPPS team to listen, understand, and develop solutions that accommodated the interests of each group. It also meant that they had to establish open and effective communication channels throughout the entire process. In many cases, collaborative partnerships serve as simply "window dressing" within community-based initiatives, and the community groups fail to become active stakeholders in the actual solution. Here this was not the case: The community partnerships and collaborations served a specific purpose of identifying and achieving common community goals.

Third, the project team was able to shift ownership of the problem, or at least specific parts of it, to these community entities because the community relationships had been firmly established. This meant that the community groups were able to take over the day-to-day management of day-laboring activities, which relieved the police and city government from having to do so. This required the COPPS team not only to understand each group's interest but also to mobilize incentives for each group to ensure their continued contributions and participation. Problem-solving officers often feel as though undertaking new projects means that the police will have even more responsibility with the ongoing management of the problem. Yet the importance of shifting ownership of problems to the community is an essential and necessary part of effective problem solving. Being able to effectively shift responsibility actually reduces police involvement. Many projects fail because this shifting of ownership was unsuccessful or because it was not attempted at all (for more on shifting ownership of problems, see Scott & Goldstein, 2005; Scott, 2005). Where police fail to effectively shift responsibility, it is at least partly because effective relationships were not formed and cultivated with relevant community groups.

A fourth distinctive feature of the project is that the problem-solving team lobbied and worked with city officials to create a new city ordinance. This was viewed as a critical component for achieving project success. In Goldstein's original conception of problem-oriented policing, establishing new regulations such as this was one of several ways identified for addressing community problems (Goldstein, 1979, 1990). Now in practice over several decades, few problem-solving projects actually utilize the creation of new regulations as a tool. This may be because it requires the assistance of city attorneys or other city officials to carry out that cannot be controlled by officers or because of the considerable effort it takes for police to lobby officials into action. But whatever the case, this project demonstrates that when the creation of a new ordinance is tethered with a comprehensive problem-solving strategy, it can be instrumental to achieving project success.

Finally, the project is also noteworthy because the officers pushed forward with their project even while faced with considerable legal ambiguity. It is quite easy to choose not to engage a problem or to otherwise do nothing when there is a lack of clear legal doctrine to rely on to guide action. Many police officers are accustomed to having their legal counsel discourage them from taking novel legal actions rather than encouraging and helping them in that process. In the case of immigration-related issues, legal uncertainty is greater given the federal ramifications. Rather than doing nothing, these officers pressed forward and pioneered a unique approach to managing day-laboring activities. The legal viability of the no-solicitation ordinance was later challenged, but in the decade and a half while it existed, many community ailments were cured.

Summary and conclusion

The Glendale project utilized fundamental principles of problem- and community-oriented policing to fix an "unfixable problem," one that had plagued the community for some time. The actions set forth were based on a firm understanding of the harms associated with the problem, a comprehensive embracement of the community, and a persistence in seeing the project through in the face of uncertainty. By shifting ownership of the problem to various community groups, Officers Ruiz and Gillman achieved a fair and effective solution that ultimately minimized demands on city services. The lessons from this project are relevant to problems beyond those pertaining to immigrant populations and extend to any that produce harms that are incurred across several distinct community groups and that have plagued jurisdictions for many years. By those two criteria alone, the applicability is indeed widespread (for more on the topic of problem-solving and day laboring, see Guerette, 2006).

References

Goldstein, H. (1979) 'Improving policing: A problem-oriented approach', *Crime & Delinquency*, 25(2): 236–258.

Goldstein, H. (1990) *Problem-Oriented Policing*, Philadelphia: Temple University Press.

Guerette, R.T. (2006) *Disorder at Day Laborer Sites*, Problem-Oriented Guides for Police, Problem-Specific Guide No. 44, Washington, DC: US Department of Justice, Office of Community Oriented Policing Services.

Rocha, V. & Hicken, M. (2011a) 'Budget deficit forces day labor center to shut down', *Los Angeles Times*, California edition, July 15.

Rocha, V. & Hicken, M. (2011b) 'Day labor center in Glendale closes', *Los Angeles Times*, L.A. Now, July 18.

Scott, M.S. (2005) 'Policing for prevention: Shifting and sharing the responsibility to address public safety problems', in N. Tilley (ed.), *Handbook of Crime Prevention and Community Safety*, Cullompton, UK: Willan.

Scott, M.S. & Goldstein, H. (2005) *Shifting and Sharing Responsibility for Public Safety Problems*, Problem-Oriented Guides for Police, Response Guides No. 3, Washington, DC: US Department of Justice, Office of Community Oriented Policing.

17

CRIME AND DISORDER AT A BUDGET MOTEL IN OAKLAND, CALIFORNIA[1]

Ronald V. Clarke

Introduction

Years ago, my wife and I visited our son at his small college town in Upstate New York. Car problems delayed us so we had difficulty finding a room and eventually we paid double our budget to stay in an up-market hotel. Before that, we had tried what seemed like a dozen different motels, the last of which showed on a dimly lit sign that it was listed by the AAA. We pulled in, and I found a lank-haired receptionist reading a comic and smoking a cigarette. His stained "wifebeater" was stretched tightly over his belly, and to complete the unwholesome spectacle, a half-naked child was playing on the grubby floor.

On my inquiry about a room, the receptionist demanded my driver's license and credit card, but I asked to see the room first. Muttering under his breath, he scrabbled among some keys on the shelf behind him, where there was also a hand-gun. Stubbing out his cigarette in the overflowing ashtray, he told me to follow him. We stumbled down a dark path, and on reaching the room he struggled to open the door, whereupon a terrible smell wafted out as though cats had lived in it and perhaps died there. I quickly made my escape. On complaining to the AAA about the motel, I was told it had been unlisted several years earlier because of complaints such as mine, but it must not have altered its sign.

So, a few years later when, as a Goldstein Award judge, I read the submission describing the transformation of the Oakland Airport Motel (OAM), my unfortunate experience in Upstate New York primed me to feel the deepest sympathy for any hapless motorist who might have tried to check in to the OAM late at night. The story of how the Oakland Police Department (OPD) (2003) transformed this facility, rife with crime and disorder, is described in this case study, the winner of the Goldstein Award in 2003.[1]

The motel's transformation was the work of the OPD's Beat Health Unit (BHU)—a noteworthy fact in its own right. Herman Goldstein (1979) had originally argued that problem-oriented policing (POP) ought to replace normal incident-driven policing, but this has proved impossible to achieve in all but the smallest departments. Larger departments seeking to implement a problem-oriented approach have generally grafted on some dedicated "POP" capacity to selected patrol units. The OPD's approach was different. They set up the BHU, run for many years by the same sergeant, Bob Crawford, which focused largely on dilapidated residences, plagued by various forms of crime and disorder that were contributing to neighborhood blight (see Green Mazerolle & Roehl [1999] for a description of the BHU).

The BHU had dealt with some 3,000 premises of this kind when it took aim at the OAM. The motel was much larger than most of the BHU's targets, and because it had recently been renovated, it had few building-code violations that could be used to leverage change. However, it was well known to OPD officers who were called there almost daily to deal with complaints about robberies, thefts, prostitution, and drug dealing. Indeed, on conducting a rudimentary form of what is now known as "risky facilities" analysis (Clarke & Eck, 2007; Eck, Clarke & Guerette, 2007), during the **scanning** phase of the project, it was discovered that the OAM had an average of nine times as many reported crimes as five other nearby motels.

During the **analysis** phase of the project, undercover BHU officers, led by Officer Brad Gardiner, recorded numerous incidents of prostitution, theft, drug deals, public urination, and pandering. An illegal auto-repair business operated in the motel's parking lot, and junk cars were regularly dumped there. Rooms were rented to minors, and some 25 guests had attained residency status at the property.

Visits to the nearby motels led the officers to conclude that poor management practices at OAM had allowed crime and nuisance to flourish. The OAM was operated by an international parent company based in Europe with many hundreds of motels in the United States and elsewhere.[2] Wider inquiries by Sgt. Crawford led him to believe that the parent company had co-opted many police agencies in the United States by employing their officers as part-time security guards.

The **response** phase was protracted, partly due to the need to engage with the parent company, and the account here is abbreviated. At first, Officer Gardiner made a concerted effort to work with the on-site manager, but with little success. This led the BHU to deliver a letter of pending legal action to the parent company's U.S. chief executive at a carefully chosen time and place—when he was likely to be at home on Christmas Eve!

The BHU had formed a partnership with the office of the Oakland city attorney to bring increased pressure on the parent company, and here too is an important lesson. Police engaged in community policing are often instructed to form partnerships with other local agencies, but these are frequently a "trap" (Knutsson & Clarke, 2006) because they are little more than talking shops. However, the city attorneys could and did do a lot more than talk. They drew up a letter again delivered to the corporation's U.S. chief executive requesting his attendance at a meeting to discuss, (1) the closure of the motel for 90 days to facilitate physical renovation and retraining of motel personnel, (2) repayment of the OPD's investigation costs, and (3) agreement to a performance bond to be paid by the parent company if the improvements failed to reduce the problems at the OAM to the level of those typical of area motels.

Only the U.S. corporate vice president for security turned up at the requested meeting. He denied knowledge of the problems but promised swift action to deal with them. He stated that he lacked authority to agree to the city's three demands, but he would pass these on to upper management.

Despite the vice president's undertakings, there was little evidence of any improvement. The city attorneys prepared a Drug Nuisance Abatement lawsuit, and a meeting was called for February 2, 2001, with the parent company's U.S. chief executive officer (CEO), the vice president of operations, OAM management, a city council member, Oakland city attorneys, and BHU staff. At the meeting, a booklet was presented outlining the crime and disorder recorded by the BHU. A certified letter was also sent to the international CEO written in English and the language of the country of his residence.

After a full day of intense negotiations, the parent company agreed to the following:

1   Make changes to the property and its management designed to reduce crime and disorder.
2   Post a $250,000 "performance" bond to signify the company's commitment to eliminating the motel's crime and disorder problems. The bond would be forfeited if the problems were not eliminated within a two-year period.
3   Reimburse the City of Oakland $35,000 for the cost of the investigation of the OAM.

The BHU declined to dictate specific recommendations for improvement for two reasons. First, it held the view that the parent company should have the expertise to manage its business properly and, second, if the BHU made recommendations that did not lead to the problems being diminished, the parent company could disclaim responsibility and might refuse to forfeit the bond.

The agreement included a 90-day grace period for the OAM to make its improvements that included the following:

• Cleaned and painted the property and removed abandoned vehicles
• Raised room rates by 50%
• Upgraded lighting and fencing
• Replaced the managers and security guards and sacked problem employees
• Instituted preemployment background checks on all new employees
• Established strict check-in procedures, prohibiting room rentals to anyone under 21, together with a list of banned individuals
• Prohibited room rentals for more than 30 days

TABLE 17.1 Calls for service at the Oakland Airport Motel

1998	1999	2000	2001	2002	2003
197	212	242	38	1	3*

* Through March 2003

This package of changes was astoundingly successful as documented in the **assessment** stage of the project. Soon after the conclusion of the agreement in February 2001, there was a precipitous "cliff-edge drop" (Ross, 2013; see also Perry et al., 2017) in the motel's police calls for service (CFS), which during the two-year monitoring phase that ended in March 2003, were all but eliminated (see Table 17.1).[3]

After the intervention, CFS for the OAM were little different from those for five nearby motels, which suggests that the OAM's crime and disorder problems did not displace to the nearby motels. This is consistent with the findings of many other studies showing negligible displacement when a concentration of opportunities at a "crime generator" (Brantingham & Brantingham, 1995), such as the OAM has been eliminated (for a classic study, see Felson et al., 1996).

Discussion

The OPD's winning submission for the Goldstein Award in 2003 was notable in many respects. Officer Gardiner's struggle with the corporate owners of the motel, reminiscent of David's epic battle with Goliath, was rewarded by the OPD's "Medal of Merit". Contrary to the usual belief, this shows that police departments can find ways to reward officers for preventing crime, not just for making arrests.

The city's dealings with the OAM's international corporate masters were exceptionally well handled. The delivery of the first letter to the home of the corporation's U.S. CEO on Christmas Eve could not have been better timed. Extracting an agreement from the corporation to compensate the city for the costs of the police investigation, as well as to post a "performance bond", was further evidence of the city's grip on the negotiations. Performance bonds have rarely been used, if ever, in problem-oriented policing, but they are of potentially wide application. The final masterstroke was the city's insistence that the corporate management develop its own measures for dealing with the OAM's problems. Altogether, the case study is an unrivaled demonstration that police can "shift and share responsibility" (Scott & Goldstein, 2005; Scott, 2005) for solving crime and disorder problems. Methods for accomplishing this are listed in Box 17.1—that employed by the OPD was number 10.

BOX 17.1 METHODS FOR CONVINCING OTHERS TO ACCEPT RESPONSIBILITY FOR COMMUNITY PROBLEMS (IN INCREASING LEVELS OF COERCION)

1 Educating others regarding their responsibility for the problem
2 Making a straightforward informal request of some entity to assume responsibility for the problem
3 Making a targeted confrontational request of some entity to assume responsibility for the problem
4 Engaging another existing organization that has the capacity to help address the problem
5 Pressing for the creation of a new organization to assume responsibility for the problem
6 Shaming the delinquent entity by calling public attention to its failure to assume responsibility for the problem
7 Withdrawing police services relating to certain aspects of the problem
8 Charging fees for police services related to the problem
9 Pressing for legislation mandating that entities take measures to prevent the problem
10 Bringing a civil action to compel entities to accept responsibility for the problem

Source: Scott and Goldstein (2005).

Further evidencing its determined approach, the BHU compared the OAM's crimes with those of five neighboring motels—in effect, as mentioned above, conducting a nascent form of a risky-facilities analysis. Subsequently, the city of Chula Vista, California, commissioned a full-fledged risky-facilities analysis of its 24 motels in preparation for another Goldstein Award submission (Chula Vista Police Department, 2009). The interim report makes a useful point about portraying the results of such an analysis (Bichler, Christie & McCord, 2003). If the intention is to understand the reasons for differences in the problems exhibited by the facilities being analyzed, it is necessary to standardize the comparisons by the size of the facilities (in their case the number of rooms in each motel). On the other hand, if the purpose is to document the burden on local police, then differences between the facilities need not be standardized by size. Figure 17.1 portrays these two different ways of showing the CFS for 24 motels in Chula Vista.

The curve for all CFS (Figure 17.1's solid line) is an inverted J-distribution usually found in risky-facilities analyses. However, the distribution does not conform

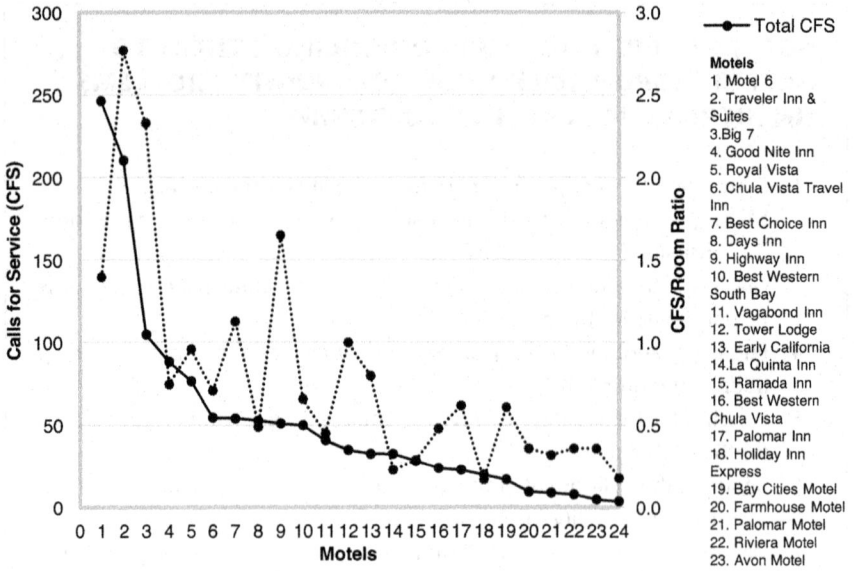

FIGURE 17.1 Calls for service at 24 motels in Chula Vista, 2005

Source: City of Chula Vista, California (Police and Developmental Services departments).

to the 80/20 rule because it takes CFS from 12 motels (50% of the total) to account for about 80% of all CFS. This indicates that in Chula Vista, there was an unexpectedly large number of motels with CFS clustered in the mid-range.

Figure 17.1 also shows, as expected, that when CFS are standardized per number of rooms (the dotted line) some motels present a dramatically different picture; for example, Motel 6 presents as less troublesome, and Highway Inn, as more troublesome. A detailed study of their design and management would be needed to explain why this is the case.

Chula Vista's focus on its motels led to an additional benefit: one of its public-safety analysts, Karin Schmerler (2005), produced a remarkably detailed Problem-Oriented Guide for Police on crime and disorder in motels. She discusses 37 different measures that motels might use under various categories such as "deterring/screening problem guests and visitors", "changing the physical environment", and "establishing and enforcing regulations and penalties". This number is greater than used at the OAM, but it is not unusually large for dealing with problems at bigger facilities such as motels, apartment complexes, parking lots, schools, sports stadiums, and urban parks.[4] In all cases, a balance must be reached between design and management changes. The former might be costly, but they require less day-to-day monitoring once implemented; however, they are no substitute for good management, which can often be harder to achieve and even harder to sustain.

Follow-up

CFS data were presented in the Goldstein Award submission for only a brief period after the intervention in 2001 and, to see whether the enormous drops were sustained, further data on yearly CFS were sought from the OPD. The Department's statistical system was changed so that yearly CFS data were not available for 2003 and 2004, but the Department's Record Management System indicates that only three incidents were recorded at the motel for 2003 and none for 2004.

Figure 17.2 shows, however, that by 2005, CFS had begun to increase ($N =$ 92). In the following year, they increased further to 161 and hovered around that number until 2013 ($N = 171$). Between 2014 and 2017, there was a further substantial increase in CFS with an average number of just over 300—greater than the number of CFS in the three years prior to the OPD's intervention. It is clear, therefore, that the remarkable improvement in CFS from the OAM was of relatively short duration. Apart from anything else, this underlines the need for longer post-intervention follow-ups of successful problem-oriented policing interventions, and, for that matter, of situational crime prevention interventions as well. As far as the present case study is concerned, however, the fact of the short life of the improvement suggests that this was not due to an erosion of the design and physical changes made but was more likely the result of a change in the motel's managers. Of greater concern is that the corporate owners apparently took no action to reverse the deterioration in CFS; while they might otherwise have acted as "super controllers" of the motel's "place managers" (Sampson, Eck & Dunham, 2010), they clearly failed in this role.

The OPD also reported that the BHU was replaced in 2005 by 35 public services officers, one for each patrol beat, funded by the Violence Prevention and Public Safety Act 2004. More than likely this eroded the city's oversight of the OAM.

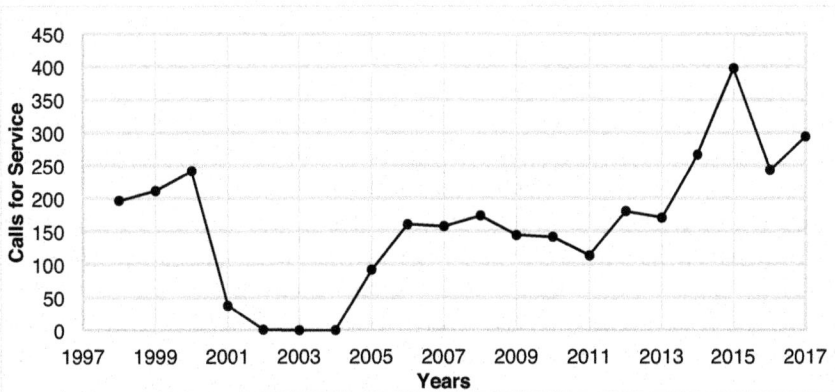

FIGURE 17.2 Calls for service at Oakland Airport Motel before and after its transformation in 2000

Summary and conclusion

Some special circumstances contributed to the stunning transformation of the OAM. Prime among these was the role of the BHU, which was a specialized entity, run for many years by the same sergeant. It had racked up some 3,000 successes in applying what were essentially problem-oriented policing methods in dealing with homes and premises contributing to neighborhood blight. In dealing with the OAM, a much larger target than usual, the BHU formed a crucial partnership with the city attorneys who had the skills and resources to bring significant legal pressure on the OAM's corporate owners. This resulted in the owners introducing a package of design and management changes that brought about a precipitate drop in the motel's crime and disorder problems. Subsequent follow-up revealed, however, that this improvement, although valuable, was short-lived. CFS at the motel began to increase within a couple of years after the intervention and, by 2017, had returned to the level that triggered the intervention in 2000.

Final thoughts

This case study of the stunning transformation of the OAM and its subsequent reversal prompts two concluding thoughts. The first is that criminal-justice authorities have paid too little attention to toxic super controllers such as the OAM's parent body. Other examples would include slum lords who increase their profits by not compelling the managers of their apartment buildings to take appropriate (and sometimes costly) security measures or the parent companies of crime-ridden hospitals and malls. Their frequently global nature, jurisdictional legal issues, and the impenetrability of corporate law all help to explain why these toxic super controllers have escaped the attention of the law. Criminologists could draw attention to their failings by undertaking comparisons of the crime rates of such facilities as motels, malls, and hospitals, either owned or not by corporate bodies.

The second concluding thought is prompted by reflecting on the work of the BHU, which provides a rare example of the institutionalization of problem-oriented policing within a police agency. Most attempts to incorporate problem-oriented policing within a police department falter quite quickly, especially when their patrons within the department move to another position. The BHU was different. It survived for many years, accumulating a stellar record of rehabilitating properties contributing to neighborhood blight. Had it not been led by the same sergeant during those years, it might not have accumulated the experience of the vital negotiating skills required for successful problem-oriented policing. The availability of supplemental local funds led to its rebirth as a dispersed team of public service officers, and without a detailed study, it is impossible to know how well these officers were able to continue the successful work of the BHU. At the very least they would have needed continuous help in undertaking the complicated negotiations involved in any successful problem-oriented project. This prompts the larger question of how police could routinely be trained in these skills without radically redefining their role and function. This is a much greater challenge than improving their analytic capability. Indeed, this prompts the even larger question of whether problem-oriented policing is at present simply too difficult for the police to "bolt on" to their usual activities.

Acknowledgments

The following members of the Oakland Police Department gave me considerable help in gathering data: Paul Figueroa, Timothy Birch, Nicole Freeman, and Michael Tacchini.

Notes

1 At that time, Oakland, California, had an ethnically diverse population close to 400,000, 45% being African American and 35% Hispanic. Most of its housing consisted of single-family homes.
2 This account honors the OPD's undertaking to not reveal the name of the parent company.
3 Clarke (2018) has argued that cliff-edge findings are as powerful as those of randomized controlled trials in indicating causality.
4 See the Center for Problem-Oriented Policing website: www.popcenter.org for guides relating to these facilities.

References

Bichler, G., Christie, J. & McCord, E. (2003) *Chula Vista Motel Evaluation Project: Interim Report Submitted to the Chula Vista Police Department*, San Bernardino, CA: Center for Criminal Justice Research, California State University.

Brantingham, P. & Brantingham, P. (1995) 'Criminality of place: Crime generators and crime attractors', *European Journal on Criminal Policy and Research*, 3: 1–26.

Chula Vista Police Department (2009) *Reducing Crime and Disorder at Motels and Hotels in Chula Vista, CA*, Submission for the Herman Goldstein Award for Excellence in Problem-Oriented Policing, Center for Problem-Oriented Policing, Arizona State University, Phoenix, AZ.

Clarke, R.V. (2018) 'The theory and practice of situational crime prevention', in *Oxford Research Encyclopedia, Criminology and Criminal Justice*, Oxford, UK: Oxford University Press.

Clarke, R.V. & Eck, J.E. (2007) *Understanding Risky Facilities*, Problem-Oriented Guides for Police, Problem-Solving Tools Series, Guide No. 6, Washington, DC: US Department of Justice, Office of Community Oriented Policing.

Eck, J.E., Clarke, R.V. & Guerette, R.T. (2007) 'Risky facilities: Crime concentration in homogeneous sets of establishments and facilities', in G. Farrell, K.J. Bowers, S.D. Johnson & M. Townsley (eds.), *Imagination for Crime Prevention: Essays in Honour of Ken Pease*, Crime Prevention Studies, Vol. 21, Monsey, NY: Criminal Justice Press, pp. 225–264.

Felson, M., Belanger, M.E., Bichler, G.M., Bruzinski, C.D., Campbell, G.S., Fried, C.L., Grofik, K.C., Mazur, I.S., O'Regan, A.B., Sweeney, P.J., Ullman, A.L. & Williams, L.M. (1996) 'Redesigning hell: Preventing crime and disorder at the port authority bus terminal', in R.V. Clarke (ed.), *Preventing Mass Transit Crime*, Crime Prevention Studies, Vol. 6. Monsey, NY: Criminal Justice Press, pp. 5–92.

Goldstein, H. (1979) 'Improving policing: A problem-oriented approach', *Crime & Delinquency*, 25: 236–258.

Green Mazerolle, L. & Roehl, J. (1999) *Controlling Drug and Disorder Problems: Oakland's Beat Health program*, Research in Brief, Washington, DC: US Department of Justice, National Institute of Justice.

Knutsson, J. & Clarke, R.V. (2006) 'Introduction', in J. Knutsson & R.V. Clarke (eds.), *Putting Theory to Work*, Crime Prevention Studies, Vol. 6. Monsey, NY: Criminal Justice Press, pp. 1–8.

Oakland Police Department (2003) *The Oakland Airport Motel*, Winner, Herman Goldstein Award for Excellence in Problem-Oriented Policing, Center for Problem-Oriented Policing, Arizona State University, Phoenix, AZ.

Perry, S., Apel, R., Newman, G.R. & Clarke, R.V. (2017) 'The situational prevention of terrorism: An evaluation of the Israeli West Bank barrier', *Journal of Quantitative Criminology*, 33(4): 727–751.

Ross, N. (2013) *Crime: How to Solve It: And Why So Much of What We're Told Is Wrong*, London: Biteback Publishing.

Sampson, R., Eck, J., & Dunham, J. (2010) 'Super controllers and crime prevention: A routine activity explanation of crime prevention success and failure', *Security Journal*, 23: 37–51.

Schmerler, K. (2005) *Disorder at Budget Motels*, Problem-Oriented Guides for Police, Problem-Specific Guide No. 30, Washington, DC: US Department of Justice, Office of Community Oriented Policing Services.

Scott, M.S. (2005) 'Policing for prevention: Shifting and sharing the responsibility to address public safety problems', in N. Tilley (ed.), *A Handbook for Crime Prevention: Theory, Policy and Practice*, London: Willan Publishing.

Scott, M.S. & Goldstein, H. (2005) *Shifting and Sharing Responsibility for Public Safety Problems*, Problem-Oriented Guides for Police, Response Guide No. 3, Washington, DC: US Department of Justice, Office of Community Oriented Policing Services.

18

CRIME AND DISORDER AT BUDGET MOTELS IN CHULA VISTA, CALIFORNIA

Gisela Bichler and Karin Schmerler

Introduction

Budget motels/hotels are important community assets. Offering economical room rates for overnight lodging, these facilities can attract a lot of people. In doing so, they have the potential to generate significant revenue through occupancy taxes, provide jobs to area residents, and contribute to the success of community events and local business by housing out-of-town visitors. For instance, the American Hotel and Lodging Association reports that the 5,596 hotels and motels in California support about 4.4% of jobs in the state and generate $156 billion in sales output (AHLA, 2017). Nationally, budget motels, charging less than $85 (£63) per night, constitute approximately 46% of properties renting rooms (estimated from data provided by AHLA, 2014).

Often clustered near highway-access ramps or along major arterial roads, properties exhibit varied physical characteristics and management styles. Smaller facilities are typically horseshoe, L-shape, or terrace structures that are single or double story. Guests park their vehicles near to their rented rooms and access rooms directly from the parking lot. Larger properties can be several stories tall and have interior corridors leading to several building egress points that open to large parking lots. While several prominent chains exist, many communities have independently owned and managed properties with diverse policies and practices, situated alongside franchised properties with corporate standards of operation.

The consequence of varying structural characteristics intersecting with notable differences in management policy and practices is that adjacent properties often exhibit vastly different crime levels (LeBeau, 2011; Schmerler, 2005). Evoking responsible crime-control-oriented management of all motel properties throughout a community requires a concerted effort. This chapter describes how the City of Chula Vista, California, used a problem-oriented policing approach to place responsibility for developing and implementing specific actions needed to curb crime levels at particular facilities with those individuals best positioned to effect change—those who own and manage the troublesome properties.

The Chula Vista motel and hotel project

Scanning

In the mid-1990s, Chula Vista was a city of approximately 150,000 people, located seven miles south of San Diego and seven miles north of the Mexican border. The city was perfectly situated to accommodate tourists visiting both the San Diego area and Baja, Mexico. For many years, however, the city's overnight lodging industry consisted primarily of cheap motels that were havens for serious crime, drug dealing, parolee violations, and prostitution. Business organizations asked for the city's help in improving the quality and safety of Chula Vista's motels in order to support future community redevelopment and growth. In response, police increased enforcement at motels and the city implemented a new law requiring all motel guests to show photo ID at check-in. Despite these efforts, police continued to respond to a high number of calls for service (CFS) at motels, which remained platforms for criminal activity and inhibited efforts to bring tourist dollars to the city. By early 2001, business leaders, elected representatives, and the police were increasingly frustrated by the seemingly intractable crime and disorder problems at the city's 27 motels.[1] With a mandate for improvement, Chula Vista Police Department (CVPD) staff, in partnership with other city staff and business groups, began working on a problem-oriented policing project to improve public-safety at motels.

Analysis

Initial findings

From an analysis of CFS data, police analysts learned that the problem was concentrated at certain motels. In fact, just five motels accounted for about 25% of the rooms in the city but generated more than 50% of all the CFS received by the police department. Officers interviewed guests and visitors who patronized city motels and found that 75% were residents of San Diego County, and many were at a local motel because they were either homeless, between homes, or not welcome in their primary residence. Motel users with in-county home addresses were 13 times more likely to be on probation and 4 times more likely to be on parole than the general adult California population.

The problem analysis conducted up to this point in the project was very helpful in identifying the nature of the problems at city motels and the factors associated with high CFS, but these findings did not fully explain the extreme variation in annual CFS per room ratios (CFS per room ratios were calculated by dividing the total CFS to that property over a 12-month period by the total number of rooms at the property.) While many motels that catered to a local clientele had high CFS-per-room ratios, some had very low ratios or virtually no calls at all. The CVPD sought to determine whether there were other factors that affected public-safety issues at motels, such as location, room price, and the amount of police attention received by the motels.

Testing hypotheses

To determine whether motels had problems merely because they were located in high-crime areas, staff mapped and color-coded motels according to their 2003 CFS-per-room ratios on top of a grid map that showed overall CFS density. The map showed that motels with relatively high CFS ratios were located right next to motels with relatively low CFS ratios. In addition, the independent motel with the second-highest CFS ratio in 2003 was located across the street from the independent motel with the lowest CFS ratio that year—and both were located in a high-CFS area. Staff consequently rejected the "bad neighborhood" hypothesis.

For quite some time, it was thought that Chula Vista motels had crime and disorder problems because they charged low nightly rates, which attracted problematic

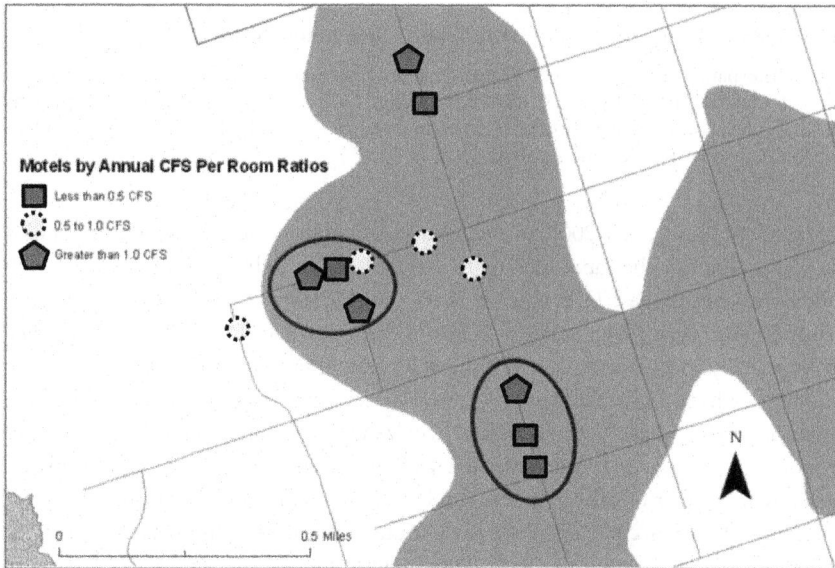

FIGURE 18.1 Northwest Chula Vista motels and hotels in high CFS hot-spot area, by annual CFS per room ratios: 2003

Source: International Association of Crime Analysts, *Exploring crime analysis: Readings on essential skills* (3rd ed.), K. Gallagher, J. Wartell, S. Gwinn, G. Jones & G. Stewart (eds.), copyright © 2017 International Association of Crime Analysts. Reprinted by Permission of the International Association of Crime Analysts.

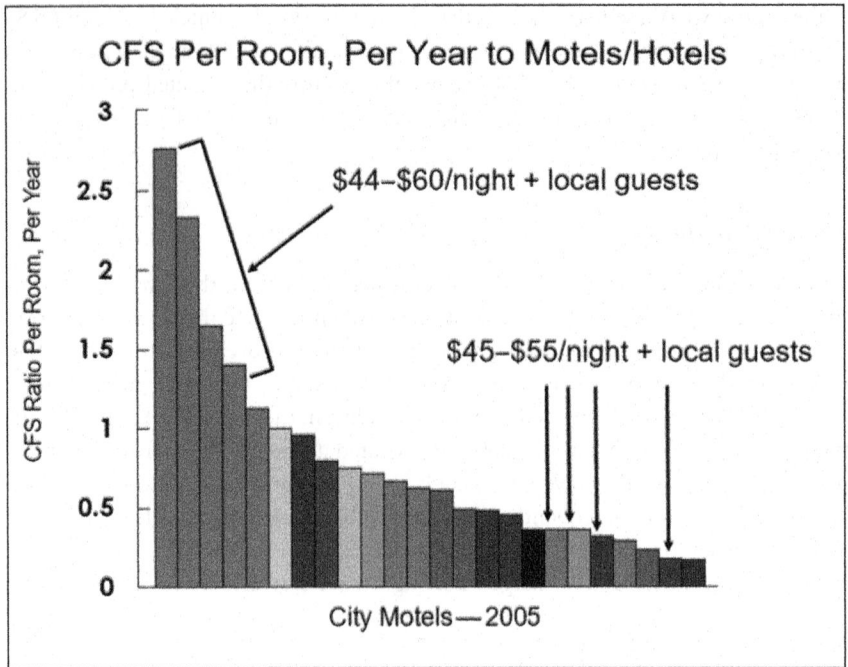

FIGURE 18.2 CFS per room per year to Chula Vista motels/hotels

Source: International Association of Crime Analysts, *Exploring crime analysis: Readings on essential skills* (3rd ed.), K. Gallagher, J. Wartell, S. Gwinn, G. Jones & G. Stewart (eds.), copyright © 2017 International Association of Crime Analysts. Reprinted by Permission of the International Association of Crime Analysts.

motel users. However, a 2005 analysis found that four motels with low CFS ratios charged essentially the same rates as four motels with high CFS ratios. In fact, the motel with the highest CFS ratio in 2005 charged almost $60 on weeknights and nearly $70 on weekends; a motel with one of the lowest CFS ratios charged $55 every night. Clearly, room prices were not the determining factor in motel CFS levels.

Another hypothesis about what caused motel problems was the level of police attention at the property. Project staff theorized that enhanced enforcement efforts at motels could reduce citizen-initiated CFS levels. However, when staff compared the annual number of officer-initiated CFS with the annual number of citizen-initiated calls between 2000 and 2004, they found little relationship between the two.

Project staff were aware that academic research on crime and place[2] indicated that place managers had a great deal of influence over the level of public safety at their properties. The Center for Criminal Justice Research at California State University, San Bernardino (CSUSB) and the CVPD interviewed 23 motel managers about their management practices and found varying levels of crime-control perspectives and that certain management practices—such as catering to a local clientele and renting to long-term guests—were correlated with high CFS at motels.

Informal conversations with motel managers in other cities corroborated this: some managers actively sought to avoid problems, relying on their prior experience to set behavioral expectations, implementing formal check-in policies, and declining to rent to guests that raised concerns. Ultimately, the police concluded that motel managers and owners could effectively control crime and disorder on their properties through good management practices—if they choose to do so. The challenge, therefore, was to get them to do so.

Response

Addressing public-safety problems at budget motels necessitated a three-stage response that began with outreach in 2003 and ended with the passage of a permit-to-operate ordinance in 2006.

Stage 1: outreach

The response began with three types of information-sharing activities. (1) Project staff shared a personalized CFS "report card" with each operator that tallied the nature and scope of crime and disorder occurring at each site. The goal was to engage motel owners and operators in a way that was meaningful for them and to ensure the owners/managers knew about the nature and scope of the problems at their properties. (2) Project staff also conducted seminars for property managers to share information on local research, laws, and best practices. (3) On-site technical assistance was offered to each operator—project staff visited sites to conduct free property reviews to identify environmental security issues. While this was enough to improve conditions at some sites, facilities with more systemic crime issues required further attention.

Stage 2: code enforcement program and public accountability

When outreach efforts failed to correct the crime and disorder problems occurring at the most troubled properties, the City of Chula Vista Code Enforcement Office stepped in. Problematic facilities were inspected, and operators were cited for problems. Then, project staff distributed reports to all motel operators ranking each motel property by CFS-per-room rate. While these efforts corrected some major problems (two properties failed to make the necessary code improvements and they were subsequently closed) and shamed some managers/owners into action, serious crime and disorder issues continued to plague some locations.

Stage 3: permit-to-operate ordinance

In 2006, faced with a number of uncooperative property operators, six city departments[3] worked together to enact a permit-to-operate ordinance that enabled the city to hold motels accountable for meeting a CFS-based public safety performance standard.[4] The CFS performance standard was set at the median CFS-per-room ratio for 2005 (the annual total number of CFS per property divided by the number of rooms available for rent at that property), which was 0.61 CFS per room. Properties failing to meet the standard were required to take appropriate corrective action or risk being denied a permit to operate in the city. In later years, properties above the CFS-per-room ratio threshold entered into detailed written agreements, such as memorandums of understanding, outlining the specific steps they would take to reduce problems, in return for receiving their permits to operate.

Assessment

Reduction in CFS and crime

After the ordinance was fully implemented and all motels were in compliance (late 2009), CFS to Chula Vista motels declined 53% citywide (from a monthly average of 112 CFS during the 2003–2004[5] performance period to a monthly average of 53 CFS by the 2008–2009 performance period). In addition, the median CFS-per-room ratio for Chula Vista motels went down from 0.61 to 0.36. The reduction in CFS was most pronounced among the motels with CFS ratios above 0.99 during the 2003–2004 performance period as is demonstrated in Figure 18.3. Crime at motels also declined: Part I and Part II crimes[6] went down 70% during the same time frame (from 345 crimes per year to 103 crimes per year), and drug arrests at motels declined 64% (from 90 drug arrests per year to 32 drug arrests per year).

Improvement in management practices

A motel management survey that followed up on the 2002 administration was conducted by CSUSB in the spring of 2008. The results from this survey indicated that fewer Chula Vista motels were targeting a primarily local clientele (30% in 2008 compared to 70% in 2002), just under a third continued to rent to long-term guests (30% in 2008 compared to 45% in 2002), and a larger percentage of motels reported having written check-in procedures (90% in 2008 compared to 55% in 2002). Some characteristics were fairly similar over the two administrations. In 2008, 50% of respondents indicated their motels were family-operated compared to 62% in 2002, and 30% of 2008 respondents said their motels were part of a chain or franchise, compared to 35% in 2002.[7]

Displacement not evident

Project staff attempted to look for two types of displacement of motel crime and disorder: target and spatial. To start, staff compiled the home zip codes and home cities of 643 people arrested at Chula Vista motels during the nearly 24-month

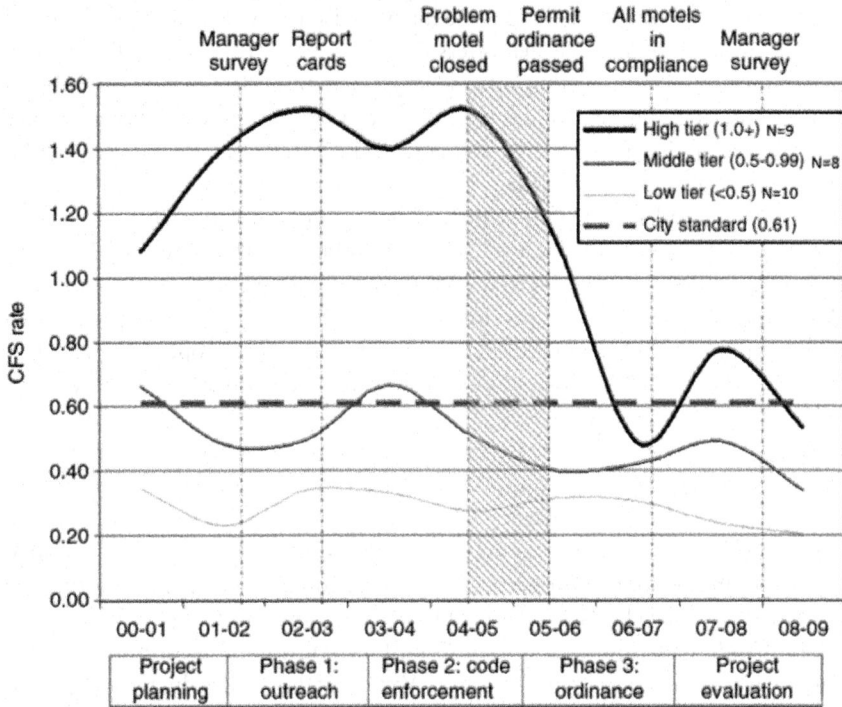

FIGURE 18.3 Change in median CFS ratios of motels in high, middle, and low ratio tiers as of 2003–2004

Source: Bichler, G., Schmerler, K. & Enriquez, J. (2013) 'Curbing nuisance motels: An evaluation of police as place regulators', *Policing: An International Journal of Police Strategies & Management,* 36(2): 437–462. © Emerald Publishing Limited all rights reserved. Reprinted by permission of Emerald Publishing Limited.

period between January 9, 2004, and December 31, 2006. Approximately 28% of all arrestees—the single largest group—hailed from the two Chula Vista zip codes where all the city motels are located. Because the largest single group of arrestees who could potentially be displaced by the motel project lived in Chula Vista, staff first looked for target displacement to city apartment complexes with eight or more units. Reviewing apartment-complex CFS for the four performance periods between October 1, 2004, and September 30, 2008, staff found that CFS to apartment complexes remained relatively steady during each 12-month comparison period, with no increase or decrease of more than 6% from one period to the next.

Immediate spatial displacement is not likely because crime problems are situation-specific (Clarke, 1997; Cornish & Clarke, 2008; Clarke, 2008; Wortley, 2008). Crime-reduction interventions targeting budget motels will not necessarily displace crime to an adjacent property, such as a bank, retail shopping mall, or fast-food outlet. Instead, crime is more likely to displace to another budget motel within a reasonable distance that offers the same set of crime-facilitating conditions. Since research finds that offenders typically travel less than three miles to commit disorder and assault (see, e.g., Wiles & Costello, 2000) and even shorter distances to sell drugs (Eck, 1995; Rengert et al., 2000), potential offenders from the Chula Vista area are most likely to displace to motels in adjacent cities, which are just several miles from Chula Vista motels. To look for spatial displacement, project staff identified 19 budget motels and obtained CFS data sets for these properties. Nine properties in National City and Southern San Diego (totaling 393 rooms) were located within three miles of Chula Vista motels: these properties comprised the possible displacement facilities. Ten properties located in the nearby Cities of El Cajon and La Mesa were used as control properties (953 rooms).

Overall, there was no evidence of displacement (Bichler, Schmerler & Enriquez, 2013). In comparison, the total net effect[8] of the permit-to-operate ordinance was positive and stronger than the overall project (all three phases), indicating that the ordinance significantly reduced crime in Chula Vista relative to changes in the control properties (El Cajon and La Mesa) while adjusting for any changes in the displacement facilities (in National City and Southern San Diego). And, while the overall project (all three stages combined) was also associated with a decline in crime at Chula Vista motels, small reductions in crime were also found among displacement and control properties located in adjacent cities. To illustrate, Chula Vista motels saw a 58% reduction in crime during the same period that displacement properties experienced a 6% decline and control properties had a 5% decline (comparing federal fiscal year crime rates from 2004–2005 to 2008–2009). Conversations with crime analysts revealed that budget motels located in other cities (displacement and control cities) were also targeted with different and unrelated crime-control initiatives launched by their respective agencies.

Follow-up

The first permits to operate were issued to Chula Vista motels on January 1, 2008. After the ordinance had been in place for 10 years, project staff reviewed the long-term impact of the initiative. At the aggregate level, CFS to Chula Vista motels were still down from preordinance levels, but the reduction in calls was only 41% (from an average of 112 CFS per month to 66 CFS per month); the reduced impact on CFS was attributable almost completely to increases in calls to the national chain motel with the most rooms in the city (see Figure 18.4). The initial reductions in crimes and drug arrests (70% and 64% respectively), still held at the 10-year mark. Although the call reduction was not as marked after 10 years, the incidents were not as serious as they were prior to the ordinance.

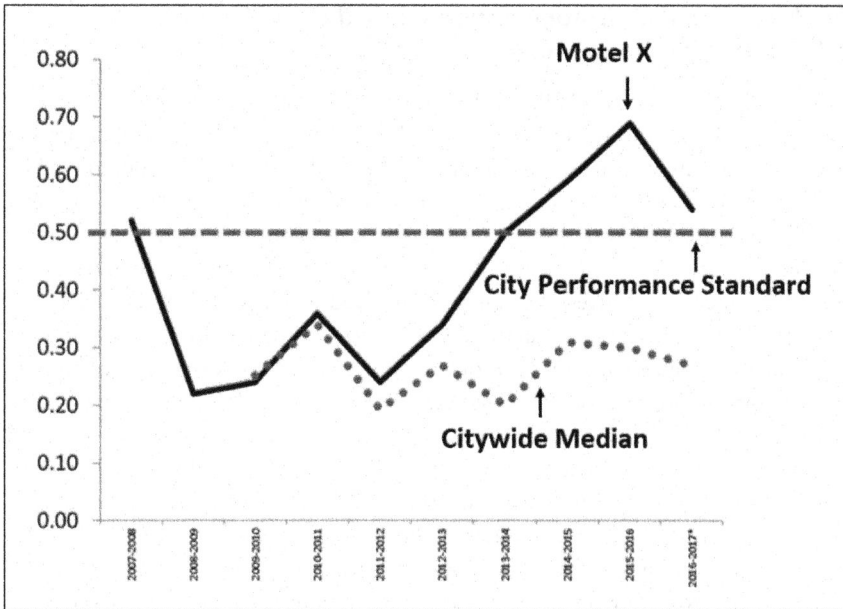

FIGURE 18.4 CFS comparison between the citywide median and the largest motel, 2012 to 2017

Source: City of Chula Vista, California, Police Department.

Discussion

The benefit of revisiting this project a decade after completing its evaluation is that as time passed, five aspects stand out as having made this project such a success.

Partnerships

Early on, the project leaders set about to build partnerships within the city, and externally with the local business community and a university-based research center. Building relations with six different departments (city attorney, finance, fire, police, planning and building, and community development) was critical to building trust and removing barriers that would otherwise have threatened the implementation of the response. Not only did each city partner contribute necessary resources, but they also stepped up their support when needed to resolve issues that arose as the project unfolded. For example, in 2003, code enforcement staff began inspecting motel properties once a year rather than once every seven years (the previous inspection schedule), and city attorney staff provided crucial legal support when problem motels were not in compliance with the ordinance and contested the status of their permits to operate.

Implementing a multistage response based on a hierarchy of shifting problem ownership

Project drivers from the CVPD initiated extensive outreach efforts (stage 1: outreach and technical assistance) prior to enforcing code violations and instituting public accountability (stage 2: code enforcement). Building on mounting public support for a more sustainable and permanent solution, project leaders successfully lobbied for a legislated solution that invoked tailored civil sanctions (stage 3: performance-based permit-to-operate ordinance). Rather than simply implementing a package of initiatives, the response involved a strategic rollout of elements designed to build momentum and to ensure public accountability and transparency in the process as efforts to correct problems at the most troubled properties became more punitive. More importantly, following Goldstein's suggested hierarchy (Scott & Goldstein, 2005), the strategies started with the simplest, least costly actions that required minimal collaboration with partners and stakeholders, such as education and straightforward informal requests. With each successive phase, the strategies escalated, drawing on more investment from partners and stakeholders while shifting the responsibility for problem resolution from law enforcement to a set of community actors. For instance, at stage 2 the emphasis shifted to targeted confrontational requests and engaging code enforcement. When these actions failed to invoke change at some properties, stage 3 was implemented, which used legislation that required motel/hotel operators to meet the CFS-based public safety performance standard or risk their permits to operate in the city. This ordinance indirectly mandated the adoption of customized preventive management practices at problem properties—a much more effective strategy and one that put the onus for results where it belonged—on motel/hotel owners.

Setting attainable and data-based performance standards

Using the median CFS ratio from the year before the ordinance was implemented meant that by default, half of the properties qualified for a permit without doing anything differently. Moreover, using a simple calculation that divides the number of CFS for a given year by the number of rooms each property had available to rent holds all properties to the same performance standard while ensuring that larger properties are not overly sanctioned. This strategy is an example of ends-based regulations. Ends-based regulations generally hold greater promise for success because they apply to all facilities equally while providing flexibility for individual circumstances (Eck & Eck, 2012). Owners and managers have the freedom to find the solution that best fits their unique property and budget.

Depth of problem analysis and assessment

Successful problem-oriented-policing projects do not rely on a single source of information at any stage of the project—this project is a model in this regard.

Instead of depending on information easily accessible through police information systems, the project team spoke with property managers (e.g., CSUSB did a survey with property management and interviews with area businesses and patrons at nearby properties), conducted observations (e.g., officers checked registration logs, and independent site audits were conducted by the CSUSB partner and code enforcement), held meetings with affected stakeholders and target properties, and examined official call and crime reports. Combined, this baseline information supports a thorough investigation of the contributory factors and conditions giving rise to the crime and disorder problems. Post-intervention, replicating this data collection provides solid evidence of programmatic impact.

Approaching the problem from a risky facilities perspective

Examining crime and disorder incidents among a set of properties (i.e., apartment complexes or bars) usually reveals that a small number of places account for most of the crime and disorder incidents (Clarke & Eck, 2007; Wilcox & Eck, 2011). The set of risky facilities are properties experiencing a high level of crime and disorder (Eck, Clarke & Guerette, 2007). Comparing high-crime facilities to low-crime facilities highlights differences that often reveal important characteristics and conditions that may contribute to the crime problems observed at risky facilities (Eck, Clarke & Guerette, 2007; Eck & Eck, 2012). Underlying most criminogenic conditions are decisions, policies, and practices within the control of property management. Acknowledging this branch of crime science, the project staff had great success in Chula Vista because, even from the beginning of the project, they set out to work with property managers, the only individuals positioned to be able to make immediate changes to improve properties. Moreover, the project staff set out to shift responsibility for crime and disorder occurring at facilities to these critical actors. Undoubtedly, this orientation contributed to the longer-term success of the project.

Summary and conclusion

Crime and disorder problems are not evenly spread across an entire set of places; rather, problems are more likely to concentrate at a small number of risky facilities. Drawing information from a diverse range of sources, the City of Chula Vista and its partners were able to make a case for holding property owners and managers responsible for improving properties and correcting policies and practices that generated and sustained problems. Much can be learned from this example of problem-oriented policing.

Acknowledgments

The authors would like to thank Chula Vista Police Chief (Ret.) Rick Emerson, who initiated this project, provided his strong support throughout, and personally presented the permit-to-operate ordinance to the Chula Vista City Council for consideration; Captain (Ret.) Don Hunter, for his leadership and optimism; Sergeant (Ret.) David Eisenberg, for his sage advice and strategic thinking; Lieutenant (Ret.) Mark Jones, for his negotiating skills; and Sergeant Scott Schneider for his shrewd insights regarding problem motel guests and facilities.

Notes

1 The number of motels in Chula Vista has varied over time. There are currently 24 motels in the city.
2 We relied in particular on Eck and Wartell (1999).
3 City attorney, finance, fire, police, planning and building, and community development.
4 A copy of the ordinance (CVMC 5.39) can be found at chulavista.municipal.codes.
5 Performance periods run from October 1 to September 30.
6 Part I offenses as defined by the U.S. Federal Bureau of Investigation's Uniform Crime Reports are murder and nonnegligent homicide, rape, robbery, aggravated assault, burglary, motor vehicle theft, larceny-theft, and arson; Part II offenses are simple assault, curfew offenses and loitering, embezzlement, forgery and counterfeiting, disorderly conduct, driving under the influence, drug offenses, fraud, gambling, liquor offenses, offenses against the family, prostitution, public drunkenness, runaways, sex offenses, stolen property, vandalism, vagrancy, and weapons offenses.
7 One caveat regarding the management survey is that the 2008 response rate was 42%, compared to the 2002 rate of 88%; also, the former was administered online and the latter in person.
8 For further explanation of the total net effect calculation, see Guerette (2009) or Guerette and Bowers (2009).

References

American Hotel and Lodging Association (2014) *Lodging Industry Trends, 2015*, Washington, DC: American Hotel and Lodging Association.
American Hotel and Lodging Association (2017) *California's Hotel Industry, by the Numbers*, Washington, DC: American Hotel and Lodging Association.
Bichler, G., Schmerler, K. & Enriquez, J. (2013) 'Curbing nuisance motels: An evaluation of police as place regulators', *Policing: An International Journal of Police Strategies & Management*, 36(2): 437–462.
Clarke, R.V. (1997) *Situational Crime Prevention: Successful Case Studies* (2nd ed.), Guilderland, NY: Harrow and Heston Publishers.
Clarke, R.V. (2008) 'Situational crime prevention', in R. Wortley & L. Mazerolle (eds.), *Environmental Criminology and Crime Analysis*, Cullompton, UK: Willan Publishing, pp. 178–194.
Clarke, R.V. & Eck, J.E. (2007) *Understanding Risky Facilities*, Problem-Oriented Guides for Police, Problem-Solving Tools Series, Guide. No. 6, Washington, DC: US Department of Justice, Office of Community Oriented Policing.
Cornish, D.B. & Clarke, R.V. (2008) 'The rational choice perspective', in R. Wortley & L. Mazerolle (eds.), *Environmental Criminology and Crime Analysis*, Cullompton, UK: Willan Publishing, pp. 21–44.
Eck, J.E. (1995) 'A general model of the geography of illicit retail market places', in J. Eck & D. Weisburd (eds.), *Crime and Place*, Crime Prevention Studies, Vol. 4, Monsey, NY: Criminal Justice Press, pp. 67–94.

Eck, J.E., Clarke, R.V. & Guerette, R.T. (2007) 'Risky facilities: Crime concentration in homogeneous sets of establishments and facilities', in G. Farrell, K.J. Bowers, S.D. Johnson, & M. Townsley (eds.), *Imagination for Crime Prevention: Essays in Honour of Ken Pease*, Crime Prevention Studies, Vol. 21, Monsey, NY: Criminal Justice Press, pp. 225–264.

Eck, J.E. & Eck, E.B. (2012) 'Crime place and pollution: Expanding crime reduction options through a regulatory approach', *Criminology and Public Policy*, 11(2): 281–316.

Eck, J.E. & Wartell, J. (1999) *Reducing Crime and Drug Dealing by Improving Place Management: A Randomized Experiment*, National Institute of Justice Research Preview, Washington, DC: US Department of Justice, Office of Justice Programs.

Guerette, R.T. (2009) *Analyzing Crime Displacement and Diffusion*, Problem-Oriented Guides for Police, Problem-Solving Tools Series No. 10, Washington, DC: US Department of Justice, Office of Community Oriented Policing Services.

Guerette, R.T. & Bowers, K.J. (2009) 'Assessing the extent of crime displacement and diffusion of benefits: A review of situational crime prevention evaluations', *Criminology*, 47(4): 1331–1368.

International Association of Crime Analysts (2017) *Exploring Crime Analysis: Readings on Essential Skills* (3rd ed.), in Gallagher, K., Wartell, J., Gwinn, S., Jones, G. & Stewart, G. (eds.), Overland Park, KS: International Association of Crime Analysts.

LeBeau, J. (2011) 'Sleeping with strangers: Hotels and motels as crime attractors and crime generators', in M.A. Andresesn & B. Kinney (eds.), *Patterns, Prevention, and Geometry of Crime*, Cullompton, UK: Willan Publishing, pp. 77–102.

Rengert, G., Chakravorty, S., Bole, T. & Henderson, K. (2000) 'A geographic analysis of illegal drug markets', in M. Natarajan & M. Hough (eds.), *Illegal Drug Markets: From Research to Prevention Policy*, Crime Prevention Studies, Vol. 11, Monsey, NY: Criminal Justice Press, pp. 219–239.

Schmerler, K. (2005) *Disorder at Budget Motels*, Problem-Oriented Guides for Police, Problem-Specific Guide No. 30, Washington, DC: US Department of Justice, Office of Community Oriented Policing Services.

Scott, M.S. & Goldstein, H. (2005) *Shifting and Sharing Responsibility for Public Safety Problems*, Problem-Oriented Guides for Police, Response Guide No. 3, Washington, DC: US Department of Justice, Office of Community Oriented Policing Services.

Wilcox, P. & Eck, J.E. (2011) 'Criminology of the unpopular: Implications for policy aimed at payday lending facilities', *Criminology and Public Policy*, 10(2): 473–482.

Wiles, P. & Costello, A. (2000) *The 'Road to Nowhere': The Evidence for Traveling Criminals*, Research Study No. 207, London: Home Office.

Wortley, R. (2008) 'Situational precipitators of crime', in R. Wortley & L. Mazerolle (eds.), *Environmental Criminology and Crime Analysis*, Cullompton, UK: Willan Publishing, pp. 48–64.

19

DISORDERLY HOMELESS ENCAMPMENTS IN EUREKA, CALIFORNIA

Sharon Chamard

It was my first autumn living in Anchorage, Alaska, and I was out for a walk on one of the many paved trails along the greenbelts that crisscross the city. A little trampled-down dirt pathway off to the side piqued my interest, and I started following it. Within a couple of minutes, I came across a small clearing with a structure constructed mainly of plywood and assorted scrap building materials and covered in a bright blue tarp. Although no one was in sight, I was overwhelmed with the feeling that I had inadvertently stumbled uninvited into someone's living room and quickly turned back.

In the years since, I have deliberately visited other encampments, many of which were not as well concealed from the main trail and clean as my first discovery. No, the majority of these stank of human waste and showed evidence of harm to the adjacent environment, such as cut-down trees, pollution of nearby creeks and streams, piles of trash and other debris, and other hazards, such as open fires.

According to the January 2018 homeless point-in-time count (Henry et al., 2018: p. 10), of the close to 553,000 people who were experiencing homelessness that winter night in the United States, one-third, or about 194,500 people, were unsheltered, that is, they had spent their previous night in a place "not designated for, or ordinarily used as, a regular sleeping accommodation for people," such as an abandoned building, car, park, or outside location (Henry et al., 2018: p. 3). There are significant regional differences. In California, the location of the case study discussed in this chapter, over two-thirds (69 percent) of homeless people are unsheltered. The state contains nearly one-half of the nation's unsheltered homeless people (despite having only 12 percent of the overall population). As a comparison, the percentages of homeless people who are unsheltered is about 5 percent in northeastern states (Henry et al., 2018: p. 15).

Eureka, a finalist in the 2017 Goldstein Awards, is a coastal city of 27,000 located in Northern California. At one time, it was a booming center of the logging and timber industry. But more recently it has suffered a declining economy, and mental illness, substance abuse, and poverty have beset the community (Eureka Police Department, 2017a).

Scanning

Eureka has had a severe homelessness problem for at least 30 years. When the problem-oriented policing project began in 2015, the annual point-in-time count showed there were 730 homeless people in Eureka, about 500 (or two-thirds) of whom were unsheltered.[1] The homeless rate (per 100,000) was extremely high— 2,200 compared to 294 in California and 210 nationally. The Eureka Police Department (EPD) classified the unsheltered homeless people into five categories: the indigent, the drug addicted, the mentally ill, criminals, and "trimmigrants"— people who came to the area to work in the then illegal marijuana industry (Eureka Police Department, 2017a).

The focus of the project was the multiple homeless encampments in an area known as Palco Marsh or the "Devil's Playground," a former logging site located adjacent to a shopping center and next to the shoreline. It was estimated that over 250 people (some of them children) were living there, some on well-established campsites.

The encampments had no water, sewer, or electric service (Kroeker, 2016). It was estimated that residents produced about 186,000 pounds of human feces each year, which flowed into the adjacent tidelands. There was a concentration of calls for service for fire, heroin overdoses, and other medical emergencies. Additionally, businesses in the neighboring Bayshore Mall experienced significant problems with theft and robbery attributed to residents in the Palco Marsh encampments. The area was a hazard in other ways too. The City of Eureka had to pay a $400,000 trip-and-fall judgment to a woman after she fell while trespassing in the marsh to bring food to homeless people (Eureka Police Department, 2017a).

Previous efforts to deal with the negative impacts of the encampments through law enforcement efforts were ineffective. Although many arrests were made for municipal code violations (639 over a two-year period from 2011–2013), the problem continued. Yet the police had to do something; the area also had multiple shootings, and EPD frequently recovered firearms there. The drug addictions and severe mental illnesses experienced by many of the campers contributed to the sense that the situation in Palco Marsh was worsening and needed to be remedied (Eureka Police Department, 2017a).

Analysis

The analysis phase of the project was comprehensive and multi-faceted, entailing online surveys of businesspeople, community members, and homeless people; a review of the problem-oriented policing literature; evaluation of conditions in the problem site; and review of call-for-service and prosecution data. In addition to these efforts by EPD, the Eureka City Council and the Humboldt County Department of Health and Human Services commissioned consultants to look more broadly at homelessness (beyond the Palco Marsh situation) and recommend ways to address the community-wide problem (Focus Strategies, 2016).

Surveys of community members found that 80 percent had changed their shopping habits and that 73 percent avoided walking in open spaces because they were afraid of homeless people. Businesspeople also reported high levels of disruption because of homelessness: 65 percent said they had lost customers, and 80 percent had received complaints about homeless people. One-half of the business survey respondents said they did not feel safe leaving work.

Ninety percent of respondents to the homeless survey said they were addicted to drugs (primarily heroin and/or meth), and more than 50 percent said they suffered from mental illness (although Eureka Police estimated that the real rate of mental illness among homeless people in Devil's Playground was over 85 percent). Ninety-one percent said they wanted housing (although on their own terms). The Devil's Playground was seen by the homeless people there as an attractive venue for encampments for three main reasons: its proximity to services, safety, and isolation or being left alone. Also important were the social networks existing in the encampments. While some people there liked solitude, others appreciated Palco Marsh because they could be around their friends, often in encampments of six to ten tents. Dog ownership was widespread: half of the homeless people who participated in the survey had dogs for companionship or protection.

Response

It was expected that the homeless population in Palco Marsh, more so than homeless people in general, would be "very challenging to engage in services and also difficult to house" (Focus Strategies, 2016: p. 6). Any successful intervention would need to simultaneously focus on housing and intensive services.

The EPD response included two elements of the community-wide response recommended by the consultants: (1) focus on rapid rehousing and (2) increase the capacity to manage mentally ill homeless people. Three other recommended measures specifically focused on Palco Marsh: (3) reduce the inflow of "trimmigrants," (4) reduce the environmental impact and visual blight created by the encampments, and (5) make Palco Marsh a less attractive venue for homeless encampments (Eureka Police Department, 2017a).

It was quickly clear that the primary goal of accommodating all Palco Marsh campers in rapid rehousing regardless of ongoing drug and alcohol addiction (an approach known as "Housing First") was not feasible because of inadequate staffing and housing resources. Members of the police department or the Eureka Department of Health and Human Services (DHHS), and homeless advocate and philanthropist Betty Chinn were able to find housing for some people, largely using their personal connections, but a comprehensive, more institutionalized program did not materialize. However, the combined efforts of EPD and DHHS resulted in an existing facility, the Multiple Assistance Center (MAC), being repurposed from transitional housing for homeless families in order to take in homeless single adults, but not those with severe mental illness or a violent criminal history. The MAC served as a triage center, providing short-term emergency shelter to an average of 33 people each night, and assessing their needs for housing and other help. The average stay at the MAC was 58 nights (Eureka Police Department, 2017a).

To deal with mentally ill homeless people, EPD partnered with DHHS to create the Mobile Intervention Services Team (MIST). In 2016 alone, MIST contacted 353 severely mentally ill individuals a total of 3,138 times to help them navigate the homeless services system and stay out of jail. MIST also worked with the hospital to create a "frequent flier" list; the heaviest users of services were prioritized for housing. This approach bore immediate fruit, as housing just two of these heaviest users resulted in hundreds fewer calls for service (Eureka Police Department, 2017a).

Many "trimmigrants" ended up in Eureka after answering ads in social media venues seeking workers for marijuana grows. EPD ran such ads on Craigslist and sent letters to several hundred respondents warning them of the dangers that awaited them in Eureka, such as murders, sexual assaults, and fraudulent employment practices (Eureka Police Department, 2017a).

Making Palco Marsh less appealing as a place for homeless encampments involved a variety of activities carried out in phases. To counter the draw of the area to those seeking isolation, efforts were made to concentrate the encampments from a sprawling area of over one linear mile to one that was considerably more compact. Importantly, before concrete action was taken to remove encampments, there was significant outreach over several months to the homeless people there. Chief Andrew Mills of EPD met with them to tell them to begin making plans to leave the area. EPD officers spoke individually with residents, handing out flyers advising them of the pending camp cleanup, and directing them to services. EPD and homeless service providers held monthly service fairs to provide resources to Devil's Playground campers. Travel funds were provided for those who wanted to leave Eureka and go back where they were from. EPD communicated with the homeless campers about the new off-limits area, even erecting physical markers to clearly delineate the boundaries (Eureka Police Department, 2017a)

The city manager of Eureka and the EPD chief held a press conference on the eviction date of May 2, 2016, reporting that no campers had been arrested at that point. To manage potential problems with dogs, Eureka Animal Control and the American Society for the Prevention of Cruelty to Animals were standing by. To ensure the cleanup would be a "straight-forward and transparent process," the media, local clergy, and independent observers were encouraged to watch police actions. Supervisors of the cleanup all wore body cameras. The Eureka city attorney was involved to ensure that the eviction process was legal. Property left behind was shrink-wrapped and stored in seven Conex trailers at the site for 90 days. Obviously abandoned property was thrown away (Kroeker, 2016).

Assessment

The phased approach gave campers plenty of notice of the imminent camp abatement and offered options for transitioning out of homelessness. By the time of the eviction, 100 people had been placed in emergency temporary housing. On the actual day of the cleanup, only 143 campsites remained, many of which were abandoned (Eureka Police Department, 2017a).

The Eureka police anticipated spatial displacement and deployed resources to quickly arrest for trespassing anyone who attempted to move their encampment to adjacent property. This tactic resulted in the arrest of eight people. A "recalcitrant group" of about 30 to 40 people displaced to a homeless services area about 1.5 miles away. An approach called "leveraged deterrence" was employed here to control the behavior of members of this group. Individuals causing problems were denied services which would be regained only after the person did something to help the community and received a voucher in return (Eureka Police Department, 2017a).

Counts of thefts showed large decreases from the year before May 2, 2016 (cleanup day) to the year after. Thefts at Bayshore Mall, adjacent to the Palco Marsh encampment, declined 43 percent, from 196 to 112. There was little indication of displacement; thefts citywide dropped from 335 to 235, a 30.5 percent reduction (Eureka Police Department, 2017a).

MIST was seen as successful because it helped many of the mentally ill campers. Outcomes of other interventions were less positive. EPD concluded that the sting campaign to deter "trimmigrants" from coming to Eureka by sending warning letters to Craigslist ad respondents had "little measurable effect." The strategy of compressing the campers into a smaller area, while making it easier for police to focus their efforts, created a more dangerous environment. EPD observed that space compression did not deter additional campers but resulted in "more of a party atmosphere" (Eureka Police Department, 2017a: p. 8).

Successful abatement of the Palco Marsh encampment achieved the goal of reducing the environmental impact and visual blight caused by the illegal camping.

Follow-up

Achieving sustainability of homeless encampment cleanups can be difficult. Without modifications to the environment that attracted homeless people in the first place, encampments are likely to be reestablished in the same locations (Devuono-Powell, 2013). In Palco Marsh, a recreational bike and walking trail was constructed through the area, effectively changing norms about acceptable behavior by directly encouraging people engaging in prosocial activity to use the space.

Prior to the eviction date of May 2, 2016, the Eureka City Council voted to allow a shipping container homeless facility to be established in the downtown area. There was a lot of opposition to this by local businesses, so it was determined that it could only remain at that location for six months (Greenson, 2016). "Betty's Blue

Angel Village" housed 40 people at one time and provided temporary housing and wrap-around services for up to 90 days, with the goal of moving residents into permanent housing. It opened the day before the Palco Marsh encampment cleanup, and in the next 24 months housed 432 people (The Betty Kwan Chinn Homeless Foundation, 2019). Early results showed some success. In the first three months, 66 people stayed at the facility. Thirty-nine percent of them found housing, 41 percent found employment, 21 percent entered substance abuse treatment programs, and 36 percent became engaged with mental health services (Betty Chin, 2016).

It is worth noting that this facility allowed people to bring their dogs with them. Many emergency shelters or transitional housing facilities do not allow pets. Half of the homeless population in Palco Marsh surveyed by EPD had dogs. One study found that about 80 percent of homeless people who were caring for pets had refused housing if they could not bring their animal with them (Cronley et al., 2009).

The broader issue of homelessness continues to be a concern in Eureka, though the community has had some success beyond the abatement of Palco Marsh. The 2017 point-in-time count in Eureka found a dramatic 60 percent drop in the number of unsheltered homeless people, from 513 in 2015 to 206 in 2017 (Eureka Police Department, 2017b).

Homelessness often coexists with other social ills. In Eureka and the surrounding areas of Humboldt County, there is a growing heroin and methamphetamine problem, possibly made worse by the abatement of the Devil's Playground. Some former encampment dwellers are purportedly using methamphetamine to stay awake at night because they no longer have a place to sleep where they feel safe. Dispersing drug use throughout a larger area has led many residents to blame homeless people for the greater number of discarded syringes on the streets. As is the case in many rural parts of the country, there is inadequate availability of treatment for drug abusers in Eureka (Del Real, 2018).

Discussion

Both the Center for Problem-Oriented Policing (Chamard, 2010) and the United States Interagency Council on Homelessness (2015) have published guides about successful approaches to address the complexity of homeless encampments. This case study is an excellent demonstration of the importance of extensive planning and partnerships. Several elements contributed to the success of the project. First, there was broad local government support for the effort and strategic planning leading up to and following the cleanup day. The "Eureka Open Space Property Management Plan" provided a framework for collaborative action by various municipal departments, including the police, the fire department, Parks and Recreation, and legal and administrative services (Eureka City Council, 2015). Legislatively, existing ordinances were reviewed and new ones passed by the city council that would allow for better enforcement of community standards relating to public spaces. Relevant new ordinances concerned panhandling, control of shopping carts, and storage of personal property in public areas. The city also received a grant to build a recreational path through the Palco Marsh area. This is an excellent example of putting a "crime detractor" in a place that could become (and, indeed, had been) a "crime generator" or even a "crime attractor" (Felson & Clarke, 1998: p. 15). Prosocial activity, such as walking or biking along a seaside trail, often has the effect of discouraging those who seek to engage in antisocial activity from spending much time in the same area.

Second, there was meaningful community engagement and involvement of the non-profit sector. It is important to ensure community support for cleanup efforts to avoid confrontations between police and homeless advocates. Social services providers also need to be enlisted to help manage the diverse needs of people living in encampments. The EPD noted a high incidence of substance abuse and mental illness among Palco March residents; this is to be expected among people who have been chronically homeless in camps or on the streets.

Third, although the "big cleanup" of the Devil's Playground in Palco Marsh happened on one day, the encampment abatement was, in reality, a slow-moving affair that stretched out over months. There was communication with the campers about what was going to happen and when. There was ongoing and direct outreach to campers by a variety of service providers to connect people with what they needed to successfully transition out of encampment life. This phased approach resulted in a fairly straightforward camp cleanup, as most people had already left and taken their belongings with them. Dramatic confrontations between police and campers were avoided.

Encampment cleanups (and efforts to deal with street homeless populations in general) have potential pitfalls that were not escaped in Eureka. Homeless encampments can only become as large as they did in the Devil's Playground if authorities allow them to grow unchecked. It may seem like a reasonable response at first. Concentrating homeless people in a certain part of the city (typically the lowest-value land) reduces conflicts over public space and can keep domiciled residents' concerns at bay. In many communities, "out-of-sight, out-of-mind" has been, for many years, how populations of the street homeless have been managed. Dispersing this population through cleanup and abatement efforts can result in increased public complaints about homeless people and their behaviors.

Unlike other criminal and disorderly activity, where some people may cease or significantly reduce that behavior if there are fewer attractive opportunities to engage in it, we all must spend some of our time sleeping. Homeless encampment cleanups thus inevitably result in some degree of spatial displacement—how much there will be is largely dependent on the availability of alternative housing resources in the community. It was a struggle for Eureka to find enough places for the campers displaced from Palco Marsh. Affordable housing was limited and the ability of local or county government to directly address that shortage was constrained, ironically because of a California law that resulted from citizen action begun in Eureka in 1950. Article 34 in the California Constitution, the Public Housing Project Law, prohibits the development, construction, or acquisition of any "low rent housing project" by a state public body without a majority vote of qualified electors in the area (Aguilar-Canabal, 2018; Dillon, 2019). Because of this impediment to publicly constructing more affordable housing in Eureka, the only option for expanding the pool of homes that could be used to implement Housing First was to find willing private landlords or prevail on non-profits to develop more units.

As it turned out, one non-profit organization did provide housing for people coming out of Palco Marsh. Betty's Blue Angel Village, where people lived in retrofitted shipping containers for up to 90 days, was actually contrary to the Housing First approach, which aims to place people directly from street homelessness into permanent (and often supportive) housing. The primary recommendation of Eureka's homeless strategy and implementation plan (Focus Strategies, 2016) was to adopt Housing First throughout Humboldt County, but local resources were inadequate to bring this to fruition. So the community was forced into expanding the availability of short-term, transitional housing, which perversely may have diverted resources that could have been used more effectively to implement Housing First.

Summary and final thoughts

The police-led intervention was one part of a larger strategy undertaken by Eureka. Homelessness has many causes, few of which can be directly addressed by law enforcement. A multi-agency approach is thus more likely to be successful than one conducted mainly by police.

Interventions that seek to move homeless people from an encampment location are likely to result in displacement if there are not substantial efforts and resources used to find alternative options for the campers. Even in Eureka, where there were measures implemented months before the encampment eradication occurred to connect people in Palco Marsh with social services and housing, there was partial displacement. A small group of the hardest-to-house people remained a problem and continued to receive significant police attention, with the goal of pushing those people into accepting resources. This situation is one that vexes emergency and homeless services providers—how do you reduce the tremendous costs created by heavy users, the so-called "frequent fliers"? The most promising approach is to use screening tools such as the Vulnerability Index—Service Prioritization Decision Assistance Tool (but see Brown et al., 2018 for discussion of the predictive validity of this tool) to rank the homeless population and then offer "no-strings-attached" housing. This harm-reduction approach is likely to be offensive to many citizens, who resent their tax dollars being spent on others who are perceived to be little more than burdens to society. However, it is actually much less expensive to put frequent fliers into subsidized permanent supportive housing than it is for them to continue to live on the streets and make extensive demands on police, fire, and emergency medical services.

Note

1 The Goldstein Award submission gives the number of unsheltered homeless as 469, but other sources reporting on the 2015 point-in-time count show this number as 513. This discrepancy may be because the point-in-time count covered all of Humboldt County, and different geographical breakouts may have used to determine a count for Eureka. In

any case, it's prudent to assume point-in-time counts of unsheltered homeless people are a rough estimate, because the numbers can vary depending on factors such as how many volunteers are available to go out to locate and count people, how detectable the homeless encampments are, what time of day or night the count is conducted, and temperature.

References

Aguilar-Canabal, D. (2018) 'For housing affordability, California must amend its Constitution: Opinion', *The Bay City Beacon*, March 25.

Betty Chinn (2016) *Greater Eureka Community Outreach Project (GECOP) Three-Month Progress Report* [Facebook page].

The Betty Kwan Chinn Homeless Foundation (2019) 'Betty's Blue Angel Village'.

Brown, M., Cummings, C., Lyons, J., Carrión, A. & Watson, D.P. (2018) 'Reliability and validity of the Vulnerability Index-Service Prioritization Decision Assistance Tool (VI-SPDAT) in real-world implementation', *Journal of Social Distress and the Homeless*, 27(2): 110–117. doi:10.1080/10530789.2018.1482991

Chamard, S. (2010) *Homeless Encampments*, Problem-Oriented Guides for Police, Problem-Specific Guide No. 56, Washington, DC: US Department of Justice, Office of Community Oriented Policing Services.

Cronley, C., Strand, E.B., Patterson, D.A. & Gwaltney, S. (2009) 'Homeless people who are animal caretakers: A comparative study', *Psychological Reports*, 105(2): 481–499.

Del Real, J.A. (2018) 'Needle by needle, a heroin crisis grips California's rural north', *The New York Times*, May 8.

Devuono-Powell, S. (2013) *Homeless Encampments in Contra Costa Waterways: Regulatory Constraints, Environmental Imperatives and Humane Strategies*. Professional report submitted for Masters of City Planning, College of Environmental Design, University of California, Berkeley.

Dillon, L. (2019) 'A dark side to the California dream: How the state Constitution makes affordable housing hard to build', *Los Angeles Times*, February 3.

Eureka City Council (2015) *Eureka Open Space Property Management Plan*, Eureka, CA: City of Eureka.

Eureka Police Department (2017a) *The Vacation of 'Devil's Playground'*. Submission to the Herman Goldstein Award for Excellence in Problem-Oriented Policing, Center for Problem-Oriented Policing, Arizona State University, Phoenix, AZ.

Eureka Police Department (2017b) 'A point in time' [Blog post], June 2.

Felson, M. & Clarke, R.V. (1998) *Opportunity Makes the Thief: Practical Theory for Crime Prevention*, Police Research Series Paper 98, London: Home Office Policing and Reducing Crime Unit.

Focus Strategies (2016) *Homeless Strategy and Implementation Plan: Phase 1*, Commissioned by the City of Eureka and Humboldt County, Focus Strategies, Walnut, CA.

Greenson, T. (2016) 'Council moves forward with container community for the homeless', *North Coast Journal*, April 26.

Henry, M., Mahathey, A., Morrill, T., Robinson, A., Shivji, A. & Watt, R. (2018) *The 2018 Annual Homeless Assessment Report (AHAR) to Congress, Part I: Point-in-Time Estimates of Homelessness*, Washington, DC: US Department of Housing and Urban Development, Office of Community Planning and Development.

Kroeker, B. (2016) *Press Briefing EPD on Evictions in Palco Marsh* [Video File], May 2.

Public Housing Project Law, Cal. Cons. Article XXXIV § 1 (1950), California State Legislature, Sacramento, CA.

United States Interagency Council on Homelessness (2015) *Ending Homelessness for People Living in Encampments*, Washington, DC: United States Interagency Council on Homelessness.

20

CRIME AND DISORDER IN A RESIDENTIAL NEIGHBORHOOD IN AUSTIN, TEXAS

Marcus Felson

Austin, Texas, has a long history of social progressivism and a quest for good government. Austin also contains pockets of poverty with minority overrepresentation and frequent police contacts. The Rundberg section of Austin is a collection of smaller neighborhoods located a few miles northeast of the center, comprising five percent of the city's population but covering 2 percent of the city's geographical area and a disproportionate share of police problems for the five-year period from 2007 to 2011. That included 11 percent of the city's violent crime, 7 percent of property crime, and 9 percent of arrests. One-third of the city's prostitution arrests were made in Rundberg. This section of the city also accounted for a large share of emergency police calls.

The setting

Rundberg straddles Interstate Highway 35, creating opportunities for the illicit drug trade and for prostitution. This area is marked by vacant lots, litter, garbage, drug paraphernalia, poor parking conditions, graffiti, and loitering. Gas stations, convenience stores, smoke shops, and liquor stores are easily accessible and foster quick criminal acts. Many of the customers and offenders come from outside Rundberg. Other problems occur around its schools. Rundberg includes a large population speaking Spanish or languages other than English. Distrust of police is found among undocumented workers fearing deportation as well as documented persons who came from nations where police were unprofessional, distrusted and feared.

The onset

In 2011, Officer Ray Kianes of the Austin Police Department (APD) began to apply crime prevention through environmental design (CPTED) to Rundberg and to create strong police–community connections. Officer Kianes reached out to the

University of Texas at Austin (UT) to join these problem-solving efforts and to participate in what would be a successful federal technical assistance funding application (Austin Police Department, 2016). From 2012 through 2015, Austin police efforts to improve the Rundberg neighborhood were federally funded. Grant funds were used to pay for police overtime pay, for enhancing law enforcement and community policing efforts, and for undercover policing activities. The Rundberg effort continued after 2015 with local support in supplies or volunteer labor and with police funding its own officers. Funds would also help the city to contract services for crime analysis, research, and evaluation. From 2016 through 2018, when federal funding was depleted, the Rundberg project became the focus of UT student Project Day. For 20 years, between 1,000 and 2,000 UT students spent one day per year in concentrated efforts to improve a chosen neighborhood. Project Day augmented the APD efforts after the federal grant funding was depleted. Certain UT professors played a role in writing proposals and reports. However, the real innovations came from the police, not from the university.

Key officers

The key figures in the Rundberg project are senior police officers Rafael Kianes and Taber White. Both thoroughly understand problem-oriented policing and are quite committed to it.[1] They knew the Center for Problem-Oriented Policing website quite well and had a feel for the subtleties in situational thinking. Both Kianes and White were skilled in dealing with people and flexible in their policing tactics. Despite their common approach, they came from contrasting cultural and geographic origins, the public housing projects of New York City and West Texas, respectively. Despite their backgrounds, both officers approached policing by helping people and asserting authority when necessary. Their commanding officers, Donald Baker and Kevin Leverenz, were supportive and knowledgeable about problem-oriented policing.

From the outset, the APD officers recognized that local citizens were more impacted by disorder than by crime itself. They decided to focus on reducing such problems as disorderly groups—in parking lots, near bus stops, and near local motels. Various work groups focused on the revitalization of problem properties, code compliance, homeless intervention, and prostitution intervention.

Focus on removing brush

Over a period of 20 years, starting in 1999, UT's Project Day emphasized planting trees and removing brush—labor-intensive and difficult work. Project leaders did not articulate why they were removing brush, except for an altruistic sense that landscaping and beautification helped improve neighborhoods' appearance. At long last, these beautification efforts came to Rundberg.

During the APD project from 2012 to 2015 and in the follow-up, there were eight community cleanups in the area. Each one involved 30 to 60 participants and lasted two to four hours. Like the university students, the APD did not articulate reasons for beautification beyond a general sense of altruism and an intuitive feeling that they were doing good. Only in retrospect do they now have a theoretical justification that helps them understand why these efforts can reduce crime and disorder.

Impairing criminal cooperation

Madensen and co-workers (Madensen et al., 2017; Madensen & Eck, 2013) help us understand why brush removal can be important. They explained how illicit markets can survive by creating a network of places within a local area. Madensen's team learned that simple maps of crime locations did not tell us why crime persisted after the conditions and/or offenders at the locations where the crimes occurred were addressed. Drug dealing and other vices were especially resilient. Madensen explained this resilience by extending crime convergence theory (Felson, 2003, 2006). She distinguished four types of crime-related sites: crime sites, convergence settings, corruption spots, and comfort spaces. Offenders traveled among these sites. They met in their convergence settings, set up crimes in corruption spots, and committed those crimes in the crime sites themselves. They also had comfort spaces where they relaxed between criminal acts. Such networks of places were especially important for drug and prostitution purposes.

Criminologists have long recognized that vacant lots or buildings can provide crime sites (Spelman, 1993; Branas et al., 2011, 2016; Garvin et al., 2012; Shane, 2012). In northern climates, many of these locations are indoors. However, in the warm climate of Austin, Texas, many such locations are located outdoors, relying on high brush and untrimmed trees for concealment and shade. That helps explain why crime in Austin is sensitive to trimming and removing brush and to careful landscaping and outdoor maintenance. Austin's creek beds help plants grow and then provide offenders with places to conceal themselves or their activities. The active brush-removal efforts in Rundberg interfered with offenders' working together to provide illicit goods or services. Although brush removal and beautification were hardly new ideas, the intensity of these efforts in Austin was noteworthy. In addition, the APD applied five innovations to make their community improvements more effective.

First innovation

The first APD innovation was to promote resident engagement with neighborhood-improvement efforts. Officers Kianes and White walked along hot spot streets, inviting community members directly and personally to attend the weekly community meeting. This face-to-face effort breathed life into these meetings and enriched the SARA process. Officers might not have been surprised that citizens wanted police to reduce crime and to improve police–citizen interactions. However, citizens also wanted police to arrange safe areas for children, not a normal part of the police portfolio. The weekly meeting resulted in the creation of the Mobile Walking Beat (MWB), which conducted door-to-door and lot-to-lot surveys to help identify community concerns, reduce language barriers, and improve perceptions of the neighborhood. Each of these beats involved four to six officers rotating across hot spots in four six-hour shifts. Rather than focusing on arresting individuals or issuing citations, officers were directed to make connections and build trust with residents, youth, and business owners. Building rapport was not designed to be a public relations effort. Rather, it was a form of gathering information to assist the APD in reducing disorder.

More important, this process generated scores of little projects, which then became the focus of police actions. Throughout the Rundberg project, officers were oriented to detail. For example, Officer Kianes wrote a letter to the superintendent of schools seeking to improve sight lines near the school—a specific but direct application of CPTED. Officers asked the local homeless men to stay away from the path where children walked to school, and the men complied with the request. Although the officers did not themselves administer health care, they put residents in touch with health care professionals. Police would need to collect more detailed information to carry out these little projects, and so they tried another innovation.

Second innovation

Normally we think of a survey as a questionnaire that leads to a tally of answers inserted into a report, with individual identities concealed. In contrast, the APD used their security survey to record information on individual complaints and then to address those complaints one by one. This innovative use of the security survey produced specific details about what had to be done.

This survey was more like a conversation. The primary question was if the person felt safe. If the answer was "yes," officers then shared information about neighborhood and city resources. If the answer was "no," officers would ask why and annotate their responses to figure out the next steps. This provided a source of data beyond official reports to police. It revealed the extent of community concerns about such problems as homeless persons, drug dealing, suspicious persons, prostitution, and public intoxication. Residents would sometimes name a specific house where drugs were sold or a specific homeless person at the bus stop who scared them every day. These specific complaints often were about disorder, not about criminal acts. At times, the main concern was a pile of trash or a broken street lamp.

Police officers became the go-to persons for getting thorns out of the community's side. In the process, officers also gained detailed information about localized crime and disorder. In effect, they were reaching out for informants rather than waiting for people to call in. Yet police were not scaring people by starting with questions about a specific crime or an offender who might retaliate. Over the years of the funded project, the MWB made over 16,000 contacts in the area, learning the specific concerns of community members while teaching them how to enhance their own safety. The APD was able to connect many residents with city and community resources and to produce a plentiful list of small "wins." They demonstrated to local people that they were listening and acting. With very specific local assistance, police were able to shrink the open-air drug market, to clean up unsightly spots, and to install lighting where needed.

Third innovation

Rundberg had become a center for illicit markets, serving the larger region. Many of these offenses occurred on weekends, often late in the afternoon and early in the morning. Illicit markets for prostitution and drugs also enhanced violence and gang activities, especially on streets near the interstate highway.

APD had been arresting people for decades in this area. However, they did this in an innovative way during the funded period, adding an offender-debriefing process to intensive arrests. These arrests were made highly visible by saturating a very small area with eight officers, one supervisor, and one transport vehicle. Officers especially arrested suspects with a recent criminal history involving drugs, gangs, prostitution, and violence. The innovative component of this process was to ask those arrested where they were from and why they were picking the Rundberg area for their criminal activity. Officers learned that 70 percent of those arrested were not residents of the Rundberg neighborhood.

Fourth innovation

A fourth innovation had to do with the homeless population. Scanning the crime data, the APD learned that homeless persons committed about 44 percent of the violent crimes in Rundberg. On the other hand, most of the local homeless people were not known to be violent, and many were victims of crime by nonhomeless persons. The homeless population in Rundberg congregated in a 22-acre section of vacant land, within which many had created informal property lines. Part of the plan was to revitalize this area in order to benefit the neighborhood. That meant that homeless people would be displaced. Commander Baker opposed a simple eviction process, fearing that it would displace the homeless to other areas. Instead, the APD devised a Care Team that helped officers link homeless individuals to social service agencies, mental health providers, and veteran's programs. Experts figured out each homeless person's specific needs, then how to provide relevant assistance. To avoid scaring homeless persons and to build trust, officers went out with social workers, bringing food, backpacks, and supplies. Orderly relocations were arranged when possible, although 5 of the 40 persons would not accept assistance. The vacant land was then purchased and sold to a new charter school, which joined in educational reforms, agreed to provide the community access to their school's playfields, and sold six acres to the city for a park. This illustrates how the Rundberg project sought to tie together the many threads of neighborhood improvement. Even when evictions were carried out, services were provided to those evicted.

Fifth innovation

In 2014, Officer Kianes created the Rundberg Educational Advancement District (READ), putting up signs that announced it. The project sought to coordinate activities, parent services, and other resources among five neighborhood schools. The Council on At-Risk Youth focused tutoring efforts on students with the greatest probability of getting into trouble. Youth advisors were to meet with groups of five to eight students, also giving personal attention to individuals. Fifty students at Dobie Middle School were supplemented by another 50 students in two feeding elementary schools and 50 ninth grades at Lanier High School.

The most innovative aspect of the READ effort was that local youths of middle school and high school age participated in the cleanup efforts in the neighborhoods. That meant that they burned calories, saw progress with their own eyes, and shared in the credit for improvements. They were engaged outside as well as inside.

Improvements

The Rundberg improvements unfolded in a period of decreasing crime in Austin. It is therefore difficult to decide the appropriate comparison group. The university research team (Springer, Yuma & Whitt, 2016) seems not to have been experienced in no-control-group hot spots were designated, and the main hot spot comparisons were made with overall city crime rates. Given that Rundberg is the city's most at-risk area, one could argue that the Rundberg share of Austin's crime and disorder should *rise* during a period of crime reduction in the rest of the city. Even maintaining the same share of crime and disorder could be interpreted as a victory.

Fortunately, the Rundberg share of Austin's crime declined somewhat. The Rundberg share of the city's violent crime was 13 percent before federal funding began and declined below 12 percent during the intervention period (April 2014–August 2015) For the Rundberg grant area from 2012 through 2017, reported property crimes declined noticeably. Unfortunately, there was no apparent way to assess the significance of this decline, except that Rundberg at least kept up with declines in the rest of the city.

Two specific crime types indicate more strongly the progress in Rundberg between 2012 and 2015. While Austin's aggravated assaults declined 20.1 percent, the corresponding decline for Rundberg was 25.7 percent. While aggravated robbery declined 4.1 percent for the city, the Rundberg decline was 20.5 percent. For the same period, Rundberg's declines were not greater for burglary of vehicle or burglary of residence.

The university research team found that crime declined in all three hot spots. Unfortunately, they had defined Hot Spot One and Hot Spot Three to contain too many blocks for assessment purposes. Those hot spots experienced declines of 5.77 percent and 20 percent, respectively. *Hot Spot Two was much smaller geographically. Its crime reduction reached 44.44 percent.* One suspects that the interventions and the evaluations would have been more successful had the other two hot spots been defined for smaller areas to allow more focus on specific problems and better measurement of outcomes.

The university research team did not build into their design an important fact: that Hot Spot One was quite different from the others, meriting a narrower geographic definition as well as a sharper problem definition. Hot Spot One straddled the Interstate highway, and its crime was fueled by prostitution and drug sales. Its violence and disorder were likely related to these two driving forces. By removing vacant land and redirecting its use, and by intensive enforcement, the APD was able to reduce Rundberg's regional role in providing illicit goods and services by more than 40 percent, as noted above. Had the university research team identified the specific budget motels, hotels, and apartment complexes that fostered prostitution and drug sales they would likely have been able to document even sharper decline. In short, the Rundberg project was probably even more successful in reducing illegal markets in Hot Spot One than the report indicated.

On the other hand, surveys demonstrated dramatic increases in the share of residents feeling safe in the community. In 2014, a survey of 800 respondents indicated that only 34 percent felt safe in the area. In 2015, this increased to 74 percent. This major subjective improvement probably reflected a combination of police engagement with a decline in social and physical disorder within the community. Sharper documentation would have been valuable. Yet the author of this chapter believes that the declines in public disorder were real, as reflected in the optimistic reports from residents.

The Rundberg officers take pride in their work with the local schools and point towards improvements in how Dobie Middle School ranks on a state and local basis. School attendance rates continued to be a bit lower than state and Austin levels but not by much. Test scores continued to be lower than state and Austin levels, but given likely improvements in the latter, they may have held their own. Some of the test scores for some grades indicated improvements. School climate measurements indicated declines between 2015 and 2016, but improvements in 2017 at least to prior levels and sometimes higher. Nine out of ten students said that teachers "know who I am" and "know what I'm good at." Most students were now agreeing: "I don't give up," "I try to calm myself down," "I get along with my classmates," and "I say 'no' to friends who want me to break the rules."

In general, the Rundberg project was a police success in applying many detailed problem-oriented ideas and at least holding back crime increases, if not helping reduce criminal behavior. Most important, social and physical disorder decreased. The Rundberg project provides many illustrations of crime-reduction applications while underscoring the need for university partners to think more cogently and specifically about how to address problems directly.

General lessons learned

It is striking how much the key officers in Rundberg learned about their territory, not just spatially but also temporally and topically. They made themselves the faces of local government service and problem solving. This occurred because APD had experience with problem-oriented policing and knew of useful resources such as the Center for Problem-Oriented Policing website, not because the local university partners assisted them.

Interestingly, the Rundberg initiatives provide the ideal opportunity for a three-photo documentation method. Such an approach could take three photographs of each small improvement, one before, one during the improvement phase, and one after improvements have been made. Each set of three could be dated and its map locations indicated. In some cases, the time of day would be relevant. Photos could be sorted and statistically analyzed. Representative sets of photos could be incorporated in reports and appendices. A database of improvements could be developed, with ongoing entry of improvements suggested, methods applied, and outcomes, including code words to assist in the organization of information for subsequent reports. A diversified application of problem-oriented policing ideas generates hundreds, perhaps thousands, of small improvements. These improvements deserve to be documented with more detail to assist replication, modification, and future applications.

Indeed, we learn several other lessons from the Austin projects. The first nine lessons are quite general:

1   Discontinuities among local organizations (local discontinuities) require extra effort to overcome, since each has its own agenda and set of projects.
2   Discontinuities over time require extra effort to overcome. The best way to do so is to develop a lasting organization or section with a problem-oriented focus.
3   Universities are often ill equipped for practical projects applying social science knowledge and for breaking down silos within themselves or with their larger community.
4   Climate influences crime reduction strategy. In the Texas climate, clearing brush can have a major impact on a local environment and help break down networks of outdoor places involved in crime.
5   Strategies and tactics of neighborhood recovery might be much more effective and lasting in a growing local economy than in a shrinking local economy.
6   Massive volunteer activities can be important for neighborhood recovery and reducing physical disorder. Universities can contribute to these efforts.
7   Proactivity should be combined with immediacy. Children should be invited to go out and play now. Middle school children should be enlisted to collect trash today. Citizen surveys should specify exactly what has to be done and when.
8   Academic contributors should take more time to explain what is happening on the ground in academic journals rather than relegating practical work to unpublished reports.
9   The crime–place network approach offers a highly effective strategy for breaking down networks of places that feed illegal markets.

Police lessons learned

The preceding general lessons are supplemented by lessons that apply more directly to policing tactics:

1   Police must give extreme attention to local detail to make problem-oriented policing succeed.
2   An officer spending a long time in the area is more likely to know these details.
3   A hot-spot map is not sharp enough for police focus. Police should keep asking questions, such as "Is this hot spot mainly about prostitution after dark? Is it mainly an after-school hot spot? Are problems focused on weekend evenings?"
4   Police should debrief persons arrested to find out why they come to the current spot.
5   Energetic door-to-door outreach is important for populating community meetings and finding out specific concerns.
6   Police need much better techniques for documenting each small action. Photographs could be taken before, during, and after a change is instituted.
7   Police should organize a problem-solving ledger to document each complaint and suggestion and what changes they instituted.
8   Citizens appreciate police officers who introduce them to service providers. They probably do not expect the officers to provide those services personally.
9   Citizens will quickly cooperate with police in reducing specific disorder spots, even when they are reluctant to name specific offenders.

Overall, the Rundberg project gives us a window into the future of multi-faceted problem-oriented policing. It shows the possibilities for a plentitude of small projects, each oriented toward a specific problem. It also reminds us to find a way to document those projects and the progress they produce.

Note

1 Both officers were interviewed while preparing this chapter.

References

Austin Police Department (2016) *Restore Rundberg: Leveraging Community Engagement to Reduce Crime and the Fear of Crime.* Submission for the Herman Goldstein Award for Excellence in Problem-Oriented Policing, Center for Problem-Oriented Policing, Arizona State University, Phoenix, AZ.

Branas, C.C., Cheney, R.A., MacDonald, J.M., Tam, V.W., Jackson, T.D. & Ten Have, T.R. (2011) 'A difference-in-differences analysis of health, safety, and greening vacant urban space', *American Journal of Epidemiology*, 174: 1296–1306.

Branas, C.C., Kondo, M.C., Murphy, S.M., South, E.C., Polsky, D. & MacDonald, J.M. (2016) 'Urban blight remediation as a cost-beneficial solution to firearm violence', *American Journal of Public Health*, 106: 2158–2164.

Felson, M. (2003) 'The process of co-offending', in M. Smith & D. Cornish (eds.), *Theory for Practice in Situational Crime Prevention*, Crime Prevention Studies, Vol. 16, Monsey, NY: Criminal Justice Press, pp. 149–168.

Felson, M. (2006) *The Ecosystem for Organized Crime*, Helsinki: European Institute for Crime Prevention and Control, Affiliated with the United Nations.

Garvin, E., Branas, C., Keddem, S., Sellman, J., & Cannuscio, C. (2012) 'More than just an eyesore: Local insights and solutions on vacant land and urban health', *Journal of Urban Health*, 90: 412–426.

Madensen, T.D. & Eck, J.E. (2013) 'Crime places and place management', in F.T. Cullen & P. Wilcox (eds.), *The Oxford Handbook of Criminological Theory*, New York: Oxford University Press, pp. 554–578.

Madensen, T.D., Herold, M., Hammer, M.G. & Christenson, B.R. (2017) 'Place-based investigations to disrupt crime place networks', *Police Chief Magazine*, April.

Shane, J. (2012) *Abandoned Buildings and Lots*, Problem-Oriented Guides for Police, Problem-Specific Guide No. 64, Washington, DC: U.S. Department of Justice, Office of Community Oriented Policing Services.

Spelman, W. (1993) 'Abandoned buildings: Magnets for crime', *Journal of Criminal Justice*, 21: 481–495.

Springer, D., Yuma, P. & Whitt, A. (2016) *City of Austin Byrne Criminal Justice Innovation Program Final Report and Replication Guide*. Prepared for the Department of Justice, the Austin Police Department, and the Restore Rundberg Revitalization Team, University of Texas at Austin Center for Social Work Research and City of Austin, Austin, TX.

PART V

Theft, robbery and burglary

21

ROBBERIES OF CONVENIENCE STORES IN HOUSTON, TEXAS

Nancy G. La Vigne and Nkechi Erondu

Introduction

In 1979, policing scholar Herman Goldstein published an article that offered a solution to those seeking a redefinition of policing in America (Goldstein, 1979). He observed that policing was largely focused on process, centering on the means to crime control and reduction rather than the ends. Examples of process-focused policing include measuring performance based on metrics such as response times and the volume of arrests, contraband confiscations, and vehicle stops made. Such means-based practices, which remain in wide use today, have fueled biased policing (Gates, 1995; Gaines, 2002; Meehan & Ponder, 2002; Tomaskovic-Devey, Mason & Zingraff, 2004; Gelman, Kiss & Fagan, 2006; Michalowski, 2010), mass incarceration (Austin & Irwin, 2000; Pattillo, Weiman & Western, 2004), and low levels of trust in the police among residents of communities experiencing high crime and a heavy police presence (Lundman & Kaufman, 2003; Tyler & Huo, 2002; Gelman, Kiss & Fagan, 2006; Warren, 2011; Russell, 2002; La Vigne, Fontaine & Dwivedi, 2017).

By contrast, outcomes-based policing focuses on the ends, such as reducing the opportunities for the commission of some crimes through preventive patrol and other measures, aiding individuals who are in danger of physical harm, resolving conflict, and identifying and apprehending those who had engaged in criminal activities. Rather than repeatedly reacting to crime problems with the same process-oriented approach day after day, Goldstein framed a role for police in which they identify the underlying precursors to crime and develop solutions to address them. This was the birth of problem-oriented policing (POP), also termed by others problem-solving policing—a concept that has been tested and found effective to address a wide array of policing problems (Goldstein, 1990; Sherman & Weisburd, 1995; National Research Council, 2004; Weisburd et al., 2008).

While POP is by no means a single, comprehensive solution to public safety—a place exists for basic police functions such as routine patrolling, responding to calls for service, controlling crowds, and investigating crime—it offers a new lens through which police can view and address the types of problems they encounter on a routine basis. Moreover, POP recognizes that police are on the frontlines of all manner of societal ills—mental health issues, substance abuse disorders, interpersonal violence, homelessness—and lack the resources to solve all those problems alone. Goldstein noted this reality in his seminal article as well, putting forth an elegant solution: use police authority to enlist other state and nonstate actors to address the underlying factors driving crime and disorder problems.

This chapter describes a POP project that employs the use of regulatory measures to tackle the common and persistent problem of convenience store crime. In the field of criminology's relatively short history of focusing on the intersection of crime and place (see Weisburd et al., 2016), convenience stores—small shops typically operating around the clock to sell gas, food, and sundries—have featured prominently. Convenience stores have long been magnets for all manner of crime and disorder, from robbery to loitering, and are so well known for their criminogenic traits that the stores are sometimes referred to as "stop-and-robs" in American parlance.

Studies of convenience store crime have shown that the probability of robberies is significantly affected by factors related to both the external environment (e.g., community maintenance, land use, street patterns) and the internal environment (e.g., business practices, such as the cash control policies and number of employees) (Crow & Bull, 1975; Jeffery et al., 1987; Callahan & Clifton, 1987; La Vigne, 1994; Dario, 2016). This is demonstrated by the relative success of various convenience store crime-prevention measures related to location/number of cashiers, number of mirrors, exterior lighting, vehicular traffic, use of security devices, and clear visibility both within and outside the store (Jeffery et al., 1987; Callahan & Clifton, 1987; La Vigne, 1994; Bellamy, 1996). Research generally supports the theory that a few minor changes in business practices or store design have the potential to reduce convenience-store crime dramatically, with some studies concluding that these interventions are most effective for repeatedly robbed stores or "risky facilities" (Bellamy, 1996; Eck, Clarke & Guerette, 2007).

Scanning

In 2007, the city of Houston, Texas, experienced an all-time high volume of violent crimes occurring at convenience stores, with 1,100 robberies, 400 aggravated assaults, and 10 homicides occurring on store properties. These crimes led to frustration on the part of owners, fear for safety among employees, and a reluctance of customers to shop at convenience stores. Meanwhile, residents in areas surrounding the stores lamented the generation of crime in their communities. Police were keenly aware of the problem and also recognized that their routine approach of repeatedly responding to calls for service and investigating the crimes was having little impact on crime reduction. The problem of convenience-store crime in Houston was so pronounced that then-Mayor Bill White established a Convenience Store Task Force, with the Houston Police Department (HPD) at the core of the task force along with the Greater Houston Retailers Association (GHRA), individual store and convenience-store-chain owners, and petroleum companies such as Exxon and Valero, given the volume of gasoline sold at convenience stores.

An initial step of the task force was to codify what defined "convenience store"—deciding on the size and determining the dividing line between gas stations that sell convenience items and convenience stores that have gas pumps—and then identify all businesses meeting that definition. Defining "convenience store" was a necessary precursor both to ensure the scope of the task force was sufficiently focused and that the correct businesses were targeted for intervention.

Analysis

Once defined, crime analysts in HPD examined the distribution of crimes by store, geography, time of day, day of the week, and various types of offending behavior patterns. In accordance with the robust literature on crime concentration (Sherman, Gartin & Buerger, 1989; Clarke & Weisburd, 1990; Brantingham & Brantingham, 1995; Eck, Clarke & Guerette, 2007; Weisburd, 2015), this analysis revealed that a small share of stores was responsible for a large share of convenience-store crimes. The vast majority of robberies occurred at smaller individually owned stores, whereas large chain stores had comparatively few violent crimes at their locations, despite the volume of business that transpired there.

HPD officers solicited input from store owners and learned that whereas the larger stores had already implemented many of the best practices in crime prevention cited in the literature, proprietors of smaller stores—often family-run businesses—lacked an understanding of crime-prevention measures, along with the resources to implement them. Interviews with owners of these stores revealed that many were immigrants, originating from countries where the principles of crime prevention were less well developed. In addition, because the stores were owned and typically operated by owners and their family members, convenience-store staff were less likely to comply with demands for money during attempted robberies, escalating the violence associated with such crimes.

A final component of the analysis was to learn about the people who were engaged in convenience-store crime to understand their demographics, motivations, and modus operandi. HPD officers learned that young men in their twenties were the most common perpetrators of convenience-store crimes, motivated by the perception that stores represented easy targets with quick rewards and a low likelihood of getting caught. The perception that convenience-store crime could be committed with impunity was reinforced by the observation that people engaged in drug dealing, panhandling, and prostitution on and around convenience-store properties were typically tolerated by store owners and management.

Response

HPD officers approached the response to the problem in a collaborative manner, developing partnerships with store owners and enlisting the support of the mayor and the city council to pass an ordinance mandating that all retailers meeting the definition of convenience store register with the city. As described below, the ordinance prescribed a number of crime-prevention measures consistent with the principles of Situational Crime Prevention (SCP). In addition, officers visited each store to encourage owners to register, educate them about the reasons for and importance of crime-prevention measures, and convey that noncompliance would result in a fine. Once registered, stores received a crime-prevention packet containing guidance and training materials, and officers followed up by visiting stores to educate owners and inspect stores for compliance.

Table 21.1 illustrates the prescribed measures of Houston's convenience-store ordinance in the context of SCP principles. A theoretical close cousin to POP, SCP

TABLE 21.1 Mandated convenience store crime-prevention measures in accordance with SCP*

Increasing Perceived Effort	Increasing Perceived Risks	Reducing Anticipated Rewards	Removing Excuses
Target hardening	*Formal surveillance*	*Target removal*	*Rule setting*
Annual safety training for employees and owners on cash handling	Trespass affidavit to facilitate police enforcement of loitering	Limiting cash on hand, with accompanying signage	"No Trespassing" signs in English and Spanish
Requirement of drop safe	*Surveillance by employees*		
Signage indicating existence of drop safe and inability of employees to open safe	Surveillance camera system		
	Silent alarm system with accompanying signage		
	Annual safety training for employees and owners on robbery prevention/response		
	Height strip at store entrance/exit		
	Natural surveillance		
	Unobstructed windows and public access doors		

* SCP also includes a "Reducing Provocations" column. However, this method was not employed as part of Houston's response to convenience store crimes.

is a framework for closing off criminal opportunities that assumes that people who are likely to engage in crime can be deterred, distracted, or disincentivized from offending by increasing the effort, enhancing the risk, reducing the reward, reducing the provocations, or removing the excuses associated with criminal acts (Clarke, 1997; Clarke & Homel, 1997).

Increasing the perceived effort of convenience-store crime was addressed by mandating the use of a drop safe and requiring annual safety training of all employees on how to use it.

Increasing the perceived risks of convenience-store crime was accomplished through a series of measures designed to enhance formal, employee, and natural surveillance. Formal surveillance was enhanced by requiring the execution of a signed trespassing affidavit from each store owner allowing police to enforce loitering on store property, as drug dealing was commonplace at many high-crime establishments. Employee surveillance was bolstered by mandating that all stores have at least two digital high-resolution surveillance cameras, one with a view of the cash-register area and the other of the store entrance/exit. Stores are required to maintain video footage for a minimum of 30 days and provide it to the police department on request. Surveillance was further enhanced by the requirement of a silent alarm system at the cashier's counter and the installation of height strips next to the store's entrance/exit. The height strip is primarily designed to prompt employees to make note of distinguishing characteristics of people who commit crimes at stores as they are exiting the premises, but its presence may also serve as a deterrent. The ordinance also aimed to enhance natural surveillance, requiring store owners to keep their doors and windows clear of signs and other obstructions so that police and passersby can have a clear view of what is transpiring inside the store.

To reduce the anticipated rewards of convenience-store crime—and specifically robbery—the ordinance coupled the requirement of a drop safe with a directive that stores must develop a policy of restricting the amount of cash in the register and routinely depositing excess cash into the drop safe. This message was underscored through mandated signage indicating that the volume of cash in the register is restricted and that employees do not have access to the safe.

A final measure of the ordinance pertains to the SCP category of removing excuses. By requiring stores to erect "No Trespassing" signs in both English and Spanish, the message is conveyed that the store has no tolerance for loiterers and people engaging in drug dealing. This message, in turn, affords staff more confidence in requesting loiterers to exit the property.

This compilation of crime-prevention measures was mandated of all stores. Enforcement of the ordinance fell primarily on police shoulders: officers first had to ensure all stores were complying with the mandate to register with the city as a convenience store, which required an extensive outreach and education campaign. Once registered, police set about ensuring the stores were adhering to the prescribed crime-prevention measures, conducting inspections, issuing warnings, and leaving behind a report to store owners on any observed violations, a copy of which was sent to HPD's command office. Persistent failure to comply with aspects of the ordinance resulted in a fine of $500.

Assessment

Initial analyses of the impact of HPD's multi-faceted response to convenience-store crimes demonstrate a resounding success. Convenience-store crimes of all types began declining at the onset of the initiative in 2007, then plummeted following the passage of the ordinance in 2009, with an 80% reduction in homicides, a 77% reduction in robberies, and similar declines in other violent crimes along with burglaries between 2007 and 2012 (see Figure 21.1). These positive results were attributed to high levels of ordinance compliance across all stores; interviews with owners indicated that they felt safer as a result of the ordinance and viewed the crime-prevention effort as a partnership rather than something that was imposed on them in an adversarial manner. While some anecdotal evidence indicated modest displacement of crime to retail stores, HPD officers viewed that as a signal that the convenience store crime-prevention measures were working as intended.

Discussion

This case study of Houston's efforts to prevent convenience-store crime presents a shining example of police leveraging civil authority to enlist compliance with crime-prevention measures. As outlined in La Vigne (2018), such regulatory measures are most likely to yield their intended impacts when they are consistent with principles embodied in the acronym **AGILE** (adaptable, germane, incentive-based,

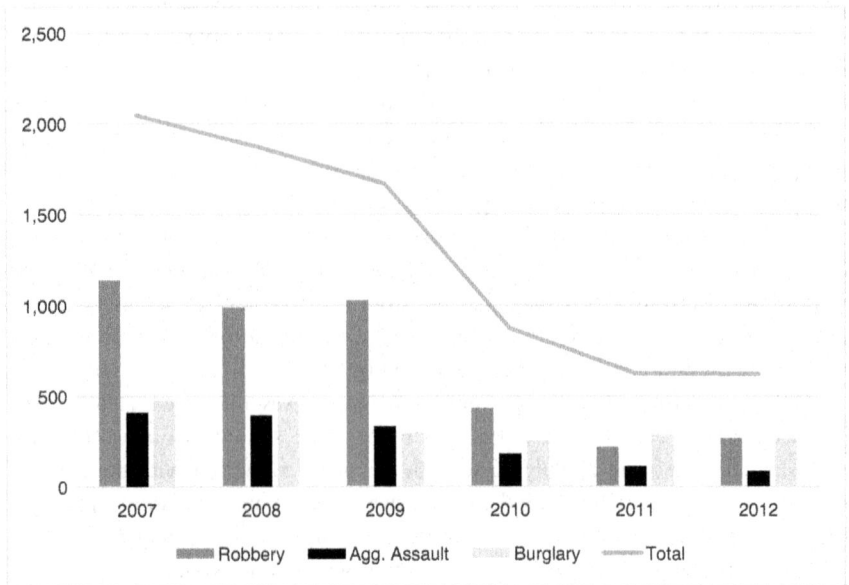

FIGURE 21.1 Part 1 crimes at Houston, Texas, convenience stores, 2007–2012

legitimate, evaluated). In the context of this Houston case study, the measures were **adaptable** to the specific context of convenience-store crime and relatively crime-specific given their focus on violence reduction. They were **germane** to the intended audience of convenience stores, retail associations, and petroleum companies that represent the key stakeholders associated with the problem. The measures were also **incentive-based**, in that the education, training, and enforcement components of the ordinance appealed to the concerns and business interests of the store owners. The fact that the measures prescribed in the ordinance were developed with the input of a task force composed of key stakeholders and focused on building trust and shared public-safety goals made the response **legitimate**, further enhancing the likelihood of compliance. And importantly, the initiative was **evaluated** to examine the impact of the ordinance on crime, potential displacement, and perceptions of safety.

Despite these best practices, the impact of Houston's response was not fully sustained over time. As illustrated in Figure 21.2, while the initial drop in crime was very likely associated with the passage of the ordinance, its impact waned over time and in later years crime at Houston convenience stores crept up again—not to preintervention levels but a meaningful increase all the same. This begs the question, Why were the crime-prevention impacts of Houston's ordinance not better sustained over time?

Communications with an HPD officer who spearheaded the POP project suggest a variety of factors might explain the lack of sustainability of the ordinance's crime-prevention impact, including implementation fatigue, the emergence of new

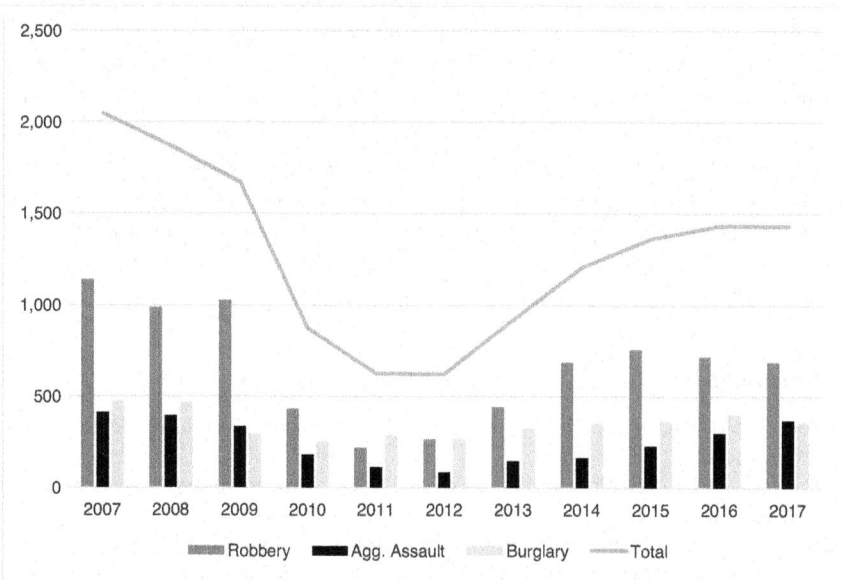

FIGURE 21.2 Part 1 crimes at Houston, Texas, convenience stores, 2007–2017

crime problems and public-safety initiatives, and changes in leadership (Watson, 2018). A key component of the success of the ordinance was the fact that a dedicated unit in HPD was tasked with routine inspections of stores and ongoing education of store owners—a time-consuming effort that dropped in priority following the crime decline. Another likely explanation for the uptick in crime is that key staff in charge of the POP project were promoted and reassigned to other units, leaving behind others who perhaps approached the inspection and education activities with less enthusiasm and vigilance. It is important to recognize that the large volume of convenience stores in Houston—roughly 1,000—makes ongoing inspection of stores a monumental and arguably infeasible task, particularly given competing public-safety priorities.

Conclusion and implications for alternative POP strategies

The Houston case study demonstrates the efficacy of employing POP in the context of convenience-store crime. However, in hindsight, the response developed by the task force could have been enhanced and better targeted by drawing from Scott and Goldstein's (2005) escalated response model, whereby the intervention begins by focusing on the least invasive (and burdensome) types of corrective actions and gradually escalates to more toothsome enforcement. Such an approach may have been a better use of police resources, although still would be burdensome given the number of stores. Perhaps an even more effective approach is akin to the Chula Vista Police Department's efforts to get motel owners to comply with crime-prevention measures, which focused on motels with crimes and calls for service that were above a certain threshold (Chula Vista Police Department, 2009). This approach essentially flips the Houston convenience-store response on its head: instead of identifying stores that are not following prescribed crime-prevention actions, which requires inspection of all establishments, officers single out businesses that exceed acceptable crime levels—a much smaller share of establishments. In the context of Houston's convenience store crime-prevention ordinance, perhaps compliance with crime-prevention mandates could only be required of stores that exceed a specific volume of crime as a proportion of total retail sales. This concept can be an effective means of passing the cost of crime back onto the businesses that are responsible for generating it (Eck & Eck, 2012).

References

Austin, J. & Irwin, J. (2000) *It's about Time: America's Imprisonment Binge*, Belmont, CA: Wadsworth.

Bellamy, L. (1996) 'Situational crime prevention and convenience store robbery', *Security Journal*, 7(1): 41–52.

Brantingham, P.J. & Brantingham, P.L. (1995) 'Criminality of place: Crime generators and crime attractors', *European Journal on Criminal Policy and Research*, 3(3): 5–26.

Callahan, P.T. & Clifton, W. (1987) *Convenience Store Robberies in Gainesville, Florida: A Intervention Strategy by the Gainesville Police Department*, Gainesville, FL: Gainesville Police Department.

Chula Vista Police Department (2009) *Reducing Crime and Disorder at Motels and Hotels in Chula Vista, CA*. Submission for the Herman Goldstein Award for Excellence in Problem-Oriented Policing, Center for Problem-Oriented Policing, Arizona State University, Phoenix, AZ.

Clarke, R.V. (ed.) (1997) *Situational Crime Prevention: Successful Case Studies* (2nd ed.), Guilderland, NY: Harrow and Heston.

Clarke, R.V. & Homel, R. (1997) 'A revised classification of situational crime prevention techniques', in S.P. Lab (ed.), *Crime Prevention at a Crossroads*, Cincinnati, OH: Anderson Publishing.

Clarke, R.V. & Weisburd, D. (1990) 'On the distribution of deviance', in R.V. Clarke & D.M. Gottfredson (eds.), *Policy and Theory in Criminal Justice: Contributions in Honor of Leslie T. Wilkins*, London: Gower, Farnborough & Hants, pp. 10–27.

Crow, W. & Bull, J. (1975) *Robbery Deterrence: An Applied Behavioral Science Demonstration: Final Report*, La Jolla, CA: Western Behavioral Science Institute.

Dario, L.M. (2016) *Crime at Convenience Stores: Assessing an In-Depth Problem-Oriented Policing Initiative*. Doctoral dissertation, Arizona State University, Phoenix, AZ.

Eck, J.E., Clarke, R.V. & Guerette, R.T. (2007) 'Risky facilities: Crime concentration in homogeneous sets of establishments and facilities', in G. Farrell, K. Bowers, S.D. Johnson & M. Townsley (eds.), *Imagination for Crime Prevention: Essays in Honour of Ken Pease*, Crime Prevention Studies, Vol. 21, Boulder, CO: Lynne Rienner Publishers, pp. 225–264.

Eck, J.E. & Eck, E. (2012) 'Crime place and pollution: Expanding crime reduction options through a regulatory approach', *Criminology and Public Policy*, 11(2): 281–316.

Gaines, L. (2002) 'An analysis of traffic stop data in Riverside, California', *Police Quarterly*, 9: 210–233.

Gates, H.L. (1995) 'Thirteen ways of looking at a Black man', *The New Yorker*, p. 59.

Gelman, A., Kiss, A. & Fagan, J. (2006) 'An analysis of the NYPD's stop-and-frisk policy in the context of claims of racial bias', *Columbia Public Law Research Paper*, No. 05–95.

Goldstein, H. (1979) 'Improving policing: A problem-oriented approach', *Crime and Delinquency*, 25(2): 34–35.

Goldstein, H. (1990) *Problem-Oriented Policing*, New York: McGraw-Hill.

Jeffery, C.R., Hunter, R.D. & Griswold, J. (1987) 'Crime prevention and computer analysis of convenience store robberies in Tallahassee, Florida', *Security Systems* (August), and *Florida Police Journal* (Spring).

La Vigne, N. (1994) 'Gasoline drive-offs: Designing a less convenient environment', in R.V. Clarke (ed.), *Crime Prevention Studies*, Vol. 2. Monsey, NY: Criminal Justice Press.

La Vigne, N. (2018) 'Applying regulatory measures to address crime problems: An agile approach to enhancing public safety', *The Annals of the American Academy of Political and Social Science*, 679(1): 202–215.

La Vigne, N., Fontaine, J. & Dwivedi, A. (2017) *How Do People in High-Crime, Low-Income Communities View the Police?*, Washington, DC: Urban Institute, Justice Policy Center.

Lundman, R.J. & Kaufman, R.L. (2003) 'Driving while black: Effects of race, ethnicity and gender on citizen self-reports of traffic stops and police actions', *Criminology*, 41: 195–220.

Meehan, A.J. & Ponder, M.C. (2002) 'Race and place: The ecology of racial profiling African American motorists', *Justice Quarterly*, 19: 399–430.

Michalowski, R. (2010) 'Keynote address: Critical criminology for a global age', *Western Criminology Review*, 11(1): 3–10.

National Research Council (2004) *Fairness and Effectiveness in Policing: The Evidence*, Washington, DC: The National Academies Press. doi:10.17226/10419

Pattillo, M., Weiman, D. & Western, B. (eds.) (2004) *Imprisoning America: The Social Effects of Mass Incarceration*, New York: Russell Sage Foundation.

Russell, K.K. (2002) 'Racial profiling: A status report of the legal, legislative, and empirical literature', *Rutgers Race and the Law Review*, 3: 61–81.

Scott, M.S. & Goldstein, H. (2005) *Shifting and Sharing Responsibility for Public Safety Problems*, Problem-Oriented Guides for Police, Response Guide No. 3, Washington, DC: US Department of Justice, Office of Community Oriented Policing Services.

Sherman, L.W., Gartin, P.R. & Buerger, M.E. (1989) 'Hot spots of predatory crime: Routine activities and the criminology of place', *Criminology*, 27(1): 27–56.

Sherman, L.W. & Weisburd, D. (1995) 'General deterrent effects of police patrol in crime "hot spots": A randomized, controlled trial', *Justice Quarterly*, 12(4): 625–648.

Tomaskovic-Devey, D., Mason, D. & Zingraff, M. (2004) 'Looking for the driving while black phenomena: Conceptualizing racial bias processes and their associated distributions', *Police Quarterly*, 7(1): 3–29.

Tyler, T.R. & Huo, Y.J. (2002) *Trust in the Law*, New York: Russell Sage Foundation.

Warren, P.Y. (2011) 'Perceptions of police disrespect during vehicle stops: A race-based analysis', *Crime & Delinquency*, 57(3): 356–376.

Watson, R. (2018) *Email Communication with Sergeant Ryan Watson*, Houston Police Department, June 7.

Weisburd, D. (2015) 'The law of crime concentrations and the criminology of place', *Criminology*, 53(2): 133–157.

Weisburd, D., Eck, J.E., Braga, A.A., Telep, C.W. & Cave, B. (2016) *Place Matters: Criminology for the Twenty-First Century*, Cambridge, UK: Cambridge University Press.

Weisburd, D., Telep, C.W., Hinkle, J.C. & Eck, J.E. (2008) 'The effects of problem-oriented policing on crime and disorder', *Campbell Systematic Reviews*, 14.

22

CONSTRUCTION-SITE THEFT AND BURGLARY IN PORT ST. LUCIE, FLORIDA

Rachel B. Santos and Roberto G. Santos

Introduction

Construction site burglary and theft is an industry-wide problem with estimates in the United States that between 1 and 4 billion dollars' worth of materials and tools, as well as large and small equipment, were stolen every year (Berg & Hinze, 2005; Jones, 2017; Lambertson, 2005; National Association of Home Builders, 2018). The impact of losses has typically been passed on to the home buyer by the construction companies and developer by increasing the home price by between 1% to 2% (O'Malley, 2005; National Association of Home Builders, 2018). Construction is often seasonal and high levels of burglary and theft can occur during periods of economic growth. Thus, developing crime prevention strategies for a community, for builders, and even individual construction sites can impact the problem overall.

While crime is an ongoing concern for a variety of environments within the construction industry, this case study addresses the problem of burglary and theft from single-family-home construction sites occurring in a city that had a growth in single-family-home construction and a systematic increase in the prevalence of the crime at these locations over several years. As this study found, the local police department was successful in educating the community and forming partnerships with builders to reduce opportunities for crime at single-family-home construction sites. Notably, the police department was able to convince builders to spend additional resources to address the problem.

This case study was a finalist for the International Herman Goldstein Award for Excellence in Problem-Oriented Policing in 2006. It provides an example of using innovative analysis techniques to understand the problem as well as creative responses to address the problem of burglary and theft at single-family-home construction sites. Importantly, the analysis and response strategies illustrated in this case study can be translated to any seasonal, temporary, or long-term construction crime problem.

Scanning

In 2004, the City of Port St. Lucie, Florida was approximately 100 square miles with a population of 118,396. The city had a significant amount of undeveloped land and was seeing unprecedented population growth. In fact, it had the fastest growth rate in the United States among large cities (100,000 or more population) between 2003 and 2004, according to the US Census Bureau (City Mayors, 2018). Preliminary analysis of crime data by the police department indicated that crime at construction sites constituted a relatively large proportion of property crime occurring in the city. Members of the department saw it as a problem worth addressing, not only because the problem was current but also because it was sure to remain one in the future absent a new preventive approach. The city still had land suitable for further residential development.

The City of Port St. Lucie is a suburban community primarily zoned for individual home sites, so most of the construction in the city and reported crime at construction sites occurred at single-family-home sites. In 2004, the city's building department personnel estimated that between 450 and 600 new building permits were issued per month and estimated more than 6,000 homes were under construction in the city at any time.

Thus, the focus of the project was on the theft or burglary of property from a single-family-home building under construction. Thefts occurring at commercial sites or multifamily sites, thefts of large construction equipment (e.g., backhoes, cranes), and vandalism of construction sites (e.g., holes in the drywall, graffiti, and general damage) were not addressed in this effort. These incidents were much less frequent, and the opportunities for these crimes and potential crime prevention strategies would be much different.

An initial analysis of single-family-home construction-site-theft incidents showed that the problem was not nearly as prevalent as the police had thought. With over 6,000 homes under construction on any given day, there were only 266 construction theft and burglary reports in all of 2004, or between 10 and 40 per month. Figure 22.1 illustrates the frequency from June 2002 to December 2004 and the linear upward trend. The increase in the second half of 2004 was due to two major hurricanes in September. These were primarily thefts of plywood that were reported in October after the storms, during the cleanup. Even without these spikes, the overall trend was increasing.

Because home construction was projected to continue and even increase in the coming years, the police department decided to continue with the initiative and conduct in-depth analysis to fully understand the scope and nature of the problem.

Analysis

A repeat-victimization analysis of individual single-family-home construction sites indicated that only 12 (4.7%) of the 254 individual sites where thefts occurred were victimized twice within 1 year. This made sense because construction sites are

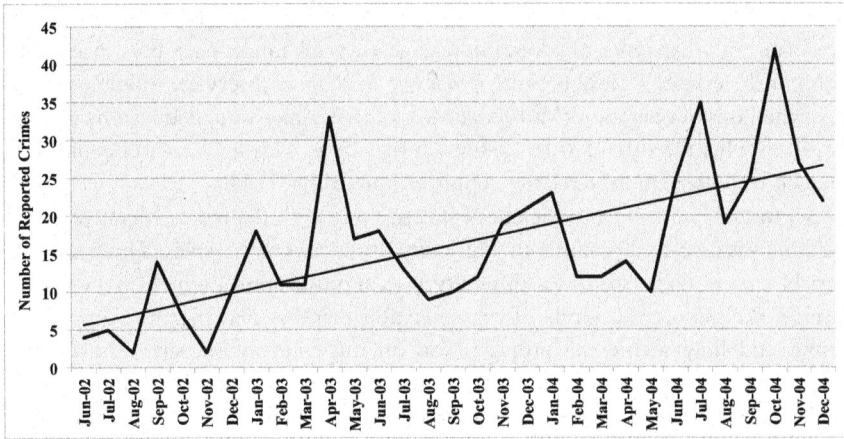

FIGURE 22.1 Single-family-home construction-site thefts, June 2002 to December 2004

transitional environments (Clarke & Eck, 2005). However, each home was under construction for 10.5 months, so there was a relatively long period of opportunities for crime. Yet, because the numbers were so low, it was concluded that repeat victimization of individual sites was not a significant concern.

The nature of the construction business in the city was that an individual company would build houses haphazardly in lots throughout the city. That is, builders would not construct all the homes in a single neighborhood or community but would have housing sites peppered throughout the city. Because of this and the difficulty this created for builders to oversee and manage all their construction sites, a repeat-victimization analysis was conducted based on builder victimization rather than site victimization. Looking at the frequency of crimes reported by the builder, the results showed that 20% of the building companies that had been victimized accounted for 69.2% of burglary and theft from single-family-home construction sites. Thus, there was indeed repeat victimization by the builder. In fact, the builder reporting the most crime represented 1.4% of the victimized builders (1 of 70 companies) and accounted for 17% of the total crime. This was nearly three times as much as the next most victimized builder. These results supported working directly with a few key builders to have the most impact on crime reduction.

The analysis also showed that there was little information in police files about the offenders committing these crimes. From January to December 2004, only five cases (1.9%) were resolved by arrest. Therefore, to capture more information about how the crimes were being carried out, a check sheet was created specifically for construction-site theft and burglary reports. The check sheet asked for information on both the builder and the subcontractors working on the site, as well as the stage of construction when the crime occurred. The categories for the stage of construction included cleared lot, concrete slab poured, exterior walls in place, roof installed, exterior walls in place, and house securable. The check sheet also asked officers to speculate on what types of tools, knowledge, or skills might have been needed to commit the crime. That is, because it was not possible to interview offenders about their methods of operation (MOs), the MOs of the crimes were deduced by officers based on what the offenders left behind at the scene. This information could then be used to understand the relative sophistication of the thieves.

Six months of data from the check sheets, along with the report narrative information, was used to determine the difficulty of the reported crimes. Three separate variables were coded to assess difficulty (i.e., sophistication), which included the level of skills/tools, the mode of transportation that was necessary to commit the crime, and how secure the property was on the construction site. The analysis results showed that 48% of the crimes required either construction skills or special tools to take the property, and 88% required a car or small truck to carry the property away (vs. simply walking away with it). In addition, in 39% of the incidents the stolen property was secured inside the building, in 36% it was outside the building and attached in some way or inside the building and unsecured, and in 25%, it was outside the building and unattached.

The reports indicated that building supplies, construction equipment, rebar, and ladders, together represented 33.8% of the types of property taken, and appliances, 16.9%. Last, using the officers' assessment of the stage of construction, just over half of the single-family-home construction-site crimes occurred when the house was "securable." Even though it was not known from the reports whether the building was actually secured at the time of the crime, this finding indicated that the crimes were happening not only when entry was likely to have been most difficult but also when the site had the most and most valuable items to take.

As part of the analysis process, the project team held a meeting to obtain input from the builders who were able to provide a better sense of the way construction worked in the city. The builders confirmed some of the analysis results—particularly that the homes were most vulnerable in the final stages of building because of the amount of property contained in the building. A separate meeting with the city building department revealed that three weeks before the official house closing, an electricity meter inspection was required, and this timing corresponded to when the house was securable. On a daily basis, after each meter inspection, the city sent the electricity company the address. Thus, this inspection process was a real-time indicator when homes were likely most vulnerable to theft and burglary.

Response

The analysis showed that this problem was not as prevalent as the police first believed, so the chief of police and the project team decided not to expend a large amount of resources and political capital to address the problem. So, instead of seeking to change city ordinances and building codes, a multifaceted response was developed centered on police responses, education of the community and builders, and shifting and sharing the responsibility of crime prevention to the most victimized builders (Scott & Goldstein, 2005).

Citywide strategies

The responses included general strategies that were implemented citywide. The first strategy included the newly hired crime analysts searching for short-term patterns on construction crime that may have been committed by the same suspect, occurred in the same area, or where the same builder was victimized several times and producing bulletins about these patterns. These bulletins were provided to patrol officers to inform their directed patrols and to detectives to provide information about property and linkages between crimes for investigation. Builders were provided bulletins on current patterns at their own or other builders' construction sites which made them aware of current activity and offered specific crime prevention advice about how to reduce crime opportunities.

The second strategy was educating potential victims and potential guardians (i.e., those who can help see and report crimes) through media, meetings, and training. In the summer and fall of 2005, the police department worked with media to provide information about the crime, strategies being implemented, and general crime prevention advice for builders and community members. The campaign included five television news spots, three radio interviews, and ten newspaper articles. The information provided came from the analysis phase of the study and encouraged individuals in particular areas of the city to be on the lookout for suspicious activity in their residential neighborhoods (i.e., increase guardianship). This was particularly important because many of the single-family-home construction sites were located on blocks that also had occupied homes. The campaign also served as a warning to offenders that the police were taking this crime seriously and taking measures to address the problem.

Throughout 2005, members of the police department's crime prevention unit attended monthly meetings of individual builders/contractors as well as the regional builders' association. Police personnel provided general crime prevention advice, results of the problem analysis, and current ongoing patterns developed as a result of the first general strategy. The relationships forged through these meetings made communication with specific builders easier and the builders more responsive to the police.

The third strategy was increasing police guardianship through individual construction site checks. The analysis showed construction sites were vulnerable in the final stages of construction, and the electric-meter checks provided a real-time notification when the home was in its final stage of construction. The crime prevention unit was notified of the meter checks on a weekly basis and distributed them to patrol officers who conducted daily checks of the sites. If the sites were found to be unlocked or property left unsecured, "crime opportunity forms" were left for the builders to warn them about the vulnerability of the site. Feedback from builders' supervisors in regular meetings indicated they were receiving the forms and making necessary changes to the site to reduce theft.

Builder-focused strategies and results

The police department worked very closely with the four builders that were most victimized. Additional analysis was conducted for each builder and responses were tailored based on the results. A pattern emerged in the analysis of the individual builder's crimes that delivery and installation practices were possibly contributing to the problem. A similar problem-solving project addressing construction site crime by the Charlotte-Mecklenburg, North Carolina, Police Department identified a similar issue (Clarke & Goldstein, 2003). In that project, the police department worked with the builders to delay the installation of appliances until after the residents moved into the home and subsequently reduced crime. Thus, guided by those results, the response for each builder in this case study included tightening delivery and installation practices of targeted property, such as appliances, pool equipment, and air conditioners.

Builder A had the most crimes in 2004 but was not building the most homes. The analysis showed that the difficulty level of Builder A's crimes was significantly "easier" than other builders' crimes, and this builder was more likely to leave property unsecured. The builder also had a relatively high number of appliances taken, and its supervisors were managing 25 to 30 homes whereas other builders' supervisors were managing only 10 to 20 homes. Builder A was convinced to reduce the number of homes assigned to site supervisors to 15, to focus on protecting the property left on-site, and to delay the installation of appliances until the very final stages of construction. Analysis of the crime after these responses were implemented showed the number of crimes reduced dramatically even though building volume stayed essentially the same during this time.

Builder B's top theft concern was appliances, and it was found that the time between the installation of appliances was several weeks, leaving the appliances vulnerable for a period. The builder changed its scheduling so that the appliances were installed right before closing. It also assigned a supervisor to check that each home in the final stages of construction was secured on a daily basis. Builder B's crimes were actually increasing before the responses were implemented, and similar to Builder A, it experienced a decrease and had only a handful of crimes after implementation. In fact, its building volume slightly increased during the response period.

For Builder E, pool equipment was being stolen, so video surveillance cameras were installed at particularly vulnerable construction sites. In addition, at the outset of the responses, the builder removed previously installed pool equipment and reinstalled it just before closing. Scheduling and policies were formally changed so that all pool equipment was installed at the end of the building process. The builder had no reported crimes after it began the responses, even with a consistent volume of home building.

Finally, Builder G had many air-conditioning units stolen, so it, too, delayed installation of air-conditioning units until later in the construction process and closer to closing. The builder also placed stickers on the air-conditioning units indicating that the property was being tracked with a GPS. In reality, it was not, but the goal was to increase the offenders' perception of the risk of being caught to deter them from taking the equipment. Builder G's crimes had been increasing before the responses were implemented, but there was a decrease that remained stable after the responses even though the builder's volume slightly increased.

Assessment

Figure 22.2 shows the monthly count of single-family-home construction site thefts throughout the city for two-and-a-half years. The responses were initiated fully in March 2005, and a period of "anticipatory benefit" is indicated in Figure 22.2 because the decrease began even before the responses were fully implemented. As Smith, Clarke, and Pease (2002) argue, crime reduction may occur before a strategy is implemented because the work being done before implementation may actually change offenders' perceptions of risk, victims' awareness, and officers' vigilance.

The analysis began nearly six months before the responses began, which included meeting with builders, the city's building department and inspectors visiting the construction sites, and having officers complete the additional checklist with each construction site crime report. Although it is difficult to confirm, it appears as though from November 2004 to March 2005 (noted by the gray rectangle) there may have been anticipatory benefits which may have been due to the increased awareness by the builders, the city government, and the police before the responses were implemented. The trend lines indicate the upward trend before the response and the downward trend during the anticipatory benefit period and after the response. Importantly, construction levels actually increased during this time (6,621 building permits in 2004 to 6,829 in 2005).

Anecdotally, some members of the police department began to notice displacement of construction site crime to burglary of homes that were completed but

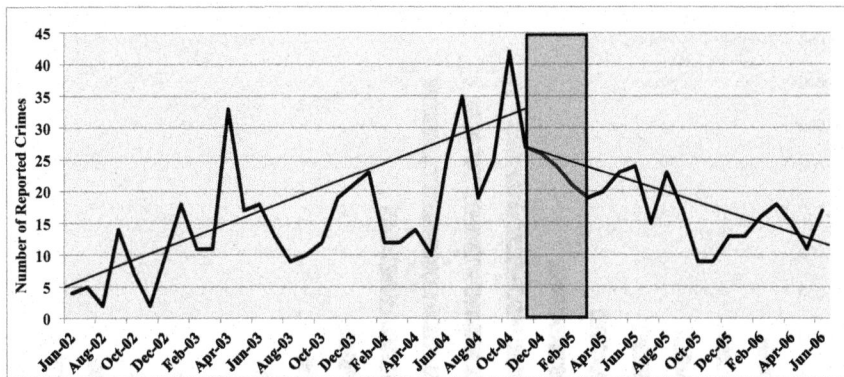

FIGURE 22.2 Single-family-home construction-site thefts per month, Port St. Lucie, Florida

were unoccupied. There might also have been a broader impact of these crime-prevention strategies on the number of vandalism incidents at single-family-home construction sites or burglary and theft at locations close to the construction sites since there was an increased level of guardianship. Unfortunately, the practical nature of this project and the data that would allow a more thorough analysis of displacement (Johnson, Guerette & Bowers, 2014) and diffusion (Clarke & Weisburd, 1994) were not available.

Discussion

This case study illustrates a very specific problem that not all communities face and those that do likely face it seasonally or for a specific period. While it was determined that the problem was not as serious as first thought, the police department did proceed because, at the time, a high level of new home construction was forecasted for the city. However, the economic downturn of 2007, which affected mortgages and new home building throughout the United States, essentially halted construction in Port St. Lucie. Figure 22.3 shows home-construction permits for Port St. Lucie from 1997 to 2014 (City-Data, 2018). Note that the project was carried out in 2004 and 2005 and assessed in the first part of 2006. As shown in this case study, the police department did have an impact on the problem during high levels of construction; however, since 2007, construction levels and related crime have remained very low.

The success of this initiative is evidenced not only in the reduction of construction site theft and burglary in the city but also in the improvements of builders' practices and the relationships established between the police department and the construction community in Port St. Lucie. There are several aspects that stand out and can serve as examples for other police departments and their communities that are seeking to address the problem of theft and burglary at single-family-home

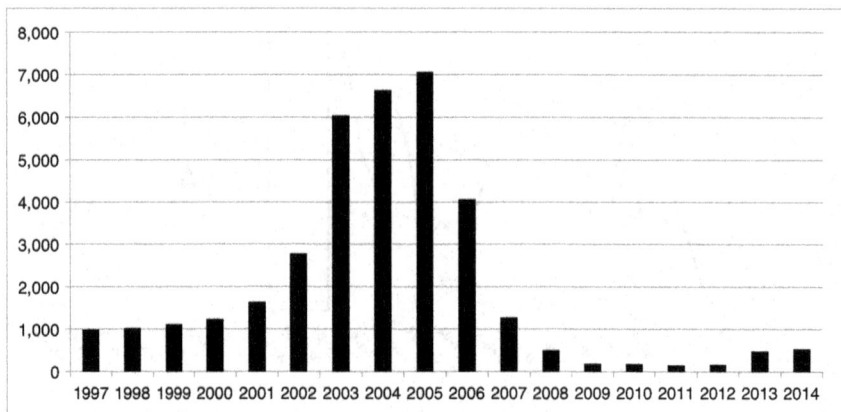

FIGURE 22.3 New-home-construction permits, Port St. Lucie, Florida

construction sites as well as those facing theft and burglary at other types of construction sites (i.e., commercial or infrastructure) or other types of crimes (i.e., vandalism and trespass) at single-family-home construction sites. The most notable aspects of crime at construction sites that influence both the analysis and responses are the transitional nature of the individual locations under construction and the local nature of the construction industry itself.

Most individual locations where crime and disorder problems arise have consistent physical structures and maintain fairly stable routine behavior, for example, convenience stores, bars, and apartment communities. In contrast, construction sites by definition are changing the entire time they exist, which means that the crime opportunities are changing as well. A construction site transitions from being a vacant lot, a foundation, a partial structure, to a securable structure. At each stage of transition, the opportunities for crime differ. For example, when a commercial location is being wired for electricity or plumbing before the building is securable, the opportunity for theft of valuable copper exists. At single-family-home sites, opportunities for trespassing and "squatting" exist when the walls and roof are finished, but the house is not securable. Importantly, once the location is no longer a construction site and becomes a retail store, residence, or completed road, the opportunities are different than they were during construction and become fairly stable since the location is no longer in transition.

Consequently, this unique characteristic of construction sites impacts the analysis of the problem and requires that data not normally captured by police be collected. In this case study, officers were asked to collect the stage of construction and the level of difficulty of the crime was assessed based on how the crime happened as it was written in the police report. The results of the analysis of these data helped identify that the sites were most vulnerable at the final stage of construction and allowed comparison among and between builders as to the difficulty of the crimes they reported. The collection of stage-of-construction data when the crime occurred is likely important for any construction-related crime problem, and other unique data might be collected depending on the specific type of construction location (i.e., commercial, industrial, infrastructure) or the type of crime (i.e., trespass, vandalism).

On a local level, construction practices can differ by state and even by individual communities. This, too, creates different and unique opportunities for crime. Therefore, it is important that any examination of a construction crime problem include an in-depth understanding of the current and local nature of the construction industry and local context. For example, in this case study, unique characteristics of local construction practices and conditions were the vast numbers of building permits that were being issued, that homes were built sporadically throughout the city and not in distinct communities, and the process for installation of appliances, air conditioning, and pool equipment left items vulnerable for a long time before closing. Interviews with builders and the city building department revealed that the electrical inspection was a real-time indicator of when the home was securable, yet vulnerable. Coupled with the analysis findings from stage-of-construction data, the responses could be effectively implemented when property was most likely to be taken.

Finally, construction is influenced by both the national and local economy, as well as other factors that can quickly and significantly increase or decrease the amount and pace of construction. Because of these rapidly changing conditions, police might be tempted to simply wait for construction to stop and the problem to go away. However, as this case study has shown, not only can crime be prevented during a specific time period of construction, but construction processes and procedures that reduce opportunities for crime can also be improved, which has a long-term impact on crime for the community and the builder.

Follow-up

A look at construction-site crime in Port St. Lucie, FL today, in Figure 22.4, shows that since the project ended, the number of crimes per year has been consistently low, which is due to the lack of building as discussed previously. However, the counts since 2017 have increased slightly, and the Port St. Lucie Police Department has implemented a few strategies to stay informed and be prepared for the problem possibly resurfacing.

That is, the PSLPD reports that while the crime analysts have consistently identified short-term patterns of construction crime since the project was concluded, they have now begun to track construction crime counts each month, particularly in District 3, to identify increases in crime and intervene before it becomes a problem. In addition, crime-prevention staff are renewing previous relationships with established builders as well as forging relationships with builders new to the area. Last, they are working closely with the city's building department to stay aware of

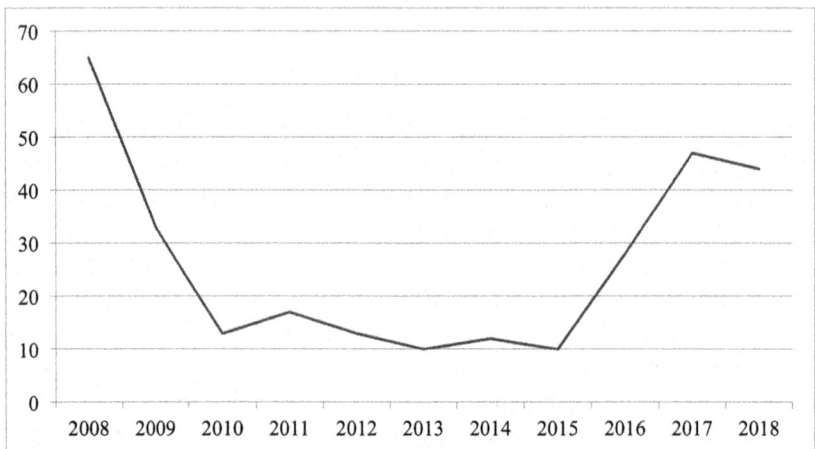

FIGURE 22.4 Thefts from construction sites in Port St. Lucie, Florida

changing trends in building permits and builders' practices as well as provide builders with crime prevention advice as they apply for new permits.

References

Berg, R. & Hinze, J. (2005) 'Theft and vandalism on construction sites', *Journal of Construction Engineering & Management*, 7(131): 826–833.

City-Data (2018) Port St. Lucie, FL. Retrieved on October 16, 2018 from www.city-data.com/city/Port-St.-Lucie-Florida.html

City Mayors (2018) *US Sunshine Cities Grow Fastest While Detroit Loses Top Ten Place*, London: City Mayors Foundation. Retrieved on January 10, 2020 from www.citymayors.com/statistics/us_cities_population.html

Clarke, R.V. & Eck, J.E. (2005) *Crime Analysis for Problem solvers: In 60 Small Steps*, Washington, DC: US Department of Justice, Office of Community Oriented Policing Services.

Clarke, R.V. & Goldstein, H. (2003) *Reducing Theft at Construction Sites: Lessons from a Problem-Oriented Project*, Washington, DC: US Department of Justice, Office of Community Oriented Policing Services.

Clarke, R.V. & Weisburd, D. (1994) 'Diffusion of crime control benefits: Observations on the reverse of displacement', in R.V. Clarke (ed.), *Crime Prevention Studies*, Vol. 2. Monsey, NY: Criminal Justice Press.

Johnson, S.D., Guerette, R.T. & Bowers, K. (2014) 'Crime displacement: What we know, what we don't know, and what it means for crime reduction', *Journal of Experimental Criminology*, 10(4): 549–571.

Jones, K. (2017) *The High Cost of Construction Equipment Theft*, Constructconnect, August 30.

Lambertson, G. (2005) 'Law enforcement focuses on construction site theft', *Construction Equipment Guide*, Issue (None), March 2.

National Association of Home Builders (2018) Retrieved on September 28, 2018 from www.nahb.org/

O'Malley, S. (2005) 'Homeland security: Thieves steal $4 billion a year from American jobsites: Here are 10 steps to help protect yours', *Building Products*, May–June.

Scott, M. & Goldstein, H. (2005) *Shifting and Sharing Responsibility for Public-Safety Problems*, Problem-Oriented Guides for Police, Response Guide No. 3, Washington, DC: US Department of Justice, Office of Community-Oriented Policing Services.

Smith, M.J., Clarke, R.V. & Pease, K. (2002) 'Anticipatory benefit in crime prevention', in N. Tilley (ed.), *Analysis for Crime Prevention*, Crime Prevention Studies, Vol. 13. Monsey, NY: Criminal Justice Press.

23

BURGLARY OF STORAGE UNITS IN CHARLOTTE-MECKLENBURG, NORTH CAROLINA

Joseph B. Kuhns

Introduction

Eventually, most everyone moves from one home to another or from one location to another. Over the course of their lives, most people take a new job, sometimes in a different part of the city, state, country, or world. Many high school graduates move to colleges and universities in other cities, states, or countries. Businesses often relocate to other areas to pursue better opportunities, lower operating costs, reduce taxes, and/or increase their customer base. Such transition often involves storing personal and business property in rented self-storage facilities. The quality of self-storage facilities varies greatly in terms of climate control, security, accessibility, and cost.

Regardless, rented storage facilities are common in the United States. In the United States, there are between 44,000 and 52,000 self-storage facilities occupying some 2.3 billion square feet of space. An estimated 9.4% of households rent a self-storage unit each year in this $38 billion industry (Harris, 2018a). Self-storage units are used for a wide range of personal and business items. Storage needs are highly seasonal in some states, and such is the case in Charlotte, North Carolina (Harris, 2018b), the setting of the current study. Summer months are peak self-storage times as students move off to college, families relocate to new homes and school districts, and warmer weather facilitates moving conditions and improved business environments that rely on temporary storage facilities (e.g., landscaping companies often temporarily store their lawn care equipment in storage units that are geographically close to customer homes and businesses).

Surveys of self-storage customers reveal that 84% are women, 88% are between the ages of 21 and 55, and 78% have lower-middle to upper-middle incomes. Moving was the primary reason for renting storage space (54%), followed by cleaning out basements/garages or just needing temporary storage space. The top reasons for preferring certain facilities versus others were the customer's perceptions of security (62%), followed by convenience and access (15%), street appeal (8%), and facility cleanliness (6%; Parham Group, 2015). Notwithstanding customer concerns about storage-unit security, many self-storage facilities are burgled.

Both residential and commercial burglaries in the United States remain a persistent challenge for police nationwide. In 2016, there were more than 400,000 nonresidential (commercial) burglaries in the United States, a 2.6% increase from 2015 (Federal Bureau of Investigation, 2016a). Of those, 6,691 burglaries occurred in Charlotte, North Carolina, which is the largest city in the state. According to an annual survey of Charlotte-area residents, home burglaries and break-ins remain a top crime and safety concern among citizens year after year (MarketWise, 2013). Most citizens fear having their homes and, perhaps to a lesser extent, their businesses broken into by strangers. Burglars are often impulsive, and studies suggest that they are not particularly selective about their targets. Most male and female burglars report a willingness to break into both homes and businesses, potentially including self-storage units (Blevins et al., 2012). Unfortunately, clearance rates for burglary hover around 13% nationally, suggesting that most burglaries remain unsolved and many burglars remain free. Complete national statistics on burglaries of storage units specifically are not readily available. However, about a third (37.1% in 2016) of law enforcement agencies participate in the National Incident Based Reporting System (NIBRS; Federal Bureau of Investigations, 2016b) and those agencies reported 10,462 burglaries of rental storage units in 2016. Further, although the state of North Carolina does not participate in NIBRS, the Charlotte-Mecklenburg Police Department maintains easily retrievable burglary location data that is examined later.

Starting in the summer of 2005, a group of four CMPD burglary detectives was tasked by their commanding officer to focus attention on burglaries at self-storage warehouse locations in Charlotte-Mecklenburg, as one step toward reducing commercial burglaries overall. This project was not specifically focused on improving burglary clearance rates but, rather, on preventing offending at self-storage locations.

Operation Safe Storage

Scanning

Operation Safe Storage was launched in response to a 28% increase in commercial burglaries in Charlotte-Mecklenburg in 2005, 7% of which occurred at self-storage warehouse storage facilities. There were 99 case reports of burglaries at self-storage units in 2005, with some of the case reports involving multiple units and multiple victims. There was an average of 3.5 victims per case report, meaning that there were nearly 350 distinct burglary victimizations that year. In one case, more than 60 storage units were broken into within a single event at one facility.

Analysis

By reading every burglary report narrative, the detectives were able to separate out burglaries of self-storage unit business offices as well as some misclassified reports, leaving a total of 291 units burgled in 71 incidents for deeper analysis. In this deeper analysis, the detectives found no significant correlation between the presence of self-storage facilities and crime within the surrounding areas. In the context of self-storage burglaries, there were no discernible patterns with respect to specific types of property stolen or the value of the stolen property. In fact, some renters could not recall the property that was stolen. However, detectives determined that some storage facility locations had not reported any burglaries or break-ins whereas other storage facilities were frequently victimized. When the detectives inspected 75 storage unit facilities, they concluded that a primary preventive factor was the use of disc (or discus) locks. The disc locks referred to here are different from the disc locks that are often used to secure bicycles or motorcycles. Self-storage faculty disc locks function similarly to regular padlocks but have a round shape that makes them more difficult to defeat with simple bolt cutters.

Disc locks were required in one of the three test facilities, and that facility had not reported any successful breaking-and-entering reports within the past year. Furthermore, one of the detectives had firsthand experience with executing a search warrant of a container that was secured with a disc lock. He indicated that it took the search team 30 minutes to remove the disc lock. Surmising that most burglars would not want to linger long while trying to break open a lock, the detectives decided that encouraging wider adoption of disc locks across self-storage facilities should be part of a broader prevention strategy.

Response

During the response phase, detectives initiated a pilot study of disc locks at three sites. One of the sites already had the disc locks in place. The police department purchased disc locks for the two other test sites. The detectives subsequently visited those two sites and asked the managers to use the disc locks in the future with all of their customers, which they ultimately agreed to do. One facility manager was initially reluctant to adopt the lock recommendation for fear that burglars would damage the storage-unit doors instead in order to gain entry. Costs for that damage would be borne by the facility owners whereas losses from damaged locks and stolen goods would be borne solely by the unit renter. The detectives were able to persuade the manager's corporate superiors to adopt the disc lock recommendation.

In addition to installing disc locks, the detectives developed and disseminated a "Best Practices Guide" to all self-storage facilities throughout the area. The guide was informed by the detectives' 75 site visits; a crime-prevention program initiated by MiniCo, a self-storage insurance company; and discussions with the North

Carolina Self Storage Association, a statewide trade association for self-storage warehouse businesses. The guide encouraged a broader range of crime-prevention strategies, which included:

1   conducting background checks on prospective renters;
2   managers remaining on the premises during business hours;
3   limiting facility access to specific operating hours or installing gates with electronic access for those who need 24-hour access;
4   ensuring that local police officers have the electronic codes to enter the premises, as needed;
5   installing surveillance cameras and improving lighting within the self-storage facilities;
6   requiring renters to use disc locks issued to them by the storage facility, the cost for which would be included in the rental price; and
7   educating renters about documenting their property by recording serial numbers, engraving some items when appropriate, and placing their most valuable items in boxes that are intentionally mislabeled, for example, as bathroom supplies, books, or dishes.

The best-practices guide was developed by the detectives and distributed to the 75 self-storage businesses in the Charlotte area. The detectives also established and maintained an ongoing partnership with the North Carolina Self Storage Association that would allow both parties to share information on future security concerns and emerging crime trends, and ensure that best prevention practices were adopted and in place in as many self-storage locations as possible.

Assessment

The project assessment involved a simple pre-post design that compared the number of burglary/breaking-and-entering incidents at test sites during the one-year period before the intervention (installation of disc locks and the dissemination of the best practices guide) with the number of incidents in the one-year period following intervention. Crime statistics from the other self-storage facilities in the Charlotte area were collected and used as a basis of comparison.

Overall, in the year following response implementation, there was an impressive 58% reduction in the number of reported burglary incidents and a 69% reduction in the number of individual units that were broken into at the three test sites. In one incident, 26 units were broken into at one of the test sites. However, none of the disc locks in place were compromised; instead, the burglars broke open the self-storage unit doors to gain entry. Meanwhile, over the study timeframe, there was a 39% increase in self-storage facility burglaries, and a 44% increase in individual units burglarized that were not test sites. It seemed clear that the responses were effective in reducing burglaries.

Update: status of the problem addressed in Operation Safe Storage

Since 2006, reported burglaries in Charlotte-Mecklenburg have dropped consistently according to data provided to the national Uniform Crime Reports system (see Figure 23.1). A number of factors might explain this broader crime reduction trend, including the role of policing and local policing strategies, substantial advances in technology, adoption of a 2012 law that increased penalties for repeat burglaries in North Carolina (NCGS 14–7.25, 2012), and broader national crime reduction trends that may be linked to incarceration practices, economic changes, and other macro-level explanations.

Again, nationwide statistics on burglaries of self-storage units are not readily available. However, the Charlotte-Mecklenburg Police Departments' Crime Analysis Division provided updated crime data on the number of burglaries of self-storage units reported from 2005 to 2017. Figure 23.2 illustrates the annual numbers of

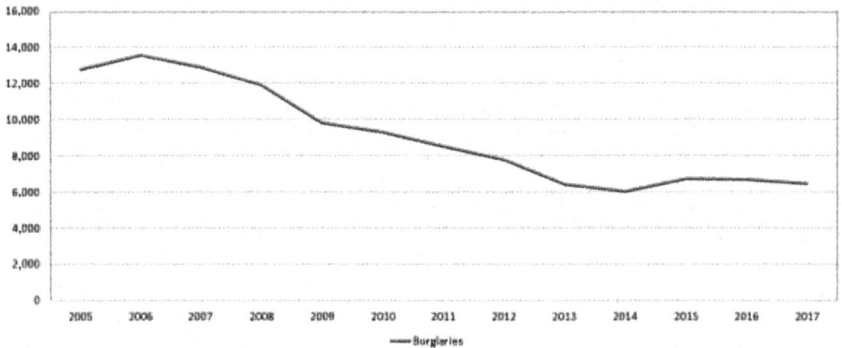

FIGURE 23.1 Total burglaries in Charlotte, North Carolina, 2005–2017

Source: Uniform Crime Reports, Federal Bureau of Investigations.

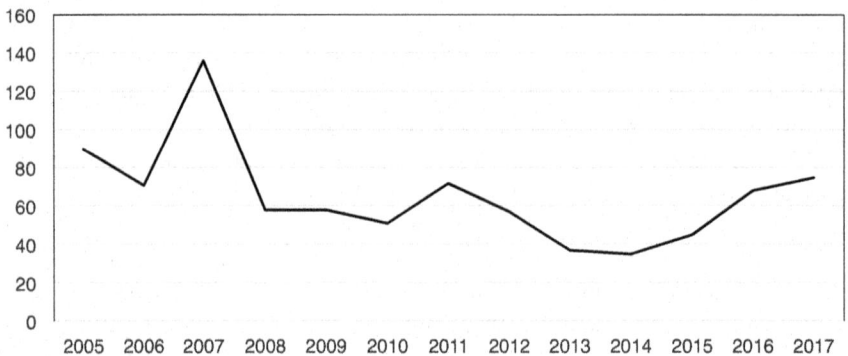

FIGURE 23.2 Burglaries of mini storage units in Charlotte, North Carolina 2005–2017

Source: Crime Analysis Division, Charlotte Mecklenburg Police Department.

mini-storage unit burglaries in Charlotte-Mecklenburg since Operation Safe Storage and through calendar year 2017. As the chart illustrates, the overall number of burglaries reported at self-storage units has fallen over the past 12 years, although a slight uptick is seemingly apparent over the last few years. Regardless, following a spike in 2007, there is a clear downward trend of reported burglaries of self-storage units in the city. Arguably, this trend could simply mimic the broader downward trend in combined residential and commercial burglaries in Charlotte-Mecklenburg over that timeframe. However, that explanation seems unlikely given that burglaries of self-storage units comprised only about 7% of reported commercial burglaries in Charlotte-Mecklenburg when Operation Safe Storage was initiated.

Finally, Figure 23.3 illustrates the total number of mini-storage-unit burglaries in the three original test sites that were the primary focus of Operation Safe Storage. Specifically, the test sites were located at 1515 E. Sugar Creek Road, 4500 Monroe Road, and 9400 Bob Beatty Road. Over the course of the last 12 years, self-storage units in the three target sites were occasionally burgled. However, in one year (2013), there were zero burglaries reported across the three target sites. Furthermore, in three other years (2009, 2012 and 2014), there was just one reported burglary across all three primary test sites (meaning, one burglary total for that year, not one burglary per site). Altogether, there were 68 reported burglaries within the three test sites over the past 14 years, representing an average of just 5.2 burglaries a year, or approximately one burglary every nine weeks. These figures include an outlier year for one of the test sites that experienced 12 reported burglaries in 2007 (representing 17.6% of all of the burglaries at the three sites during the 14-year timeframe). Given these updated numbers and the initial results from the project, one can reasonably conclude that the three primary test sites initiated and have maintained adequate security protocols and those efforts have been effective in deterring self-storage-unit burglaries.

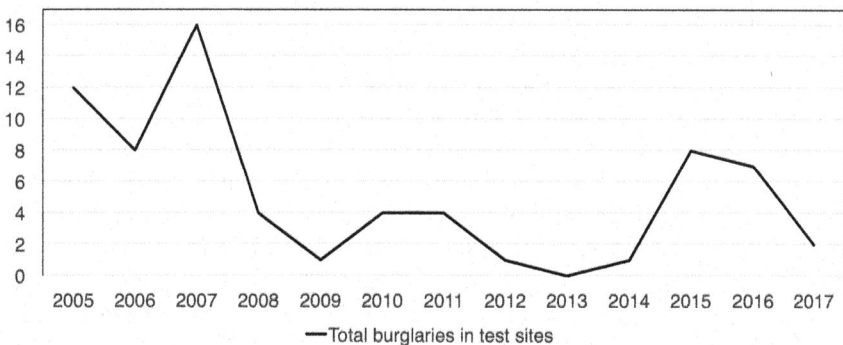

FIGURE 23.3 Burglaries of three mini storage target test sites in Charlotte, North Carolina, 2005–2017

Source: Crime Analysis Division, Charlotte Mecklenburg Police Department.

Discussion

Operation Safe Storage was an interesting and clearly effective project that offers several important lessons for other police agencies to consider. First, it serves as a useful example of how a problem-oriented approach to a crime problem can be implemented effectively and relatively inexpensively. Detectives began their scanning process and initial analysis approach by closely examining one specific form of commercial burglary and focusing attention on that "problem within a problem." Detectives personally visited 75 self-storage facilities, considered which crime prevention approaches might work, and developed a plan of action. During the initial phases, the detectives established meaningful partnerships with self-storage managers and relevant trade organizations and effectively engaged stakeholders while working to shift and share some of the responsibilities for addressing burglaries of self-storage units (Scott & Goldstein, 2005). The adopted responses were multifaceted yet cost-effective and are rather easily transferrable to other businesses with similar concerns. Arguably, the project results were noteworthy within the project timeframe and even when examined with 14 years' worth of follow-up data. Simply considered as a model problem-oriented policing project, Operation Safe Storage offers much to the field.

Project sustainability

Many successful problem-oriented policing projects will generate a "cliff-edge" effect—a dramatic decrease in the problem once the planned responses are implemented (Clarke, 2008; see also Perry et al., 2017). Sometimes the levels of crime and/or disorder begin to climb back up as time passes. This is often due to staff changes or changes in departmental leadership that pull resources and departmental focus away from the project, and therefore limit the sustainability of the results achieved through the initial responses. These challenges were certainly apparent in Charlotte over the 14-year timeframe. There were many leadership and personnel changes since 2005, including two new chiefs. Only one of the four original officers working on the project was still working at CMPD by August 2018. Regardless, the impact of Operation Safe Storage, in terms of reduced self-storage burglaries, particularly in the target sites, has sustained over time.

One potential explanation is that the primary response to the problem that had the greatest impact, the installation of disc locks, did not require continued monitoring, resources, or support from the police department. Furthermore, since the implementation of Operation Safe Storage, there have been significant advancements in self-storage locking options (Goodman, 2017) and access technology that could further serve to reduce, or even eliminate, burglaries of these units. Automated vehicle identification systems, license plate readers, and mobile alert systems that can text renters should there be an intrusion in the facility have proved to be cost-effective and efficient for many storage facilities (Gilliam, 2017; Pavlasek, 2011). It is unclear whether these advancements are effective. In 2011, NIBRS recorded

8,092 burglaries of rental storage units; by 2016, there were 10,462 recorded, a 29.2% increase over that timeframe. However, additional cities, counties, and states have likely joined NIBRS over time. Therefore, it is unclear whether burglaries of rental storage units nationally are stable, rising, or perhaps falling (on a rate-adjusted basis). Furthermore, it is unknown how many new self-storage facilities opened in Charlotte or how many existing facilities closed over the study timeframe.

Situational crime prevention

When considered from a different but related perspective, Operation Safe Storage effectively adopted and implemented a situational crime prevention approach that could serve as a useful model for other cities and police agencies. CMPD burglary detectives substantially increased the effort required to burglarize self-storage units through target hardening (via the installation of disc locks) and by controlling access/screening exits (via recommending monitored gates and codes for entry). Perceived risks for potential offenders increased through the extension of guardianship, natural surveillance, the utilization of place managers, and enhancing formal surveillance (all by ensuring that managers were on-site during regular business hours and by installing video cameras and improving lighting). Potential rewards for burglars were effectively reduced by encouraging future renters to conceal their high-value targets (through deceptive boxing and mislabeling) and through proactive identification of personal property (by recording serial numbers and item descriptions and engraving, as appropriate) in the event that a burglary did occur (Center for Problem Oriented Policing, 2018). Although situational crime prevention language was not specifically mentioned in the original project description, crime prevention through environmental design was discussed, and many of the primary elements of situational crime prevention are easily identified within the Operation Safe Storage project.

Final thoughts

Over the past decade, the author helped to develop and implement problem-oriented policing projects in Trinidad and Tobago and in Raleigh and Charlotte, North Carolina. He trained police officers and students to do so. In some cases, he helped train police supervisors to help their subordinate officers implement successful problem-oriented policing projects. One of the prominent themes of his training talks was to encourage everyone to simply find and adopt what we already know, and implement what works, before trying to reinvent the crime-prevention wheel or invent a new wheel. In the Internet era, with powerful search engines, it is not difficult to find out what other police agencies are doing and simply replicate their projects locally. It is no longer particularly challenging to find a problem-oriented policing project that offers solutions for very specific local crime and disorder challenges. Indeed, the Problem-Oriented Policing Center website makes it easier and easier for police officers and crime-prevention practitioners to learn from others and to share and replicate successful projects. The Problem-Oriented Policing conference also disseminates many of those important lessons and studies to officers and others around the world.

Early adopters of problem-oriented policing might recall the Gainesville, Florida, Police Department project that focused on convenience store robberies (Clifton, 1985). There are clear parallels between that earlier problem-oriented policing project and Operation Safe Storage. In Gainesville, the officers identified a specific pattern of robberies that were occurring in similar locations (i.e., convenience stores). They worked with a national convenience store trade association and developed some best-practice guidelines, implemented a range of crime prevention strategies and modifications in Gainesville convenience stores, and achieved remarkable reductions in convenience store robberies over a short period. Over time, the results of that project were shared with other convenience store owners and trade association leaders (although not without controversy—the convenience store trade association filed, but ultimately lost, a federal lawsuit over the local ordinance that mandated two clerks on duty at all times [see Sampson & Scott, 2000]). Since then, convenience stores have become safer and more difficult to victimize as broader adoption of situational crime prevention strategies made it more and more challenging for potential offenders (see Exum et al., 2010).

In the case of Operation Safe Storage, we would strongly encourage readers to review this project, consider its simplicity and overall effectiveness, and share the results with local police leaders and storage facility managers. The adoption of disc locks offered a simple and inexpensive solution to a persistent and very specific crime problem. The combination of disc lock adoption along with other crime prevention strategies, many of which were also cost-effective, yielded positive short-term results and the results appear to have persisted over time. More to the point, the simple crime prevention steps used in this project could be easily implemented in the 50,000-some self-storage facilities across the nation. Most every police agency has one or more of these facilities within its jurisdiction. As such, sharing the strategies and lessons from Operation Safe Storage could reach a very large audience and could potentially reduce burglary rates. Given the challenges of clearing burglary cases, burglary prevention efforts are clearly needed, and specific forms of burglary require specific forms of situational prevention. Operation Safe Storage offers some helpful burglary prevention lessons that literally could be adopted in thousands of locations across the country and around the world.

References

Blevins, K.R., Kuhns, J.B., Lee, S., Sawyers, A. & Miller, B. (2012) *Understanding Decisions to Burglarize from the Offender's Perspective*, Dallas, TX: Alarm Industry Research and Educational Foundation.

Center for Problem Oriented Policing (2018) *Twenty-Five Techniques of Situational Prevention*. Retrieved on August 2018 from www.popcenter.org/25techniques/

Clarke, R.V. (2008) 'Situational crime prevention', in R. Wortley, L. Mazerolle & S. Rombouts (eds.), *Environmental Criminology and Crime Analysis*, Cullompton, UK: Willan Publishing.

Clifton, W. (1985) *Convenience Store Robberies in Gainesville, Florida: An Intervention Strategy by the Gainesville Police Department*, Gainesville, FL: Gainesville Police Department.

Exum, M.L., Kuhns, J.B., Koch, B. & Johnson, C. (2010) 'An examination of situational crime prevention strategies across convenience stores and fast food restaurants', *Criminal Justice Policy Review*, 21(3): 269–295.

Federal Bureau of Investigations (2016a) *Crime in the United States, 2016*, Washington, DC: US Department of Justice.

Federal Bureau of Investigations (2016b) *National Incident-Based Reporting System, 2016*, Washington, DC: US Department of Justice.

Gilliam, C. (2017) 'Advancements in self-storage access control technology', Inside Self Storage. Retrieved on January 10, 2020 from www.insideselfstorage.com/security/advancements-self-storage-access-control-technology

Goodman, R. (2017) *10 Best Storage Locks to Secure Your Storage Unit*, United Locksmith. Retrieved on January 10, 2020 from https://unitedlocksmith.net/blog/10-best-storage-locks-to-secure-your-storage-unit

Harris, A. (2018a) *U.S. Self-Storage Industry Statistics*, Spare Foot Storage Beat. Retrieved on January 10, 2020 from www.sparefoot.com/self-storage/news/

Harris, A. (2018b) *U.S. Self-Storage Industry Statistics by State*, Spare Foot Storage Beat. Retrieved on January 10, 2020 from www.sparefoot.com/self-storage/news/

MarketWise (2013) *2013 CMPD Community Survey: Final Report*, Charlotte, NC: Marketwise. Retrieved on January 10, 2020 from https://charlottenc.gov/CityManager/CommunicationstoCouncil/Memo%20attachments/2013%20CMPD%20Citizen%20Survey%20Report.pdf

NCGS 14–7.25 (2012) *Habitual Breaking or Entering Status Offense*, Raleigh, NC: North Carolina State Legislature.

Parham Group (2015) *Who Are Our Customers? Customer Profile Survey Results*. Retrieved on January 10, 2020 from https://learnselfstorage.com/blog/2015/10/07/who-are-our-customers-2/

Pavlasek, K. (2011) *New Advance in Self-Storage Security: Mobile to Mobile Systems*, Inside Self Storage. Retrieved on January 10, 2020 from www.insideselfstorage.com/security/advancements-self-storage-access-control-technology

Perry, S., Apel, R., Newman, G.R. & Clarke, R.V. (2017) 'The situational prevention of terrorism: An evaluation of the Israeli West Bank barrier', *Journal of Quantitative Criminology*, 33(4): 727–751.

Sampson, R. & Scott, M.S. (2000) *Tackling Crime and Other Public Safety Problems: Case Studies in Problem-Solving*, Washington, DC: US Department of Justice, Office of Community Oriented Policing Services.

Scott, M.S. & Goldstein, H. (2005) *Shifting and Sharing Responsibility for Public Safety Problems*, Problem-Oriented Guides for Police, Response Guide No. 3, US Department of Justice, Office of Community Oriented Policing Services, Washington, DC.

24

AUTO THEFT IN WINNIPEG, MANITOBA[1]

Rick Linden

Introduction

Winnipeg, Manitoba is Canada's eighth-largest city, with a population of nearly 700,000 people. From 2003 to 2008, Winnipeg had North America's highest rates of motor vehicle theft. In 2004 and 2006, when auto theft rates peaked, Winnipeg had Canada's fourth-highest crime rate and a vehicle theft rate that was four times the national average. In 2006, nearly one in every five Criminal Code offences in Winnipeg was a vehicle theft, and the vehicle theft rate was 67 per cent higher than that of the next highest Canadian city[2] and four times the national average.

The auto theft problem began in 1993 when the number of vehicles stolen in Winnipeg nearly tripled. Rates continued rising until they reached 1,932 stolen vehicles per 100,000 population in 2004. After a slight decline in 2005, they rose again in 2006. These thefts were costly and the danger to Winnipeg residents was a major concern because of the recklessness of the auto thieves. In 2007, two people were killed by drivers of stolen vehicles, and in one highly publicized case, an early morning jogger was seriously injured after being deliberately run down by a youth driving a stolen car. In one 16-month period in 2007/08, eight drivers deliberately tried to run down police officers with stolen vehicles. Vehicle thieves also frequently attempted to ram police cars. Some youth engaged in other dangerous behaviour, such as jamming down vehicle accelerators and launching driverless vehicles down city streets and into parking garages.

Most Winnipeg residents had either been directly victimized by auto theft or knew someone who had been victimized, and personal accounts and media reports made it clear that the public felt vehicle theft was a major problem. In addition to being a major focus of the media, auto theft was also a topic frequently raised by the opposition party in the provincial legislature.

In 2001, the province established the Manitoba Auto Theft Task Force made up of representatives from Manitoba Justice, Manitoba Public Insurance (MPI),[3] Winnipeg Police Service (WPS), Royal Canadian Mounted Police, Manitoba Prosecution Service, and the University of Manitoba.[4] The initial efforts of the task force involved measures such as bait cars, fingerprinting all recovered stolen vehicles, and restricting licensing for drivers convicted of vehicle theft. Rates fell 12 per cent in 2002, so the task force was optimistic that these early efforts had met with some success. However, rates soon resumed their upward climb as these measures were not sufficient to deal with Winnipeg's highly motivated vehicle thieves. During the last quarter of 2004, the problem was spiralling out of control and in November of that year reached an annualized rate of more than 3,000 stolen vehicles/100,000 population. At this point, the Task Force developed a plan for the Winnipeg Auto Theft Suppression Strategy (WATSS).

Problem analysis: the vehicle theft problem in Winnipeg

Why did auto theft rates rise so dramatically in Winnipeg, and why did they remain high for so long? The answer is that auto theft had become an important part of youth culture in parts of the city. Virtually all the stolen vehicles were used for joyriding or as temporary transportation and were eventually recovered. A small number of high-end stolen vehicles were sold, and there were some small-scale chop shops, but the primary motivation for stealing cars was excitement, not money. Interviews with young offenders found that they stole cars for excitement and to show off for their peers and that they were very committed to continuing to steal cars (Anderson & Linden, 2014).

Offence patterns

Most vehicle thefts are reported so we had good data on theft targets and geographic patterns of theft. Vehicles were stolen from all parts of Winnipeg, although theft rates were highest in the core area. There were no consistent monthly or day-of-week patterns. More than 90 per cent of all stolen cars were recovered, so the vast majority were not being sold or chopped. Only about 10 per cent of thefts resulted in arrests.

Certain types of vehicles were targeted, particularly Chrysler products built in the early 1990s. These vehicles were easy to steal and had high theft-risk rates. The fact that these vehicles could be stolen by children as young as 10 years of age showed the role that target vulnerability played in the rise of the auto theft culture and was an issue that had to be addressed if we were to significantly reduce auto theft rates.

Offender patterns

While we had good documentation of the offence patterns, we also needed to learn more about the offenders. Young offenders were involved in most vehicle thefts. Why were some young people so attracted to auto theft?[5] In one of the POP Guides,

Scott Decker (2005) has outlined how offender interviews can provide information critical to reducing crime. We conducted a study in which 43 incarcerated young auto thieves were interviewed (Anderson & Linden, 2014). The sample included all the auto theft offenders living in three closed-custody institutions. Many of the youth had been incarcerated for other, more serious, offences, but their records included convictions for vehicle theft. The main findings were the following:

- Most came from single-parent families. Over half had run away from home at least once. There was a high rate of criminal involvement among immediate family members. Respondents did poorly in school. They were two to three years below expected grade levels and had high rates of truancy, suspension, and expulsion.
- The average age of first involvement in vehicle theft was 12, and the average age when the youth began stealing cars themselves was 13.
- Respondents were involved in a range of offences in addition to vehicle theft. They had high rates of alcohol and drug use and enjoyed a thrill-seeking lifestyle.
- Most thieves did little planning and seemed willing to steal cars any place and any time. They used the vehicles for joyriding and for short-term transportation and usually just abandoned the vehicles. Many would try to steal several vehicles in a day.
- Peers were important. Many respondents reported gang associations. Virtually all had friends who stole cars, most reported peer pressure to steal cars, and they obtained status from their peers for stealing cars. This supports the conclusion that there was an extensive adolescent car theft culture in some parts of Winnipeg.
- Some targets were clearly more attractive than others. There was a strong preference for stealing older Chrysler vehicles.
- Most respondents were not concerned about the consequences and any fear they had was not sufficient to overcome the thrill of stealing cars or the peer pressure.

Review of effective programs

The task force conducted a detailed review of the research on vehicle theft prevention. The review concluded that electronic vehicle immobilizers were effective[6] and found that some youth programs had potential (Linden & Chaturvedi, 2005).

We also learned that the Regina Police Service had a successful intensive supervision program for young offenders on conditional release. Regina had a vehicle theft problem very similar to Winnipeg's and, prior to their program, had Canada's highest vehicle theft rate. Their prevention program led to a reduction in vehicle theft of 33 per cent between 2001 and 2003, which dropped their auto-theft rate below that of Winnipeg (Regina Police Service, 2004). Task force members visited Regina to learn about this program, and a modified version of this initiative became a core component of the WATSS, along with immobilizers and social development programs for youth.

Analysis summary

The problem analysis told us a great deal about Winnipeg's vehicle-theft problem:

- Rates were extremely high, and youth were involved in most of the thefts.
- Many of the youth had histories of involvement with Child and Family Services and came from unstable family situations. Substance abuse issues were common and there was a high prevalence of diagnosed or suspected fetal alcohol spectrum disorders (FASD) and other cognitive impairments.

(Baydack, Buchel & Linden, 2010)

- More than 90 per cent of stolen autos were recovered, most within 24 hours, and most were inexpensive older vehicles. This indicated that the problem was joyriding, not theft for profit.
- Clearance rates were around 10 per cent, indicating that conventional investigative and enforcement tactics had limited impact. Analysis of court statistics showed that sentences for vehicle theft were typically very light, again suggesting that conventional youth-justice measures would not alleviate the problem.
- The Most At-Risk Vehicle list—initially 50,000 vehicles—included extremely vulnerable vehicles, particularly Chrysler minivans built in the early 1990s that had a yearly theft-risk rate as high as one in four. The vehicles on the list made up just 10 per cent of the total vehicle pool but accounted for 62 per cent of total theft claims.
- Some neighbourhoods had higher rates than others, but the pattern of thefts was city-wide.
- Auto theft was part of the youth culture in some Winnipeg neighbourhoods. This conclusion was based on interviews with young offenders and was reinforced by interviews with police, probation officers, and prosecutors.
- A scan indicated that intensive community supervision of high-risk offenders, some types of electronic immobilizers, and some youth programs had been successful in reducing vehicle theft in other jurisdictions.

The WATTS: program components

WATSS had three components: (1) education and supervision of youth, (2) mandatory electronic immobilizers, and (3) social development programs for at-risk youth.

Education and supervision of youth

The task force developed a tiered program for youth having different levels of risk of involvement in vehicle theft. Staff reviewed files on all young offenders involved in vehicle theft and classified them into Levels 2, 3, and 4. Level 1 youth were not identified individually, but programming was delivered in neighbourhoods with high levels of involvement in vehicle theft. The actions taken at each level are detailed next.

Level 1: youth-at-risk

Level 1 youth lived in areas where vehicle theft was a problem. Presentations were given in schools, including elementary schools that fed into schools where vehicle theft was a problem. The program was delivered by teachers, police school resource officers, and youth service organizations. Students who exhibited one or more of a list of risk factors were involved in the CHOICES youth program run by the Winnipeg School Division which had five activity streams—classroom, wilderness, mentoring, family, and follow-up club.

Level 2: early involved

Level 2 youth were those with one arrest for vehicle theft. The actions for these youth focused on prevention and on diversion out of the justice system using alternative measures. Under Canadian law, youth under 12 cannot be charged. A number of the youth apprehended for vehicle theft were under 12, and a program run by Manitoba Justice called Turnabout was used for these underage youth. This program linked the youth and their families with community resources such as clinical referrals, multi-systemic programming, anti-gang programs, and recreational opportunities.

Level 3: repeaters

Level 3 offenders received more resources and specialized programs. Youth corrections workers worked with young offenders and their families under specialized case management programs and required them to participate in programs specifically targeted at vehicle theft. Youth with addictions were involved in substance abuse programs. Many Level 3 youth also participated in a one-on-one mentoring program delivered by Big Brothers Big Sisters.

Level 4: very high risk to re-offend

Level 4 offenders received similar programming to Level 3 youth. However, they were subject to a higher degree of supervision. Level 4 youth were typically in the community under conditions of release such as curfews. WATSS provided intensive supervision to enforce these conditions. Youth were contacted in-person every day by probation officers or police and contacted by phone every three hours. Youth who violated their conditions of release were apprehended by the police, so they did not have the opportunity to re-offend. Prosecutors (who were members of the task force) would normally advocate for custody for youth who re-offended or otherwise violated their conditions of release. Initially, there were about 200 Level 3 and 4 offenders, so additional staff were required. Fourteen specialized youth corrections staff were hired to form a new Auto Theft Unit. Their role was to ensure that all release conditions were met and to develop programming for the highest-risk youth and their families to help reduce their criminal involvement. The police Stolen Auto Unit worked closely with the probation staff to provide intensive supervision for high-risk youth.

Electronic immobilizers

The second component involved installing electronic immobilizers in high-risk vehicles. Electronic immobilizers disable a vehicle's starter, ignition, and fuel systems unless a coded transponder is used to start them. Research in several countries showed that immobilizers were effective (Tabachneck et al., 2000; Potter & Thomas, 2001). MPI initially subsidized the installation of electronic immobilizers and then offered to provide free immobilizers to owners of the most at-risk vehicles. As noted later, this voluntary program was later expanded and made compulsory for these vehicles because the voluntary participation rate of owners of most-at-risk vehicles was too low[7] to have an impact on theft rates.

Social development programs for at-risk youth

The third component addressed the social causes of auto theft by working with young people and their families to reduce the number of young people who find auto theft an appealing form of recreation. Much of this work was done by youth probation staff. Support programs for high-risk offenders and their families were run with community partners including the Winnipeg School Division, Big Brothers and Big Sisters, and New Directions for Children, Youth, Adults and Families. The goals were to move current offenders away from auto theft and to end the flow of new recruits to this dangerous and costly pastime.

Re-analysis: responding to another increase in vehicle theft rates

The WATSS initially appeared to be successful. Theft rates declined by just 8 per cent between January and August 2005 but by 27 per cent from the beginning of the WATSS from September 2005 to December 2005. However, an increase of 26 per cent in the first quarter of 2006 indicated more changes were required. A major change to the program resulted from work done by Winnipeg Police Service Patrol Sergeant Kevin Kavitch, a supervisor in the Stolen Auto Unit who found a correlation between the number of the top 50 offenders who were in the community each day and the number of cars stolen on that day (See Figure 24.1). While this finding was by no means surprising, it did focus attention on the need for additional resources to ensure that the program would succeed.

This analysis clearly showed that the more of these high-risk youth who were on the street each day, the more cars that were stolen. Other crime analysis supported this conclusion. For example, the police knew that certain young offenders preferred particular models of vehicles, and when they were in custody or under effective supervision in the community, thefts of these vehicles dropped. These findings highlighted the need for improving the focused deterrence approach used in the intensive supervision program.

The Auto Theft Task Force reported directly to the provincial minister of justice, so a briefing was arranged at which P/Sgt. Kavitch was able to present his findings personally to the Minister. The task force proposed adding more police officers to improve community supervision. As a result, the Department of Justice funded five more positions for the WPS Stolen Auto Unit, allowing the unit to provide round-the-clock shift coverage. The police also shifted more of their resources to dealing with high-risk offenders rather than investigating vehicle thefts.

Another weakness of the initial version of WATSS was that the voluntary immobilizer program did not have sufficient penetration to avoid displacement. If would-be thieves could not start the first Dodge Caravan they encountered because it had an immobilizer, it was easy to find a similar vehicle without one. Thus, the Manitoba government passed legislation stating that effective September 2007 it would be compulsory for the 50,000 most at-risk vehicles to have immobilizers installed before they could be registered or reregistered. The list included all vehicles

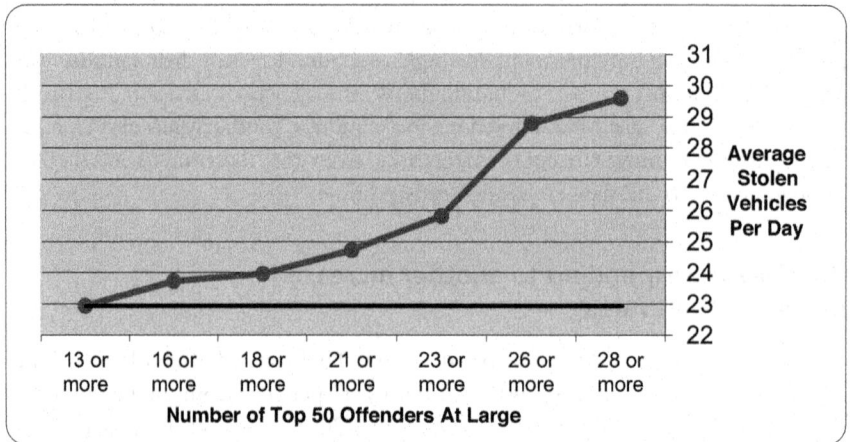

FIGURE 24.1 Relationship between number of top 50 offenders in the community and stolen vehicle rates

Source: Winnipeg Police Service.

with odds of up to 1 in 100 to be stolen in a year. The immobilizers and installation costs were paid by Manitoba Public Insurance.[8]

This mandatory program was phased in over 12 months. However, crime analysts noted that as favourite targets were protected, offenders began to target other vehicles, particularly those equipped with the General Motors (GM) Passlock II immobilizer. While these GM immobilizers did offer some security, several experienced offenders had learned how to defeat them and passed this knowledge on to their peers. Consequently, when installations of immobilizers on the first list were completed in September 2008, a second list of most-at-risk vehicles was established. This list involved another 50,000 vehicles. Immobilizer installations in these vehicles were completed by September 2009. There was no new evidence of serious displacement to other types of vehicles.

Another part of the immobilizer initiative was lobbying the federal government to mandate the installation of effective electronic immobilizers in new vehicles sold in Canada. The task force collaborated with other groups, including the Manitoba government, in this effort and after several years of lobbying, the federal government passed a regulation (Canadian Motor Vehicle Safety Standard 114) mandating that all new vehicles sold in Canada after September 2007 were required to have effective immobilizers installed.

Coordination

This comprehensive strategy required a high level of coordination. This began with the Auto Theft Task Force that oversaw all elements of the strategy. Below the task force were working groups for each of the four levels of youth. The most important was the Level 4 group, which met weekly and which was made up of representatives from the WPS, youth corrections, prosecutions, and MPI. Frontline staff from these different agencies worked together on a daily basis as a team and eliminated many of the normal organizational boundaries. This effective coordination meant that offenders were often arrested within hours of being breached for violating release conditions.[9] This resulted in non-compliant high-risk offenders being taken off the streets as quickly as possible. This teamwork was a key to the strategy's success.

The prosecutor's office also worked closely with the other WATSS participants. Designated vehicle theft prosecutors made a significant contribution to the program by carefully preparing cases and by educating judges about the seriousness of vehicle theft and about the continued involvement of chronic offenders.

There was also a high degree of coordination within the WPS. The department augmented the work of the Stolen Auto Unit by starting the Platoon Representative program. Each platoon in the five uniform divisions had one or two designated representatives who received specialized training and who worked with the Stolen Auto Unit on vehicle theft within their districts. This program was a key element in the Strategy as the representatives provided their platoons with information about current offenders, hot spots, and other intelligence. They also passed on intelligence from their platoon members to the Stolen Auto Unit.

The cooperation of different agencies led several of those involved to state that one of the things they most enjoyed about the assignment to the task force or the working groups was that they finally got a chance to see the justice system working as a true system.

Implementation issues

Many potentially successful crime-reduction initiatives have failed because of implementation problems. The WATSS used several measures to ensure the strategy was implemented as planned.

Leadership

Strong leadership was in place at all levels. Frequent meetings and open discussion ensured that everyone knew about the strategy and worked together to implement it. Turnover of personnel was kept to a minimum to ensure continuity, although there were several times when the replacement of key personnel put the program's success at risk.

Accountability

Because of their role as a major funder, MPI developed a business plan that specified targets for practices, such as the number of contacts made with individuals under supervision, and mandated three external evaluations during the first two years of the strategy. The task force and working group structures facilitated accountability. Most issues were raised and resolved at the task-force or working-group level.

Communications

Internal communication was a priority. Changes in the program were quickly disseminated and the task force and working groups enabled constant input from the people working at the street level. Bottom-up and top-down communication led to many important changes in the program.

Results: did WATSS reduce vehicle theft?

After several false starts, the reductions after 2006 were dramatic (Figure 24.2). Between January 2007 and December 2009 vehicle theft rates dropped by 67 per cent. This compares with a decline of 34 per cent for Canada as a whole and of 40 per cent in Regina, 44 per cent in Edmonton, and 46 per cent in Abbotsford, which were the other Canadian cities with the highest rates of vehicle theft. Because the program was in the implementation phase in 2007, most of the drop occurred in 2008 and 2009—and the reductions in these two years was 63 per cent. Between 2006 and 2011, when vehicle theft rates levelled off across Canada, the reduction in

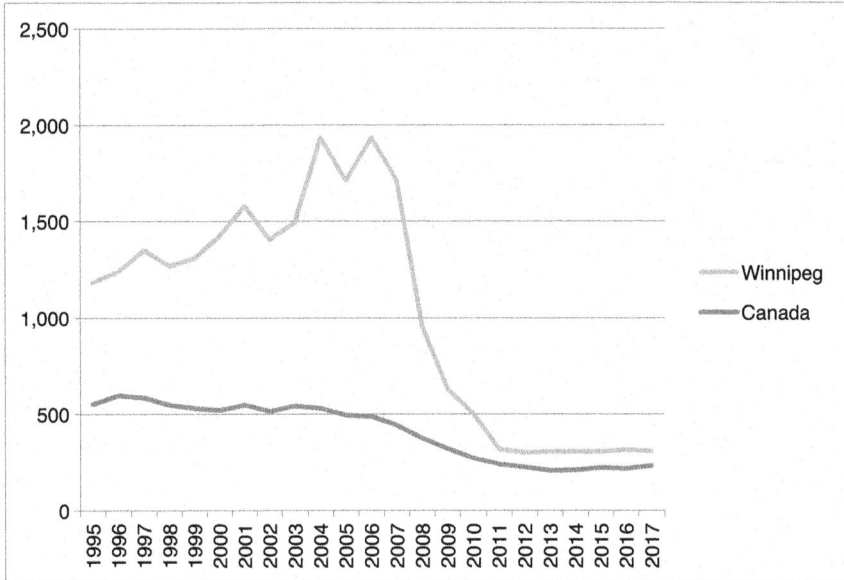

FIGURE 24.2 Motor vehicle theft rates—Winnipeg and Canada, 1995–2017

Source: Statistics Canada: Police-Reported Crime Statistics in Canada.

Winnipeg was 84 per cent compared with 51 per cent for Canada as a whole. These reductions—which can be described as a cliff-edge drop (Ross, 2013; see also Perry et al., 2017) that could likely only have been caused by the interventions—were far greater than for any other Canadian city. From 2011 to 2017, the vehicle theft rate in Winnipeg remained constant at slightly over 300 thefts per 100,000 (Figure 24.2), a rate which is about one-third higher than the national rate, which also remained constant over that period. This is consistent with the fact that Winnipeg's overall crime rate is higher than the national average.

The intensive supervision program continued until October 2017. By that time, the federal regulation requiring immobilizers for all motor vehicles sold in Canada meant that 99 per cent of all vehicles in the province had electronic immobilizers so the vehicle fleet was well protected from the young offenders who were responsible for Winnipeg's vehicle theft problem.[10] Vehicle theft rates went up by 16 per cent in 2018, but it is not clear whether this was just part of an overall increase in crime[11] or whether it was at least, in part, due to the termination of the focused-deterrence component of WATSS.

The WATSS had a major impact on community safety as the reduction in vehicle theft represented a reduction of 16 per cent in Winnipeg's overall crime rate. This was the major reason why the city's crime rate dropped from the fourth highest among Canada's largest cities in 2006 to the eighth highest in 2008.

There were also substantial financial benefits. The total investment (mostly for the immobilizer program but also including salaries for the WPS Stolen Auto Unit and the Auto Theft Workers employed by Manitoba Justice) was about CN$52 million. Manitoba Public Insurance forecasted ongoing savings of at least CN$30 million per year so the program more than paid for itself in a relatively short period.

Displacement or diffusion of benefits?

There were concerns that reducing vehicle theft would lead to an increase in carjackings and in crimes such as burglary and robbery. However, there were few carjackings in Winnipeg (between 30 and 50 per year) and rates of burglary, robbery, and theft from autos also declined between 2006 and 2009 when the greatest reductions in vehicle theft occurred. Thus, the evidence suggested a diffusion of benefits rather than displacement to other offences. This was likely because the intensive supervision by police and probation encouraged high-risk youth to stay out of trouble and because the work of probation staff helped some to change their behaviour.

The lessons of the WATSS

The WATSS has several innovative features. First, the intensive supervision component demonstrates the success of the individualized deterrence strategy that was used so successfully in Boston's Operation Ceasefire (Kennedy, 2009). Concentrating resources on individual high-risk offenders is one of the most promising crime-reduction strategies and potentially can be applied to many other offences such as gang-related crime, including homicide (Scott, 2017) and intimate partner domestic violence (Sechrist & Weil, 2018).

Second, the WATSS demonstrates the potential of comprehensive crime-reduction strategies that combine several types of intervention focused on a particular crime problem. The WATSS combined focused deterrence involving the police and probation with situational prevention (immobilizers) and crime prevention through social development (youth programs dealing with underlying causes). It is difficult to separate the effects of the different components of the WATSS, but the data support the view that both the focused-deterrence and the immobilizer components played significant roles in the reduction.[12] The enhanced supervision began in mid-2006 and the mandatory immobilizer program began in September 2007. Thefts dropped by 11 per cent in 2007 and because the immobilizer program did not begin until September 2007, only about 15,000 vehicles had received immobilizers by the end of that year. Thus, the reductions in 2007 could likely be attributed to the focused-deterrence component. There were further drops of 44 per cent in 2008 and 34 per cent in 2009,[13] which showed the collective impact of both program components operating together.

Third, a major success of the WATSS involved the ability of people from different parts of the justice system and from different units within the WPS to work together. While organizational issues did arise, there was a commitment from senior leaders from the WPS and other agencies to resolve these quickly.

Finally, partnerships were critical to the success of the program. Neither the offender supervision nor the immobilizer components could have been done without the funding and the expertise provided by MPI. Prosecutors and youth corrections staff were a vital part of the team, and many went beyond their normal duties to ensure the program's success. The WPS—and particularly the Stolen Auto Unit—were enthusiastic participants and were able to work around a few of their senior leaders who were not as committed to the program.

The WATSS highlights the value of taking a disciplined, problem-oriented approach to crime reduction. Reducing vehicle theft in Winnipeg was difficult because of the strength of the auto theft culture among many Winnipeg youth, and the efforts suffered numerous setbacks. However, continued refinements of the program enabled the task force to achieve very significant reductions in vehicle theft. The role of MPI was also critical to the program's success. WATSS was a very expensive program, and while the government was very supportive, the province would not have provided the level of funding required to ensure its success. As a non-profit Crown corporation that insures all motor vehicles in the province, MPI was able to make a business case to invest in the WATSS.

Notes

1 The author would like to acknowledge the funding support of the AUTO21 Network of Centres of Excellence. Many people were instrumental in the program's success, including Greg Graceffo, Marilyn McLaren, Gord McIntosh, Dave Chomiak, Kevin Kavitch, Barry Ward, and Reg Phillips.

2 Winnipeg's rate was also about 35 per cent higher than in Fresno and Modesto, California, which had the highest rates in the United States throughout much of the decade.

3 Manitoba has a provincial auto insurance company that insures all vehicles in the province. The role of MPI was critical to the success of the program.

4 The author of this paper was the chair of the task force.

5 The question might also have been worded as "Why was auto theft so attractive to young people that some would go out in −30 C weather to spend the day stealing, driving and abandoning cars?"

6 At the time the review was conducted, the evidence on immobilizers was much more limited than it is today. The main studies we examined were Tabachneck et al. (2000) and Potter and Thomas (2001).

7 Under the voluntary program, only 5 per cent of most-at-risk vehicles were protected.

8 The installation of 100,000 immobilizers was a major task as the installations were complicated and had to be carried out by certified technicians. A program in Australia had experienced thousands of breakdowns attributed to improper immobilizer installation (Vehicle Security Installation Bureau, 2008), and a repeat of this experience would have led to public resistance to the mandatory program. To avoid this, the immobilizer manufacturers and the Vehicle Security Installation Bureau worked closely with a small number of installers (including the Canadian Automobile Association) and established a training and inspection process to ensure that standards were met. MPI only allowed approved shops to be part of their mandatory program. As a result, there were very few complaints concerning the operation of the immobilizers. The immobilizers approved for the program had to meet the standard CAN/ULC 5338–98, which was adopted by the National Highway Traffic Safety Administration in the United States in 2016.

9 Arrests made by members of the WPS Stolen Auto Unit increased from 180 in 2005 to 424 in 2008.

10 Almost all the vehicles stolen in recent years had been left running or were a result of keys being stolen, indicating that immobilizers were very effective. One interesting trend, which reflects the need to use keys to steal most vehicles, is that attempted thefts are now almost negligible. In 2006, 47 per cent of reported vehicle thefts were actually attempted thefts. By 2018, attempts made up only 11 per cent of vehicle thefts.

11 While official 2018 crime statistics will not be released until July 2019, a list of major crimes including homicide, sexual assaults, shootings, robbery, break and enter, and vehicle theft also increased by 16 per cent.

12 An independent evaluation (Baydack, Buchel & Linden, 2010) found that the social development component of the WATSS, which included a broad range of different programs, had a positive, but very modest, impact on the reduction in auto theft rates.

13 By October 2009, more than 100,000 vehicles had immobilizers installed under the mandatory program.

References

Anderson, J. & Linden, R. (2014) 'Why steal cars: A study of young offenders involved in auto theft', *Canadian Journal of Criminology and Criminal Justice*, 56: 241–259.

Baydack, N., Buchel, A. & Linden, R. (2010) *An Evaluation of the Empowering Justice Project for Youth Auto Theft Offenders*, Winnipeg: PRA.

Decker, S. (2005) *Using Offender Interviews to Inform Police Problem Solving*, Problem-Oriented Guides for Police, Problem-Solving Tools Guide No. 3, Washington, DC: US Department of Justice, Office of Community Oriented Policing Services.

Kennedy, D.M. (2009) *Deterrence and Crime Prevention*, London and New York: Routledge.

Linden, R. & Chaturvedi, R. (2005) 'The need for comprehensive crime prevention planning: The case of motor vehicle theft', *Canadian Journal of Criminology and Criminal Justice*, 47(2) (April): 251–270.

Perry, S., Apel, R., Newman, G.R. & Clarke, R.V. (2017) 'The situational prevention of terrorism: An evaluation of the Israeli West Bank barrier', *Journal of Quantitative Criminology*, 33(4): 727–751.

Potter, R. & Thomas, P. (2001) *Engine Immobilisers: How Effective Are They? Report for the National Vehicle Theft Reduction Council*, Adelaide: National Vehicle Theft Reduction Council.

Regina Police Service (2004) *Regina Auto Theft Strategy*, Submission to the Herman Goldstein Awards for Excellence in Problem-Oriented Policing, Center for Problem-Oriented Policing, Arizona State University, Phoenix, AZ.

Ross, N. (2013) *Crime: How to Solve It: And Why So Much of What We're Told Is Wrong*, London: Biteback Publishing.

Scott, M.S. (2017) *Focused Deterrence of High-Risk Individuals*, Problem-Oriented Guides for Police, Response Guide No. 13, Washington, DC: US Department of Justice, Bureau of Justice Assistance.

Sechrist, S. & Weil, J. (2018) 'Assessing the impact of a focused deterrence strategy to combat intimate partner violence', *Violence against Women*, 24(3): 243–265.

Tabachneck, A., Norup, H., Thomason, S. & Motlagh, P. (2000) *VICC-Approved Theft Deterrent Systems: A Study into the Impact of VICC-Approved Theft Deterrent Systems on Insurance Claim Frequency and Loss Cost*, Don Mills, Ontario: Vehicle Information Centre of Canada.

Vehicle Security Installation Bureau (2008) *Proven Solutions That Support Road Safety*, Powerpoint Presentation, Winnipeg, Manitoba: Vehicle Security Installation Bureau.

PART VI

Reflections

25

PROBLEM-ORIENTED PUBLIC SAFETY

David M. Kennedy

Introduction

Tabitha Birdsong was murdered, knifed to death, on a public street in Kansas City, Missouri, in the first week in November 2018. She was found with a restraining order in her pocket, taken out against her estranged husband, Gene Birdsong. She had left him years before, moved away from him, sometimes gone into hiding. She had reported him to the police, often calling one detective several times a week. He was twice convicted of domestic battery against her. He was charged with raping another woman. Tabitha Birdsong took out multiple restraining orders, telling the court she was "terrified" for her safety; he repeatedly violated them, and she repeatedly reported him for violating them. He harassed her friends and family, who came to fear for their own safety; hacked her Facebook page; stole her food stamps. She gave up custody of her young daughter out of fear for the child's safety. Her friends called police to warn them that she was in danger. The night before she was killed, a male friend refused to let her into his home because he saw that Gene was with her. She was found dead the next morning, a block away. Gene Birdsong, covered in blood, was arrested that same day. "There's only so much we can do," said Detective Doug Rison, one of the police officers Tabitha Birdsong called frequently. Asked if he was concerned that she would be killed, Rison said he had not been. "She seemed to be staying up on trying to help herself out, and you don't see that a lot with victims. But that didn't cross my mind, no." Domestic violence advocates did not have anything to offer, either. "You think if you check all those boxes, you'll be safe," said Maryanne Metheny, the chief executive officer of Hope House, a local domestic violence shelter and support center. "But that isn't always the case."[1]

Tabitha Birdsong's death and the reality of intimate partner violence are a special case of a general phenomenon in public safety. Many, many people knew of the Tabitha Birdsong's situation, that she lived in fear, that she had been physically and otherwise harmed, and that those around her were being harmed and at risk of further harm, and nobody did anything effective about it. Intimate partner violence itself is extraordinarily serious; we know our responses to it are ineffective, we see them fail repeatedly and disastrously, those things have been true for a very long time, there seems little prospect for progress, and we largely accept that situation as normal. Both situations are common. Terrible things happen, both individually and more broadly; we know that they are terrible; we know that what we are doing is ineffective; and largely we keep on doing them. Until recently, urban homicide and gun violence fit that description (and in some places, those responsible still act that way). American drug epidemics have always fit that description: public policy did little to affect the trajectories of the first heroin epidemic of the late 1960s and 1970s, the powder cocaine epidemic of the early 1980s, the crack epidemic of the late 1980s and mid-1990s, the recent and returning methamphetamine epidemic, or—so far, at any rate—the current opioid epidemic. If we take the commonsense term *practical* to mean "making a meaningful difference," then nothing practical is being done about the growing number of American spree shootings. Nothing practical is being done about burgeoning cybercrime. Nothing practical is being done about sexual assault. And despite the now-well-established record of innovative and successful public-safety and crime-prevention interventions—including those inspired directly and indirectly by the thinking of Herman Goldstein—those interventions and that thinking are not the norm. Those approaches and habits of mind have, for the most part, not been thought of in regard to, or applied to, what we might think of as large, important, "high-level" problems. Part of the thrust behind the basic problem-oriented model, and frequently associated frameworks such as situational crime prevention, has, in fact, been to break problems down to small components: this bar, this drug market, this disorderly apartment building. That thrust has pushed the approach away from high-level problems: intimate partner violence, the opioid epidemic. The result and the norm are that nothing practical is being done about many other important public safety issues.

Herman Goldstein's idea of problem-oriented policing has, in fact, been adapted to address some such high-level problems, including intimate partner violence. It represents an alternative to traditional thinking about such problems and can, in practice, offer a way out of the lack of policy development and practical movement around such problems. This article addresses the American experience with addressing high-level public-safety problems in order to frame the limitations of traditional thinking and to suggest the merits of a routinized use of higher-level problem-oriented public safety.

System and structure: the failed duality of thinking about public safety

America began shifting its thinking about domestic violence in the 1970s, driven by a movement by advocates to reject the conventional belief that domestic violence was private, normal, and unimportant. Formal guidance to police departments at the time prescribed noninterference in domestic assaults: Michigan's began with "avoid arrest if possible"; went on to emphasize the complexity, uncertainty, and weakness of court proceedings; and ended with "don't be too harsh or critical" (Zorza, 1992). That movement has been powerful and sustained and has driven substantial shifts in public opinion and public policy, including police and prosecution policy. Domestic violence has become widely understood as a spectrum of behavior encompassing a wide range of controlling actions, psychological and physical abuse, and harms visited on other family members, friends, and pets (National Coalition Against Domestic Violence, 2019). It has been recognized to cause intergenerational impact (Abramsky et al., 2011; Smith et al., 2018). It has been located in the broad dynamics of patriarchy and toxic masculinity (Hall, 2019). A range of interventions has been developed and deployed, including shelters, victims' services, protocols for victims' safety, risk assessments, batterer treatment, legal orders of protection, policies for mandatory arrest of offenders, protocols for victimless prosecution, understanding of and responses to particularly high-risk actions such as nonfatal strangulations; restrictions on abusers' rights to purchase and possess firearms, and the like (Sullivan, 2018; Xie & Lynch, 2017; Everytown for Gun Safety, 2019; Battered Women's Justice Project, 2019; Klien, 2009).

It is universally recognized by both advocates and law enforcement that none of this has been satisfactory. Domestic violence has been in a long, slow decline nationally but remains at profoundly unacceptable levels, and research suggests that one of the main drivers of that decline is the withdrawal of women from intimate relationships, in part because of the reality of domestic violence (Dugan, Nagin & Rosenfeld, 2000). In terms of public attitudes, domestic violence is still not the anathema it should be. If domestic violence is rooted in deep social structures such as patriarchy, those structures have not been addressed and corrected. The first social response to abuse frequently remains inquiry into why the victim became involved, and remained or remains involved, with the abuser. Options such as shelters require victims to upend their lives and are tacit admissions that abusers cannot be stopped. For victims to draw on the criminal justice system requires them to take actions that are burdensome and often expose them to further risk. Criminal justice responses are broadly ineffective, do not offer victims effective protection, do not serve to effectively deter or incapacitate abusers, and do not offer victims what they want. Probably the single most significant shift in police practice around domestic violence, mandatory arrest of abusers, has been shown to put the most vulnerable victims at further risk (Schmidt & Sherman, 1993; Sherman, Schmidt & Rogan, 1992). Probably the single most significant non–law enforcement innovation aimed at abusers and batterer treatment has been shown to be ineffective (National Institute of Justice, 2011). Domestic violence remains an extremely serious public-safety problem; repeat offending and repeat victimization are common, and very serious individual, family, and community harm remains the norm. Tabitha Birdsong was not an anomaly; such appalling situations and outcomes are frequent and can reasonably be considered normal. It is routinely the case that someone whose name we know is being horribly abused and threatened by someone whose name we also know, and we do nothing effective to stop it.

The ways in which we have thought about and responded to domestic violence mirrors the ways in which public safety issues are generally framed and addressed. As far back as the 1967 President's Commission on Law Enforcement and the Administration of Justice, which formally framed those habits of mind, thinking about public safety has been divided into thinking about *prevention*—root causes, social, culture, and the like—and the *criminal justice system* and its actions. The commission was clear about where it thought the real work had to be done. "In the last analysis, the most promising and so the most important method of dealing with crime is by preventing it—by ameliorating the conditions of life that drive people to commit crimes and that undermine the restraining rules and institutions erected by society against antisocial conduct," the commission wrote (President's Commission, 1967: p. 1).

> The underlying problems are ones that the criminal justice system can do little about. The unruliness of young people, widespread drug addiction, the existence of much poverty in a wealthy society, the pursuit of the dollar by any available means are phenomena the police, the courts, and the correctional apparatus, which must deal with crimes and criminals one by one, cannot confront directly. They are strands that can be disentangled from the fabric of American life only by the concerted action of all of society.
>
> *(President's Commission, 1967: p. 58)*

Attention to prevention leads to a framing of collective responsibility and facilitative interventions; attention to the criminal justice system leads to a framing of individual responsibility and the application of authority. Where domestic violence is concerned, attention to structure led to issues of deep social dynamics, the meaning of maleness and masculinity, batterer treatment, and protection of and services to victims. Attention to the criminal justice system led to mandatory arrest, innovative investigative and prosecutorial practices, the invention of new legal tools such as orders of protection, and statutory changes such as those permitting the seizure of abusers' firearms. This pattern can be seen for essentially any meaningful public-safety issue; it is how we think about things and therefore how we act. Gang violence brings steps by law enforcement to dismantle gangs, investigate and prosecute gang crimes, and track gangs and gang members and by lawmakers to write new statutes criminalizing gang membership; it brings steps by service providers and advocates to teach young people to stay away from gangs, to ease gang members' pathways out gangs, to interrupt gang disputes, and to help gang members change their lives and by lawmakers to improve the conditions of communities that produce gangs. The current opioid epidemic is debated in terms of drug enforcement versus "public health," with enforcement representing steps toward interdiction, enforcement attention to traffickers, and legal and prosecutorial measures to hold dealers accountable for subsequent overdose deaths and public health focused on addressing the community conditions that drive addiction, harm reduction, medical treatment for overdoses, expanding treatment availability and modalities, and the like. Emerging practice in the opioid epidemic shows that criminal justice agencies can practice prevention, as in the widespread deployment of naloxone by police agencies; such overlap does not fundamentally change the duality of public safety thinking, and is in fact frequently characterized in terms of "police adopting a public health approach."

It should be recognized that these are not simply operational approaches, but are deeply felt normative positions. They represent different attitudes toward morality and fundamental issues of right and wrong, particularly with respect to individual versus collective accountability; different political ideologies, with criminal justice associated with the right and prevention with the left; different professional orientations; different camps; even different identities.[2] Proponents of criminal justice frequently regard proponents of prevention as naïve and weak; proponents of prevention frequently regard proponents of criminal justice as thuggish and violent.

This is a framework that routinely fails us. Neither criminal justice nor prevention, either alone or in any combination, has done away with gangs, prevented young men from joining them, gotten those in them to leave them, prevented gang violence and other crime, or made a meaningful improvement in the lives of communities affected by gangs and gang violence. Neither criminal justice nor prevention has had any meaningful positive impact on America's string of drug epidemics. They have not worked for domestic violence. They have not worked for sexual assault. They have not worked for spree shootings. They have not worked for any number of other important public-safety issues. There may be instances in which they have worked—they may have addressed problems that would otherwise be with us but are not—but if so, it is difficult to identify them. It is more the case that the world presents us with important public-safety problems, that we think about them in terms of criminal justice and prevention, that that way of thinking is routinely ineffective and unhelpful, and that we are so used to it that we take it as normal and inevitable.

When this way of thinking fails, we have predictable responses. Proponents of criminal justice go to system issues—resources and system failure—and to the broader society. Resources can mean either more material resources—people, equipment, funding—or more state power and authority, such as more law and sanctioning power. System failure points to the inevitable failure of the criminal justice system to act and coordinate effectively: police point to weak prosecutors and corrections, prosecutors point to poor police investigations and inadequate laws, and so on. The look to the broader society is, in effect, an embrace of the prevention position: the issue in question is a social problem, is beyond the reach of authorities and requires action by parents, families, the church, and the community. Proponents of prevention point overwhelmingly to inadequate commitment and resources. Commitment and resources can be high level, as with a lack of national political commitment to eradicating poverty, racism, and patriarchy, or particular, for example, to a supported work program for gang members or a shelter system for domestic violence victims.

In neither case, with respect to such diagnoses, is there generally anything very practical offered nor anything within the immediate control of the people and institutions involved. Police failing to prevent gang violence are not in a position to change gang statutes or the behavior of prosecutors or community norms around violence. Domestic violence advocates are not in a position to (directly) increase funding or to have a meaningful impact on patriarchy. In each case, the basic move is from an already large and serious problem on the ground to something even larger and further out of reach: the criminal justice system, family breakdown, gun availability, racism, gender dynamics.

We are so used to making this move that it is worth underscoring what it means in practice. Faced with an inability to address a serious problem in any proximate way, proponents of both prevention and criminal justice prescribe action that is *further* away from their span of control, *more* difficult, takes *more* resources, takes *more* time, and generally lacks any real operational reality. We cannot sort out how to address Tabitha Birdsong's husband—whose name we know, who is right in front of us, and who is at least theoretically open to local action by criminal justice and prevention actors—so we say we have to change patriarchy—how, exactly?—families—how, exactly?—judges—how, exactly? Our instinct, when our public-safety policies do not work, is almost invariably to move from the difficult to the essentially impossible. The result is, very frequently, an open recognition on all sides that what is being done is not working and will not work, that there is nothing they can do about it, and that that situation will not be fixed or get better.

It is worth noting that criminal justice, particularly policing, has changed to a considerable degree over the last decades through the framing and adoption of "evidence-based" practice. That change—the norm that policing strategies should only be employed if supported by evaluation research—can further highlight things that do not work and foster the employment of things that do. Evaluation can do nothing, however, to produce new and effective interventions where there currently is none. It cannot address the common situation of there being an important public safety problem, no effective response, and no progress or pathway toward developing one.

Herman Goldstein and a "problem" orientation to public safety

Forty years ago, Herman Goldstein published his seminal article "Improving Policing: A Problem-Oriented Approach" (Goldstein, 1979). It argued, essentially, that when what police were doing was not working, they should step back, take a fresh look at the problem they were dealing with, figure out something new that might work, try it, and assess whether it worked. That simple but profound idea worked its way deeply into policing; has produced a rich and growing body of theory, practice, and evaluation research; and—among other things—justly earned Goldstein the 2018 Stockholm Prize in Criminology, out of which this volume emerged. In his Stockholm acceptance speech, Goldstein set out that his original idea was that police were

- to identify specific problems the public expected them to handle,
- to dig deeply into understanding each problem, and
- to think freshly and creatively about the best possible tailor-made response.

As the police searched for that response, they were urged to place a high value

- on preventive action,
- on responses that preferably do not depend wholly on the criminal justice system, and
- on alternatives that engaged the community, other public agencies, and members of the private sector having a direct interest in the problem (Goldstein, 2018).

This does not appear to be a bad charge for those public safety professionals faced with a long-standing and important problem that self-evidently is not responding to current efforts and clearly will not respond to anything anybody is contemplating doing going forward. Looking back on "Improving Policing," it looks eerily prescient in this regard; altering Goldstein's abstract so that references to "police" and "policing" are replaced by references to "public safety," it reads:

> public safety practitioners have been particularly susceptible to the "means over ends" syndrome, placing more emphasis in their improvement efforts on organization and operating methods than on the substantive outcome of their work. This condition has been fed by the professional movement within the public safety field, with its concentration on the staffing, management, and organization of public safety agencies. More and more persons are questioning the widely held assumption that improvements in the internal management of public safety departments will enable public safety practitioners to deal more effectively with the problems they are called upon to handle. If [public-safety] practitioners are to realize a greater return on the investment made in improving their operations, and if they are to mature as a profession, they must concern themselves more directly with the end product of their efforts.
>
> Meeting this need requires that public safety practitioners develop a more systematic process for examining and addressing the problems that the public expects them to handle. It requires identifying these problems in more precise terms, researching each problem, documenting the nature of the current public safety response, assessing its adequacy and the adequacy of existing authority and resources, engaging in a broad exploration of alternatives to present responses, weighing the merits of these alternatives, and choosing from among them.

Improvements in staffing, organization, and management remain important, but they should be achieved—and may, in fact, be more achievable—within the context of a more direct concern with the outcome of public safety practice.

Just so. If it is the case that our current methods are not working around critical public-safety issues—and that is the case—and, if it is the case, that our habits of mind around addressing such issues are predictably ineffective—and they are—our methods and habits of mind should change. Or, as Goldstein wrote 40 years ago, again edited only to alter references to policing to references to public safety,

> [t]o address the substantive problems of public safety requires developing a commitment to a more systematic process for inquiring into these problems. Initially, this calls for identifying in precise terms the problems that citizens look to public safety practitioners to handle. Once identified, each problem must be explored in great detail. What do we know about the problem? Has it been researched? If so, with what results? What more should we know? Is it a proper concern of government? What authority and resources are available for dealing with it? What is the current [public-safety] response? In the broadest-ranging search for solutions, what would constitute the most intelligent response? What factors should be considered in choosing from among alternatives? If a new response is adopted, how does one go about evaluating its effectiveness? And finally, what changes, if any, does implementation of a more effective response require in the institutions producing public safety?

This is clearly a higher-level and more ambitious notion of "problem-oriented" than has been the norm in problem-oriented policing. It contemplates addressing larger and more challenging problems, and it explicitly expands beyond policing. If we take "public-safety professionals" as anyone who can or should be making contributions to addressing any given public safety problem—and recognizing that any given public-safety problem might benefit from attention from criminal justice practitioners, the medical community, educators, various levels of government, social service providers, community organizations, the business community, members of the public, and the like, it expands very far beyond policing indeed. It is a move opposite that generally seen in problem-oriented policing, which is to think in terms of as small and narrow a problem definition as possible. But if we take the current baseline to be the "prevention" and "criminal justice system" frameworks, then this move is exactly what problem-oriented thinking has always done: to move from those extremely large and unwieldy categorizations to much smaller ones. "Intimate partner violence" is a much bigger problem than, say, disorder at a poorly managed bar, but it is a much smaller problem than eradicating patriarchy or reforming the criminal justice system.

Problem-oriented public safety

My own work in public safety has been directly influenced by Goldstein and his framework for problem-oriented policing. The Boston Gun Project, framed and carried out in partnership with Anne M. Piehl and Anthony A. Braga, is generally considered to be at the high end of problem-oriented practice (see, e.g., Tilley, 2010), and won a Goldstein Award for Excellence in Problem-Oriented Policing in 1998. The Boston Gun Project combined original research into youth violence in Boston with a steady, iterative consideration—informed by the research—of what might make for an effective intervention. I managed that process and applied four simple tests to intervention ideas as they surfaced in the Gun Project working group:

- Will it make a big difference?
- How long will it take?
- Can we do it?
- Do we want to?

Writing about these four simple questions as they were later applied in the U.S. Department of Justice's Gun Project–inspired Strategic Approaches to Community Safety Initiative (SACSI), Dalton wrote:

> The first question requires the working group to consider the strategy's potential impact. If the solution cannot plausibly have a large impact on the violence problem, then it is discarded. For example, while offering parenting classes in violent neighborhoods may lead to more prepared parents and better cared-for children in the target population, it is not likely that this solution would have a significant impact on violence—at least not in the short term. This leads to the second question, "How long will it take?" In the parenting classes example, the answer is, "Too long." This strategy would need at least half a generation to take hold, which is longer than the working group can wait. The third question, "Can we do it?" requires the working group to assess whether the people in the room have the resources and the influence to implement the solution. In the case of offering parenting classes, the answer is probably "No." This sort of work is really not in the domain of the criminal justice practitioners at the table. The last question, "Do we want to?" requires the SACSI working groups to consider their norms and values and those of the community they represent. Asked about parenting classes, many working groups would answer, "Yes," it would be nice if parents in troubled neighborhoods were given access to parenting classes. However, SACSI working groups tended to be uncomfortable with solutions that were too costly (e.g., mandatory minimum sentences for drug users) or overly broad (e.g., citywide curfew for all kids under 18). As simple as they are, these questions set a very high standard. Most of the tactics suggested by SACSI working groups failed to meet at least one of the four parameters.
>
> *(Dalton, 2003)*

Core "criminal justice system" and "prevention" ideas invariably fail these tests. Criminal justice system changes might logically (at least sometimes) produce large results and rapid results; changing police and judicial behavior to create effective deterrence for gun crime, for example, might do so. Such changes are not within reach of those suggesting them, however, and what it would take to create that deterrence through broad punitive action would not pass moral muster with a large number of important constituencies (assuming it would pass legal muster). Eradicating patriarchy might produce large impacts on intimate partner violence but will perforce take a long time and—again—is not within reach of those suggesting it. Put most any ordinary crime-prevention and public-safety policy prescriptions up against these standards, and ordinary common sense will tell us that they will fail.

Different ways of thinking about important public-safety problems can meet these standards, however. Most of the cities involved in the SACSI project ended up also using the Boston approach to reduce gun violence, but one city, Memphis, Tennessee, took on that city's high rate of sexual assault. It developed important insights about the dynamics of rape in Memphis—for example, poor school transportation practices facilitated situations in which female students were assaulted as they took rides with strangers—and over the course of several years developed and implemented an intervention associated with a 49% reduction in reported sexual assault (Roehl, 2006). The 2017 Goldstein Award winner, work done by the Cincinnati Police Department with criminologist Tamara Herold, applied place-based criminology to develop a structure in which police used their existing methods and skills to identify violent-crime hot spots, investigate their dynamics, and provide that analysis to municipal actors with the capacity to develop and implement a non–law enforcement intervention. Violence reductions in the Cincinnati pilot sites were dramatic; like other such demonstration work, there seems no reason that the approach, now that it has been figured out, cannot be replicated and taken to scale (Madensen et al., 2017).

In my own work, situated since 2009 in the National Network for Safe Communities at John Jay College of Criminal Justice, my colleagues and I have sought to use the basic structure and methodology of a problem-oriented approach to advance public safety: to identify public-safety problems of particular import to the most vulnerable communities; conduct research on those problems, in partnership with a wide range of local partners (a typical team includes police, prosecutors, community corrections, service providers, faith leaders, community activists, and local researchers); design and implement an intervention; evaluate impact; adapt and replicate the intervention elsewhere; and incorporate the research and operational lessons learned into scholarship, public discourse, and public-safety practice. Our work has included problem foci on homicide and gun violence (Kennedy, 2001), overt community drug markets (Kennedy, 2009), domestic violence (Sechrist & Weil, 2018), prison safety (Operation Place Safety (Program), Washington (State), and Washington State Library, 2014), the opioid epidemic (Kennedy & Ben-Menachem, 2018), and other such areas. In each of these areas, the problem-oriented focus has led to new frameworks and new interventions. Our action research approach to intimate partner violence is described in this volume and begins with a commitment to exactly the situation that resulted in the murder of Tabitha Birdsong: that we know full well that a particular person is harming another particular person and do not intervene effectively. In its first implementation, it produced almost immediate reductions in homicide and, over time, reductions in calls, calls with injuries, repeat calls, and offender recidivism.

All the interventions produced by this process were guided by a commitment to understanding the particular facts and dynamics inhering to a particular, important public-safety problem and to producing an effective intervention that could be implemented by the people and institutions involved in the action research undertaking; that would produce substantial, meaningful impact in the near term; and that would pass legal and moral muster. Explicit in this framing has been that any prescription that did not meet these standards—would not produce large effects, would take a long time, could not be implemented by the people involved in the project, or crossed normative boundaries—was not a real prescription. That framing excludes—both implicitly and explicitly—prescriptions that rely on out-of-reach system and social changes. As the manager of many of these projects, my personal shorthand for the latter has been "Any statement of the form 'somebody should do something about X'"—patriarchy, racism, guns—"is not allowed."

In doing work in this way, another pernicious effect of the "system" and "prevention" frameworks becomes evident. The habits of mind of looking to system failure and broad social issues prevent careful examination of the actual problem in front of us. If there is a rape problem, we look to the failure of police to test enormous backlogs of rape kits and to rape culture, both of which are hard to change. We do not look for, and find, school transportation deficits, which might be a good deal easier to change. The Harvard Gun Project team learned from frontline practitioners in Boston on literally the first day they sat down together what the practitioners already knew: homicide in Boston was an issue hugely concentrated among a small number of high-risk groups, a basic finding since replicated innumerable times nationally and internationally and that has fundamentally changed violence prevention. That happened in 1995: ten years into the national homicide spike that came with the crack epidemic, and into a resulting long national debate about gun availability, "superpredators," the juvenile justice system, mandatory minimums, rap music, and the like that had proceeded nearly entirely without any inquiry into the actual nature and dynamics of the violence.

Framed another way, and informed by the large body of practical criminology that has developed since the President's Commission, the "system" and "prevention" frameworks point us away from what we now know to be true: that much crime and a large volume of what make up many important public safety problems are *situational* (see, e.g., Clarke, 1980). It may be that a young black man is carrying a gun because he has terrible character, or because his community has been and is being subjected to racism. It may also be because he has to traverse gang turf to get to school or because someone else whose name we know, or can figure out, is trying to kill him. The latter are much easier to address than either of the former.

Our received ways of thinking about public safety once again systematically move us away from what is particular and immediate to what is general and distal.

It is thus possible that these problem-oriented processes can produce both fundamentally new insights into important public-safety issues and fundamentally different and more effective ways of addressing them. The record thus far suggests that it is possible to get substantial returns on ludicrously small investments. The early work of the original Boston Gun Project, which took on homicide at a city scale and piloted an action-research framework for doing that kind of thing, was supported by a Justice Department grant of under $400,000—estimates of the public cost of a single homicide range as high as $17 million (DeLisi et al., 2010)—and the outlines of what became the actual operational approach had been developed within about six months of beginning. The Memphis sexual assault work was supported by a Department of Justice research-and-intervention grant of $250,000 (Roehl, 2006). I was paid a few thousand dollars for my part-time look into domestic violence and focused deterrence some fifteen years ago. I do not know what the University of North Carolina, Greensboro researchers were paid for their study of domestic violence in High Point; I can be confident that it was not much. To my knowledge, those were the *only* new resources put into that undertaking: everything else, including all the work put into designing, implementing, managing, and continuing to refine the strategy by the High Point partnership and Susan Herman's and my participation as outside advisors, was done with existing resources and *pro bono*. To put it another way, this potential transformative contribution to a vital national problem was done *in people's spare time*. It was not even that hard; developing the original notion that framed the intervention only took a couple of months, and the work in High Point that built on that was taken extremely seriously by the people involved but required no special skills or resources.

That has been the history of such work. A previous effort in High Point took on the overt drug markets associated with the crack era and developed a strategy that was ultimately widely employed nationally: that was also a spare-time, *pro bono*, and in-kind effort. Tracy Meares, then a professor at the University of Chicago School of Law, put together what came to be known as the "Chicago PSN" gun violence intervention in a month at the request of then U.S. attorney Pat Fitzgerald; the approach cut homicide in its target neighborhoods by nearly 40% and opened up new thinking about how to map procedural justice and police legitimacy in violence prevention. Meares did that work *pro bono* (Meares, 2019 Papachristos, Meares & Fagan, 2007). Herold's place-based work in Cincinnati was done for under $30,000 of new investment (and, as tends to be the way with this work, an enormous in-kind investment from the partners involved; Herold, 2019). The issue with taking this different approach to addressing important public-safety problems is not that it is extremely difficult or extremely expensive: it is simply that we do not think of doing so.

It is also not hard to think about how to do so. The SACSI process framed the undertaking as

- develop a strategic partnership.
- use research and information to assess the specific nature and dynamics of the targeted problem.
- design a strategy to have a substantial near-term impact on that targeted crime problem.
- implement the strategy.
- evaluate the strategy's impact and modify the strategy as indicated (Dalton, 2002).

If that sounds a lot like Herman Goldstein's problem-oriented policing schema, that is because it is: the Boston project was itself framed as a problem-oriented policing project, and SACSI drew directly from Boston. In his Jerry Lee Lecture to the Stockholm Criminology Symposium when Goldstein was awarded his prize, Harvard's Malcolm Sparrow—an old friend and colleague of mine, whom I happen to know was first introduced to problem-oriented policing at about the same time I was, in the mid-1980s—reflected on his decades of mapping the problem-oriented framework on to nonpolicing settings such as environmental and tax compliance. Such "problem-centric" work, he argued, should follow a basic pattern:

Stage 1: Nominate potential problem for attention
Stage 2: Define the problem precisely
Stage 3: Determine how to measure impact
Stage 4: Develop solutions/interventions
Stage 5 (a): Implement the plan
Stage 5 (b): Periodic monitoring/review/adjustment
Stage 6: Project closure, and long-term monitoring/maintenance

(Sparrow, 2018)

Surely that—or something very much like it—is correct, and surely it is correct that when we know, as we so often do, that what we are doing with respect to an important public safety problem *is not working and will never work*, we should stop simply doing what is not working and will never work and be serious about developing something that will. When we *know* that there will be another Tabitha Birdsong, and another, and another; that rape victims will keep getting raped; that children will keep getting abused; that overdose victims will keep dying; that schools will keep becoming killing grounds; because the ways we are thinking about intimate partner violence, and sexual assault, and child abuse, and the opioid epidemic, and spree shootings, are not working and will never work, we should *do something different.* Forty years ago, Herman Goldstein said to the world of policing, in essence, when what you are doing is not working, step back and think of something that will. Everything else in problem-oriented practice is an elaboration on that powerful charge. I believe Goldstein was more right than perhaps even he knew, and certainly more right than we have given him credit for. We should take his advice with respect to the big problems as well as the smaller ones.

Were we to do so, we would find that we are considerably better positioned than we were forty years ago. One of the major, and most practical, developments in the world of criminology and public safety over that time has been the emergence of a range of theoretically informed, powerful, and practical frameworks for analyzing and addressing problems. Situational crime prevention, routine activities theory, repeat victimization, repeat offending, crime prevention through environmental design, a range of place-based frameworks, focused deterrence, thinking about markets and market disruption, thinking about legitimacy and procedural justice, and others offer perspectives and guidance that make "stepping back and thinking of something that will" work a good deal easier, less formless, and frankly less terrifying than it was previously.

The existing record, as sparse as it is, shows that such work is possible. It also shows that it can be driven by existing public-safety agencies, at the direction of top-level figures and by low-level practitioners, by academics in partnership with practitioners, spurred by federal and state funders and by the philanthropic world. That sparse record is in fact enormously promising. The problem, I would submit, is not with the work itself, but with its sparseness, and the habits of mind that have led to that sparseness. Some fifty years ago, the President's Commission on Law Enforcement and the Administration of Justice taught us that public safety was, on one hand, about massive dynamics of prevention and, on the other, about massive criminal justice system issues. That has in practice been a nearly useless way of thinking and acting. I would submit that Herman Goldstein, some ten years later, gave us the single best alternative we know for thinking about and acting on public safety problems. We have not yet taken in the salience of his insight. We should do so and act accordingly.

Notes

1 This account is drawn from Melinda Hennenberger, "'Victims have to help themselves,' says OP cop: Tabitha Birdsong did that and died anyway," *Kansas City Star*, November 18, 2018. www.kansascity.com/opinion/opn-columns-blogs/melinda-henneberger/article 221736785.html; Glenn Rice and Kaitlyn Schwers, "KC police begin homicide investigation after dead body found near Roanoke Park," *Kansas City Star*, November 6, 2018, www.kansascity.com/news/local/crime/article221194750.html; and Tony Rizzo, "She had an order of protection against him: It was in her pocket when she was killed," *Kansas City Star*, November 8, 2018, www.kansascity.com/news/local/crime/article221364950.html.
2 My thanks to Daniel Webster at John Hopkins for the insight regarding identity.

References

Abramsky, T., Watts, C.H., Garcia-Moreno, C., Devries, K., Kiss, L., Ellsberg, M., Jansen, H.A.F.M. & Heise, L. (2011) 'What factors are associated with recent intimate partner violence? Findings from the WHO multi-country study on women's health and domestic violence', *BMC Public Health*, 11(109). doi:10.1186/1471-2458-11-109
Battered Women's Justice Project (2019) *Our Work*. Retrieved on January 13, 2020 from www.bwjp.org/our-work.html

Clarke, R.V.G. (1980) 'Situational crime prevention: Theory and practice', *British Journal of Criminology*, 20(2): 136–147.

Dalton, E. (2002) 'Targeted crime reduction efforts in ten cities: Lessons for the Project Safe Neighborhoods Initiative', *United States Attorneys' Bulletin*, 50(2): 16–25.

Dalton, E. (2003) *Lessons in Preventing Homicide*, East Lansing, MI: Michigan State University, School of Criminal Justice.

DeLisi, M., Kosloski, A., Sween, M., Hachmeister, E., Moore, M. & Drury, A. (2010) 'Murder by numbers: Monetary costs imposed by a sample of homicide offenders', *Journal of Forensic Psychiatry & Psychology*, 21(4): 501–513.

Dugan, L., Nagin, D.S. & Rosenfeld, R. (2000) 'Explaining the decline in intimate partner homicide: The effects of changing domesticity, women's status, and domestic violence resources', *Sage Family Studies Abstracts*, 22(1).

Everytown for Gun Safety (2019) *Guns and Violence against Women: America's Uniquely Lethal Domestic Violence Problem*, April.

Goldstein, H. (1979) 'Improving policing: A problem-oriented approach', *Crime & Delinquency*, 25(2): 236–258.

Goldstein, H. (2018) 'On problem-oriented policing: The Stockholm lecture', *Crime Science*, 7: 13. doi:10.1186/s40163-018-0087-3

Hall, C.M. (2019) 'Merging efforts: The intersections of domestic violence intervention, men, and masculinities', *Men and Masculinities*, 22(1) (April): 104–112. doi:10.1177/1097184X18805565

Herold, T. (2019) *Personal Communication*, February 7.

Kennedy, D.M. (2001) *Reducing Gun Violence: The Boston Gun Project's Operation Ceasefire*, Washington, DC: US Department of Justice, Office of Justice Programs.

Kennedy, D.M. (2009) 'Drugs, race and common ground: Reflections on the High Point intervention', *NIJ Journal*, 262: 12–17.

Kennedy, D.M. & Ben-Menachem, J. (2018) 'Rutland, Vermont, case study: Using DMI to combat covert opioid markets', *The Police Chief*, March.

Klien, A. (2009) *Practical Implications of Current Domestic Violence Research for Law Enforcement, Prosecutors and Judges*, Special Report for National Institute of Justice, Contact number 2007M-07032, June.

Madensen, T.D., Herold, M., Hammer, M. & Christenson, B. (2017) 'Place-based investigations to disrupt crime place networks', *The Police Chief*, April.

Meares, T. (2019) *Personal Communication*, February 13.

National Coalition against Domestic Violence (2019) *What Is Intimate Partner Violence?* Retrieved from https://ncadv.org/learn-more

National Institute of Justice (2011) *Batterer Intervention Programs Often Do Not Change Offender Behavior*, National Institute of Justice, July 5.

Operation Place Safety (Program), Washington (State) and Washington State Library (2014) *Operation Place Safety: First Year in Review*, Olympia, WA: Washington State Department of Corrections.

Papachristos, A.V., Meares, T.L. & Fagan, J. (2007) 'Attention felons: Evaluating Project Safe Neighborhoods in Chicago', *Journal of Empirical Legal Studies*, 4(2): 223–272.

President's Commission on Law Enforcement and Administration of Justice (1967) *The Challenge of Crime in a Free Society: A Report by the President's Commission on Law Enforcement and Administration of Justice*, Washington, DC: US Government Printing Office.

Roehl, J. (2006) *Strategic Approaches to Community Safety Initiative (SACSI) in 10 U.S. Cities: The Building Blocks for Project Safe Neighborhoods*, US Department of Justice, Document 212866, February, 3.

Schmidt, J.D. & Sherman, L.W. (1993) 'Does arrest deter domestic violence?', *American Behavioral Scientist*, 36: 601–609.

Sechrist, S.M. & Weil, J.D. (2018) 'Assessing the impact of a focused deterrence strategy to combat intimate partner domestic violence', *Violence against Women*, 24(3) (March): 243–265. doi:10.1177/1077801216687877

Sherman, L.W., Schmidt, J.D. & Rogan, D.P. (1992) *Policing Domestic Violence: Experiments and Dilemmas*, New York: Free Press.

Smith, S.G., Zhang, X., Basile, K.C., Merrick, M.T., Wang, J., Kresnow, M. & Chen, J. (2018) *The National Intimate Partner and Sexual Violence Survey (NISVS): 2015 Data Brief: Updated Release*, Atlanta, GA: National Center for Injury Prevention and Control, Centers for Disease Control and Prevention.

Sparrow, M.K. (2018) 'Problem-oriented policing: Matching the science to the art', *Crime Science: An Interdisciplinary Journal*, 7: 14. Quote adapted from Figure 5.

Sullivan, C.M. (2018) 'Understanding how domestic violence support services promote survivor well-being: A conceptual model', *Journal of Family Violence*, 33(2): 123–131. doi:10.1007/s10896-017-9931-6

Tilley, N. (2010) 'Whither problem-oriented policing', *Criminology & Public Policy*, 9(1): 6.

Xie, M. & Lynch, J.P. (2017) 'The effects of arrest, reporting to the police, and victim services on intimate partner violence', *Journal of Research in Crime and Delinquency*, 54(3) (May): 338–378. doi:10.1177/0022427816678035

Zorza, J. (1992) 'The criminal law of misdemeanor domestic violence, 1970–1990', *The Journal of Criminal Law and Criminology*, 83(1): 46–72, 49.

INDEX